OXFORD

TWENTY-FIRST CENTURY

APPROACHES TO LITERATURE

Matthew Rubery is Professor of Modern Literature at Queen Mary University of London. He is the author of *The Untold Story of the Talking Book* (Harvard, 2016) and *The Novelty of Newspapers: Victorian Fiction after the Invention of the News* (Oxford, 2009). He also co-curated "How We Read: A Sensory History of Books for Blind People," a public exhibition held at the UK's first annual Being Human festival.

Leah Price is Distinguished Professor of English at Rutgers University. Her books include *What We Talk About When We Talk About Books* (Basic, 2019), *How to Do Things with Books in Victorian Britain* (Princeton, 2012), and *The Anthology and the Rise of the Novel* (Cambridge, 2000). She has written on media old and new for the *New York Times, London Review of Books, Times Literary Supplement, San Francisco Chronicle,* and *Boston Globe.*

OXFORD
TWENTY-FIRST CENTURY
APPROACHES TO LITERATURE

Further Reading

Edited by

MATTHEW RUBERY
AND
LEAH PRICE

OXFORD
UNIVERSITY PRESS

Great Clarendon Street, Oxford, OX2 6DP,
United Kingdom

Oxford University Press is a department of the University of Oxford.
It furthers the University's objective of excellence in research, scholarship,
and education by publishing worldwide. Oxford is a registered trade mark of
Oxford University Press in the UK and in certain other countries

Published in the United States of America by Oxford University Press
198 Madison Avenue, New York, NY 10016, United States of America

British Library Cataloguing in Publication Data

Data available

Library of Congress Cataloging in Publication Data

Data available

ISBN 978–0–19–880979–1 (Hbk.)
ISBN 978–0–19–286553–3 (Pbk.)

ACKNOWLEDGMENTS

We would like to thank Helen Small and Paul Strohm, editors of the Oxford Twenty-First Century Approaches to Literature series, for their help in conceptualizing this volume. At Oxford University Press, our thanks go to Jacqueline Norton, Aimee Wright, Catherine Owen, and other staff for their editorial assistance. Thanks are owed as well to Matthew Brown, Jason Camlot, Daniel Shore, and the anonymous readers for their helpful advice. We are also grateful for the support of Deidre Lynch, David James, and Maia Silber, as well as to the English departments at Harvard and Queen Mary. Our final thanks, of course, go to our contributors.

CONTENTS

SENSES

BRAINS

FUTURES

LIST OF ILLUSTRATIONS

NOTES ON CONTRIBUTORS

Salvatore Antonucci is an undergraduate researcher at Michigan State University specializing in English, philosophy, and digital humanities.

Paul B. Armstrong, Professor of English at Brown University, has written several books on the phenomenology of reading and modern fiction, including *How Literature Plays with the Brain: The Neuroscience of Reading and Art* (2013) and *Play and the Politics of Reading: The Social Uses of Modernist Form* (2005). He is also editor of Norton Critical Editions of *Heart of Darkness* (2006; rev. edn 2017), *Howards End* (1998), and *A Passage to India* (forthcoming 2020). His book *Stories and the Brain: The Neuroscience of Narrative* (2020) is forthcoming.

Amy M. Belfi is Assistant Professor in the Department of Psychological Science at Missouri University of Science and Technology. She received her PhD in Neuroscience from the University of Iowa and completed postdoctoral training at New York University. Her research focuses on the behavioral and neural mechanisms underlying aesthetic experiences such as reading poetry, viewing images, and listening to music.

Christopher Cannon has taught at the University of California, Los Angeles, the University of Oxford, the University of Cambridge, New York University, and Johns Hopkins University, where he is now Bloomberg Distinguished Professor of English and Classics. He has written books on Geoffrey Chaucer's language, literary form after the Conquest, the cultural history of Middle English, and, most recently, elementary education in the fourteenth century. He is now at work on an edition of the complete works of Chaucer and a monograph on dictation.

Steven Connor is Grace 2 Professor of English in the University of Cambridge, and Director of the Centre for Research in Arts, Social Sciences, and Humanities (CRASSH). His books include *Living by Numbers: In Defence of Quantity* (2016), *Dream Machines* (2017), and *The Madness of Knowledge: On Wisdom, Ignorance and Fantasies of Knowing* (2019).

Johanna Drucker, Breslauer Distinguished Professor of Bibliographical Studies at the University of California, Los Angeles, is internationally known for her work in the history of graphic design, typography, experimental poetry, and digital humanities. Recent publications include *Graphesis: Visual Forms of Knowledge Production* (2014) and *Downdrift: An Ecofiction* (2018). In 2014 she was elected to the American Academy of Arts and Sciences.

Andrew Elfenbein is Professor of English at the University of Minnesota—Twin Cities. He is the author of *Byron and the Victorians* (1995), *Romantic Genius: The Prehistory of a Homosexual Role* (1999), *Romanticism and the Rise of English* (2009), and *The Gist of Reading* (2018). For Longman Cultural Editions, he has edited Oscar Wilde's *The Picture of Dorian Gray* and Bram Stoker's *Dracula*.

Lori Emerson is Associate Professor in the Department of English and the Intermedia Arts, Writing, and Performance Program at the University of Colorado at Boulder. She is also Director of the Media Archaeology Lab. Emerson is the author of *Reading Writing Interfaces: From the Digital to the Bookbound* (2014) and the co-editor of numerous collections.

Rita Felski is William R. Kenan Jr. Professor of English at the University of Virginia and Niels Bohr Professor at the University of Southern Denmark. She is currently completing a trilogy of books on rethinking the aims and methods of literary studies: *Uses of Literature* (2008), *The Limits of Critique* (2015), and *Hooked: Art and Attachment* (forthcoming).

Elaine Freedgood teaches in the Department of English at New York University and in NYU's Prison Education Program. She is the author of *Victorian Writing about Risk: Imagining a Safe England in a Dangerous World* (2000) and *The Ideas in Things: Fugitive Meaning in the Victorian Novel* (2006). She is also the editor of *Factory Writing in Nineteenth-Century Britain* (2003). Her current book is on how to undo the literary critical invention of realism.

Lisa Gitelman teaches English and media studies at New York University. She is the author most recently of *Paper Knowledge: Toward a Media History of Documents* (2014).

Wendy Griswold is Professor of Sociology and Bergen Evans Professor in the Humanities at Northwestern University. Her books include *Bearing Witness: Readers, Writers, and the Novel in Nigeria* (2000), *Regionalism and the Reading Class* (2008), *Cultures and Societies in a Changing World* (2012), and *American Guides: The Federal Writers' Project and the Casting of American Culture* (2016). She is a Guggenheim Fellow.

Christopher Grobe, Associate Professor of English at Amherst College, is the author of *The Art of Confession: The Performance of Self from Robert Lowell to Reality TV* (2017). His other writings on literature and performance can be found in *PMLA*, *NLH*, and several edited collections. Currently, he is writing a cultural history of realist acting, or "the art of seeming human."

Isabel Hofmeyr is Professor of African Literature at the University of the Witwatersrand in Johannesburg and Global Distinguished Professor in the English Department at New York University. Her most recent book is *Gandhi's Printing Press: Experiments in Slow Reading* (2013). Along with Antoinette Burton she edited *Ten Books That Shaped the British Empire: Creating an Imperial Commons* (2014). She currently heads up a Mellon-funded project "Oceanic Humanities for the Global South" with partners from South Africa, Mozambique, Mauritius, India, Jamaica, and Barbados.

Joseph A. Howley is Associate Professor of Classics at Columbia University. His research and teaching interests focus on the intellectual culture of the Roman Empire, and the ancient, transhistorical, and global histories of the book. He is the author of *Aulus Gellius and Roman Reading Culture* (2018). His current project is entitled *Slavery and the Roman Book*.

Melissa Klamer is a PhD candidate in English at Michigan State University, working at the intersection of Victorian life writing and digital humanities. She is an active Editor on the Digital Mitford Project, transcribing and coding the letters of Mary Russell Mitford.

Georgina Kleege teaches creative writing and disability studies at the University of California, Berkeley. Her recent books include *Sight Unseen* (1999), *Blind Rage: Letters to Helen Keller* (2006), and *More than Meets the Eye: What Blindness Brings to Art* (2017).

Anežka Kuzmičová leads the Integrating Text & Literacy (InT&L) group at Charles University, Prague. She has published widely on topics including readers' mental imagery, immersion and empathy, the physical reading environment, and the digitization of reading. Her interdisciplinary reading research aims at supporting Reading for Pleasure pedagogy.

Jonathan Lazar is Professor in the College of Information Studies, Associate Director of the Trace Center for Research and Development, and core faculty in the Human-Computer Interaction Lab, all at the University of Maryland. He is the author/co-author/editor of twelve books, including *Research Methods in Human-Computer Interaction* (2nd edn, 2017) and *Ensuring Digital Accessibility through Process and Policy* (2015).

Christina Lupton is Professor and Head of the Institute of Modern Languages at the University of Copenhagen. She writes on book and media history, eighteenth-century literature, and twentieth-century literary and social theory, and is the author of *Reading and the Making of Time in the Eighteenth Century* (2018).

Deidre Lynch is Ernest Bernbaum Professor of Literature at Harvard University, an editor of *The Norton Anthology of English Literature* (2018), and author, most recently, of *Loving Literature: A Cultural History* (2015). Her other projects on the history of books and readers include "Cultures of Reading," a special double issue of *PMLA* (2018–19), co-edited with Evelyne Ender.

Cody Mejeur is Visiting Assistant Professor of Game Studies at University at Buffalo. They served as graduate lab lead in the Digital Humanities and Literary Cognition lab at Michigan State University. They have published on games and education, representation in games, and the narrative construction of reality.

Natalie Phillips is Associate Professor of English at Michigan State University, and co-founder of the Digital Humanities and Literary Cognition Lab (DHLC). Her first book, *Distraction: Problems of Attention in Eighteenth-Century Literature* (2016), traces how changing Enlightenment ideas about the unfocused mind reshaped literary form.

Andrew Piper is Professor and William Dawson Scholar in the Department of Languages, Literatures, and Cultures at McGill University. His work focuses on the relationship between the history of technology and reading. He is the author most recently of *Enumerations: Data and Literary Study* (2018).

Jessica Pressman is Associate Professor of English and Comparative Literature at San Diego State University. She is the author of *Digital Modernism: Making It New in New Media* (2014), co-author, with Mark C. Marino and Jeremy Douglass, of *Reading Project: A Collaborative Analysis of William Poundstone's "Project for Tachistoscope {Bottomless Pit}"* (2015), and co-editor of two other volumes.

Leah Price is Distinguished Professor of English at Rutgers University. Her books include *How to Do Things with Books in Victorian Britain* (2012), *The Anthology and the Rise of the Novel* (2000), and *What We Talk about When We Talk about Books* (2019). She has written on media old and new for the *New York Times, London Review of Books, Times Literary Supplement, San Francisco Chronicle*, and *Boston Globe*.

Stephen Ramsay is an Associate Professor of English and a Fellow at the Center for Digital Research in the Humanities at the University of Nebraska-Lincoln. He teaches programming to students in the arts and humanities, and has lectured widely on subjects related to the digital humanities. He is the author of *Reading Machines: Toward an Algorithmic Criticism* (2011).

Matthew Rubery is Professor of Modern Literature at Queen Mary University of London. He is the author of *The Untold Story of the Talking Book* (2016) and *The Novelty of Newspapers: Victorian Fiction after the Invention of the News* (2009). He also co-curated "How We Read: A Sensory History of Books for Blind People," a public exhibition held at the UK's first annual Being Human festival.

Rebecca Sanchez is Associate Professor of English at Fordham University. She is the author of *Deafening Modernism: Embodied Language, Visual Poetics and American Literature* (2015) and the co-editor of Pauline Leader's *And No Birds Sing* (2016). Her work on literary and cultural modernism and disability studies has appeared in numerous journals and edited collections.

Cannon Schmitt, Professor and Director of Graduate Studies in English at the University of Toronto, is the author two books, *Darwin and the Memory of the Human: Evolution, Savages, and South America* (2009) and *Alien Nation: Nineteenth-Century Gothic Fictions and English Nationality* (1997), and essays in *Representations, ELH, Victorian Studies*, and elsewhere. At present he is completing a book on the sea in Victorian fiction and the possibility of literal (and technical) reading.

Gillian Silverman is Associate Professor of English and Director of the Women's and Gender Studies Program at the University of Colorado Denver. She is the author of *Bodies and Books: Reading and the Fantasy of Communion in Nineteenth-Century America* (2012). She is currently at work on a study of reading practices and their relation to the human sensorium.

Karah Smith is an alumna of Michigan State University with degrees in English, Psychology, and Digital Humanities. She has served as the Digital Humanities and Literary Cognition Lab (DHLC) Manager.

G. Gabrielle Starr is Professor of English and Neuroscience, and President of Pomona College in Claremont, California. Her research on aesthetics has been supported by the Guggenheim Foundation and the Andrew W. Mellon Foundation.

Garrett Stewart is James O. Freedman Professor of Letters at the University of Iowa. His studies of literary reading include most recently *The Deed of Reading: Literature • Writing • Language • Philosophy* (2015), *The Value of Style in Fiction* (2018), *The One, Other, and Only Dickens* (2018), and *Book, Text, Medium: Cross Sectional Reading for a Digital Age* (forthcoming 2020).

Elaine Treharne is Roberta Bowman Denning Professor of Humanities, and Director of Stanford Text Technologies at Stanford University. She is the author of many books and articles on early medieval British literature and on manuscripts from ca. 600 to 1200, and her next major publication will be *The Phenomenal Book*. She is a Fellow of the Society of Antiquaries, the Royal Historical Society, and the English Association.

Whitney Trettien is Assistant Professor of English at the University of Pennsylvania, where she teaches and writes on text technologies from print to digital. She is currently completing her first monograph, *Cut/Copy/Paste*, on the creative reuse of fragments in seventeenth-century books.

Rebecca L. Walkowitz is Distinguished Professor and Chair of English and Affiliate Faculty in Comparative Literature at Rutgers University. Past President of the Modernist Studies Association, Walkowitz is the author or editor of ten books, including as author *Born Translated: The Contemporary Novel in an Age of World Literature* (2015) and *Cosmopolitan Style: Modernism beyond the Nation* (2006), and as editor, with Eric Hayot, *A New Vocabulary for Global Modernism* (2016) and, with Douglas Mao, *Bad Modernisms* (2006). She is now writing a book about the concept of the Anglophone and the representation of world languages in contemporary writing.

Maryanne Wolf is the past Director of the Center for Reading and Language Research at Tufts University and the new Director of the Center for Dyslexia, Diverse Learners, and Social Justice at UCLA. She is the author of *Proust and the Squid: The Story and Science of the Reading Brain* (2007), *Tales of Literacy for the 21st Century* (2016), and *Reader, Come Home: The Reading Brain in a Digital World* (2018).

Lisa Zunshine is Bush-Holbrook Professor of English at the University of Kentucky, a Guggenheim Fellow, and the author and editor of eleven books, including *Why We Read Fiction* (2006), *Strange Concepts and the Stories They Make Possible* (2008), *Getting Inside Your Head: What Cognitive Science Can Tell Us about Popular Culture* (2012), and *The Oxford Handbook of Cognitive Literary Studies* (2015).

INTRODUCTION

LEAH PRICE AND MATTHEW RUBERY

What does "reading" mean in the twenty-first century? If any group of people can agree on an answer, you might expect it to be literary critics. After all, reading is the end as well as the means of most of our business and some of our pleasure. Whether an app informs us that our SMS has been read or we are nagging students to "do" (as we say) "the reading," the verb feels too obvious to require glossing. You are—we hope—reading effortlessly right now.

And yet the term has never had a satisfactory definition. Reading turns out to be both the most frequently discussed and the least agreed on procedure in the literary disciplines. No sooner did reading become mentionable, sometime in the middle of the past century, than its boundaries became battlegrounds. Poststructuralist literary critics changed "reading" from a literal verb to a figurative noun: once any object could be read, any intellectual operation became "a reading." These Cold-War-era theorists joined a long line of critics invoking "close reading" to distinguish themselves from amateurs who skim or paraphrase their way around texts. The advent of digital media around the turn of the millennium, however, hastened the splintering of both groups and, conversely, made visible ways of reading that cut across that professional/amateur divide. Intensive critical analysis is now merely one methodology among many as literary critics continue spinning out taxonomies of reading styles: deep, descriptive, denotative, distant, hyper, just, mere, paranoid, reparative, slow, surface, symptomatic, uncritical, even large. We now read against as well as with the grain. The narcissism of small differences corrals us into adjectival pigeonholes.

Debates about "The Way We Read Now"—as the title of one recent forum put it—have resonated widely throughout literary studies. Three of those "ways" have provoked particularly fierce debate: styles of reading described as distant, hyper, and surface. You might understand them as reading more, reading less, and reading less into. Where close readers zoom in on apparently insignificant details in individual works, distant readers exploit computational methods to analyze large corpora of texts—usually but not always digital—that no single person could read, in the maximal sense of the word, in a lifetime.[1] Proponents of hyper reading, meanwhile, suggest that rather than restricting the discipline's scope to complex works of literature in print requiring sustained concentration, literary studies should broaden its purview to include more diverse, and arguably less attentive, modes of reading that some associate with digital media.[2] (Though you could, of course, object that much of the world's reading has always been hyper.) And lastly, surface readers suggest that we should refrain from looking through the text's apparent meaning to seek out the coded messages perceptible only to an ever-vigilant, usually politically motivated critic.[3]

But as all three vocabularies develop, binary oppositions are beginning to cross-cut each other. The antonym of computer-assisted "distant reading" may turn out to be less the close reading beloved of twentieth-century literary critics than the "slow reading" that is becoming a political rallying cry in the twenty-first: pace replaces space as the metaphorical field in which literary critics situate themselves.

These otherwise very different rivals to close reading nudged scholars such as Merve Emre to consider what other forms of "uncritical reading" (to borrow Michael Warner's formulation) we ourselves have been engaging in all along.[4] In how we read as much as what, we are all omnivores now. Literary critics are increasingly confessing to, and learning from, what the cognitive neuroscientist Mark Seidenberg calls "Sorta Reading": sloppy, careless, intermittently attentive.[5] The figure populists and patronizers once agreed to call "the common reader" turns out to be at once more varied and unknowable than that term would suggest, and less easy to distinguish from ourselves.

Reading, in short, is coming to trouble literary critics precisely as it becomes more ubiquitous in our—and everyone else's—everyday lives. And what about the pixelated elephant in the room? Recognizing that reading's in a perpetual state of crisis isn't incompatible with noticing that the emergence of digital media is causing people in many parts of the world—outside as well as inside the academy—to do it more variously, and more self-consciously, than ever before. No longer, then, is reading, in George Steiner's words, "done rather than spoken about."[6] Sometimes it feels as if we speak—or worry—about little else. Or at least, we imagine ourselves to

---

[1] Franco Moretti, *Distant Reading* (London: Verso, 2013), 43–62.

[2] N. Katherine Hayles, *How We Think: Digital Media and Contemporary Technogenesis* (Chicago: University of Chicago Press, 2012), 55–79.

[3] Stephen Best and Sharon Marcus, "Surface Reading: An Introduction," *Representations* 108.1 (2009): 1–21.

[4] Michael Warner, "Uncritical Reading," in *Polemic: Critical or Uncritical,* ed. Jane Gallop (New York: Routledge, 2004), 13–38; Merve Emre, *Paraliterary: The Making of Bad Readers in Postwar America* (Chicago: University of Chicago Press, 2017). See also Rita Felski, *Uses of Literature* (Oxford: Blackwell Publishing, 2008).

[5] Mark Seidenberg, *Language at the Speed of Sight: How We Read, Why So Many Can't, and What Can Be Done about It* (New York: Basic Books, 2017), 73.

[6] George Steiner, "Critic/Reader," *New Literary History* 10.3 (1979): 423–52; 439.

be speaking about reading: for Heather Love has recently argued that literary critics misdescribe as debates about reading methods what are really "questions of affect and ethics," dispositions more than methods.[7]

This volume takes difficulties in defining reading not as an occasion for hand-wringing but as the latest opportunity to probe the term's intricacy and speculate about its potential reach. One thing that makes reading such a generative term is its contradictions: reading is of the mind (you get lost in books) and of the body (viewing, touching, sniffing the page); reading can be silent or voiced, solitary or sociable (and the parallel play of news readers on the subway makes clear that those two oppositions don't necessarily go together); reading helps you empathize with other people and retreat from them; reading is a way of engaging with the world as well as an escape from that very world; reading can change your life or make nothing happen.[8] For every claim about reading, there is an equally obvious counterclaim.

"I read a book": every word in that statement is up for grabs. Alone or in a group? With your eyes, ears, or fingers? In print or on screen? The same sentence covers multiple scenarios: a person turning the pages of a paperback novel in her living room, skimming an electronic text on her phone while crossing the road, or listening to an audiobook on a bus to work. Or even some combination of the three (people continue to print hardcopies from their screens even as they toggle between a PDF and an MP3). At a time when reading is as likely to take place in front of a screen as a page, and to be supported by a server farm as by a lectern, it's worth asking whether book reading will remain the template—if it ever was—for the uses to which we put the larger universe of texts. If Guglielmo Cavallo and Roger Chartier are correct that "forms produce meanings," then our work is cut out for us.[9]

Our knowledge of reading is changing in step with the media and scholarly tools we use to apprehend it—tools that depend not just on our historical moment, but on the boundaries of that "we." In the same years that saw literary critics interrogating reading with increasing frequency and intermittent anxiety, other disciplines began to offer competing descriptions of the practice.[10] During the second half of the twentieth century, work from a variety of historiographical traditions—employing methods ranging from macro statistical analyses to micro observation—exposed how differently past cultures had understood what reading is and does. Early in the present century, cognitive and computational scientists turned their gaze to the mechanisms of reading which literary critics still took for granted. As Seidenberg recently observed, "people manage to be good at reading without knowing much

---

[7] Heather Love, "Merely Ameliorative: Reading, Critical Affect, and the Project of Repair" (forthcoming).

[8] David Henkin, *City Reading: Written Words and Public Spaces in Antebellum New York* (New York: Columbia University Press, 1998).

[9] Guglielmo Cavallo and Roger Chartier, ed., "Introduction," in *A History of Reading in the West* (Oxford: Polity, 1999), 1–36; 2.

[10] Evelyne Ender and Deidre Shauna Lynch, "Learning to Read," *PMLA* 130.3 (2015): 539–45.

about how they do it."[11] Think of it as the difference between knowing how to read and how to read knowingly.

The gap is observable not just in how we read now but in how we talk about reading now. At one end of the spectrum, teams of researchers working in labs sometimes speak of reading as a mechanical, even algorithmic process of decoding graphic signs. At the other end, those in the humanities talk about reading largely in terms of interpretation, occasionally imposing outside agendas onto the text or, in Roland Barthes's phrase, "overcoding."[12] If literary critics use "reading" as a euphemism for interpretation, for others it means, just, well ... reading. Even scholars of a navel-gazing or novel-gazing temperament have begun to recognize the way we read as only one among many.

Or, perhaps, many among many, for even within any given discipline, no single way of engaging with text dominates. Historical accounts from Henri-Jean Martin and Lucien Febvre's *The Coming of the Book* (1958, translated 1976) to Shafquat Towheed, W. R. Owens, Katie Halsey, and Rosalind Crone's three-volume *The History of Reading* (2011), by way of Guglielmo Cavallo and Roger Chartier's *A History of Reading in the West* (1997, translated 1999), Alberto Manguel's *A History of Reading* (1996), and Steven Roger Fischer's homonymous *A History of Reading* (2003), enact, as much as they narrate, the tension between the "intensive" reading of a few texts and the "extensive" reading of many.[13]

Delimiting Reading

Dissension, then, but also consensus—for literary critics who agree on little else have invented (in some cases) or swallowed (in others) a series of shared assumptions about reading. That reading must be virtual, silent, disembodied; that the reader must be autonomous, knowable, and, most basically, human: these are some of the myths contested here. Our contributors struggle to denaturalize reading—whether that means dethroning literary reading or novel reading or interpretive reading, attending to those aspects of reading that are usually taken for granted as too easy, extending our gaze beyond literary critics to other disciplines, or looking beyond the "ideal reader" (as we called her in the 1960s) to a reader with cognitive or physical disabilities.

---

[11] Seidenberg, *Language at the Speed of Sight*, 3.
[12] Roland Barthes, *The Rustle of Language*, trans. Richard Howard (Berkeley, CA: University of California Press, 1989), 42.
[13] Lucien Febvre and Henri-Jean Martin, *The Coming of the Book: The Impact of Printing, 1450–1800* (London: Verso, 2010); Shafquat Towheed, W. R. Owens, Katie Halsey, and Rosalind Crone, eds., *The History of Reading*, 3 vols. (Basingstoke: Palgrave Macmillan, 2011); Cavallo and Chartier, eds., *A History of Reading in the West*; Alberto Manguel, *A History of Reading* (London: HarperCollins, 1996); Steven Roger Fischer, *A History of Reading* (London: Reaktion Books, 2003).

You are what you read: Deidre Lynch's (Chapter 8) intellectual history shows the self-sufficient subject being forged through reading—or, more precisely and more surprisingly, through the act of choosing what to read. Hume's long-accepted claim that "we are pretty much masters [of] what books we shall read" erases, she shows, our dependence on other people who regulate the supply of books. This can mean adults who give a child books, but it can also mean teachers who beat the child for failing to learn a task from books, as Christopher Cannon (Chapter 2) points out. Though there may not be a right way to read a book, there's certainly a wrong way.

Brain scanners take their place in this volume as one more scene of reading along with the classroom, the library, and the park bench. The experimental subject who features in Natalie Phillips, Salvatore Antonucci, Melissa Klamer, Cody Mejeur, and Karah Smith's study (in Chapter 6) is more literally hemmed in, asked to read while lying still in a cramped MRI scanner. Other obligations are legal, like the import tariffs reconstructed by Isabel Hofmeyr in Chapter 3. In her materialist history, "weight, date and place of manufacture" are as likely as genre to serve as classification terms; in fact, the most attentive close readers might not be bibliophiles but bureaucrats. Highly specialized vocabularies are what most other audiences feel it's okay to skip over. Otherwise, readers remain dependent on others for expertise, those forms of technical knowledge that Elaine Freedgood and Cannon Schmitt (Chapter 10) call "epaulets in prose." Neuroscientific terms can function like epaulets for English professors themselves: where once literary criticism aspired to fashion its own methods into a science, it's now likelier to outsource rigor by invoking cognitive scientists' findings about literary texts.

Another challenge to autonomy lies in reading's dependence on intermediaries, such as Rebecca Walkowitz's (Chapter 27) translators, Rebecca Sanchez's (Chapter 18) American Sign Language interpreters, and Elaine Treharne's (Chapter 7) medieval preachers. In the latter case, intermediaries block reading as much as they facilitate it: medieval preachers once prevented audiences from touching books. In the classical world, slaves were also central to the circulation (and triangulation) of ancient texts. The Roman master could be socially powerful but physically powerless: Joseph Howley's (Chapter 1) prehistory of prosthetic reading points out that Roman book-slaves "performed assistive work for those whose eyesight was failing or who were not able to write with their own hands." To be a "dependent" reader, in Lynch's terminology, can stem from wealth as well as poverty, from self-indulgence as much as weakness. The interest of translation may lie in its power to rub readers' noses in their dependence. "Irreducible to one," a text "in other words" forces us to confront what Walkowitz calls "the self's reliance on other selves."

Other essays confront theory with practice. As Steven Connor's (Chapter 4) study of "vernacular reading activity" points out, "what most people do when they perform the action, or undergo the experience, popularly understood as reading appears to be beneath the notice or beyond the ken of literary studies." Idealizing reading requires commentators to narrow the range of forms that reading takes—to deny that less exalted uses of print count as "reading." In 2017, for example, two biblioactivists defended literary reading by declaring that "reading in this sense is quite different from the skimming and scanning of images and text which young people think they are 'reading' on the Internet."[14] Their scare quotes recycle for the digital age the logic of a Victorian curmudgeon who asked of magazine readers, "Was that miserable dipping and skimming of the surface of that printed page to be called reading?"[15]

Not disembodied, not self-sufficient, the reader who emerges in these pages is also not only or always an objective interpreter. Felski's "postcritical reading" places a value on attachment rather than critical distance and feeling rather than thought, taking seriously non-literary critical reading practices without mimicking them. Engaging, paradoxically enough, in the very "defamiliarizing and denaturalizing" that she critiques, Felski undertakes an almost ethnographic analysis of literary critics' emotional tone of "knowingness, wariness, and skepticism." In its place, she sketches out a model of readerly attachment as "Velcro rather than superglue"—a metaphor that makes room for friction as well as dynamism. The stickiness equated with paralysis when students get "stuck" on a passage (as in Whitney Trettien's (Chapter 26) account of collaborative reading) can also go along with love.

Lisa Gitelman (Chapter 31) questions, more fundamentally, whether reading is even the primary activity to which texts are subjected. Like Christina Lupton (Chapter 13), she draws attention to the negative spaces carved out by potential or impossible reading: "the small amount any of us ever could read versus the enormity we can't." Yet as Trettien remarks, for some artists' books, such as Heather Weston's *Read (Past, Tense)*, "to respect the book's desires is simply to refuse to read it." Not reading receives nearly as much attention as reading in the ensuing chapters, where the refusal to read may reflect a calculated response to information overload as much as an opting out within the postliterate society envisioned by Marshall McLuhan's *The Gutenberg Galaxy*. As Wendy Griswold (Chapter 5) points out, the factor limiting reading worldwide is neither literacy nor access to books; rather, it's the desire to read.

Measuring Reading

For those who do read, the cognitive sciences enable new ways of responding to Georges Poulet's classic question, "Now what happens when I read a book?"—or, as an updated version might go, "Now what happens *in my head* when I read a book?"[16]

---

[14] Martha C. Pennington and Robert P. Waxler, *Why Reading Books Still Matters: The Power of Literature in Digital Times* (New York: Routledge, 2018), 157.

[15] Charles Alliston Collins, "Our Audience," *Macmillan's Magazine* 8 (1863): 161–6; 161.

[16] Georges Poulet, "Phenomenology of Reading," *New Literary History* 1.1 (1969): 53–68; 56.

Lisa Zunshine's Chapter 22 on mindreading places a formal question (what mental operations a text prompts in its readers) in dialogue with a thematic one (what psychological operations a fictional text attributes to its characters). In showing that round characters are also deep in the older, pejorative sense of being cunning, Zunshine links social prominence to formal character space, and formal character space to moral qualities—unraveling, in the process, the political implications of competing psychological models. Competing models of consciousness are at work in Anežka Kuzmičová's Chapter 23, by contrast, which marvels at the fact that, given the vagaries of individual experience and attention spans, two people reading a novel can ever reach consensus.

As the scene of reading shifts from library to lab, advice about what to read and why emanates from a new set of disciplines. The cognitive sciences have at the very least updated literary criticism's figures of speech. Reading is not eating, as Jan Radway reminded scholars three decades ago. But from George Eliot's plow and cheese to Carlo Ginzburg's cheese and worms, metaphors have always driven our understanding of reading. Kuzmičová rejects the metaphor of consciousness as a bucket into which content is poured, instead comparing the reader to a colander through which the text flows—though either way, we still end up in the kitchen.

One reason may be that readers don't just have minds. Texts are encountered by bodies, whether that means brains (for Phillips et al., and Gabrielle Starr and Amy Belfi (Chapter 24)); eyes (Johanna Drucker (Chapter 14), Georgina Kleege (Chapter 17), Sanchez, and Jonathan Lazar (Chapter 19)); ears (Garrett Stewart (Chapter 9), Christopher Grobe (Chapter 15), and Kleege again); hands (Treharne, Chapter 7); or skin (Gillian Silverman, Chapter 16).

Neuroimaging offers one way to grasp the brain's role in the reading process; as Robert Darnton observed, book historians have always found it easier to document "the external history of reading" than the internal one.[17] Snapshots of the reading brain tantalizingly offer the means to move beyond that impasse. Yet, as Starr and Belfi point out, even something as apparently simple as pleasure turns out to be exceedingly complex in neurological terms. Nor should pleasure be taken for granted when discussing literature. Maryanne Wolf's chapter on dyslexia and Leonardo da Vinci offers a further reminder that the brain's neural circuitry is not one-size-fits-all; da Vinci found it easier to design flying machines than to read Latin. Neither is the very category of pleasure reading. Should what we do in the classroom count as reading for pain?

The chapters on print disabilities reflect the movement among some practitioners of disability studies away from fictional representations of people with disability toward the experience of disability itself: from reading *about* dyslexia to reading *with* dyslexia, for example. Contesting the usual model in which sight alone is

---

[17] Robert Darnton, "First Steps toward a History of Reading," *Australian Journal of French Studies* 23 (1986): 5–30; 7.

acknowledged as the sense relevant to reading, Kleege considers modes of "reading visually" and "reading aurally." In the process, she debunks the moralizing assumption that listening is more passive than looking—and, by extension, that audiobooks are the lazy way out. The converse is true in Sanchez's when we shift from embodied reading to reading on bodies: deaf audiences' predominately visual engagement with signed literatures may be one of the few forms of reading for which screens are not second-best to paper.

An equally polemical urge informs Silverman's plea to take seriously the "holding, grasping, and turning" that accompany the cognitive processes of reading. Too often, she shows, literary critics are no more comfortable thinking about touch than the nineteenth-century experts who rejected precursors to braille as too tactile, or the rabbis who use a pointer to approach the Torah. In contrast, the readers whom you will encounter here don't simply interpret texts: they touch pages, squint at words, arrange their hands and their necks, dwell "at the somatic threshold of enunciation" (Stewart), or use their mouths to activate the "potential for sound that lies buried in the silent page" (Grobe). They are giving voice to a text literally as much as figuratively.

Bodies change over time, too. The reader whom we encounter in Lupton's essay ages, returning to the same text at different moments of life or expecting, during the first reading, that it will be followed by others. Repeat reading is anything but repetitive reading. Where Walkowitz makes it hard to identify an original text, Lupton demolishes the myth of an original reading. Not everyone ages gracefully, of course. Other contributors emphasize the continuum between ability and disability (think of how many readers wear glasses). As Lazar insists, "accessible reading benefits all readers." Everyone will at some point in their lives probably need assistive technologies—from large type and screen magnifiers to text-to-speech software—to help them read. We might all be disabled readers one day.

As any late adopter will tell you, reading varies with the medium being read. A number of chapters trace how screens shape textual encounters in innovative ways while still requiring similar degrees of interactivity as print—page-turners versus page-tappers.

Signs are everywhere we look. Cutting across the tension between verbal and material aspects of the text, Drucker emphasizes instead a tripartite distinction between substance, site, and effect. Starting from the familiar example of the word "STOP," which carries a different kind of authority in a streetscape than on a screen, Drucker urges us to move beyond the formal dimension of texts to their performative function. "Identification, demarcation, prohibition, permission, announcement" are all as embedded in space as in institutions. Yet written signs that straddle digital and analog worlds, as in GPS positioning, challenge older models of site-specificity as well as the very boundaries between those worlds. And whereas reading books has itself been described as a form of virtual reality, Lori Emerson reverses this relationship by considering attentive reading as a way to prevent the world from becoming *too* virtual.[18]

Another axis along which literary-critical methods are coming to diverge is scale. This volume exemplifies that diversity, since the essays range from macroanalyses of large corpora of thousands of texts all the way down to microanalyses of individual phonemes, morphemes, and lexemes (Grobe's "O"; Connor's "i"; Stewart's "ey"). Reading can certainly be too distant. But can it be too close? The latter studies force the question by breaking language down at a granular level seldom contemplated by the casual reader. A poem's entire meaning can hinge on the interpretation—or even inflection—of a single letter.

A familiar distinction made between the humanities and sciences is that only the latter's findings are falsifiable. Formalist criticism in particular would seem to bear this out by relying solely on the critic's ingenuity to tease out meanings from a text. But other experimental methods, especially those derived from the disciplines of psychology, neuroscience, and computer science, suggest that even this division is misleading as humanist ideas are increasingly being subjected to forms of quantifiable verification. You won't find any breezy assertions here that reading stories makes us better people. While science may not resolve all of our controversies, notes Paul Armstrong (Chapter 20), its methods can at least rule out claims that are demonstrably false.

The attention to counting evident in computationally driven approaches bears this out. Andrew Piper (Chapter 12) finds "quantity" everywhere he looks, not just in the content we read, but in metadata such as "page numbers, chapter headings, volume number, publication date, series number, call number, or ISBN"—and this before and beyond the digital turn. Andrew Elfenbein (Chapter 21) likewise questions the scale on which reading can best be studied, and with what tools. In turn, he asks what questions become unaskable when we equate thinking about reading with thinking about medium. Where might the conversation go if we swapped virtuoso formalist readings for ones that are merely "good enough"? His essay draws on cognitive psychology, if not to provide new answers, then to expand the vocabulary in which literary critics formulate questions.

Projecting Reading

Utopian and dystopian registers are never far apart in conversations about reading. Reading habits are evolving in line with the media on which we read, and much of the data accumulated by electronic devices will be a boon for historians

[18] See, for example, Marie-Laure Ryan, *Narrative as Virtual Reality: Immersion and Interactivity in Literature and Electronic Media* (Baltimore: Johns Hopkins University Press, 2003).

seeking evidence of how people interact with texts. Kindle's "Popular Highlights," for example, makes it possible to determine exactly what passages grab the attention of readers (who, as Trettien reminds us, are themselves being read by Amazon). The very distinction between analog and digital reading may be nearing obsolescence now that all reading is shaped to some extent by digital technologies and behavior. As Jessica Pressman (Chapter 28) puts it, "electronic reading has become just reading." Yet technology solves some problems while introducing others. In this case, assistive technologies that help people read raise the specter of aggressive technologies taking over that very role—machines not only helping us read but reading *instead* of us. Pressman's use of the phrase "human reader" would have once been redundant.

More radically, some of the following chapters ask what happens when the readers in question are no longer human at all. We say glibly that reading makes us human. But machines can read too—and perhaps better. Certainly, they can read more. Over a century ago, Israel Zangwill wondered whether "the critic will ever be replaced by an automaton, something analogous to the camera that has replaced the artist."[19] The enslaved readers described by Howley prefigure the invisibility of the machines described by Pressman and Stephen Ramsay (Chapter 30); evidently, human consciousness is no longer a prerequisite for literacy. Pressman shows how enmeshed reading has become in "a participatory network of media and actors in which humans are no longer the central node." In that context, a question posed by Ramsay takes on new urgency: "if reading has historically served as a way to define the self, then what does it mean when some entity that cannot meaningfully be said to have a self begins to engage in the activity?"[20] Any discomfort felt toward reading books on screens instead of on paper pales in comparison to that generated by a nonhuman entity telling you which book to read next.

How To Read This Book

A brief word about how to use this volume. The following chapters might be thought of as provocations rather than the last word on various aspects of reading. Their remit is to provide a vocabulary adequate to the challenge of talking about reading in the twenty-first century; to introduce new ways of conceptualizing the term's forms, boundaries, and uses; and to broaden the frame of discussion beyond a narrow conception of the term. The challenge that we posed our contributors was to investigate reading in its own right rather than as a sub-section of histories of the book, sociologies of literacy, or theories of literature. To do so, however, required

---

[19] Israel Zangwill, *Without Prejudice* (New York: Century Co., 1896), 3.
[20] Stephen Ramsay, "Reading Oneself," unpublished manuscript, January 1, 2018, 1–10; 7.

mixing and matching methods (cognitive, economic, literary, historical, pedagogical, philosophical, psychological, sociological) that have too often been cramped in separate toolkits. Contributors have been encouraged to avoid lengthy retrospectives of previous scholarship, to use footnotes sparingly, and, since space is limited, to point audiences to the (a pun was inevitable) "Further Reading" section at the end of each chapter.

Enough throat-clearing. As we cede the floor to our contributors, listen to the novelist Italo Calvino: "You are about to begin reading.... Relax. Concentrate. Dispel every other thought. Let the world around you fade."[21]

---

[21] Italo Calvino, *If on a Winter's Night a Traveler*, trans. William Weaver (San Diego, CA: Harcourt Brace, [1999]), 3.

SCENES

1

IN ANCIENT ROME

JOSEPH A. HOWLEY

Writing the ancient history of reading requires uneasy collaborations with our ancient sources. We are at their mercy: in the absence of the rich material evidence from other periods of book history, we are left to construe ancient reading in large part from its depictions in literary sources. The historian of ancient reading must listen carefully to her subjects while remaining equally mistrustful of them and herself. For there are some things on which our sources are silent, and others on which they are vocal; but even when vocal, it still falls to us to distinguish between reading activities that our sources find normal and those they find noteworthy or unusual, and to correctly extrapolate from the specific to the general.

For example: Cicero walks into his friend Lucullus's library, and there amidst the scrolls, he finds another friend, Cato, "basically gorging himself" on volumes of Stoicism.[1] From this scene, the opening vignette of Book Three of Cicero's *De finibus*, historians of ancient reading have concluded that this sort of thing—wealthy associates wandering into each other's libraries to read—must have happened all the time. And thus did we think we knew something about private library culture in the late Roman republic.

But we were wrong. As the classicist Stephanie Frampton has recently shown through careful rereading of this scene and other accounts of Roman libraries, Cicero is describing *abnormal* behavior: to a Roman, staying in the room where the books are stored, surrounded by them, reading them there, is comically strange.[2] Romans, Frampton shows, took their books from where they were stored and read them somewhere else. For decades, in rereading this scene we have filled in all the wrong context around a moment glimpsed briefly and in passing.

The questions we ask of ancient reading have been shaped by trends within the study of antiquity broadly, and beyond it, in the study of reading in more recent

---

[1] Cicero, *De finibus* 3.7: "…maximaque copia quasi helluari quasi…videbatur."
[2] Stephanie Frampton, "What to Do with Books in the *De finibus*," *Transactions of the American Philological Association* 146.1 (2016): 117–47.

time periods. In what follows, I want to suggest that we also take our cue from the ancients themselves. To understand what they are and are not telling us about their own reading, we should consider what they *know* about their reading: what they can and cannot see in *their own* reading. We will briefly map the limits and dimensions of Romans' own perceptions of what it is to read, and what it is to read someone else's reading; in their perceptions as well as their blind spots, acknowledged and unconscious both, we will find the building blocks of a more productive hermeneutic of ancient reading in ancient sources.

The Nourishment of Ambrose

Another fragmentary moment: a young Augustine and his friends come across their teacher Ambrose reading silently to himself. They wait for the teacher to acknowledge them, or share what he's reading, but he continues to read in silence. Eventually, they leave, discussing after they have gone different possible explanations for Ambrose's unusual behavior.

This scene from Augustine's *Confessions* is surely the most abused and put upon passage in the modern history of ancient reading.[3] It has for decades been used as proof that *nobody in antiquity* (save truly exceptional persons like Ambrose and Augustine) was even *capable* of reading silently. The ancient reading experience has been cast as functionally and even neurologically different, with ancient writing incomprehensible except through the ear, even to readers themselves; not until the monasteries of the eleventh and twelfth centuries, the story has gone, would silent reading as we know it come to Europe. This entire mountain of argumentation and assertion has been balanced, like an inverted pyramid, on this one brief moment in Augustine's *Confessions*. Poor Augustine—hasn't he suffered enough?

This notion was capably demolished in print by Bernard Knox in 1968, but not until William Johnson staged a second assault in 2000 did many in the field begin to take its absurdity seriously.[4] One still encounters the idea within classics, and certainly beyond it; as R. W. McCutcheon has recently shown, the "no silent reading because of Augustine" canard owes its longevity in no small part to how well it serves sweeping, teleological accounts of Western reading written by scholars of other eras, who have favored a sort of Whiggish history of the book, marching on from ancient barbarism to modern sophistication.[5] The fallacy has also thrived

[3] Augustine's *Confessions* 6.3.3.
[4] B. M. W. Knox, "Silent Reading in Antiquity," *Greek, Roman and Byzantine Studies* 9 (1968): 421–35; William A. Johnson, "Toward a Sociology of Reading in Classical Antiquity," *American Journal of Philology* 121.4 (2000): 593–627.
[5] R. W. McCutcheon, "Silent Reading in Antiquity and the Future History of the Book," *Book History* 18 (2015): 1–32.

on the way historians have made the ancient book seem especially alien, by emphasizing the unwieldiness of the scroll, or by describing ancient books as universally without word separation and therefore impossible to construe silently (in fact use of interpuncts varied with time, place, language, and genre; and the inflected endings of Greek and Latin words would have easily facilitated silent reading of continuous script).

Let us be clear: literate people in the ancient Roman world could read silently and did so with some frequency. They also read aloud and were read to, with some frequency. Each reading behavior would be practiced in a different social setting, and with different social significance, just as a modern person might listen to the same album on a stereo at a house party, on a tinny Bluetooth speaker at the beach, or on their headphones on the subway—but might get odd looks for wearing their headphones at the party. Augustine's observations of Ambrose reflect shock not at his reading skill, but at his social choices. It's all about context.

But Augustine the author is not himself interested in reading, or only in reading: here, reading is a metaphorical representation of his relationship with Ambrose. The passage comes early in *Confessions* 6, among Augustine's first impressions of Ambrose, and as an illustration of the nature of their relationship at first, before it grew more intimate:

> I had not yet begun to moan in my prayer that You would come to my aid, but my restless soul was intent on inquiring and debating, and I thought Ambrose to be a singularly happy man (as the world judges such things), so honored was he by the rich and powerful; his celibacy was the only thing about his life that seemed a burden. What hopes he had for himself, and how he struggled against the temptations of his position, what consolations he had for his troubles, the face he showed only to himself, what he held in his heart, how much pleasure he took in feasting on Your bread—I neither knew, nor could begin to guess at any of this, and nor was he aware of my own agitations or the hazardous snares that surrounded me. I could not ask him the questions I wanted to ask, in the way I wanted to ask them, kept as I was from his ear and his mouth by the crowds of busy men to whose infirmities he ministered.
>
> When he was not with them—a tiny fraction of his time—he replenished either his body with a bit of necessary sustenance or his mind with reading. But when he read, his eyes were led along the columns of text and his inner mind grasped the sense, but his voice and tongue were at rest. Often when we were in his presence (for no one was prohibited to enter, but nor was it his custom for anyone coming in to be announced), we would see him reading in this way, silently and never otherwise, and we would sit for a long time in silence (for who would dare impose on someone so intent?) and then leave, and we imagined that when he was taking a break from the din of other people's speeches, he did not want to spend what small amount of time he could get for restoring his mental faculties paying attention to someone else or having to worry that, if he had some listener hanging on every word he read aloud, and the author Ambrose was reading should have phrased something especially obscurely, he would have to explain it to his audience, or hold forth on even more difficult questions; and if his time were

taken up with that responsibility he would get through fewer books than he wanted to. That said, the preservation of his voice, which very got very easily worn out, could have also been a good reason for reading silently; anyway, whatever was going on in his mind, he had a good reason for what he did.[6]

The first of these paragraphs is often passed over, but it is important: the narrator is interested here not in Ambrose's reading habits but in Augustine's own inability to construe or comprehend them. The point is the distance between strangers, a distance which reading figures. Reading is one of those private, internal mental experiences that, like one's struggles with religion or celibacy or ambition, is unknowable to others unless they choose to reveal and communicate it. Ambrose's behavior is remarkable not because silent reading was rare but because solitary reading in a social setting was abnormal: reading means privacy, and solitary reading—even with others around—means *solitude*.

In his memoir of returning to teach high school English after over a decade away from it, Garret Keizer describes an epiphany that comes to him as he discovers what it is that makes his young students, stereotypically averse to reading, come alive as readers:

> I discover how much the students love reading aloud—especially what was always meant to be read that way. Girls vie for the part of Emily in *Our Town*; the unlikeliest boys take a shot at Whitman's *Song of Myself*. I come to suspect that it is not reading my students hate so much as reading in isolation. The same radical privacy that I seek in books, my mind's way of eating its lunch alone, is what turns their stomachs. I learn of two girls in my tenth-grade classes who got through *Ethan Frome* by reading aloud to each other over Skype, not unlike George Gibbs and Emily Webb chatting between their upstairs bedroom windows, just with different kinds of windows. They are acutely *social* creatures, these kids, and it is a slow learner indeed who fails to grasp that fact even as he prattles on about building a more social democracy.[7]

For decades, modern readers have peered at the two-millennia-old skeleton of Ambrose's reading and wrapped it in the pebbled, scaly skin of an old-fashioned dinosaur, seeing only the mechanics of reading and misconstruing utterly the social dynamics around it. Keizer's inverted echo of Augustine reminds us that modern adults may commit the same error: a 50-year-old may look at a 15-year-old reluctant to sit and read a book, and conclude that they do not like reading, when in fact what they dislike is *being alone*—and alone is how we read.

The idea that reading constitutes not just privacy but *radical* privacy, a complete separation from others, newly illuminates Augustine on reading. Augustine describes Ambrose's reading in order to illustrate his lack of intimacy with the other

---

[6] Augustine, *Conf.* 6.3.3. Translation mine.
[7] Garret Keizer, *Getting Schooled: The Reeducation of an American Teacher* (New York: Picador, 2015), 264.

man; but he is also preparing us for an even more dramatic and famous reading scene to come in *Confessions* 8—the epiphany in the garden.

Augustine and his friend Alypius have just heard a story about someone else's epiphanic conversion, and, tormented by his warring desire and reluctance to commit himself to Christianity, Augustine goes to wander alone. Anguished, he hears a childlike voice from a neighboring house chanting *tolle lege, tolle lege*—"pick up and read, pick up and read"; interpreting it as a divine command, he picks up a book Alypius has with him and reads a passage of *Romans* 13 that seems to speak directly to the war going on in his soul:

> I neither wanted nor needed to read any further. Indeed, immediately with the end of this sentence, it was as if freedom from care were a light that poured into my heart, dispelling all shadows of doubt. Then with a finger or something else marking the place, I closed the book and with a tranquil face I filled Alypius in. And he filled me in on what had been going on within him, which I did not know, in this way. He asked to see what I had been reading. I showed him, and he indeed noticed more than what I had read. Indeed, I did not know what came after, but the text went on, "Yea, receive the one who is weak in faith." Alypius applied this to himself, and disclosed this to me. He was given confidence by this admonition. . . .[8]

The conversion that reading prompted transpired in the private places of Augustine's mind: he must expose that inner experience to his friend (just as he has exposed it to us). Likewise, Augustine does not know what has been going on in Alypius's mind. The intensity of Augustine's conversion is followed by an equally intense moment of intimacy with a fellow traveler, a mutual exposing of one's inner experiences by means of pointing to a book and telling each other how what is seen on the visible page relates to what is felt and thought in the privacy of the heart and mind.

We always read alone: another's reading is always taking place somewhere that we cannot go. The distance between Ambrose and his disciple Augustine, or between Augustine and his friend Alypius, might as well be 1,000 miles—or 2,000 years.

Reading Where Everyone Can See You

We always read alone, and yet we try to invite others in. Augustine discloses his conversion-reading to Alypius, just as Augustine disclosed it to us—and just as he disclosed his own futile attempts to "read" Ambrose's reading at a distance. What others know of our reading is what we tell them.

Book history has cast Augustine as two-faced Janus, between a "pagan" Roman past and a Christian present, looking in both directions at once. This is woefully imprecise: Augustine speaks to us from that long period of overlap in which

---

[8] Augustine, *Conf.* 8.12.29–30.

some Romans were Christians (and vice versa), and Roman reading culture was transforming into Christian reading culture. And for all Augustine's innovation in his depiction of the interior experience of conversion, it is long Roman traditions of practicing and representing reading that both set the stage for this move and make it intelligible to us (as to his contemporary audience).

Like us, the ancient Romans read in many different kinds of situations; unlike us, they often read socially, and not just in the classroom: at a dinner banquet, at a festival, at the bathhouse, or at an author's house to hear his latest work. Like so much of Roman culture, these social contexts were intensely performative of qualities like class and gender: habitually and mercilessly, Roman reading practices dragged private moments out into a public space for advertisement and scrutiny.

In his *Letters*, the senatorial writer Pliny the Younger describes a Roman practice called *recitatio*: half book-launch party, half public reading, the *recitatio* let an author introduce part or all of a new work to a select, limited "public" of invited guests. The responses of the audience, then, were fraught with significance for all involved; Pliny writes angrily of attending a recitation where some attendees did not clap or in any other way show their appreciation of what was obviously good work.[9] Appreciation in reading was something to perform externally, where others could see it.

Of course, the dynamics of the crowd could be treacherous, especially when the prestige of the author might compel the audience to express favor, or when fashion intersected with taste. The poet Persius, in his first *Satire*, imagines composing serious literature so suited to the public's simple tastes that it evokes a palpably erotic response: "Then you will see every towering Tom, Dick, and Harry, with proper manner and calm voice abandoned, trembling as the poems enter their loins, and their innermost parts are tickled by verses that leave them weak in the knees."[10] Worse, the taste of the approving and applauding crowd is uncritical, undiscerning, and worthless: "I deny that your 'Bravo!' and your 'Good show!' are the measure or limit of what is good," he snorts.[11]

If the recitation of new literature demanded that Romans perform their aesthetic reactions, then the collective reading of older books compelled performance of more intellectual response. The reading culture documented by the essayist Aulus Gellius, a century later, favored literature from the distant past over more recent work. Old literature was marked by and valued for its tokens of antiquity, words and phrases no longer in common use but characteristic of the favored archaic style. Does a word catch your ear as interesting? Raise a question for the group, and perform your act of noticing, or answer such a question, and perform your erudition:

> At the table of Favorinus, in gatherings of his friends, it was customary for some old specimen of lyric poetry or history to be read, sometimes in Greek, sometimes in

---

[9] Pliny, *Epistulae* 6.17.   [10] Persius, *Satire* 1.19–21.   [11] Persius, *Sat.* 1.48–9.

Latin. So, one day, in a Latin poem, the word "Iapyx," the name of one of the winds, was read out, and it was asked which wind this was, and from which direction it blew, and what the explanation was of so unusual a word; and we begged Favorinus that he should teach us about the names and quarters of the other winds, since there is no general agreement about their names or the difference between them, nor even how many there are.[12]

Those who can answer such questions are *well-read*. Gellius brings a diagnostic approach to the intellectual dimensions of performed-past-reading. In this mode, he examines others' speech and conduct as indicators of their *past* reading.

The Roman motif of *lucubratio*—"burning the midnight oil"—allowed authors to frame the literary labors (*studia*) of their leisure time as efforts for the public good; thus was reading done in private spaces made public performance. By the same logic, Gellius peered closely at the people he encountered in public spaces, and construed their private reading accordingly: a man bellowing out overly obscure words in the courtroom revealed himself to be an "opsimath," who had only just read these words recently in some old book and thought he could impress others with their antique incomprehensibility. Meanwhile, a friend of Gellius's gets a pass for using the outdated form *pluria*—not, Gellius says, because he was trying to show off, but simply because he was a habitual reader of good old books, and some of the language he found there must have lodged itself in the front of his mind. In both Latin and Greek, as in English, the adjectives for "well-read" or "cultured" or "learned"—*eruditus*, πεπαιδευμένος—are perfect passive verbs: we judge someone intelligent now because they have in the past been subjected to good reading.

Romans resisted the solitude of reading, everting their internal experiences for others to see, and peering closely at their friends and foes for signs of what was happening in the lonely places of construal. This too can inform the way we read ancient reading: if we look for what Romans themselves are unintentionally revealing, we see that it is their most vociferous claims to be reading alone that we must treat with the greatest skepticism.

Reading with Other People's Bodies

Ideally, the study of ancient reading would find in our fragmentary literary evidence a series of pinhole cameras, tiny apertures somehow reflecting a complete view of what lies on the other side. But as it is, we see through a glass darkly, and this is because that glass is made of people; testimonia of ancient reading were acts of conscious performance when first written, and remain so today. We must subject them to careful literary reading to better understand what they are saying, but we

---

[12] Gellius, *Noctes Atticae* 2.22.1–2.

must also find a historicizing and symptomatic mode of reading to help us see what they are *not* saying, particularly where their authors themselves have blind spots: our witnesses cannot tell us about what they cannot see.

In announcing the first iPhone, Steve Jobs spoke of how the responsive touch-interface on the phone would cause the device itself to melt away, creating the illusion of interacting with pure data. The aesthetic of the "invisible" device is a form of what Matthew Kirschenbaum has called *screen essentialism*, the lie that computer interfaces tell us about the processing and data substrates that underlie that interface layer, which further elide the webs of networked infrastructure ("the cloud") that drive such devices and the systems of labor and natural resource exploitation that produced them.[13]

Roman book culture, too, has its essentialist ideologies of omission and elision, obscuring one of its most significant material substrates: enslaved human beings. A Roman version of Robert Darnton's classic "communication circuit," in which each stage of a book's physical creation and circulation is diagrammed, would be dense with enslaved labor.[14] When composing new works of literature, a Roman author would dictate to a secretarial slave (*notarius*); that secretary, or else a scribal slave (*librarius*), would turn draft into fair copy; further *librarii* would copy the book to be sent to friends or patrons. And when it was time for some of that social reading I discussed above, the person reading the book to the assembled dinner guests was a *lector* or *lectrix*, a reader-slave, trained especially in the oral delivery of the written word.

I may overstate the case: Romans could and sometimes did draft and read unassisted; books may have been copied by free *librarii* paid for their labor. But the wealthier a Roman household, the larger and more differentiated its enslaved staff, and use of enslaved labor to produce and consume books constituted a kind of ideal paradigm (think of antique vinyl on high-end stereo systems) among the most affluent classes, of whom the classical canon has always been a document, and in whom the discipline has traditionally been most interested.

Musing on the embodied history of ancient reading, one classicist has observed that reading is something we do with our entire body.[15] In ancient Rome, reading was as often as not something you did with someone else's body. In Latin (as sometimes in English), verbs ascribing personal agency could easily elide the labor of subordinates; in Roman book culture, this means slaves. In other words, when Romans tell us they are reading, what they mean (sometimes) is that *they are being*

---

[13] Matthew Kirschenbaum, *Mechanisms: New Media and the Forensic Imagination* (Cambridge, MA: MIT Press, 2008).

[14] Robert Darnton, "What is the History of Books?" *Daedalus* 111.3 (1982): 65–84.

[15] Simon Goldhill, "Body/Politic: Is There a History of Reading?" in *Contextualizing Classics: Ideology, Performance, Dialogue. Essays in Honor of John J. Peradotto*, ed. Thomas M. Falkner, Nancy Felson, and David Konstan (Lanham, MD: Rowman & Littlefield, 1999), 89–120.

read to by a slave. This, rather than the old no-silent-reading canard, is the most important way in which we must alienate ancient reading for ourselves.

This erased labor is especially visible in compilatory or miscellaneous literature, like the "encyclopedia" of Pliny the Elder or the essays of Aulus Gellius. The equestrian administrator Pliny boasts of his own efforts in logistical terms:

> From reading about 2,000 volumes from 100 authors (very few of which other scholars touch, so obscure is their content), I have stored up 20,000 facts worthy of attention—because, as Domitius Piso says, we need treasuries, not books—in 36 volumes.[16]

In direct response to Pliny's model of undifferentiated aggregation, Gellius presented his own efforts as more idiosyncratic and reflective of his careful intellect:

> I, on the other hand, since I had at heart the words of that most noble Ephesian (that is, "much learning does not teach the mind"), indeed exercised and exhausted myself with the unrolling and going over of a great many scrolls during every respite from business in which I could steal the leisure, but I took only a few items from them[...].[17]

Each describes an idiosyncratic *lucubratio*. Pliny's claim is repeatedly to comprehensiveness; Gellius foregrounds a kind of critical, forward-leaning engagement in which he searches out answers to obscure questions, leaving no stone unturned or commentary un-commented-upon. Each man asks us to imagine only himself and his books, yet both did all this work—reading, searching, comparing, excerpting, compiling—with the assistance of an enslaved staff.

Gellius's slaves are almost invisible; we must infer them from the rare occasion on which, instead of "I read this" or "I copied this," he happens to say "I *had this copied*"; in this way is enslaved reading labor customarily elided in Romans' language. Indeed, Gellius gives a stronger impression of being in the "company" of the dead authors he reads than of the living slaves who attend him. Pliny's enslaved workflow is part of the portrait drawn of him by his admiring nephew, Pliny the Younger, who famously comments on his uncle's industry by describing him hurrying about on his official business with a *lector* on one side of him and a note-taker on the other (or sometimes just one, if there wasn't room in the litter). The judgment of the slave-owner was the filter through which the things read passed, but the actual reading—the extracting of things from one set of books, in preparation for using them for another set of books—was the work of slaves. These slaves become extensions of their masters' literate faculties: Cicero complains he cannot compose without his amanuensis Tiro, and when Pliny the Younger's favorite reader-slave is taken ill, Pliny moans that books will just not sound the same any more.

It has been easy for classical scholars to collaborate with the way our literary corpus, the product of the slave-owning class, has rendered slaves largely invisible, their subjectivity beyond recovery. I wonder what it would mean for us to truly

---

[16] Pliny, *Natural History* Pr. 17.   [17] Gellius, *NA* Pr. 12.

acknowledge and reckon with this fact: in some if not many cases, an encounter a Roman describes as being between themselves and a text *is in fact mediated by the immanent and invisible presence of an enslaved person.* Scholarship flinches from this reality, preferring to envision scribes and reader-slaves as members of the household staff, or even speculating (without evidence) that they were "probably" freedmen or wage laborers instead of slaves.[18] Doubly invisible are the female reader-slaves, well-attested in the epigraphic record (sometimes with winking names like "Clear-sighted" or "Speech") and mentioned almost not at all in the literary material (and so in scholarship).[19]

What interpretive framework should we use to understand the presence of these invisible—these erased—enslaved individuals in the reading practices of the wealthiest Romans? Perhaps we should turn to media studies, and consider the relationship between Roman book and Roman reader-slave as that between storage medium and playback device (diskette/disk drive, LP/turntable, cassette/VCR): this would seem to capture, perhaps unfortunately, some of the Roman sense of their book-slaves as equipment rather than people. Or perhaps we should turn to the concept of the prosthesis, to think about (as modern scholars have occasionally noted) how Roman book-slaves performed assistive work for those whose eyesight was failing or who were not able to write with their own hands. Here we might have a modern history of prosthetic reading, pre- and post-industrial, to tap into.

More mundane and less horrifying aspects of the ancient book experience also seem beneath the notice of our ancient elite witnesses: how much did books cost? What did papyrus feel like? How did old books look or smell different from new books? As often happens, what they took for granted and so saw no reason to comment on is most enticing to us to know about. On the other hand, although book historians have long been frustrated by the silence of Imperial-era sources on the transition from scroll to codex, which the material record tells us was underway by the turn of the third century CE, perhaps we should take this silence itself as significant, an expression of a Roman aristocratic conviction that format was beneath their notice. Silence itself may be read, with care.

It is here that much of the excavation remains to be done: better understanding not only what our ancient sources are telling us, but also what they are not telling us. Some things we see clearly, some through a glass darkly; some we cannot see, strain as we might; and some things, perhaps, we would prefer not to see at all.

---

[18] See, for example, George W. Houston, *Inside Roman Libraries: Book Collections and Their Management in Antiquity* (Chapel Hill: University of North Carolina Press, 2014), a fine and invaluable study.

[19] Raymond J. Starr, "Reading Aloud: Lectores and Roman Reading," *The Classical Journal* 86.4 (1991): 337–43.

The Reading Room is Crowded

In retrospect, it becomes clear that modern readers' repeated pilgrimages to the shrine of *Confessions* 6.3.3 are as revelatory about them as they are of the text itself. Readers in the middle and later twentieth century, for example, went in search of enlightenment about "orality," under the influence of thinkers like Marshall McLuhan and Walter Ong.[20] What reflections might we find of ourselves in our own histories of ancient reading? How might the present future of reading and ancient reading reflect one another?

The world of ancient reading and books was an intensely multimedia and multi-format one. Romans might hear a book read to them, or read it with their eyes, or hear it quoted by heart by a friend; they might encounter the same book in all of these formats. They might read or be read to from a scroll, or a codex. This, like the messily hybrid world of print and manuscript in the early modern period, is a condition to which we are now returning: academics and the general public alike enjoy a range of both print and electronic reading formats and devices, some purpose-made (the e-ink reader) and some merely applications on another platform (smartphones or tablets). Amazon's absorption of not only print and digital book distribution but also digital audiobook distribution has allowed them to synchronize media, inviting you to put down your Kindle reader and resume the audiobook from the same place. The noun *book* and the verb *to read* are approaching levels of messiness to rival those that marked them in antiquity.

The flattening of competition in platforms such as Amazon's Kindle distribution system are obscuring other realities of labor and capital: it is as easy to buy a self-published book on Amazon, or a mendaciously repackaged public domain text, as it is the product of a massive corporate publisher. In the academic space, versioning and the attendant profit motives are redefining "textbook."

But it is Augustine's and Keizer's radical solitude of reading that seems most implicated. Romans reading in a scholarly mode were given to imagining the traditions and authorities that constituted their reading material's antecedents—the chains of commentary and influence that produced the book in front of them—and were also inclined to consult commentaries for exegetical insight; like the hungry ghosts clustering around the hot blood Odysseus spills at the edge of the underworld, or like the wax ancestor masks that loom behind the eulogist at a Roman funeral, the writers and fellow readers of past and present gathered hazily over some kinds of Roman reading. Features like the ability to look a word up in a dictionary or

---

[20] *Inter al.*: Marshall McLuhan, *Understanding Media: The Extensions of Man* (New York: McGraw-Hill, 1964); Walter Ong, *Orality and Literacy: The Technologizing of the Word* (New York: Routledge, 2002).

Wikipedia with a tap, or Kindle's built-in "X-Ray" annotations, promise something similar (X-Ray incidentally fulfills another Roman slave-role: the *nomenclator*, who reminds you who everyone is).

Another Kindle feature, "Popular Highlights," offers to bring all the sweaty-palmed social anxiety of Roman dinner party reading to the privacy of your own e-reader. Enabled by default, this feature indicates passages in the book you are reading that have been most highlighted by other readers of the same book (the feature does not work, of course, on books that the user has loaded into Kindle manually, rather than purchased from the platform). Almost as soon as e-reader developers and designers had reproduced the experience of reading books digitally, they also reproduced the experience of opening a library book in which a dozen people have already written. The effect is a curious kind of banal haunting: such highlights, by virtue of the underlying algorithmic logic, are a kind of common denominator of appealing insights or turns of phrase. The feature may be disabled, but the assumption is clear: you wouldn't want to read *alone*, would you?

The story of Augustine's *Confessions* and the "no silent reading" canard warns us against continuing to valorize specific and isolated textual loci. Here the methods of philology, literary studies, and history must work hand-in-hand, as they always do when classics is at its best. The future history of ancient reading will be written with closer reading, broader reading, and reading that treats the ancient evidence on its own terms while also pushing back against our sources' willful omissions and blind spots. But per Augustine himself, it may also be written by making our peace—whatever that will mean—with everything in the private spaces of our subjects' reading minds that is as inaccessible to us now as it would be if we were staring at them across a quiet classroom.

How did the ancients read? We can answer with adverbs of the group (socially, alone), of the body (visually, aurally, orally), of the mind (voraciously, memoriously, cautiously); we can answer with what Latin calls the ablative of means (by means of their eyes, by means of a slave); but we must inevitably conclude that they read *unknowably*—as do we all.

FURTHER READING

Fitzgerald, William. *Slavery and the Roman Literary Imagination.* Cambridge: Cambridge University Press, 2000.

Frampton, Stephanie. "What to Do with Books in the *De finibus*." *Transactions of the American Philological Association* 146.1 (2016): 117–47.

Goldhill, Simon. "Body/Politic: Is There a History of Reading?" Thomas M. Falkner, Nancy Felson, and David Konstan, eds. *Contextualizing Classics: Ideology, Performance, Dialogue: Essays in Honor of John J. Peradotto.* Lanham, MD: Rowman & Littlefield, 1999, 89–120.

Harnett, Benjamin. "The Diffusion of the Codex." *Classical Antiquity* 36.2 (2017): 183–235.

Horsfall, Nicholas. "Rome without Spectacles." *Greece & Rome* 42.1 (1995): 49–56.

Howley, Joseph A. *Aulus Gellius and Roman Reading Culture: Text, Presence and Imperial Knowledge in the Noctes Atticae.* Cambridge: Cambridge University Press, 2018.

Johnson, William A. "Toward a Sociology of Reading in Classical Antiquity." *American Journal of Philology* 121.4 (2000): 593–627.

Johnson, William A. *Readers and Reading Culture in the High Roman Empire: A Study of Elite Communities.* Oxford: Oxford University Press, 2010.

Johnson, William A., and Holt N. Parker, eds. *Ancient Literacies.* Oxford: Oxford University Press, 2009.

Keizer, Garret. *Getting Schooled: The Reeducation of an American Teacher.* New York: Picador, 2015.

Ker, James. "Nocturnal Writers in Imperial Rome: The Culture of *Lucubratio*." *Classical Philology* 99.3 (2004): 209–42.

McCutcheon, R. W. "Silent Reading in Antiquity and the Future History of the Book." *Book History* 18 (2015): 1–32.

Milnor, Kristina. *Graffiti and the Literary Landscape in Roman Pompeii.* Oxford: Oxford University Press, 2014.

Starr, Raymond J. "Reading Aloud: Lectores and Roman Reading." *The Classical Journal* 86.4 (1991): 337–43.

Stock, Brian. *Augustine the Reader: Meditation, Self-Knowledge, and the Ethics of Interpretation.* Cambridge, MA: Harvard University Press, 1996.

Valette-Cagnac, Emmanuelle. *La Lecture à Rome. Rites et pratiques.* Paris: Belin, 1997.

2

IN THE CLASSROOM

CHRISTOPHER CANNON

The 4- or 5-year-old child entering "reception" in the UK (what schools in the United States tend to call "kindergarten") might open his or her first reader and find nothing to read in it at all. One of the first books in the ubiquitous series that calls itself "The Oxford Reading Tree" is called *At School*, and, while these words are printed on the cover, the book itself consists of five openings in which a narrative unfolds in pictures.[1] In the first of these openings a small boy is dragged up a path by a woman (who must be his mother) toward a doorway where another woman crouches, holding out a small stuffed bear. The next opening shows the boy hiding behind a cloakroom door and a girl his own age holding out another toy to entice him into the room. In the third opening the boy has entered a classroom already crowded with children at play. In the fourth we see the formerly reluctant boy joining in (vigorously stirring a pot of blocks on a toy cooker). The last opening reverses the first with the teacher again at the door, but rather than dragging the boy up the path, the boy's mother is now dragging him *away* from the school where he clearly wants to stay. Not least because no teaching is required in order to read this book, a child might well be given it on his or her first day of school, where that day would also unfold in its pages.

It has, in some ways, been ever thus: the reader accommodates the student to reading by absorbing the student's world, drawing him or her into the tuition it provides by reflecting that world back as if in a mirror. The first reader a medieval child would have encountered moved more quickly to words, but its very first text, the *Distichs of Cato*, began with two-word commands that described what such a child should be expecting to do on his first day of school: "Read books" ("Libros lege"), "Play with the hoop" ("Trocho lude"), "learn literature" ("Disce litteras").[2]

---

[1] "The Oxford Reading Tree" (Oxford: Oxford University Press, 2018) (https://www.oxfordowl.co.uk/for-home/reading-owl/oxford-reading-tree-levels/).

[2] *The Distichs of Cato* (as *Dicta Catonis*), in *Minor Latin Poets*, ed. J. Wight Duff and Arnold M. Duff (Cambridge, MA: Harvard University Press, 1961; first published 1934), 585–663.

The New England Primer, the first schoolbook printed in the US, also began with simple commands designed to shape an early reader's behavior in the classroom: "Love your School," "Mind Your Book," "Play not With Bad Boys," and "Be Not a Dunce."[3] McGuffey's *Eclectic Readers*, the most widely used schoolbooks in the US from the middle of the nineteenth into the twentieth century, situated the "little reader" in a farmyard rather than a schoolroom but proceeded as if the school were itself on the farm and its first simple sentences were a catechism that pointed to each farmyard animal as if that animal were right there: "Is it an ox"? "A sly hen," "Can she fly?" The absorptive pedagogy by which all of these early readers taught was summed up in McGuffey's culminating command: "Do as we do."[4]

Such realism is a constant in early readers because it eases the new student into the unfamiliarity he or she must begin to master, but it is worth focusing on this fundamental similarity in the first steps of reading in the classroom from the Middle Ages until now because these steps are also fundamentally different. In the centuries before our own, the primary school student was also asked to lean forward into what might be described as the future familiar, into the schoolrooms he or she would eventually inhabit as well as into the life that schoolroom reading was preparing him or her for. The *Distichs* grew the schoolboy up particularly fast (this early, and well into the Renaissance, it was only boys who had the opportunity to read in a classroom): if he honored his parents and played with hoops in its first pages, he was also enjoined in those same pages to love his wife ["Coniugem ama"], drink wine with moderation ["Vino tempera"], teach his own children ["Liberos erudi"], and shun prostitutes ["Meretricem fuge"]. The New England Primer not only offered stern moral lessons ("In Adam's Fall/We Sinned All") but insisted that time's winged chariot was already drawing near ("While youth do cheer/Death may be near"). It might be that the McGuffey's first reader is on its way to "The Oxford Reading Tree," since it is richly illustrated, already teaching through pictures, and often sees the farmyard through the child's eyes: "A bad dog. It bit a man." But this student is already asked to imagine him- or herself, not only surveying the animals on the farm, but at work there: "A red cow. Has she hay?" "A big ox. Let him go." And what the young boy holds in these pictures, as his very first possession, is not a pencil, tablet, or book, but an axe ("My axe is by me").

The slow progress of both perspective and pedagogy in "The Oxford Reading Tree" might therefore be seen as the form learning to read must take in a culture in which helicoptering is a kind of parenting and the thing a schoolroom must never

---

[3] *The New England Primer: to which is added, the shorter catechism of the Westminster Assembly of Divines* (Concord: Rufus Merrill, 1850); Sabin Americana, Gale, *Cengage Learning*, 18 (http://galenet. galegroup.com.proxy1.library.jhu.edu/servlet/Sabin?af=RN&ae=CY102293597&srchtp=a&ste=14) (accessed January 18, 2018).

[4] William Holmes McGuffey et al., *McGuffey's New First Eclectic Reader: For Young Learners* (Cincinnati, OH: Wilson, Hinkle & Co., 1863); *Nineteenth Century Collections Online* (http://tinyurl. galegroup.com/tinyurl/5hDtw2) (accessed January 18, 2018).

do is leave a child behind. Such a reader is the leading edge of the strong view that a child must be made "ready" for literacy and that print knowledge (as it is sometimes called in such contexts) should not be sprung on the unsuspecting child. A modern journal addressed to reading teachers describes how children can be led toward literacy in a "singing classroom" where a song is playing each day even before lessons begin so that children might memorize the lyric as they unconsciously learn a tune, and can then talk about what the song's words mean and illustrate those meanings before ever seeing them written.[5] Singing with such attention to signification *is* a form of literacy of course, and the other literacies a child might pass through in the modern classroom while getting ready for books are now thought to include building with blocks (because blocks may signify the objects—the car or house or row of shops—they stand in for), drawing (which can convey particular ideas), and imaginative play (in which bits of clothing can produce characters and the child's own actions can tell a story).[6] As philosophy taught us in its own writing lesson recently enough, words need not be understood "in the narrow sense of linear and phonetic notation," and so the view that the Nambikwara of Brazil drew only "wavy horizontal lines" when given paper and pencil (as anthropologists had put it) was blinkered by an ethnocentrism that could not see that wavy lines used "as if" they were writing *were*, in fact, writing (as Jacques Derrida insisted) in every sense we mean by that term.[7] And so we may also rightly say that the child paging through the pictures in *At School*, transforming them as I did above into a narrative, *is* reading even if he or she is not reading words.

In measuring the speed of current habits of reading in the classroom, however, we must also reckon with the extent to which *At School* is in fact the *end* of the preparatory teaching embraced by "The Oxford Reading Tree." Even before *At School* is placed in any child's hands, he or she is made ready for it by large "character cards" that introduce the student to the boy at the center of the story as if he has some larger existence beyond this or any of the method's books. His name is Kipper, a sign made the more vivacious by the revelation that Kipper is in fact the word "Christopher" morphed into this gender-neutral common noun, not as a diminutive, but because the boy could not initially pronounce his own name. The woman dragging Kipper, these cards show, is simply "Mum" (as "Dad" in other books is simply "Dad"), and Kipper's nuclear family is further fleshed out by Biff, Kipper's twin, so called because it was the best "Barbara" could do in pronouncing her own name. The history the character cards reveal to be congealed in its simplest pictures

[5] Becky Iwasaki, Timothy Rasinski, Kasim Yildirim, and Belinda S. Zimmerman, "Let's Bring Back the Magic of Song for Teaching Reading," *The Reading Teacher* 67.2 (2013): 137–41.

[6] Jolyn Blank, "Fostering Language and Literacy Learning: Strategies to Support the Many Ways Children Communicate," *Dimensions of Early Childhood* 40.1 (2012): 3–11; 4.

[7] See Claude Lévi-Strauss, "A Writing Lesson," in *Tristes tropiques* (New York: Criterion, 1961), 294–304; and, for his critique of this account, Jacques Derrida, *Grammatology*, trans. Gayatri Chakravorty Spivak (Baltimore: Johns Hopkins University Press, 1976), 101–40.

reaches beyond the classroom and, like the illustrations in McGuffey's readers, pulls the world around the school into the book—assuming, of course, that that world is a suburban England in which the person who does the school run must be his mother and, paired with every mother, there is a dad and one sibling. "The Oxford Reading Tree" works to resist the ethnocentricism of Kipper's family with two children of color, Wilf and Wilma, who are also introduced on character cards as Kipper and Biff's best friends. But the realism of this pedagogy also takes a different form when students are presented with the "big book," a page-for-page version of *At School* with pages several feet high—as if, reversing the absorptions of the book's realism, books themselves begin to expand to the size of the classroom—a size that allows the teacher to guide the whole class through this wordless text before they are given the smaller book to page through on their own.

The philosophy that educators tend to cite in journals such as *The Reading Teacher* or *Dimensions of Early Childhood* or the *Journal of Teacher Education* when talking about such preparations is John Dewey's emphasis on "experience" in education. Jean Piaget and Lev Vygotsky are often mentioned along the way as constructivists, who, like Dewey, believed that knowledge is most fully and easily acquired when it is found, not in books, but in the "transaction" (a term Dewey liked) that occurs between an "individual"(another crucial word) and his or her environment.[8] The pedagogy such a philosophy reformed was described as traditional and identified less with the early reading texts I have mentioned—the *Distichs of Cato*, *The New England Primer*, McGuffey's readers—than as a method that, as Dewey put it, may have provided experiences, but experiences "of a wrong kind," the repetition that not only made the student "callous to ideas" but robbed him or her of "the impetus to learn"; a pedagogy that bent the child to the knowledge being purveyed rather than bending itself to the child's "situation."[9] As Dewey was himself quick to recognize, experience was a slippery concept—almost any practice or idea that analysis wants to put out of the way can be fitted into it—but Dewey's philosophy also draws a firm line between the classrooms in which reading was taught before the latter half of the twentieth century and the classrooms in which something like "The Oxford Reading Tree" is employed. *At School*, like so many similar books, assumes that any cognitive difficulty the child encounters when learning to read—anything like the feelings that mean Kipper's mum must drag him to school—can be made to evaporate, just as they do for Kipper, in a classroom where literacy is represented *as* play. What such a pedagogy firmly rejects is an educational philosophy in which difficulty is understood as the defining quality of elementary learning. Early readers such as *The New England Primer* represent the alphabet's first lesson not as a movement from fear to pleasure as in Kipper's happy case but a process in which (as in the *Primer's* lesson for the letter "F") the

---

[8] John Dewey, *Experience and Education* (New York: The Macmillan Company, 1938), 44.
[9] Dewey, *Experience and Education*, 26.

"foolishness bound up in the heart of a Child" is to be "driven from him" not by a warm welcome and enticing toys but "the rod of Correction," where the resistant learner may be called an "idle Fool" and the remedy for any reluctance "at school" is to be "whipt."

The Tongue Says What the Heart Loves

Literacy training in the Middle Ages and well through the Renaissance was traditionally called *grammatica*, the first of the seven liberal arts, and always represented by a female figure—female because of the grammatical gender of "grammatica"—wielding a rod or a handful of twigs. This figure represented the classroom circumstances of any medieval or Renaissance schoolboy whose teacher employed beating as a method, but the rod and the violence it promised were themselves representations of how the teaching of reading was understood in these earlier periods, not as the acquisition of knowledge, but as the stamping out of error, as if it was impossible to read without proceeding wrongly at first. Learning was therefore a process of admonishment, as if the student's intellect was not so much to be prepared as to be hammered into a suitable shape. And yet, just as *At School* represents as normal what must be a limit case, Grammatica represented a threat much more than a schoolroom reality. We know that beating was a feature of elementary teaching until very recently, but to read the books that preceded *At School* is to find not as much violence as playfulness. "The Priest and the Wolf" ("De Presbitero et Lupo"), for example, a popular fable found in English schoolbooks in the Middle Ages, also absorbs the circumstances of the classrooms in which it was used, but because the lesson it describes is an animal fable, like so much older schoolroom literature, it also makes a joke of the pedagogy it recreates (see Box on p. 33). Its narrative begins with the priest teaching the wolf the alphabet, which the wolf learns with ease at first, repeating "A" after the teacher's prompt, as he does with both "B" and "C." But when the priest gives him a little quiz, asking him to repeat all that he has learned so far, instead of chanting "A B C," he says that the best he can do is "AGNUS" (lamb) since nothing happening in the classroom can distract him from the thought of lunch. The story finishes with a proverb that presses the grammar lesson into a general, ethical truth ("the tongue says what the heart loves"), but that general truth still applies to the classroom in which the student's natural dispositions (all that he already "loves") might distract him from the lesson his teacher wants him to care about. At this level, the strategy, and one might even say the subject, of "The Priest and the Wolf" is the same as *At School* since the latter text also shows how learning almost necessarily requires overcoming an initial resistance. Although the shape of the joke in *At School* and "The Priest and the Wolf" is different, they both make the

The Priest and the Wolf

A priest taught a wolf his letters. The priest said, "A" and the wolf replied likewise. The priest said "B" and the wolf replied likewise. "C" said the priest, and the wolf replied likewise. Now put it all together, said the priest, and recite the alphabet. And the wolf responded: I do not yet know the alphabet. To which the priest responded: just say what you think is correct. And the wolf said, "To me what seems most correct is 'LAMB' [AGNUS]." Then the priest said, "as it is in the heart, so it is in the mouth." And the moral of this story is: The tongue announces what the heart loves. And so we see here that it is often the case that we understand best what we already know in our hearts.

De Presbitero et Lupo

Presbiter quidam docuit lupum litteras. Presbiter dixit: "A" et lupus similiter. Presbiter ait "B" et lupus similiter. "C" dixit presbiter, et lupus dixit similiter. Modo congrega, ait presbiter, et sillabica. Et respondit lupus: sillabicare nondum scio. Cui presbiter: Ut tibi melius videtur, sic dicito. Et ait lupus: Michi optime videtur quod hoc sonat "AGNUS." Tunc presbiter ait: Quod in corde, hoc in ore.

Moralitas: Lingua clamat quod cor amat. Hinc sepe datur intelligi quod verum sit in corde teneri.*

reversing of this resistance their humorous point, in the modern instance because fear is so quickly and completely transformed into affection and in the medieval case because the wolf demonstrates that he cannot learn his letters by spelling a word he has never been taught. Insofar as the joke in the medieval case also showed the medieval schoolboy that learning to read might be easier than he thought, "The Priest and the Wolf" was also getting the student who read it ready for literacy training.

"The Priest and the Wolf" differs very much from *At School*, however, in the amount of prior knowledge its recursive lesson presumes, and this demand both reveals and constitutes an even more fundamental difference than attitudes toward punishment and violence in the teaching of reading before John Dewey and since. The schoolboy who was reading the Latin fable had to recognize only simple words and understand only the most rudimentary rules of syntax (many of the sentences of "The Priest and the Wolf" are only three words long), but, even as this text was preparing him for the lessons that followed, he was already reading it. "The Oxford Reading Tree" not only holds off on words in *At School*, but when its books begin to

* *Romuli anglici cunctis exortae fabulae [Romulus LBG]* 2: 642 in *Les fabulistes latins*, ed. Léopold Hervieux, 2nd edn, 2 vols. (Paris: n.p., 1893–9). The translation here is my own.

include them they are doled out like medicine, one at a time ("Biff" or "Mum"), without syntax because they are all nouns, until the story's very last words ("No, it's Dad"). The wolf's leap from letters to words in "The Priest and the Wolf" not only transforms an early learner's resistance into a joke, it precisely tracks the rapid movement from letters to whole texts that characterized literacy training in earlier periods. *The New England Primer* moved with similar speed, from the alphabet on its first page to letter combinations on its second and third, with a whole poem for the student to read on page four ("Fear God all day/Parents obey/No false thing say,/By no sin stray…"). A medieval primer moved even faster, with an alphabet, then the Lord's Prayer, the Ave Maria, and the Creed, all on a single sheet of parchment. This is to say that a certain amount of the violence in the classroom prior to Dewey was *cognitive*, as the readings put in front of the schoolboy lashed him forward from novelty to novelty, leaving no space for consolidation of his abilities before demanding yet another leap. Grammatica and the violence her rod promised could therefore also be said to represent the violence that may regularly attend breaking through the barrier from ignorance to knowledge. A fifteenth-century schoolbook describes the feelings at issue in one of the English sentences set for students to translate: "A hard Latyn to make, my face wexyth blakke." This exercise once again absorbs the teaching it performs—since "making a Latin" was to translate an English sentence like this one—but it also absorbs the discomfort of a student faced with such a task and the extent to which his fear or frustration could be read right out of his expression.

We Understand Best What We Already Know in Our Hearts

The goal of classroom reading both early and late is what we might imagine the *Distichs of Cato* to command ("Love literature" ("litteras ama")) and what we now call, more simply, "a love of reading"—that is, even as schoolbooks absorb the student's experience to themselves, we also want those books to move outward to become a lived and constant part of the child's, and then the full grown child's, experience beyond the classroom. Modern studies about how to achieve this extension of the remit of the classroom to life do not always endorse the view that the slow pedagogy so common now is better than the leap that used to be demanded. When asked to define reading, some students today will indeed say that reading is a pleasure, others will say that it is a task (saying words correctly), still others will describe it as work (what must be done to accomplish something else) or even a rung on a social ladder (a source of status), but it is the children who seem to have been exposed to it earliest who love reading most.[10] The children who find reading

---

[10] Elizabeth Bondy, "Seeing It Their Way: What Children's Definitions of Reading Tell Us About Improving Teacher Education," *Journal of Teacher Education* 41.5 (1990): 33–45.

a chore are those who arrive at school unable to tell the difference between the front and back of a book. Although classrooms may avoid it, in other words, the leap into literacy may still be occurring at home, or perhaps even out and about, before the boy or girl enters the modern classroom and learning is slowed down.

To be sure, modern pedagogy does not always insist on slowness. In some curricula there is an emphasis on "whole word" instruction, not unlike the kinds of teaching the medieval and *The New England* primers demanded, with the student given whole texts early on with the assumption that slow steps can be boring and therefore counter-productive. Some school systems have made a firm and resolute move back to what has long been called "phonics," the rote learning of letters and their sounds, not unlike the lesson the priest is giving the wolf in the medieval fable and exactly the sort of drill that Dewey reprehended. As a result, much of the discussion about how to teach reading in journals or in policy statements looks like a kind of bargaining between warring forces with no obvious conclusion. The National Literacy Strategy promulgated by the Labour government in the UK advocated a kind of grand compromise called the "searchlights model," which assumed that "reading is best taught by using a range of strategies simultaneously," with the student turning from cue to cue, "phonics" or "knowledge of context" or "word recognition" or "grammatical knowledge," and reading the text by dint of whatever strategy worked best.[11] But a 2005 House of Commons report observed that this eclectic method had no empirical basis (no studies proved it was effective), and one of the consequences of the government's insistence on such variety was to edge out any opportunity in the curriculum for reading and writing to be systematically taught.[12] One might expect technology to have intervened in some way in this negotiation. There is certainly a sense that the web demands new kinds of literacy, that students must be prepared for online reading by training with web browsers and in the synthesis of the texts that can be amassed when moving between a variety of sites. And yet there are very few websites or programs or apps that do more than change the medium in which a student encounters the texts he or she must learn to read. Alongside an increasing use of these media is the conviction, sometimes stated but always implicit in practice, that "technology does not teach."[13]

And the debate may really be moot if it is true, as the best early readers suggest, that reading cannot really be taught.[14] Something like this idea serves as a kind of allegory in *At School*, whose spare narrative, like so many of the simple stories we

[11] House of Commons Education and Skills Committee, "Teaching Children to Read," *Eighth Report of Session 2004–5* (London: Stationery Office, 2005), 10–12.

[12] House of Commons Education and Skills Committee, "Teaching Children to Read," 15–18.

[13] Peter McDermott and Kathleen A. Gormley, "Teachers' Use of Technology in Elementary Reading Lessons," *Reading Psychology* 37 (2015): 121–46.

[14] According to Jacqueline Lynch, "many preschool teachers felt that there was a correct or 'best' way to encourage children's reading and writing development and they were unaware of the 'best' way." "Preschool Teachers' Beliefs about Children's Print Literacy Development," *Early Years* 29.2 (2009): 191–203; 198.

tell children, is haunted at the edges by the uncanny. That is, while on its face it makes perfect sense that Kipper is reluctant to enter a school on his first day, why is the classroom already full of children who are comfortable? Why is it only Kipper's first day and not the first day of school for all of the other children? Is he just late? Kipper could have just arrived at a new school, of course, but since the story seems intent on universalizing his experience—designed to sympathize with the discomfort each of its readers might have felt when arriving at school for the first time—the school really ought to be new to every child in the story. The narrative only makes sense, then, because of a temporal sleight of hand that makes the school a pleasant space by peopling it with what are, in effect, Ghosts of the Classroom Yet to Come, future Kippers who are as comfortable at the beginning of the story as Kipper will be, with their assistance, by its end. These ghosts are therefore future Kippers whose comfort in the classroom acknowledges that in order for children to learn this reader's lesson, they must know it before their first day "at school."

Of course children are helped to read by the guidance they are given by teachers and in books, particularly those children who have difficulty in relating letters to sounds and writing to meanings. To the extent that helping a child decode a text in the classroom makes him or her happier about the task, it must also conduce to the pleasure in reading that is, of course, the goal of reading in the classroom. But, as in the case of my children, or even my own recollection of how I learned to read, there is a long moment when letters are pictures that do not instantly conjure up a sound and groups of letters are like bricks whose shape can only be painstakingly related to meaning, and then there is a transition—so lightning-fast that it is imperceptible— when words suddenly *are* meaning and the only thing left to learn is more words. The speeds and strategies of pedagogy that turn around this little miracle might be understood as different ways of recognizing that reading is an innate skill, in effect called forth, like speech, by our ability to acquire language as such. And there are, indeed, advocates of an approach that capitalizes on the similarity of learning to read to the acquisition of spoken language, and who would therefore expose even infants to whole texts since there is no reason not to leap across the invisible boundary to literacy as early as possible.[15] But the older and newer sorts of pedagogy I have been contrasting here are drawn together by the subtle ways that they acknowledge this fact. The wolf in "The Priest and the Wolf" concludes—as did many animal fables in the Middle Ages—with a second moral that generalizes the first, insisting that it is not just appetite that is innate in the student but understanding ("we understand best what we already know in our hearts"), that, just as the wolf finally proves, he could read all along. Despite its graphic insistence that words should be kept at bay, moreover, *At School* offers this same acknowledgment in words so subtle that they are themselves like pictures, and so close to the edge of the frame that they act like the anamorphosis at the corner of a portrait which can only

---

[15] Dominic W. Massaro, "Acquiring Literacy Naturally," *American Scientist* 100 (2012): 324–33.

be made out if you have eyes to see it. As Kipper is being dragged into school, at its gate—and therefore just outside the boundaries of its teaching—there is a small sign that says "nursery school." This sign is not meant for Kipper, of course, and yet it must be meant for the child getting ready to read who opens *At School* on his or her first school day. This sign presumes that the child can read even before any teaching, and so reading in the classroom consists most often of acknowledging, and then fostering, what many children—maybe even most children—already know.

FURTHER READING

Bohning, Gerry. "The McGuffey Eclectic Readers: 1836–1986." *The Reading Teacher* 40.3 (1986): 263–9.

Burke, Catherine, and Ian Grosvenor. *School*. London: Reaktion Books, 2008.

Cannon, Christopher. *From Literacy to Literature: England, 1300–1400*. Oxford: Oxford University Press, 2016.

Carpenter, Charles. *History of American Schoolbooks*. Philadelphia: University of Pennsylvania Press, 1963.

Cazden, C. B. *Classroom Discourse: The Language of Teaching and Learning*. Portsmouth, NH: Heinemann, 2001.

Cipolla, Carlo M. *Literacy and Development in the West*. Harmondsworth: Pelican, 1969.

Crain, Patricia. "New Histories of Literacy." *A Companion to the History of the Book*, ed. Simon Eliot and Jonathan Rose. Chichester: Wiley-Blackwell, 2007, 467–79.

Egan, Kieran and Michael Ling. "We Begin as Poets: Conceptual Tools and the Arts in Early Childhood." *The Arts in Children's Lives: Context, Culture and Curriculum*. Dordrecht, The Netherlands: Kluwer, 2002, 93–100.

Kolb, David A. *Experiential Learning: Experience as the Source of Learning and Development*. Englewood Cliffs, NJ: Prentice-Hall, 1984.

Lerer, Seth. *Children's Literature: A Reader's History from Aesop to Harry Potter*. Chicago: University of Chicago Press, 2008.

Mann, Jill. *From Aesop to Reynard: Beast Fable in Medieval Britain*. Oxford: Oxford University Press, 2009.

Marrou, H. I. *A History of Education in Antiquity*, trans. George Lamb. Madison, WI: University of Wisconsin Press, 1982; first published in English, 1956.

Orme, Nicholas. *Medieval Schools: From Roman Britain to Medieval England*. New Haven: Yale University Press, 2006.

Roskos, Kathleen A. and Patton O. Tabors. *Oral Language and Early Literacy in Preschool: Talking, Reading and Writing*, 2nd edn. Newark, DE: International Reading Association, 2009.

3

IN THE CUSTOM HOUSE

ISABEL HOFMEYR

Books Overboard

Most nineteenth-century sea-travelers would have been familiar with the phrase "the Chops of the Channel." The term referred to the jaws, or chops, of the English Channel and hence to its entrance, signaled to the north by Land's End and the Scilly Isles. The stretch of sea was fabled—the setting of early skirmishes against the Spanish Armada in 1588, and for ocean-weary English sailors, a herald of home.

To ship's passengers, the Chops signaled yet something else, namely that it was time to sort through their books in preparation for encountering Customs officials in port. As an 1849 passenger's manual explained, these officers paid particular attention to copyright violations, especially pirated US editions of English authors. These reprints "can endure no longer than the voyage" (as the manual phrased it), and many such volumes must have been tossed into the Chops, to sink slowly into the nether reaches of Davy Jones's library.

Yet disposing of volumes overboard did not end the preparation that book-burdened voyagers had to make. As the manual gratuitously reminded its readers, books are "cumbrous appendages to the traveller." Like friends, they could improve on greater acquaintance, but could equally cause "inconvenience or disappointment."[1] And inconvenient these textual companions certainly proved to be. Passengers had to sort their books by place and date of publication as well as by language. In terms of place, travelers had to distinguish those volumes printed in British possessions from those originally produced in Britain but exported elsewhere. Books produced outside the British Empire constituted yet another pile. Bookish passengers also had to keep an eye on the date of publication, sorting their volumes into those that appeared before and after 1801. That year marked the Act of Union between Great Britain and Ireland; the latter was a long-standing center of reprinting and the

---

[1] Henry Sayer, *The Homeward-bound Passenger's Companion, via the Cape; Compiled for the Use of Residents in India, and the British Possessions Adjacent Thereto; with a Tariff of Customs Duties* ([London]: C. Beckett, 1849). Quotations from pp. 10–11, 36.

copyright status of books printed there before and after 1801 differed.[2] Each of these various categories attracted a different duty reckoned by imperial hundredweight (112 pounds). Maps and drawings were levied with a tax of one penny each, and pictures and paintings, one shilling per square foot.

The handbook may sound simply like so much overwrought Victorian bureaucracy, deserving of being consigned to the Chops. For our purposes, however, the handbook is useful since it trained passengers to think like Customs officials. Instead of classifying their books by genre or author, travelers had to assess them in terms of weight, date, and place of manufacture (no more light reading or weighing of arguments here). In addition to engaging with the micro-qualities of their books, passengers had to factor in larger issues, attending to the pathway of the book itself and how this intersected with international law. With a stress on materiality and scale, these methods of interpretation start to sound rather modern. Add in the maritime setting of the Chops, and one has a contemporary-looking agenda: materialism, mobility, scale, ecology. Somewhat unexpectedly, the Victorian Custom House and its officials offer a useful vantage point from which to consider twenty-first-century themes.

Why would one want to do this? Customs and Excise is an obscure and little-studied institution. The red and green lanes in the airport remind us that they're there, and we might have encountered Customs officials as B-grade detectives in novels and films about drug smuggling, but we have little idea of how they work in practice.[3] Yet, in a posthuman, object-oriented age, Customs and Excise become of more than passing interest. As the arm of the state that governs mobile objects (or "matter in transit," as one official said), Customs and Excise and their procedures can illuminate contemporary themes of the human and nonhuman. An observation from two early historians of Customs is apposite here: "Customs history, properly studied, may be found fruitful of striking lessons. Possibly the most novel of these is the vital importance of discriminating clearly between names and things."[4] How did Customs officials go about their business of dealing with names and things, and what relevance might this have for scholars of reading?

Customs: Theory and Practice

Customs and Excise is an instrument of taxation and revenue generation. In England, Customs (taxing of goods traveling over borders) is the older part of the equation dating back to the thirteenth century while Excise (taxing of goods

---

[2] My thanks to Meredith McGill for explaining the significance of this date.

[3] Gerald Seymour, *The Untouchable* (London: Hodder & Stoughton, 2014).

[4] Henry Atton and Henry Hurst Holland, *The King's Customs: Vol II: An Account of Maritime Revenue, Contraband Traffic, the Introduction of Free Trade, and the Abolition of the Navigation and Corn Law, from 1801 to 1855* (New York: August M. Kelly, 1967; originally published 1910), vi.

within borders) is a seventeenth-century departure used to raise funds for the Parliamentary forces during the English Civil War. As William Ashworth demonstrates in his superb history, from its inception, Customs was a feudal-ridden institution bristling with sinecures and perquisites.[5] Excise, by contrast, was rapidly forced to become modern in part because it was so widely hated—excise officers had right of search and entry especially in relation to liquor production, making the excise man a universally reviled figure.

Under close public scrutiny, excise officers had to make their procedures visible and defensible. The nature of their work (checking the composition, weight, measure, quality, and production processes of goods) promoted scientific standardization while advancing ideas of public health. These procedures standardized and policed the qualities of goods, making visible how, and with what substances, commodities had been made. As Ashworth argues, "To tax a good frequently required it to be rendered visible both in terms of its ingredients and in the way it was produced."[6] These excise procedures rubbed off onto Customs, which by the nineteenth century had become more modernized, a process hastened by the amalgamation of the two departments, a common early twentieth-century event in many parts of the Anglophone world.

In discussing how best to make sense of Customs, Ashworth offers some pertinent advice, namely to examine "the everyday labor of those employed by [Customs], and a survey of the physical and social geography in which they operated....What was it like to work in the bustle of the hectic, smelly and cosmopolitan space of the London Custom House?"[7]

Taking a more empire-wide purview, this chapter sketches out how Customs officials went about their business. These daily protocols of the dockside in turn shaped the way they read and interpreted the printed matter that passed through their hands. The focus is mainly on southern Africa with some glimpses of Customs work in British India, Canada, Australia, and the US.

As Ashworth indicates, in order to tax, one has first to define, and much Customs business hinged on deciding what an object actually was so that it could be assigned to a duty category. This ontological work was spread across a number of points that made up the Customs process. This chain was triggered when any vessel crossed into a 12-mile zone from the coast, the point at which the procedure of importation was deemed to begin (export, by contrast, was complete after 3 miles out to sea). The Master of the incoming vessel had twenty-four hours to present his manifest (description of cargo on board for that port) to the clerks in the Long Room (the name borne by all administrative sections of Custom departments across the British Empire and taken from Christopher Wren's 1671 design for a Custom House on the

---

[5] William Ashworth, *Customs and Excise: Trade, Production and Consumption in England 1640–1845* (Oxford: Oxford University Press, 2003).

[6] Ashworth, *Customs and Excise*, 147.   [7] Ashworth, *Customs and Excise*, 174.

Thames).[8] A tidewaiter from Customs was sent out to the ship to keep watch and to search for concealed cargo whether hidden in double hulls or woven into ropes, as smuggled tobacco often was. Meanwhile, on land, the importer framed a bill of entry for his goods, estimating the amount of duty that was paid to clerks in the Long Room. At this point the cargo could be unloaded, a process observed by a landing waiter and then by an examiner who cross-checked documents and scrutinized the cargo, checking its marks and number (the identifying symbols written onto cargo), the number of cases, nature of the goods, their weight, gallonage, quality, and so on. If satisfied, the examiner signed a delivery warrant and the goods could proceed. If not, he detained the goods for further inspection.[9]

As this description indicates, the procedures of Customs were invariably byzantine and cumbersome, due in part to the feudal history of such departments but also to the logistical difficulties involved in moving goods through a port city which was simultaneously a maritime boundary (although not all Customs posts were port-based).

This context shaped the daily dockside protocols that sought to manage the uncertainty inherent in moving people and goods from sea to land. Port cities are, after all, deceptive places, funneling goods and people from far away *entrepôts*. How did one know that a person was who he or she claimed to be? Like people, objects too could dissemble, a persistent problem for officials, as the South African Customs and Excise archive indicates. Might a walking stick in fact be a lethal weapon?[10] Could a shaving brush contain anthrax?[11] Was a coin fashioned into a brooch, real or not (and which was worse)?[12]

These uncertainties were inscribed in the ecology of the port city itself. Port cities aim to pave the ocean and assert sovereignty over the conjuncture of land and sea. While any form of sovereignty is potentially flimsy, hydrocolonial modes are especially so since they are subject to the ocean, both in its physical laws and by the people, objects, and animals delivered by vessels docking in the port.

Foreign objects often fell under suspicion: they might be diseased, putrefying, contaminated, seditious, obscene, illegal, or counterfeit. The hold of a vessel hummed with microbes, weevily maize, rotting cargo, dogs, parrots, reptiles, cattle (both dead and alive). Ships burped bilge water, extruded diseased human bodies, deposited

---

[8] Anne Fletcher, *The London Custom House: Souvenir Guidebook* (London: London Custom House, 2000), 8.

[9] This account is drawn from Western Cape Archives and Records Service, Cape Town, SDK 25, 1930, Customs and Excise. Inspection Report; E. B. McGuire, *The British Tariff System* (London: Methuen, 1939), 131–63.

[10] National Archives Repository, Pretoria, SAB, HKE 11, T5/7, 1958, Consolidated List of Prohibited and Restricted Imports and Exports Issued by Customs Departments.

[11] National Archives Repository, Pretoria, SAB, DEA 203, A10/11X, 1946, Prohibited and Restricted Imports. Anthrax in Brushware.

[12] National Archives Repository, Pretoria, SAB, JUS 1228, 1/171/30, 1932, *Coinage Bill*.

animal carcasses, secreted seditious pamphlets and obscene objects, and disgorged undesirable aliens. The ship was indeed an ark of "nuisances," a term from sanitary inspection much beloved of port authorities.

This uncertainty can also be understood ecologically. Custom Houses, often built on reclaimed land, sought not only to rule but also to dispel the waves, an ambition apparent in job titles like tide surveyor, tide department, or tide waiter, terms which undercut their own authority by stressing human dependence on time and tide. Titles of various offices attached to the harbor—port captain, water police, beach magistrate, receiver of wrecks (the latter two governing shipwrecks, flotsam, and jetsam)—exuded authority, even as they reminded their holders that they were dependent on the ocean and its physical vagaries.

Compounding the complexity of port city logistics were the particular contradictions inherent in Customs procedures. While the bulk of imports passed smoothly through the process, borderline cases occupied much time since Customs officers always sought the highest duty category while importers angled for the lowest. Each disagreement between Customs officials and importers generated a file, and the state archives in South Africa abound with such material as committees attempted to adjudicate how objects should be categorized. Was a substance butter or margarine? Could medicinal herbs be classified as tea? Were soup squares the same as stock? Was Gloy (a brand of book-binding glue) identical to glue? Was there any difference between poppy seed in a packet (which could be detained under the opium laws) and poppy seed for culinary use? Fabric proved particularly tricky as officials debated whether a particular bolt of cloth should be entered as printed tartan or gingham with swatches included (calling to mind that other famous swatch of fabric which shows up in Hawthorne's Custom-House).[13]

The arbiter of these disputes was the tariff handbook, which specified the various categories into which articles were to be assigned for purposes of duty. This process may sound fairly straightforward until one actually sees a tariff handbook, invariably a volume of several hundred pages. In the British imperial world, such handbooks hubristically promised to account for every object in the empire, if not the world, but in their very form acknowledged the impossibility of this task—tariff books were generally interleaved, every alternative page left blank to allow officials to write in amendments and to note comments and recommendations for changes, which were then forwarded to head office for inclusion in the next year's edition.[14]

---

[13] National Archives Repository, Pretoria, SAB, DCU 76, 670/06, 1906, Contravention Customs Union Regulations. JE Bigwood—Standerton. 2 Cases Margarine; DCU 85, 1416/06, 1906, Underentries of Duty: Foo Lee and Company. Tea Described as Herbs: Under Entry; DCU 82, 1091/06, 1906, H Moschke, Pietersburg. "Soup Squares," Re Classification Of; DCU 71, 415/06, 1906, Re Duty Leviable on "Gloy"; DCU 74, 574/06, 1906, Importation of Poppy Seed; DCU 81, 1032/06, 1906, "Gingham" (Flanelette) Tariff Item 175. Imported by Mosenthal Brothers, Limited.

[14] South African Railways and Harbours, ed., *Official Railway Tariff Book* (Johannesburg: Office of the General Manager of Railways, 1911).

One only has to flip through these volumes to grasp the intricacies of making adjudications about commodities. With dizzying speed, one moves from haberdashery to haggis to hair, from palisade fencing to pancake flour (always, of course, with the get-out clause "EOHP"—"except as otherwise herein provided").

In the face of these contending tides of meaning, officials were inevitably driven to the objects themselves, sniffing, tasting, and feeling the items in front of them in an attempt to classify them. They minutely checked thread counts in fabric, they opened cartons to verify the weight of items, they tested alcohol to see whether labels matched content.

The type of labor involved in such procedures is well-captured in the instructions from a Calcutta Customs manual on how to check thread count (reckoned by area of fabric in relation to weight). The length part of the equation was fairly straightforward and involved measuring the selvage. Gauging width, however, presented various problems, and Customs officials were enjoined to proceed as follows:

> A double-fold of the cloth should be laid on the table and the creases stroked out, so that it may lie perfectly flat. The measuring rod should then be placed across the cloth, and the finger and thumb run down the rod on each side of it across the cloth so as to once more flatten the creases. Care should be taken in doing this to see that whilst the creases are smoothed out, stretching is avoided and the warp threads remain perpendicular to the rod. The measurement should then be recorded.

Officials also had to think about the type of material:

> In taking these measurements the peculiarities of the cloth under measure should not be lost sight of. Thus cloths, like grey shirtings, that are pressed but not folded gain slightly, but by no means uniformly, in breadth in the course of pressing; whilst those that are folded, like mulls, lose in the folding more than they gain in the pressing....Loose cloths like mulls, especially if shrunk in the course of manufacture, are naturally liable to bag and stretch more than others, and owing to their flimsiness it is difficult to apply the first method of measurement satisfactorily; such cloths also are liable to drag in the weaving towards the end of a long piece, and the folds will sometimes not coincide with the weft. Due allowances should be made for these characteristics.[15]

These procedures required that Customs officials apprentice themselves to the objects they worked with, learning the minute peculiarities of the commodities under their jurisdiction. In effect, Customs officials functioned as assayers, learning to define and determine composition by touch, feel, and handling.[16] In larger Customs stations, examiners and surveyors could specialize in particular areas, and in big US establishments, officials were recruited from particular industries to capitalize on their dedicated expertise in certain classes of goods. In smaller establishments, jack-of-all-trades officers developed skills of identification and classification across an astonishing array of commodities.

---

[15] L. F. Morshead, comp. *Merchandise Marks Manual* (Calcutta: Government Printer, 1910), 35–6.
[16] I am indebted to Geeta Patel for this insight.

Such examiners spent their days amongst a gallimaufry of objects, from the predictable (sugar, rice, coal) to the obscure (galloons, gimps, and petershams—twisted, worsted, or reinforced cord used in upholstery and millinery). Examiners had to be "object literate" and to know the "character" of each item, moving from the gigantic (furnaces, bridge parts, motor cars) to the miniscule (needles, fish hooks, press studs).

These economies of attention produced an intimacy between official and object. In response to a query about the status of poppy seed for use by bakers, a collector of customs sent the following almost loving account of a fancy bread:

> The seed is not only used for garnishing bread and cakes but a bread cake, a sample of which I send under separate cover, made by the importers of the seed, which has, in addition to garnishing, a small quantity—about a teaspoonful—a sweetening mixture added, in the center of the article of food.[17]

The examiners' intimate knowledge of commodities encompassed a quasi-biographical appreciation of the object's trajectory from its origin to its destination. With regard to cloth, examiners were aware of the market for which it was headed and how it might change once there. In southern Africa, any surveyor would have known that German and Italian prints and sateens, once imported, changed their guise and entered the market as loincloths for the "native trade."[18] Item 47 of the South African tariff was entitled "Shawling," defined as "wraps for covering the back and shoulders," more specifically "cotton scarves, handkerchiefs and mats exceeding in size 1,600 square inches, that is 40 inches square or its equivalent whether imported singly or joined together by a fringe or weft."[19] Most officers, however, were aware that once in the market, such "shawling" transmogrified into "kidungas, cadungas, Zanzibar shawls...Congo Mats and are sometimes invoiced as Printed Calicos, Gordon Tartans, Animal Pattern Calicoes."[20] In one instance an examiner rejected a consignment of flannelette under item 47 since the fabric was generally used for cheap underskirts and hence could not be classified as shawling.[21] A conflict about whether a white honeycomb bed covering was a quilt or a blanket was settled by an official who decreed the item a quilt since it was used as such "by every European family" in Johannesburg.[22]

Examiners and surveyors had to pay painstaking attention to how objects were inscribed, a skill necessitated by trademark and copyright legislation as well as the Merchandise Marks Act, an imperial provision of 1887 specifying that all commodities passing through Customs bear a mark of origin indicating where they had

---

[17] National Archives Repository, Pretoria, SAB, DCU 74, 574/06, 1906, Importation of Poppy Seed.
[18] National Archives Repository, Pretoria, SAB, DCU 82, 1072/06, 1906, German Prints.
[19] National Archives Repository, Pretoria, SAB, DCU 82, 1074/06, 1906, Selampores.
[20] National Archives Repository, Pretoria, SAB, DCU 82, 1074/06, 1906, Selampores.
[21] National Archives Repository, Pretoria, SAB, DCU 81, 1022/06, 1906, Printed and Calicos.
[22] National Archives Repository, Pretoria, SAB, DCU 79, 987/07, 1907, Interpretations of the Tariff.

been made ("Made in England," "Made in Australia," and so on).[23] This legislation not only specified that objects had to be marked but also *where* the inscription had to appear: on the stem of pipe, the face of clock, every two yards on selvedge of fabric, on the address section of postcard, on the rind of the bacon, the flange of the printing block, and so on. The question of how this information was to be imprinted on the object produced yet further regulations, and the handbooks on the topic are veritable thesauruses of inscription replete with instructions on how objects had variously to be "impressed, embossed, die-stamped, cast, engraved, etched, printed, applied, stamped, incised, stenciled, painted, branded, molded, punched, cast," along with an appropriate range of adverbs: indelibly, visibly, conspicuously, durably. [24]

A further dimension pertained to the language and script in which the mark of origin was to be inscribed. Any script could be used as long as Roman lettering was also present. Any language could be present, but in the British Empire, English generally had to appear as well. Yet, in following this injunction, importers had to be careful since language itself could legally be construed as a mark of origin. As one handbook explained, "if any names, trade-marks, or descriptions in the English language or any English words at all appear on the goods, wrappings or containers, they are considered... as purporting to be of British origin." Goods produced outside Britain but with English markings had to carry clear signs of what was called "counter-indication" showing that despite the English words on the product, the commodity had not been manufactured in Britain. Exporters from the US were advised that "the words 'Made in the U.S.A.' in letters as large and as conspicuous as any other English wording, should be printed on every article, label, or wrapper bearing any words in the English language." In some cases, the mania for inscription went to extraordinary lengths. In the case of writing paper, "if so much as a water-mark containing English lettering appears in sheets of paper, a counter-indication of origin must also be watermarked into each sheet, wherever the water-mark occurs."[25] In other instances Roman lettering, like the "K" and "S" stamped onto Japanese copper ingots, did not require counter-indication: "such letters are not exclusively English, being common to all nations who use the Latin alphabet."[26] In yet other cases, English, when appearing on waste paper, became less a mark of origin than of exclusion since such paper could not be imported into Britain.[27]

Like all forms of intimacy, this pastoral care of objects assumed a disciplinary form as Customs officials "corrected" or "reformed" objects before they could be

---

[23] Howard Payn, *The Merchandise Marks Act, 1887, with Special Reference to the Important Sections and the Customs Regulations and Orders Made Thereunder, Etc.* (London: Stevens & Sons, 1888).

[24] All quotations from Roberta P. Wakefield, *Foreign Marks-of-Origin Regulations* (Washington, DC: United States Government Printing Office, 1947).

[25] Wakefield, *Foreign*, 83.

[26] Anandram Mewaram Jagtiani, *A Practical Companion to the Indian Merchandise Marks Act IV of 1889* (Karachi: Mercantile Press, 1901), 66–7.

[27] George Clements, *Clements' Customs Pocket Manual* (London: Smith and Elder, 1842), vii.

released into the market. False trademarks could be scrubbed off a product which was then allowed to proceed on its way.[28] Obscene images in articles like "novelty pencil sharpeners" and "keyhole tumblers" were likewise erased (but only by European labor).[29] Examiners tore off covers of objectionable magazines and blacked out offending passages. In Australia, the New South Wales Collector of Customs boasted of his particular method—a stamp with a rosette pattern which not only obliterated the pernicious text but had a disconcerting effect on the eye.[30] Films were likewise "reformed" with sections being defaced or excised before they were permitted to limp out of Customs.

As Deana Heath has shown in her perceptive account of Australian Customs, this work of detention, seizure, and censorship formed part of a larger imperial pattern of "quarantined culture."[31] White settler regimes constructed ever-more closely guarded boundaries in an attempt to keep out, neutralize, or reform "foreign bodies" and "undesirable persons." These practices of exclusion and quarantine were largely carried out by Immigration Restriction Departments, which emerged in the last quarter of the nineteenth century and policed the global color line with considerable ferocity. Customs as a form of port city governance long predated these institutions, and their role in shaping practices of hydrocolonial authority has yet to be factored into this larger story. Their obsession with mark of origin and the inscription of objects resonated with immigration restriction procedures of excluding those with the wrong bodily "mark of origin" and the notorious writing and dictation test by means of which would-be immigrants, as a condition of entry, could be required to write a dictated passage in a European language and in Roman script.

Object-Oriented Reading

The intention of Customs, as we noted earlier, is to discriminate between names and things. Yet things often trumped names. Names may have predominated on documents like manifests, bills of lading, bills of entry, invoices, stop notes, search warrants, registers, ledgers, bonds, and tariff handbooks that were variously perused, carried, stamped, initialled, and filed by a cast of administrative characters: tide waiters, landing waiters, examiners, surveyors, clerks, boatmen, and messengers. Objects, however, also played a role in how they came to be classified. Customs

[28] Western Cape Archives and Records Service, Cape Town, CKN 3/9. 14/9/33.

[29] Western Cape Archives and Records Service, Cape Town, CKN 3/9, 6/9/39; National Archives Repository, Pretoria, SAB, DEA 199, A10/5X, 1958, Prohibited and Restricted Imports. Indecent and Objectionable Articles.

[30] Deana Heath, *Purifying Empire: Obscenity and the Politics of Moral Regulation in Britain, India and Australia* (Cambridge: Cambridge University Press, 2010), 140.

[31] John Frank Williams, *The Quarantined Culture: Australian Reactions to Modernism, 1913–1939* (Cambridge: Cambridge University Press, 1995).

personnel were hence object-oriented readers, interspersing their two-dimensional reading of documents and handbooks with the three-dimensional assaying of cargo which they categorized by means of touch, feel, and handling.

Even when it came to printed publications, object-oriented modes dominated Customs protocols. When assaying print objects, one might anticipate that examiners paid most attention to the words in the publication under scrutiny. Yet in many instances, writing was not necessarily prioritized since it constituted only one dimension of the object as a whole. Instead the printed object was apprehended in its entirety or adjudged by a range of material features. French novels were hence often categorized as undesirable simply for being French or on the basis of their illustrations.[32] Book covers provided another avenue for assaying a publication, with the offending jacket being enough to have the object banned or burned.[33] In other instances, officials followed a sampling method in which random passages from suspect texts were selected, rather like an excise official testing a consignment of alcohol.[34] In Australia, this method attracted satirical comment from opponents of Customs censorship who feared that "any landing waiter … might find in a volume of Zola a phrase which might appear to be indecent to his prurient or too vivid imagination."[35] The anti-establishment *Sydney Bulletin* declared that a Customs official "may be all right for dealing with the undervaluation of pianos and piece-goods, but in the name of commonsense how is such a man allowed to regulate the literature of a country?"[36]

The ways in which Customs dealt with copyright provides yet another example of such material reading protocols. Generally officials treated copyright less as a sign of an abstract property right than as an indication of origin, that is, that the book has been manufactured or produced in the place in which copyright was registered. In part this development was shaped by the confusing layers of copyright legislation which Customs officers confronted: colonial law pertaining to the colony, imperial law to the empire, and the Berne Convention to much of the world. It was hence difficult to ascertain which law applied where, and officials of necessity had to make things up as they went along, applying the logic of their everyday dockside routines to problems as they cropped up. One important aspect of such daily routines, as we have seen, was mark of origin. When confronted with questions about the copyright status of publications, officers sought evidence that the book had been "composed, manufactured or copyrighted" in Britain, subjecting the book to a logic of origin

---

[32] National Archives Repository, Pretoria, TAB, LTG 19, 25/54, 1906, Customs Detention of Certain Books.

[33] National Archives Repository, Pretoria, DEA 199, A10/6X, 1922, Prohibited and Restricted Imports. Objectionable Literature.

[34] Western Cape Provincial Archives and Records Services, Cape Town, T 912, 2145, 1902, 1905, Detention of Book "Vechten and Vluchten van Beyers en Kemp."

[35] Heath, *Purifying Empire*, 107.   [36] Heath, *Purifying Empire*, 104.

and source.[37] In these procedures, they were supported by the Merchandise Marks Act which specifically indicated that British copyright could "be taken to be [an] indirect indication of British manufacture."[38] Copyright was routinely seen as a type of trademark, and pirated reprints were treated as suspect, less because they infringed intellectual property rights and more because they contained a "false trade description."[39] In attempting to ascertain if works were illegal reprints, officials paid close attention to material features of manufacture, looking for poor quality of paper, indistinct printing, inferior binding, or absence of the publisher's address on the title page.[40] "Reading" hence involved an assaying of material features of the text as a manufactured object.

At times, this material mode of apprehension took a radical form in which seditious or obscene goods acquired imagined microbial properties. Banned films were described as being unfit for human consumption; objectionable condoms were deemed "harmful to health";[41] indecent items were considered injurious to the public well-being; while undesirable publications apprehended in the post were likened to foreign bodies.[42] In Australia, suspect magazines were regarded as physical contaminants, immune even to the bleaching agent used in the manufacture of their pages. As one official noted, this disinfectant should have been able to "militate against disease" but in the face of such grave assault was rendered useless.[43] A logic of contamination and infection prevailed. In instances where one pirated piece of music or book was detected, the whole consignment came under suspicion and was generally detained.[44] These arguments could at times be turned against Customs: an importer whose periodicals had been detained argued that these publications were "perishables" and that detention would impair their freshness.[45]

These strategies were of course linked to the anti-foreign body policies that saturated British imperial immigration and border control from the last quarter of the nineteenth century. Combining concerns about global hygiene, eugenics, food adulteration, and moral purity, such policies shaped ever-more paranoid maritime boundary-making across the empire. This climate in turn enabled Customs to extend their reach through enhanced forms of censorship. In southern Africa, these

[37] Western Cape Provincial Archives and Records Services, Cape Town, KAB, T 815, 1505, 1904–1905, Complaint by Mr Speelman Regarding the Detention of Certain Books by the Customs.

[38] Payn, The Merchandise Marks Act, 21.

[39] Morshead, comp. The Merchandise Marks Manual, 30.

[40] Western Cape Provincial Archives and Records Services, Cape Town, CKN 3/8 89/9/21.

[41] National Archives Repository, Pretoria, SAB, DEA 199, A10/5X, 1939. Prohibited and Restricted Imports. Indecent and Objectionable Articles.

[42] National Archives Repository, Pretoria, DEA 199, A10/6X, 1922, Prohibited and Restricted Imports. Objectionable Literature.

[43] Heath, Purifying Empire, 115.

[44] National Archives Repository, Pretoria, SAB, DCU 89, 1850/06, 1906, Importation of Pirated Copyright Music.

[45] National Archives Repository, Pretoria, DEA 199, A10/6X, Prohibited and Restricted Imports. Objectionable Literature.

functions expanded rapidly during the Anglo-Boer war (1899–1902), with Customs officials, especially in the Cape, taking on a major role in censoring pro-Boer material. These officials formulated and refined the reading protocols which would be adopted and extended by subsequent censorship regimes.[46] Growing anti-Communism from the 1920s onwards gave Customs further occasion to extend their scope. However, as the Cold War started to gain ground and become an international "security issue," and as more films started to circulate (something for which Customs lacked viewing facilities), censorship was taken over by the Department of the Interior (with their specially built "censorship theatre") and then by a fully-fledged censorship apparatus under the apartheid regime.[47]

This increased surveillance meant that officials had to read suspect publications in a more systematic and bureaucratized way. Instead of following ad hoc procedures, examiners had to plough through the whole publication and produce a report on the text. Officials grumbled:

> The labour entailed is very considerable for it will be appreciated that in a whole newspaper or periodical there may only be one article which is objectionable, but it is necessary to peruse the whole newspaper in order to discover it.[48]

Even the supposed frisson of reading obscene publications palled after a while, especially where recruits had expected a boy's own adventure of "chasing smug- glers" or "sitting back in a fast motor boat running around outside the port," as Heath notes in the Australian case. Instead they found themselves "dumped in a cramped office and ordered to pore over imported publications looking for obscene words or images."[49]

These methodical ways of reading may seem to indicate a departure from object-oriented reading, a turn away from the material nature of the book to just its textual dimensions. Yet traces of the older assaying method lingered, with books being scrutinized like organic matter for their most dangerous ingredients. This procedure is apparent in the genre of the censor's report, which generally summar- ized the plot (or argument) and then provided quotations of the most seditious passages. In 1904, Hjalmar Reitz's novel *De Dochter van den Handsopper* (*Daughter of the Handsupper*, i.e., those Boers who put up their hands and joined the British)

---

[46] Western Cape Provincial Archives and Records Services, Cape Town, T 815, 1505. 1904–1905. Complaint by Mr Speelman Regarding the Detention of Certain Books by the Customs; T 912, 2145. 1905. Detention of Book "Vechten en Vluchten van Beyers en Kemp"; AG 1367, 296, 1904, Detention of Book "The Mobile Boer"; AG 1441, 4790, 1904, Book Entitled "De Dochter van den Handsuffer [Handsopper]": Detention of.

[47] National Archives Repository, Pretoria, DEA 209, A10/26X. Prohibited and Restricted Imports. Censorship of Films. Precedent. TES 696, 1963, Censors: Appointment and Remuneration of Members. Board of Censors: Staff For.

[48] National Archives Repository, Pretoria, DEA 199, A10/6X. 1933, Prohibited and Restricted Imports. Objectionable Literature.

[49] Heath, *Purifying Empire*, 123.

fell victim to a Customs examiner in Cape Town. The resulting report provided a plot summary with selected passages to illustrate the anti-British tenor of the text. The report notes that on "page 72" a party of Boers had captured a train and its contents, and amused themselves by reading the private letters of the British officers. The report then provides a quotation from the novel:

> The English of a private soldier or of his wife is glorious and betrays a high degree of civilization and a treasure of lofty ideas. In one letter a little boy writes to his father: "Daddy why don't you kill all the Boers and come home to mother and me.". . . A wife writes to her husband "If I were Lord Kitchener I would have the nasty Boers shot down like dogs."[50]

The passage is of course intended as a sarcastic indictment of the war-loving British, a point the censor considers self-evident since no gloss is appended to the quotation.

This mode of reading could be understood as isolating the most infected portions of the text, or compared to assaying fabric, running one's hand over the surface of the text to locate its creases and imperfections. Officials were reading the material in every sense of the phrase—reading the words as well as the physical features of the text. In an era where we debate how to read both textually and materially, these assaying practices of the Custom House assume a new relevance and offer a vantage point from which to explore themes of object-oriented reading.

FURTHER READING

Heath, Deana. *Purifying Empire: Obscenity and the Politics of Moral Regulation in Britain, India and Australia*. Cambridge: Cambridge University Press, 2010.

Hofmeyr, Isabel. "Colonial Copyright, Customs and Port Cities: Material Histories and Intellectual Property." *Comparative Literature* 70.3 (2018): 264–77.

Moore, Nicole. "Surrealism and Pulp: The Limits of the Literary and Australian Customs." *Censorship and the Limits of the Literary: A Global View*, ed. Nicole Moore. London: Bloomsbury, 2015, 105–18.

---

[50] Western Cape Archives and Records Service, Cape Town, AG 1441, 4790. 1904. De Dochter van den Handsuffer [Handsopper].

4

IN PUBLIC

STEVEN CONNOR

Most of what literary critics like to describe, prescribe, and circumscribe as reading has only a shingly kind of foothold in what most people, most of the time, think is happening when they do the thing they think of as reading. Symmetrically, what most people do when they perform the action, or undergo the experience, popularly understood as reading appears to be beneath the notice or beyond the ken of literary studies. What follows points to some striking and possibly formative changes in the landscape of non-institutional reading that, like most forms of vernacular reading activity, appear to have gone unobserved by critics within literary studies.

Reading is like thinking. We do it, purposively and systematically, without knowing exactly what it is we are doing or how we are doing it. As with thinking, most of our understanding of the process of reading is governed by fantasy-projection— things we assume we must be doing, or would like to think we may be doing, when we read. Like many fantasy-projections, this one is designed to ensure and secure the pleasing idea that reading is a rare and precious accomplishment, one that determines who and what we are. By looking at the kinds of radiation and diffraction which the act of reading has undergone over the last century or so, I want to be able plausibly to propose a general ecology of reading, in being, in matter, in which we take part rather than necessarily making the pace.

Modern literature disperses reading across different kinds of scene and occasion. In large part, this is an uneasy response to the increasing prominence of advertising, though in fact this is itself part of a larger history of writing and reading in public, or visible proclamation, to which the modern word (dating in print from 1949) "signage" economically refers. Signage, a word that seems to hint at alliance with terms like "foliage," "garbage," and "verbiage," as well as more neutral terms like "carriage," is the insistence of the visible letter in the public world. Dickens evokes signage in the passage of *Bleak House* which reflects on what it must mean to be illiterate in a modern city:

> It must be a strange state to be like Jo! To shuffle through the streets, unfamiliar with
> the shapes and in utter darkness as to the meaning, of those mysterious symbols, so

abundant over the shops, and the corner of streets, and on the doors, and in the windows![1]

Not to be able to make out meaning in no way means not capable of meaning. Dickens recurs to the name of Jo for an example of a kind of elementary machine reading in *Great Expectations*, in which Joe Gargery's method of reading is delightedly to pick out the letters of his own name:

> "Why, here's a J," said Joe, "and a O equal to anythink! Here's a J and a O, Pip, and a J-O, Joe." ... "Give me," said Joe, "a good book, or a good newspaper, and sit me down afore a good fire, and I ask no better. Lord!" he continued, after rubbing his knees a little, "when you do come to a J and a O, and says you, 'Here, at last, is a J-O, Joe,' how interesting reading is!"[2]

Dickens performs a similar action with "I am" in the words that follow on little Jo's awareness of his unawareness, in a passage that in writing on Jo's behalf mimes the process whereby Jo is both subject of and subject to the words that read out loud his illegibility:

> To be hustled, and jostled, and moved on; and really to feel that it would appear to be perfectly true that I have no business here, or there, or anywhere; and yet to be perplexed by the consideration that *I am* here somehow, too.[3]

Bleak House appeared in the same year in which commercial toilet paper was first marketed in Britain. This seems emblematic in a number of ways. First of all, *Bleak House* is a novel in which paper and waste are closely associated, with its many sacks of moldering, yet also smolderingly incendiary, bags of official documents. But, more importantly, it is a novel that testifies to the cheapness of paper and to the ubiquity of surfaces on which to sign and signal, along with the growing autonomy of those processes from the human subjects they hustled and jostled and kept in various kinds of motion. Literary writing shared those surfaces, with the advertisements for many kinds of commodity that were crammed into the spare spaces surrounding the text in the serial parts of nineteenth-century fiction. But the space of reading was also exteriorized. As Walter Bagehot remarked of Dickens's writing in 1858:

> London is like a newspaper. Everything is there, and everything is disconnected. There is every kind of person in some houses; but there is no more connection between the houses than between the neighbours in the lists of "births, marriages, and deaths." As we change from the broad leader to the squalid police report, we pass a corner and we are in a changed world.[4]

---

[1] Charles Dickens, *Bleak House*, ed. Norman Page (Harmondsworth: Penguin, 1972), 274.
[2] Charles Dickens, *Great Expectations*, ed. Charlotte Mitchell (London: Penguin, 2003), 45–6.
[3] Dickens, *Bleak House*, 274.
[4] Walter Bagehot, *The Works and Life of Walter Bagehot*, ed. Mrs Russell Barrington, 10 vols. (London: Longman's, Green and Co., 1915), 3: 84–5.

Bagehot sees London as pre-adapted to the "essentially irregular and unsymmetrical" constitution of Dickens's mind, which operates in "graphic scraps."[5] The word "graphic" aptly embodies the oscillation between iconicity and legibility of these outward and visible signs. Although "graphic" refers as much to writing as to drawing, when *The Graphic* weekly newspaper first began to appear in 1869, the word referred to the fact that it was an illustrated paper, like the *Daily Graphic* that began publication in New York in 1873. The graphic space of London is both fragmented and impermanent; both businesses and the visible signs that announce them come and go overnight, as in the evocation in *Sketches by Boz* of the draper's shop that suddenly springs into existence:

> a handsome shop, fast approaching to a state of completion, and on the shutters were large bills, informing the public that it would shortly be opened with "an extensive stock of linen-drapery and haberdashery." It opened in due course; there was the name of the proprietor "and Co." in gilt letters, almost too dazzling to look at.[6]

For the written letters of the two Jo's hover between the condition of apprehension and comprehension, both faster and slower than reading, as for example in Dickens' memory of the sign on the door of a coffee house to which he resorted as a young child:

> in the door there was an oval glass-plate, with COFFEE-ROOM painted on it, addressed towards the street. If I ever find myself in a very different kind of coffee-room now, but where there is such an inscription on glass, and read it backward on the wrong side MOOR-EEFFOC (as I often used to do then, in a dismal reverie), a shock goes through my blood.[7]

Events are sometimes described in Dickens's writing in terms of the ways in which they might be rendered in newspapers or public notices, like play-bills, as in the account of the spat between tipsy ladies in Seven Dials in *Sketches by Boz*: "The scuffle became general," and terminates, in minor play-bill phraseology, with "arrival of the policemen, interior of the station-house, and impressive *dénouement*."[8]

Every surface in the city seems to become a support for inscriptions and items to be read. With the development of packaging from the early nineteenth century onwards and its growing convergence with information—advertisements and instructions for transmission or use—objects and their designations came more and more to be identified. Lewis Carroll's two *Alice* books play with the growing tendency for every object in the world to bear a label, as in the bottle labelled "DRINK ME" or the jar promisingly labelled "ORANGE MARMALADE," which Alice snatches from a shelf during her fall into the rabbit-hole, then tidily puts back

---

[5] Bagehot, *Works and Life of Walter Bagehot*, 79, 80.
[6] Charles Dickens, *Sketches by Boz*, ed. Dennis Walder (London: Penguin, 1995), 81–2.
[7] John Forster, *The Life of Charles Dickens*, 2 vols. (London: Chapman and Hall, 1876), 1: 29.
[8] Dickens, *Sketches by Boz*, 93.

on another shelf when it turns out to be empty, "for fear of killing somebody" if she drops it.[9] Labels and objects came closer together with increasing speed and density of transport. As David Trotter observes, travel by rail in particular seemed to turn travelers into parcels or postal objects. He quotes John Ruskin complaining in 1856 that rail travel "is merely 'being sent' to a place, and very little different from becoming a parcel; the next step to it would of course be telegraphic transport."[10]

This is the beginning of what Michel Serres has identified as the appropriation of space through sign-pollution: just as the tiger marks its territory by urinating on it, so we take possession of the world by drowning it in signage:

> On each mountain rock, each tree leaf, each agricultural plot of land, you have advertisements; letters are written on each blade of grass; the big name brands draw their giant images on the immense glaciers of the Himalaya. Like the legendary cathedral, the landscape is swallowed by the tsunami of signs. All species have vanished and we remain *alone in the world*, among ourselves.[11]

The sensitivity to the iconicity of script in the nineteenth century is suggested by the fact that it was in this century that graphology, the reading of the psychological signatures of written signs, was formalized, in particular by the appearance of Adolphe Desbarrolles and Jean-Hippolyte Michon's *Les Mystères de l'écriture* in 1872. Sherlock Holmes, so adept a reader of every kind of physical and physiological signature, is also a believer in what a previous era might have called the doctrine of signatures, now applied literally to the interpretation of the look of letters in the analysis of character through handwriting, as indicated in an interchange with Watson early in *The Sign of Four*:

> "What do you make of this fellow's scribble?"
>
> "It is legible and regular," I answered. "A man of business habits and some force of character."
>
> Holmes shook his head.
>
> "Look at his long letters," he said. "They hardly rise above the common herd. That *d* might be an *a*, and that *l* an *e*. Men of character always differentiate their long letters, however illegibly they may write. There is vacillation in his *k*'s and self-esteem in his capitals."[12]

The experience of modern life can be seen as a state of incessant address, a word which contains primary ideas of alignment, erection, or setting upright, as when

---

[9] Lewis Carroll, *Alice's Adventures in Wonderland* and *Through the Looking Glass and What Alice Found There*, ed. Roger Lancelyn Green (Oxford: Oxford University Press, 1982), 18, 20.

[10] John Ruskin, *Modern Painters. Vol. 3: Of Many Things* (London: George Allen, 1906), 311; David Trotter, *Literature in the First Media Age: Britain between the Wars* (Cambridge, MA: Harvard University Press, 2013), 271.

[11] Michel Serres, *Malfeasance: Appropriation through Pollution?*, trans. Anne-Marie Feenberg-Dibon (Palo Alto: Stanford University Press, 2011), 70.

[12] Arthur Conan Doyle, *The Penguin Complete Sherlock Holmes* (London: Penguin, 1981), 96.

one dresses a piece of stone. The authority of the Times New Roman typeface, commissioned in 1929 from Stanley Morison, derives in large part from its imitation of the script incised on Trajan's triumphal column in Rome. The history of public proclamations depends on the enforced elevation of the eyes to what lies not passively beneath one's gaze but in front or above. Banners and placards are held above the head.

It is not surprising that such proclamations should aspire to the greatest altitude of all, the sky. Skywriting appeared for the first time on Derby Day 1922, when an airplane traced the words "DAILY MAIL" in the sky over Epsom, the feat being repeated the following day over Hyde Park and St Paul's. Advertising had moved into airspace long before this, with messages inscribed on balloons and airships, but this was the first attempt to use the imaginary space of the sky as an inscriptive surface. The feat was performed by Major Jack Savage, who had been a pilot with the Royal Naval Air Service during the First World War, and, by 1924, his air-advertising business would be employing seventeen pilots working across five countries.[13] This scene is much less well-known nowadays than its recapitulation in the opening chapter of Virginia Woolf's *Mrs Dalloway*, in which an advertising airplane draws the gazes of pedestrians in London's West End:

> Suddenly Mrs. Coates looked up into the sky. The sound of an aeroplane bored ominously into the ears of the crowd. There it was coming over the trees, letting out white smoke from behind, which curled and twisted, actually writing something! making letters in the sky! Every one looked up.[14]

J. Hillis Miller articulates a common response to this scene, which sees the letters as furnishing a principle of continuity in an otherwise multiplied and unstable social world:

> Such transitions seem to suggest that the solid existing things of the external world unify the minds of separate persons because, though each person is trapped in his or her own mind and in his or her own private responses to external objects, nevertheless these disparate minds can all have responses, however different they may be, to the same event, for example to an airplane's skywriting. To this extent at least we all dwell in one world.[15]

And yet, of course, the reverse is also true. Far from being among the "solid existing things of the external world" that bind us into a common experience, it was apparent to all that, as *The Times* assured its readers in 1922, "aerial advertisements cannot be written in indelible smoke."[16] The letters of the skywriting airplane are

---

[13] James Taylor, "Written in the Skies: Advertising, Technology and Modernity in Britain since 1885," *Journal of British Studies* 55 (2016): 755.

[14] Virginia Woolf, *Mrs Dalloway*, ed. G. Patton Wright (London: Vintage, 1992), 16.

[15] J. Hillis Miller, *Fiction and Repetition: Seven English Novels* (Cambridge, MA: Harvard University Press, 1982), 180.

[16] "Sky Writing by Aircraft: Wide Scope in War and Peace," *The Times* (August 18, 1922), 5.

cryptic, intermittent, and literally vapid, brought to intelligibility only through the itself intermittent act of reading undertaken by spectators. The letters written against the sky blur into it, just as the act of inscribing letters blurs into the other elements of the scene that this opening chapter of *Mrs Dalloway* assembles, notably the mysterious car moving through the London streets:

> It had gone; it was behind the clouds. There was no sound. The clouds to which the letters E, G, or L had attached themselves moved freely, as if destined to cross from West to East on a mission of the greatest importance which would never be revealed, and yet certainly so it was—a mission of the greatest importance.[17]

Mission, transmission, emission, and omission melt smokily together, the process of making up and making out letters forming a sort of mobile, impermanent bond, gluey and fluid at once, like toffee perhaps, in the act of collective making-legible— collectivity and collegiality being etymological kin.

The message written on the sky in the inaugural act of skywriting "DAILY MAIL" was in fact a wholly phatic one, since the product it advertised was a newspaper, which had already become the modern world's most insistent vehicle for advertising messages. In its reporting of the event, the *Daily Mail* bragged that it was "the largest advertisement the world has ever known."[18] The message is accordingly here the medium, less a sign than a signature, the purpose of which is to signify its own making. This is made clear by the admiring account of the *Daily Mail* stunt published in the *Illustrated London News*, which produced a drawing of an imaginary display of the letters "ILN" inscribed in smoke above the Houses of Parliament along with a diagram of how the feat would be achieved.[19]

Our contemporary preoccupation with the spectacles of commodity means that most commentators on the skywriting passage in *Mrs Dalloway* neglect the menace that is associated with the airplane. Vincent Sherry, who observes the strong associations between the advertising airplane and the recently concluded war—one of the most engaged observers being the veteran Septimus Smith—is among the exceptions, while Paul K. Saint-Amour goes further in seeing in the airplane's "embodiment of illegible alterity" the demand for "an imperiled aerial reading."[20] In the screenplay for *Things to Come*, H. G. Wells imagines the message "SURRENDER" being written by airplanes in the sky.[21] Drawing on a long poetic history of making out battles in heaven in the form of cloud-masses, the aeronautical correspondent of *The Times* not only imagined the deployment of skywriting for propaganda

---

[17] "Sky Writing by Aircraft," *The Times*, 17.

[18] "Writing on the Sky," *Daily Mail* (June 1, 1922), 8.

[19] Michael North, *Reading 1922: A Return to the Scene of the Modern* (New York: Oxford University Press, 1999), 82–3.

[20] Vincent Sherry, *The Great War and the Language of Modernism* (Oxford: Oxford University Press, 2003), 265; Paul K. Saint-Amour, *Tense Future: Modernism, Total War, Encyclopedic Form* (Oxford: Oxford University Press, 2015), 115.

[21] H. G. Wells, *Things to Come* (London: Cresset Press, 1935), 91.

purposes in war, he (presumably he) went as far as to suggest that not only would one be able to read the signs of combat in the air from smoke and vapor trails, there would be mechanical battles in and over those very signs: "One can imagine... the sort of aerial conflict that would arise when, if the operating machines were not successfully attacked, efforts would be made to blot out their messages with heavy smoke clouds."[22]

Where proponents of the art of skywriting emphasized its vast reach and legibility, the distinctive feature of Woolf's rendering of skywriting is that it embodies meaning in emergence, construal rather than appearance. An analogue is to be found in *Bleak House*, a novel that is full of forms of cryptic signature and spelling out, in the performance of writing by the illiterate but lexically avaricious Krook, the letters of JARNDYCE singly inscribed on and erased from the wall of his room in turn, without ever leaving two letters visible together.[23] Krook's spelling out alternates between ostension and concealment, like the enigmatic words MENE, MENE, TEKEL, PARSIN inscribed on the wall during Belshazzar's Feast.[24] It is not so much signification as signaling, in the form in which it was adopted in Morse code and ouija boards alike. Public reading often involves this kind of cryptic insistence of the letter, which decomposes words into their written elements, making visible the material forms which must ordinarily be kept invisible, or rather unapparent, as they are "read through" in the act of reading.

The fact that its central character, Leopold Bloom, is a canvasser of advertisements helps make Joyce's *Ulysses* as alive to the mobile materiality of writing as *Bleak House*, nowhere more so than in the ambulant forms of the sandwichboard men advertising the stationer Hely's. As with the skywriting in *Mrs Dalloway*, the contingencies of city life threaten all the time to decompose the word that the marching men collectively compose:

> A procession of whitesmocked sandwichmen marched slowly towards him [Bloom] along the gutter, scarlet sashes across their boards. Bargains. Like that priest they are this morning: we have sinned: we have suffered. He read the scarlet letters on their five tall white hats: H. E. L. Y. S. Wisdom Hely's. Y lagging behind drew a chunk of bread from under his foreboard, crammed it into his mouth and munched as he walked... He crossed Westmoreland street when apostrophe S had plodded by.[25]

The apostrophe of public display always seems to involve some apotropaic averting (apostrophe and apotropaism both derive from ἀπό away + στρέφειν to turn) in its address, some conspicuous yet cryptic elision or illegibility amid the appearance. If this is a reading which resists or repels immediate understanding, it also by that very token invites it, the text becoming a riddle or rebus which draws readers in or draws viewing subjects into the act of reading and so into the condition of readers.

---

[22] "Sky Writing by Aircraft," *The Times*, 5.   [23] Dickens, *Bleak House*, 106–7.
[24] Daniel 5:25.
[25] James Joyce, *Ulysses*, ed. Jeri Johnson (Oxford: Oxford University Press), 147–8.

The Skywriting Corporation, established in 1923 by Allan J. Cameron and Leroy Van Patten, launched a campaign for Lucky Strike cigarettes, inditing the slogan "L S M F T" (Lucky Strike Means Fine Tobacco) across American skies. Reading here is not something you do, exactly, so much as something done to, through, or with you; the medium works by means of you.

Cars and airplanes are not the only means of vehiculating the word. Almost every device for putting things and persons in motion—trains, automobiles, escalators, and elevators—suggested new modes of display, advice, warning, and instruction. Words could either occupy and stabilize the reading eye during transit or, with the development of ticker-tape displays and kinetic neon signs, they could impart motion to writing and reading, in what Michael North has called "a literal cinematography" or "logocinema."[26] The first road signs were milestones, which often, like epitaphs, encouraged the traveler to pause and reflect. With the development of road-markings in the early twentieth century, accompanying and regulating the growth of motor vehicles, the lines on the road came more and more to make it rather than merely to mark it out.

Robbie Moore suggests that the stock-market ticker-tape produced a new kind of reading, one that could never quite be practiced in any reading present:

> The reader of the ticker looked for the relations between ticks, seeking not a discrete piece of information but a direction, a pattern. It was a reading practice which yearned towards the future, a reading practice whose ultimate goal was not to understand the message sent, but to anticipate the message yet to be sent.[27]

The reading machinery of public displays is anticipated and mirrored by the device known as "The Readies" invented by Bob Brown in the early 1930s. Brown's reading machine, which essentially scrolls words in a line across the reader's visual field, anticipates the dematerialization of the word in contemporary reading devices. His hope was that words might eventually be

> recorded directly on the palpitating ether.…The word "readies" suggests to me a moving type spectacle, reading at the speed-rate of the day with the aid of a machine, a method of enjoying literature in a manner as up-to-date as the lively talkies.[28]

Brown promised that his machine would not only make traditional kinds of reading easier and more convenient, but that it would also help in the development of a new kind of reading purged of the implication of soliloquy or sub-vocal sonority. The dedication of Brown's 1930 book *The Readies* is "TO ALL EYE-WRITERS AND

---

[26] Michael North, *Camera Works: Photography and the Twentieth-Century Word* (Oxford: Oxford University Press, 2005), 66.

[27] Robbie Moore, "Ticker Tape and the Superhuman Reader," in *Writing, Medium, Machine: Modern Technographies*, ed. David Trotter and Sean Pryor (London: Open Humanities Press, 2016), 138.

[28] Bob Brown, *The Readies* (Bad Ems: Roving Eye Press, 1930), 40, 27.

ALL READERS WHO WANT AN EYEFUL,"[29] and he proposed a model of the unreeling tape to replace that of the interior monologue:

> Why wasn't there a man-made machine like the running tape-of-thought device in the mind which would carry words endlessly to all reading eyes in one unbroken line, a reading machine as rapid and refreshing as thought, to take the place of the antiquated word-dribbling book?[30]

Brown's optical reading may be regarded as the obverse or even adversary of what came to be known as "close reading." For the kind of reading that was made both possible and necessary by Brown's machine starts to erode the idea of reading as an action consciously performed by a reader on an object. Rather, it resembles the automatic reading with which Gertrude Stein experimented when a psychology student at Harvard.[31] "I was almost a book myself," wrote Brown.[32] The avant-garde and experimental texts that Brown assembled as specimens for his machine seem closely entrained with the diffractive and distractive, yet curiously insistent, reading practices made common in the modern world. Indeed, Brown makes the connection explicit between his mooted reading machine, as well as the avant-garde experiences of text in motion stimulated by it, and these new reading experiences:

> We are familiar with news and advertisements reeling off before our eyes in huge illuminated letters from the [t]ops of corner buildings, and smaller propaganda machines tick off tales of commercial prowess before our eyes in shop windows. All that is needed is to bring these electric street signs down to the ground, move the show-window reading device into the library, living and bed-rooms by reducing the size of the letter photographically and refining it to the need of an intimate, handy portable, rapid reading conveyor.[33]

One of the most important symptoms and outcomes of public reading's intensification has been the increase in sensitivity to the effect of typefaces. In the first centuries of printing, the varieties of typeface were very limited and slow to evolve, so that their materiality had little chance to mingle with and inflect meaning and response. The explosion and prodigious variability of typographic form during the twentieth century, and especially in the era of word-processing, that made different fonts and faces easily available to writers as well as readers has produced something like a psychotypographic complex among readers, allowing the look of letters to be ever more constitutive of their meaning, tonality, and effect.

Perhaps the most important and intense psychotypographic force is wielded not by any particular typeface but by what is known, from the arrangement of the compositor's box, as the upper case. Majuscule, or capital letters, were stored in the

---

[29] Brown, *The Readies*, n.p.
[30] Bob Brown, *Readies for Bob Brown's Machine* (Cagnes-sur-Mer: Roving Eye Press, 1931), 168.
[31] Leon M. Solomons and Gertrude Stein, "Normal Motor Automatism," *Psychological Review* 3 (1896): 492–512.
[32] Brown, *Readies for Bob Brown's Machine*, 154.   [33] Brown, *The Readies*, 33.

upper case because they were needed much less often than lower case letters, on a ratio of around 1 to 5; their meaning derives in part from this relative rarity. Capitals break into the continuity of words to signify the structural as well as semantic functions of language. They mark the beginnings of sentences and therefore express the sense or force of sense, the *haec*, *hic*, and *nunc* of signification, as well as signifying certain kinds of special importance, above all religious, but also political and social. That is, like Serres's *here lies*, they signify the fact of signification itself. When used on their own, capitals signify the imperative and the imperious, embodying urgency, prerogative, and demand. Capitals are seldom cursive and can usually be constructed through a combination of straight lines, vertical, horizontal, and diagonal. As such, and given the fact that they are much easier to engrave than cursive letter forms, they suggest the monumental, the impersonal, and the mechanical. Only the most skillful or vainglorious pilot would ever attempt copperplate skywriting, or a seriffed font. Capitals suggest both the power needed to overcome the resistance of stone and the cruelty of that which may be incised into flesh, as in the capitals seared simultaneously into the text of Samuel Beckett's *How It Is* and the helpless posterior of Pim. The names of corporations and institutions are formed from acronymic sequences of capital letters. The force of capital letters actually resists and decomposes word formation, as suggested by the punitive or domineering function of certain capital letters, like Nathaniel Hawthorne's scarlet A, Pauline Réage's subordinated O, or Fritz Lang's and Ian Fleming's M, or the power encoded in words like H-bomb or G-spot. Magical rituals that employ writing will usually be in the form of capital letters.

Because capitals signify this impersonal and mechanical power of signification, they have a particular attraction for anyone susceptible to word-magic, like psychotics, visionaries, stroke survivors, and poets. Most of us understand well enough that you should only open an email containing a subject-line typed in capitals if you are an aficionado of death threats and paranoid ravings. In that the upper case signifies the abstractly public and perhaps machine-like dimensions of language—Lacan's "big Other"—this represents the attempt to blend private and public utterance, declaration and inscription.[34] The effacement of capitals, by contrast, and especially the demotion of the most commanding capital of all, the I, enacts informality, vulnerable sensitivity, expressive spontaneity, and democratic non-domination.

The capital letter is an emblem of the capitality of the letter as such, the autonomous power of the glyphic that comes from its power to constitute and exceed its occasion, a capitalization founded on decapitation. We live in an era of machine-reading, in which we have not only taught machines to read but learned to read more and more of the mechanism of our own reading. The world's visual clamor,

---

[34] Jacques Lacan, *The Seminar of Jacques Lacan. Book II: The Ego in Freud's Theory and in the Technique of Psychoanalysis 1954–55*, ed. Jacques-Alain Miller, trans. Sylvana Tomaselli (New York: W.W. Norton, 1991), 236.

whether on the street or in the wilderness, breaks in constantly on the Hieronymic seclusion of the reader, sunk in his or her book, myopically averting the world's advertisement, lions, scorpions, dancing girls. For now, in a world in which there is only code, the world itself appears to be engaged in the work of attention-theft, reading itself out loud.

FURTHER READING

Bohn, Willard. *The Aesthetics of Visual Poetry, 1914–1928*. Chicago: University of Chicago Press, 1986.

Kinross, Robin. *Modern Typography: An Essay in Critical History*. London: Hyphen Press, 2004.

Leonard, Gary. *Advertising and Commodity Culture in Joyce*. Gainesville, FL: University Press of Florida, 1998.

Portella, Adriana. *Visual Pollution: Advertising, Signage, and Environmental Quality*. New York: Routledge, 2016.

Rickards, Maurice. *The Public Notice: An Illustrated History*. London: David & Charles, 1973.

Schutt, Stefan, Sam Roberts, and Leanne White, eds. *Advertising and Public Memory: Social, Cultural and Historical Perspectives on Ghost Signs*. New York: Routledge, 2017.

Stewart, Garrett. *The Look of Reading: Book, Painting, Text*. Chicago: University of Chicago Press, 2006.

Treu, Martin. *Signs, Streets, and Storefronts: A History of Architecture and Graphics along America's Commercial Corridors*. Baltimore: Johns Hopkins University Press, 2012.

5

ACROSS BORDERS

WENDY GRISWOLD

While the dream of a borderless world is ancient, envisaged by builders of empires and monotheistic religions among others, technological revolutions seem to quicken the dreamers' pulses. The rise of international digital media and other forms of globalization have renewed the fantastic apparition of people being everywhere and nowhere, floating above the strictures of place. Recognizing that such dreams inevitably falter or are unevenly realized, we need to figure out what has changed and what has not in the wake of the globalization-digitization upheavals. This is as true for reading as for everything else.

We can quickly dispose of the idea that digitization has simply given rise to a world without borders, a democratic fellowship of humanity sharing concerns about human rights and the future of the planet. If anything, the opposite seems to be the case as the same media both transcend distance and foster chauvinism. Nationalisms, benign and malignant, find recruits, stoke emotions, and motivate actions through social media. Immigrants maintain a social presence online in their places of origin as well as in places of destination, while anti-immigrant groups rally the likeminded. And censors put up firewalls to keep out materials deemed threatening; it has proven easier to smuggle biblical passages into North Korea via balloons than via the Internet.

Another imagined digital-age scenario that hasn't panned out is the disappearance of print. On the contrary, e-book sales have plateaued, print books (and, to everyone's surprise, bookstores) have held steady, and there is little danger of the reading class or their progeny giving up reading.[1] This last clause has some implications, of course. The "reading class" is the educated, socially advantaged

---

[1] The past several years have seen a drumbeat of reports like "In Books, Print Makes a Stand," all expressing surprise that the "newfangled formats" have not displaced print, and that the book industry is doing just fine. Zeke Turner, "In Books, Print Makes a Stand," *Wall Street Journal*, October 16, 2017. The 2017 Frankfurt Book Fair (the industry's largest) reported that e-book sales were down while printed-book revenue was up 4.5 per cent. Interviews of industry professionals at Frankfurt came up with a variety of explanations—screen fatigue, political angst, better-designed print books—but the overall trend appears robust.

group of people who read in their leisure time. Its percentage of the population varies—close to half of adults in Finland, single digits in Malawi—but every country has one. These people both model and pass on social advantages and cultural tastes, intertwined and mutually constructive as Pierre Bourdieu has demonstrated, so such characteristics as parental education and the presence of books in the house correlate with whether children become readers. The advent of digital media doesn't seem to make much difference.

This essay will use Nigeria as a running empirical case for examining the relationship between reading, on the one hand, and globalization and digitization, on the other. I am using Nigeria because I know something about its readers and writers, and because the Nigerian literary complex—a number of world-class writers, a large reading public at home and abroad, an established publishing industry, online sophistication—is in as good a position as any to cross borders.

To begin with, Nigerian readers exemplify the persistence of print. In 2000, I published a book on Nigerian readers, writers, and fiction that came out just as the Internet was starting to be widely available in Anglophone Africa.[2] Many observers of the literary scene, including me, believed this might "change everything," as both the youth and the people involved in the commercial and educational sectors celebrated the advent of globalization. So I began studying educated African (and other) youth's reading practices in the digital era, a study using focus groups, interviews, and short surveys. Initially focused on Africa, I conducted research in Nigeria, Ghana, Malawi, and South Africa. The early stages of this research suggested that while young Africans embraced digital technology, the impact on their reading practices was minimal: Going online was glamorous, but reading had social honor, and readers saw the two as occupying different cultural sectors.[3] My subsequent research, within and beyond Africa, has further confirmed this, even as educated youth—the seed stock of the reading class—have become digital natives who have grown up with smartphones. One of the questions I ask student focus groups is, "If you had equal access to whatever you like to read in your leisure time, if there were no difference in cost or availability, would you prefer to read it in print or on a screen?" Invariably about three-quarters say print.[4]

---

[2] Wendy Griswold, *Bearing Witness: Readers, Writers, and the Novel in Nigeria* (Princeton: Princeton University Press, 2000).

[3] Wendy Griswold, Erin M. McDonnell, and Terence E. McDonnell, "Glamour and Honor: The Relationship between Reading and the Internet in West African Culture," *Information Technologies and International Development* 3.4 (2006): 37–52.

[4] Other researchers have found a similar preference for print; see, for example, Naomi S. Baron, *Words Onscreen: The Fate of Reading in a Digital World* (Oxford: Oxford University Press, 2015). And this is just as well, for there is a growing body of evidence that print is better than screens for reading comprehension and retention; see, for example, Anne Mangen, Bente R. Walgermo, and Kolbjørn Brønnick, "Reading Linear Texts on Paper versus Computer Screen: Effects on Reading Comprehension," *International Journal of Educational Research* 58 (2013): 61–8. Even *Wired* suggests that "the smart reading device of the future may be paper" (Brandon Keim, "Why the Smart Reading Device of the Future May Be…Paper," *Wired*, May 1, 2014 (https://www.wired.com/2014/05/reading-on-screen-versus-paper/)).

My focus today will be two borders: access and desire. The first term is the more capacious, the second more operational. Both are produced by technology and directed by social evaluation.

Access and Desire

In the twenty-first century, what keeps people from reading? There can be only two answers: They are unable or they are unwilling.

People might be unable to read for two main reasons: They are illiterate or they don't have reading materials available. Of course there are others, such as having impaired vision, or poor light, or insufficient free time, but literacy and availability are the major impediments. Of these two, the battle for literacy has been largely won, despite a few persistent pockets in places like Afghanistan and South Sudan where war piled on top of a traditionally low rate of literacy has stalled progress.[5]

Availability is a different matter. Distribution of print materials is spotty, especially in rural and/or developing areas, and easily disrupted. Books, when available at all, are expensive. Access to digital media is not yet universal, with various digital divides persisting in denying the Internet to some people, especially poor people in the developing world, the same demographic likely to have lingering illiteracy.

According to this line of thinking, if people were *able* to read—if they had the skills and the reading material, print or digital—they *would* read. Scholars and researchers, those of us who make our livings reading, tend to assume this, but in fact it is not the case. The key consideration is not whether people have access but whether people who do have access—who are literate and able to procure reading materials—have other ways to spend their leisure time. A series of studies in the Netherlands, a country with historically high rates of reading, has shown that a drop began in the 1950s with the advent of television, and this has been reading's principal and successful competitor in most of the West.[6] In Italy the early competition came more from movies. At the turn of the twentieth century, south-

[5] As of 2016, 90 per cent of adult men and 83 per cent of women were literate; literacy is all but universal in Europe and North and South America (with a few exceptions in poor nations like Guatemala and Haiti). It approaches universality in China and is getting close in developing countries like Indonesia and Brazil. War-ravaged and/or poor countries in sub-Saharan Africa lag behind; adult literacy is less than 50 per cent in Burkina Faso, Chad, Cote d'Ivoire, Guinea, Liberia, Mali, Niger, and South Sudan. Afghanistan is another country where literacy, low to begin with, has stalled and where sharp differences between male–female and urban–rural literacy remain. UNESCO Institute for Statistics (http://data.uis.unesco.org/Index.aspx?DataSetCode=EDULIT_DS&popupcustomise=true&lang=en#); *The World Factbook* (Washington, DC: Central Intelligence Agency, 2017); and "Enhancement of Literacy in Afghanistan (ELA) Program," UNESCO Office in Kabul (http://www.unesco.org/new/en/kabul/education/enhancement-of-literacy-in-afghanistan-ela-program).

[6] Wim Knulst and Gerber Kraaykamp, "Trends in Leisure Reading: Forty Years of Research on Reading in the Netherlands," *Poetics* 26 (1998): 21–41.

ern Italy had much lower rates of literacy than northern; by the time the South began to catch up in terms of education, films, radio, and later television offered attractive alternatives, and the South has never caught up to the North.[7] Today the attractive alternatives are social media and texting. Parents and teachers in the Western world for decades have urged their children, generally to no avail, to get off the television/video games/computers/smartphones and read a book.

So the high wall is not access but desire. The border between readers and those who could read but don't is often self-imposed, and non-readers generally have no wish to cross it. In the twenty-first century, we will see, indeed, are seeing, a return to the historical norm whereby not everyone wants to read unless they have to (for work or studies), even if they are perfectly capable of doing so. A minority has the skills, the access, and—most critically—the desire. The percentage varies from place to place: high in Nordic countries, Western Europe, North America, Japan, urban China; lower in Latin America; lowest in sub-Saharan Africa and the Arab world. All else being equal, educational level being the primary variable, the reading habit is higher in cities than in rural areas, and higher among women than men. Desire is intense both among longstanding members of the reading class and also in areas where the thirst for information about the world is newly available, as in the case of Kabul's recent boom in book publishing and bookstores.[8]

Let us imagine that the borders of access have been crossed, as they have for most, and that the border of desire has been acknowledged. While not everyone wants to read, some do and can. These people constitute the reading class, and they are socially powerful almost everywhere, able to do and get what they want. So what do they want? And how does what readers want square with what authors and publishers want? Are there any borders left for global members of the reading class?

Globalization and digitization have led to rosy predictions along the lines of "African writers are going global." The idea is that once writers have Facebook pages and once readers have Internet access, something like Pascale Casanova's "world republic of letters…independent of political boundaries" where everyone is a citizen and where readers and writers are unconstrained by wherever they happen to be will finally be realized.[9] While this scenario is not altogether wrong, it needs to be qualified.

Many recent scholars and commentators have assumed a linear development thesis along the lines that once digital access is achieved, hitherto marginal literary communities will enter the circulation of global discourse in a way that had not been possible with print media. Formerly, the idea goes, African writers depended on pre-established colonial relationships and metropolitan publishers (in London, Heinemann, Longman, and Macmillan, for Anglophone countries) to have any

---

[7] Wendy Griswold, *Regionalism and the Reading Class* (Chicago: University of Chicago Press, 2008).

[8] Rob Nordland and Fahim Abed, "Most Afghans Can't Read, but Their Book Trade Is Booming," *New York Times*, February 3, 2018 (https://www.nytimes.com/2018/02/03/world/asia/afghanistan-kabul-books-publishing.html).

[9] Pascale Casanova, *The World Republic of Letters* (Cambridge, MA: Harvard University Press, 2007).

chance of reaching an international readership; now they can just circulate their writing online. Africans involved in the book trade, as well as the writers them-selves, have festooned their products and activities with "global" and "international" labels. My research suggests instead four sometimes contradictory conclusions:

1. *Most writers* have embraced new media as a way of reaching larger audiences.
2. *Some writers* can be considered global in terms of their readership.
3. *Women writers* have the advantage in terms of crossing borders and attaining global recognition.
4. *Few readers* desire to read authors from outside their own countries or places with which they are familiar.

In the twentieth century it was unlikely for a Nigerian writer to reach a global market. A few lucky giants of the first generation—for example, Chinua Achebe, Flora Nwapa—caught the attention of British publishers like Heinemann and Longman and reached readers in the English-speaking world. A few others—for example, Buchi Emecheta, Ben Okri—were able to establish careers once they had moved to London. The vast majority either published their books in Nigeria with virtually no distribution inside or abroad, or published with firms like Macmillan's Pacesetters Series that were distributed only to an African market. They might achieve considerable success locally, more in terms of being known than in making a living from their writing, but they were unknown outside that community. Geographic borders were barriers to cultural transmission for most writers and most readers.

Digital technologies and new media have changed all this. Nowadays it appears that every Nigerian writer maintains and manages an online presence via Facebook, blogs, Instagram, Twitter, YouTube (African poets are particularly adroit at YouTube readings, as the research of Susanna Sacks has demonstrated).[10] Electronic distribution has made the output of African writers accessible all over the world.

However, there are three caveats. First, the definition of a *Nigerian* novel or author is becoming blurred. Second, going digital does not mean going global, not in terms of readership; the "Nigerian authors" that the outside world is likely to read tend to be atypical cosmopolitans who write about issues that the outside world is interested in. And, third, they are likely to be women.

Almost two decades ago I wrote a book with the subtitle *Readers, Writers, and the Novel in Nigeria.* Implicitly acknowledging that the readers could be in Brooklyn, the writers in London, the novels sold in bookshops in Berlin, the subtitle confidently assumed that such things as Nigerian readers, authors, and novels actually existed

---

[10] Susanna L. Sacks, "Slam Poetry in Malawi: Digital Media Aesthetics and Translingual Poetic Forms," in *Digital Technology and Languages in African Communities and Classrooms: Innovations and Opportunities*, ed. Leketi Makalela and Goodith White (Bristol: Multilingual Matters Press, forthcoming).

and could be identified. Needless to say, the digital, technological, and demographic tides of the twenty-first century have washed away any such categorical stability (which probably wasn't there in the first place). The fluidity of the present collides with the specificity of social diagnosis that the novel has traditionally offered. What readers remain—and, again, people have alternatives if all they seek is entertainment—are those seeking such specificity, about Nigeria or anything else.

The global elite is moving away from the local, crossing the old borders, and this is especially true in the case of female authors. For the book just mentioned, I looked at every twentieth-century Nigerian novel I could identify (476 in total), running from the 1950s through the late 1990s. Fifteen per cent of the authors were women. A few years later I compiled a list of novels that had been published after my book. Although this list was less comprehensive, I identified 132 titles from the late 1990s to 2005. Eighteen per cent were by women; while mildly encouraging, this didn't suggest much of a trend.

Compare this to the truly global list of novels published and distributed by Cassava Republic, which has the explicit mission "to build a new body of African writing that links writers across different times and spaces" and has received a great deal of attention in the UK and US.[11] Thirty novels are available through Amazon.com or directly from the publisher (who has a London office and is opening one in the US). Of these, twenty-three (77%) are by women. And while Cassava Republic has an explicit mission of promoting African writers, it has no explicit gender agenda. Nor is it just African-oriented presses that are tilting female. Overall, it is remarkable how a new generation of writers born in Nigeria features so many prominent women authors—Chimamanda Ngozi Adichie (b. 1977; *Half a Yellow Sun, Americanah*), Adaobi Tricia Nwaubani (b. 1976; *I Do Not Come to You by Chance*), and Helen Oyeyemi (b. 1984; *Boy, Snow, Bird*)—authors who publish with mainstream Western presses and whom critics have lavished with attention and praise.

Why have women suddenly moved to the foreground? Why have they been able to capitalize on digital and physical border-crossing more than men? There could be a number of factors in play. The literacy gap in Nigeria and elsewhere is closing, meaning more female readers; women everywhere read fiction more than their male peers, giving an advantage to writers who deal with issues of interest to women;

[11] Based in Abuja, Cassava Republic Press has been in operation since 2006. Cassava Republic (https://www.cassavarepublic.biz/pages/about-us). For the 2016 London launch, see "Nigerian Publishing House Cassava Republic Comes to the UK this April," What's On Africa, April 13, 2016 (http://whatsonafrica.org/nigerian-publishing-press-cassava-republic-launches-london-april/). For its 2017 entry into the American market, see Ed Nawotka, "Cassava Republic Brings Africa to America," *Publishers Weekly*, June 30, 2017 (https://www.publishersweekly.com/pw/by-topic/international/international-book-news/article/73739-cassava-republic-brings-africa-to-america.html). See also Mark Williams, "Social Media and Instagram Are Making Books Sexy Again—in Nigeria," *New Publishing Standard*, November 24, 2017 (http://www.thenewpublishingstandard.com/social-media-and-instagram-are-making-books-sexy-again-in-nigeria/).

publishers and critics concerned with promoting diversity may see a double benefit in favoring women of color; cosmopolitanism benefits intellectually ambitious women more than it does men because it releases the former from patriarchal expectations (in Nigeria, highly educated women who are too serious about their work have been stigmatized as "acadas," either sexually undesirable or having used their "bottom power" to achieve success). I suspect another factor is that while both men and women can promote their literary careers online, this might be especially beneficial for women who are more geographically limited by family responsibilities.

To sum up the picture so far: authors from the periphery are attempting to go global via social media. A fortunate and talented few—especially women—have captured attention in the West and beyond; Adichie's works have been translated into some thirty languages, mostly European but also Japanese, Malayalam, Hebrew, Sinhala, Vietnamese, and Arabic. So what about back home? Have readers and the book trade gone global as well?

Among the research sites I am exploring are book fairs where publishers and booksellers display their wares, depict their trajectories, and make connections. I attended the Nigerian International Book Fair 2017 in Lagos, where I spoke with a number of publishers as well as booksellers at leading Lagos bookstores, and, to get another perspective and see if Nigeria is atypical, I also attended the Nairobi International Book Fair the following September. Based on my observations and conversations, the shift toward globalization of markets, readers, and literary circulation has been greatly exaggerated. While both events adopted the label of "international," in fact virtually all of the booths set up by publishers and other members of the book trade were locally oriented. And beyond textbooks, booksellers tell me that their customers want the same things they wanted twenty years ago: formulaic fiction by Western authors (Frederick Forsyth and John Grisham are very popular) and motivational or Christian books. There is little demand for quality literature by foreign authors. As for quality work by Nigerian or Kenyan authors, the booksellers shrug and say that expats are the ones who buy these books. Despite a revolution in access, the tastes and desires of the local reading class have not changed.

Chinelo Okparanta, one of the most successful Nigerian border-crossers, exemplifies the fluidity and limits of the current situation, the complexities of readership, and how women are involved. Born in Port Harcourt, she moved to the United States at the age of 10 and was educated there. She is variously referred to as Nigerian, American, Nigerian-American, and "Nigeria's US-based author." Her fiction, set both in Nigeria and the US, focuses on women's lives, gender oppression, and female same-sex love. Ever since her short stories began appearing in places like *The New Yorker*, she has enjoyed extraordinary attention and acclaim in the West: London-based *Granta* named her one of their "New Voices for 2012"; she began to garner prizes such as the O. Henry Prize for the year's best short stories; and when *Granta* published her collection *Happiness, Like Water*, it received glowing praise from the likes of the *New York Times Sunday Book Review* and

National Public Radio. And also from the Lesbian Gay Bisexual Transexual and Queer (LGBTQ) cultural tastemakers, which awarded it the Lambda Literary Award for best Lesbian General Fiction in 2014. Her debut novel *Under the Udala Trees* similarly drew praise from mainstream, Black (e.g., *Essence*), and LGBTQ critics and writers; again receiving the Lambda award for 2016, it has won prizes and been on the "best book" lists of everything from the *Wall Street Journal* to *Cosmopolitan*.[12]

The response in Nigeria has been more measured. Both YNaija and Pulse, news sites aimed at young, urban Nigerians, included the novel on their ten-best lists for the year (though it was number ten for Pulse), but the press has paid no attention to it.[13] It was shortlisted for the Etisalat Prize for Literature in 2014 but lost out to a South African novel, Songeziwe Mahlangu's *Penumbra*, a work that has been largely ignored in the West.[14] At the Ake Book Festival in 2016, Okparanta received a mixed response: "Boos as well as cheers greeted one audience member who told Okparanta that 'the natural order of life is against LGBT because the Bible said he [God] made male and female.'"[15] The ambivalence in Nigeria is not surprising. On the one hand, the Nigerian literary world still takes its cues from London and New York to a considerable extent, so someone who has conquered that world would usually be celebrated. On the other hand, Nigerians are extremely conservative when it comes to same-sex relations. A draconian law from 2014 prohibits not only same-sex marriage but also any "public show of same-sex amorous relations"; the law seems to have encouraged vigilante violence, and few Nigerians outside of the activist community have objected. Ninety-five per cent of Nigerians are against gay marriage, ninety per cent against cohabitation or LGBTQ organizations.[16] So a writer dealing sympathetically with lesbian issues has difficulty getting traction with the local reading class.[17]

---

[12] Cited on Chinelo Okparanta's website (https://www.chinelookparanta.com/book-reviews).

[13] Zaynab Quadri, "10 Oustanding Nigerian Books for this Year," *Pulse*, December 16, 2015 (http://www.pulse.ng/books/pulselist-2015-10-outstanding-nigerian-books-for-this-year-id4464207.html); Wilfred Okiche, "The 10 Most Notable Books of 2015," *YNaija*, December 13, 2015 (https://ynaija.com/the-fishermen-blackass-under-the-udala-tree/).

[14] Another indication that it is not the case that novels that have won acclaim in Africa have crossed borders into the West. Both *Happiness, Like Water* and *Penumbra* were published in 2013, and both are available from Amazon.com; as of February 2018, *Penumbra* has received two customer reviews, *Happiness, Like Water*, fifty-nine (*Under the Udala Trees*, published three years later, has ninety-five).

[15] Sarah Ládípò Manyika, "The Nigerian-American Writer Who Takes on Taboos," *OZY*, December 19, 2017 (http://www.ozy.com/rising-stars/the-nigerian-american-writer-who-takes-on-taboos/82567).

[16] "'Tell Me Where I Can Be Safe': The Impact of Nigeria's Same Sex Marriage (Prohibition) Act," *Human Rights Watch*, October 20, 2016 (https://www.hrw.org/report/2016/10/20/tell-me-where-i-can-be-safe/impact-nigerias-same-sex-marriage-prohibition-act). Figures are from p. 18.

[17] Okparanta is perfectly aware of this. At the Ake Book Festival during a panel on "Legs Open, Eyes Closed: The New Sensuality in African Writing," she argued that "when we talk about sex, we are talking about power. Shame is the power that we give others to wield over us, so when I write I take back my power." "Galaxy of Africa's Literary Stars," *This Day*, December 15, 2016 (https://www.thisdaylive.com/index.php/2016/12/15/galaxy-of-africas-literary-stars-2/).

Meanwhile back in the West, critics are not the only ones who love Okparanta's fiction. Goodreads, with sixty-five million registered members, offers a sense of her popularity.[18] While we do not know the gender breakdown, evidence from book-club membership and reading patterns in general suggests that it would skew female. We know that women read more than men do, especially more fiction, and that they favor new books, reading them twice as often as men do.[19] So it comes as no surprise that Goodreads names *Under the Udala Trees* as one of the thirteen most popular Nigerian books—or that over half of these books are by women.[20]

Position and Location

When we think about people and borders, it is useful to distinguish between position and location. Position is where a person is; location is how a person makes meanings from where she is. In the twenty-first century, position seems to have become less important. Digital media allows readers to access writers from anywhere and writers to reach out globally (most readers, most writers, I hasten to add; there are still issues of access and digital divides, though much less so than in the recent past). Moreover, the very position of people, both authors and readers, is less stable than it was in the past. Lesley Nneka Arimah was born in the UK, grew up in various places including Nigeria, and lives in Minnesota. Wikipedia calls her a Nigerian writer; the *New York Times* calls her a "British-Nigerian-American writer," and the University of Chicago Library houses her book in the "William Vaughn Moody Collection in American Literature." She herself is coy, saying she is "Nigerian-ish," and that she "was born in the UK and grew up wherever her father was stationed for work, which was sometimes Nigeria, sometimes not" (Burney 2017). Position is fluid, with authors transcending borders, moving from place to place, in and out of the world republic of letters as they see fit.

Readers' positions are less fluid. (The mobility of the reading class should not be confused with the mobility of people fleeing war and poverty; we need to remember that we are talking about an advantaged group here.) While a few cosmopolitans like those expats in Africa want to read African writers, by and large people choose to read locally, about their own country, region, city; when they relocate, they read about their new country, region, city. To be cosmopolitan usually just means to be

---

[18] "Number of Registered Members on Goodreads from May 2011 to September 2017 (In Millions)," Statista (https://www.statista.com/statistics/252986/number-of-registered-members-on-goodreadscom/).

[19] On women vs. men reading, see Andrew Perrin, "Book Reading 2016," *Pew Research Center: Internet & Technology*, September 1, 2016 (http://www.pewinternet.org/2016/09/01/book-reading-2016/). On women favoring contemporary books, see "Elizabeth," "Sex and Reading: A Look at Who's Reading Whom," Goodreads Blog, November 19, 2014 (https://www.goodreads.com/blog/show/475-sex-and-reading-a-look-at-who-s-reading-whom).

[20] "Nigeria," Goodreads (https://www.goodreads.com/genres/nigeria).

local, culturally savvy, in more than one place. Readers read about some places but not all places.

Why might this be? Readers have bodies, material rather than virtual, and those bodies spend time in particular places. Thus readers do their location, their meaning-making, from a specific place, not from some planetary everywhere. Location, it appears, entails borders. Social constructions though they may be, borders help orient people. By drawing lines, they demarcate a place worthy of attention, separating what is inside them, an area of interest and concern, from what is outside them and therefore less compelling.

The reasons for this come both from the brain and from society. Human beings are neurologically wired and socially conditioned to pay attention to some things, to things that might matter, and to ignore the rest. So just as readers tend to select reading materials related to their gender, their ethnicity, their religion, their occupation, and so on, they also prefer to read about the place or places with which they are most familiar.[21] An American reader who has lived in Italy but not France will be more inclined toward fiction set in Italy than in France. Again we see that the borders are not impenetrable, but the readers themselves tend to honor them.

Reading across borders in the twenty-first century? It is easier than ever before to read works from other places and cultures. Writers and publishers and (some) educators use every digital and social media device they can to encourage it. Those barriers of access that remain will evaporate. Most readers, however, will not have the desire to read beyond their own positions. They are local, perhaps multilocal, but not translocal in their interests and satisfactions, and their reading choices will reflect this. Although the borders will be wide open, few people will make the journey to cross them.

FURTHER READING

Arimah, Lesley Nneka. *What It Means When a Man Falls from the Sky*. New York: Riverhead, 2017.

Atogun, Odafe. *Taduno's Song*. New York: Pantheon, 2016.

Baron, Naomi S. *Words Onscreen: The Fate of Reading in a Digital World*. Oxford: Oxford University Press, 2015.

Barrett, A. Igoni. *Blackass*. Minneapolis, MN: Graywolf Press, 2015.

Casanova, Pascale. *The World Republic of Letters*. Cambridge, MA: Harvard University Press, 2004.

Griswold, Wendy. *Bearing Witness: Readers, Writers, and the Novel in Nigeria*. Princeton: Princeton University Press, 2000.

---

[21] Wendy Griswold and Hannah Wohl, "Evangelists of Culture: One Book Programs and the Agents Who Define Literature, Shape Tastes, and Reproduce Regionalism," *Poetics* 50 (2016): 96–109.

Griswold, Wendy. *Regionalism and the Reading Class*. Chicago: University of Chicago Press, 2008.

Griswold, Wendy, Erin M. McDonnell, and Terence E. McDonnell. "Glamour and Honor: The Relationship between Reading and the Internet in West African Culture." *Information Technologies and International Development* 3.4 (2006): 37–52.

Griswold, Wendy, and Hannah Wohl. "Evangelists of Culture: One Book Programs and the Agents Who Define Literature, Shape Tastes, and Reproduce Regionalism." *Poetics* 50 (2016): 96–109.

Knulst, Wim and Gerber Kraaykamp. "Trends in Leisure Reading: Forty Years of Research on Reading in the Netherlands." *Poetics* 26 (1998): 21–41.

Manyika, Sarah Ládípò. *Like a Mule Bringing Ice Cream to the Sun*. Abuja: Cassava Republic, 2016.

Newell, Stephanie. *Writing African Women: Gender, Popular Culture, and Literature in West Africa*. London: Zed Books, 1997; 2017.

Okparanta, Chinelo. *Under the Udala Trees*. Boston, MA: Houghton Mifflin Harcourt, 2015.

Omotoso, Yewande. *The Woman Next Door*. New York: Picador, 2016.

Onuzo, Chibundu. *Welcome to Lagos*. London: Faber & Faber, 2017.

Sacks, Susanna L. "Slam Poetry in Malawi: Digital Media Aesthetics and Translingual Poetic Forms." *Digital Technology and Languages in African Communities and Classrooms: Innovations and Opportunities*, ed. Leketi Makelela and Goodith White. Bristol: Multilingual Matters Press, forthcoming.

Turner, Zeke. "In Books, Print Makes a Stand." *Wall Street Journal*, October 16, 2017.

UNESCO Institute for Statistics. *Adult and Youth Literacy: National, Regional, and Global Trends, 1985–2014*. Montreal: UNESCO Institute for Statistics, 2013.

6

NEUROIMAGED

NATALIE PHILLIPS, SALVATORE ANTONUCCI,
MELISSA KLAMER, CODY MEJEUR, AND KARAH SMITH

In an interview with Neil deGrasse Tyson on *StarTalk*, Salman Rushdie said that stories captivate us so deeply that we become immersed in their fictional world. As a writer, Rushdie said, "what I want to do—or hope to do—is to create that world that readers like being in [and] want to inhabit." As readers, we have the power to cognitively transform words on the page into vibrantly imagined experiences. We build a world in our minds, scene by scene, character by character, detail by detail until it comes to life. Rushdie suggests this experience can be transformative:

> The great thing about literature is, I think it does change people. I think it changes readers, one reader at a time, but neither the writer, nor the reader knows when it's going to happen.[1]

When it comes to talking about the transformative power of fiction, Rushdie voices a familiar sentiment. This romantic idea has long enticed literary scholars and bibliophiles alike, including George Eliot, who believed the purpose of fiction is to "enlarge [our] sympathies." Yet Rushdie's comment raises deeper questions about reading: when and why do stories persuade us? What invites a reader to inhabit a world, and in what ways—big or small—can it change them?

How does reading change someone's mind?

Recent work in neuroscience suggests that reading doesn't just change our minds, it changes our brains. This happens, in no small part, because when we "inhabit a fictional world," to use Rushdie's phrase, we also simulate that fictional world in *our minds*.

Brain regions that come alive while we're reading about the actions of fictional characters are often the same ones we'd use if we performed those actions in real life. Thinking about the neuroscience of reading, then, moves swiftly beyond merely exploring which brain regions are active in reading, language processing, or

---

[1] "Salman Rushdie," *StarTalk*, hosted by Neil deGrasse Tyson, season 4, episode 11, *National Geographic*, December 10, 2017.

comprehension. When we read a sentence like "Bobby kicked the ball" or "Karen grabbed a beer," it activates the motor cortex, the brain region used to control motion in everyday life. We cognitively simulate each imagined action with extraordinary specificity, deploying distinctive parts of the motor cortex used to move an arm or leg ourselves. And this goes beyond actions. As we read a novel, we involuntarily recreate, or cognitively reproduce, the fictional environment before us.

Rather than just visualizing a setting or scene—already a complex cognitive act—this mental simulation translates words and phrases into a multisensory world, full of imaginary tastes, textures, sounds, and smells. As we know from a study in Spain, just reading the word "cinnamon" activates the primary olfactory cortex, the brain region used to process real-world smells.[2] Take, for example, Oscar Wilde's *The Picture of Dorian Gray*. From the very first sentence, we are simulating—one could even say feeling or virtually sensing—a rich mixture of sights, sounds, and smells:

> The studio was filled with the rich odor of roses, and when the light summer wind stirred amidst the trees of the garden there came through the open door the heavy scent of the lilac, or the more delicate perfume of the pink-flowering thorn.[3]

As we try to imagine the studio, our memories of the "odor of roses" or the "scent of…lilac" intermix with the "more delicate" perfumes, a sensory environment enriched by the imagined sound of trees rustling in the "light summer wind." Already multiple neurological processes are engaged, including the visual, auditory, and olfactory senses, as we recall past experiences and use them to create this first evocative setting that will open into a full, immersive story world. Yet Wilde's metaphors take us even further, engaging senses we wouldn't expect to be associated with the sights, sounds, and smells of a studio. As researchers at Emory discovered, when we read about an old man having a *leathery voice*, for example, it doesn't just engage our auditory cortex.[4] Our sense of touch—the somatosensory cortex—is also activated; to imagine how his voice sounds we first have to think of the *feel* of leather and transpose it to sound. So when we read about the "*heavy* scent of the lilac" or the "*light* summer wind," we are still using our senses even if their stimuli are only present figuratively (here, feeling something heavy and light). Metaphors compound sensory experience, creating ever-increasing cognitive complexity by activating diverse neural systems associated with various senses and feelings. This process allows us to enter the story: cognitively speaking, we're *in* that fictional world, recreating the multisensory experiences we read about. And the more evocative the language, the richer the world readers get to inhabit.

[2] Julio González et al., "Reading Cinnamon Activates Olfactory Brain Regions," *NeuroImage* 32.2 (2006): 906–12; 906.

[3] Oscar Wilde, *The Picture of Dorian Gray* (New York: Penguin, 2003), 5.

[4] Simon Lacey, Randall Stilla, and K. Sathian, "Metaphorically Feeling: Comprehending Textural Metaphors Activates Somatosensory Cortex," *Brain & Language* 120.3 (2012): 416–21 (doi:https://doi.org/10.1016/j.bandl.2011.12.016).

If just one sentence by Oscar Wilde can do all this, we can only imagine what reading a full novel (or, I dare say, a series of them) does to—and for—the brain. By understanding these neurological processes, we can see that reading actively employs and alters the brain, dynamically changing the reader in the moment-to-moment experience of a novel. These changes may not be lasting or world-altering on their own. Yet, by examining how these moments of emotional identification, sensory engagement, and imagination work at a micro-level in reading, gradually shaping and reshaping the brain, we can begin to explore how literature comes to change our minds. Reading the brain can lead to new insights about what reading means and does, revealing how it shapes our experiences of fictional and actual worlds around us.

Reading and the Brain

When we think about reading, we tend to think about reading a book, perhaps in a library, in a coffee shop, or in our favorite armchair at home. We rarely think of reading inside a brain scanner. For those who exclude the digital, this wouldn't count as reading at all; you can't flip through the pages of a novel inside a magnetic resonance imaging (MRI) scanner. Instead, MRI reading means reading inside a magnetic bore and head-coil, only able to see the text on the computer screen behind you because it is reflected through a mirror above your eyes. If you flip pages at all, you do so only figuratively, by pushing a button in your hand to advance to the next slide.

Reading inside an MRI scanner may not seem like the most natural way to engage with fiction, poetry, prose, or film, yet the knowledge we can gain from doing so has the potential to transform not only existing research practices but also how we conceptualize reading more broadly. First and foremost, this work draws us into complexities we don't often consider as literary scholars. Simply to "see" words on a page, much less understand them, we first activate the primary visual cortex. As our eyes skim rapidly over the page (we read, not linearly, but in short leaps and bounds), we must unravel the visual puzzle to decode what letters are present and in what order. And that's just to identify each word. As we read, moreover, we sub-articulate the words we see, using the same brain regions we'd use to move our lips as if reading them aloud. This process involves, at the simplest level, accessing the visual images of letters, how they would sound and be pronounced, and each word's lexical meaning (often multiple), before we even begin to comprehend what each phrase, sentence, or story means. To put this simply, reading—be it a novel, billboard, or cereal box—is extraordinarily complex. As studies of reading have advanced, the neural networks believed to be involved have become increasingly intricate. Early neuroscientific work suggested a relatively "simple" one-way network flowing from regions responsible for visual processing to those associated with language processing and reading comprehension. Contemporary research, however, depicts multiple cognitive regions working in concert, often bi-directionally, in an ongoing cycle of parallel processing.[5]

And none of this work even begins to touch on what happens in the brain when we read a work of literature. It is difficult to find an fMRI (functional magnetic resonance imaging) study where people read naturally at their own speed, or engage with a text longer than a few sentences. The new field of literary neuroscience has only just begun to navigate these challenges, revealing the vast potential of what's left to learn about how and why we read literature.

In our first fMRI study, now known in the media as "Your Brain on Jane," our team of researchers at the Digital Humanities & Literary Cognition Lab (DHLC) looked at the cognitive complexity of two forms of literary attention we can bring to a book. Using a chapter from *Mansfield Park* by Jane Austen, we compared close reading, or formal literary analysis, to pleasure reading, moments when one becomes lost in a good book—or, perhaps more literally, in a good screen. Even at an individual level, brain images comparing these two styles of attention reveal a cognitive diversity that expands the neural regions traditionally believed to be involved in reading (Figure 6.1).

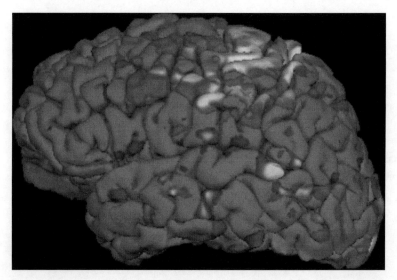

Figure 6.1 An fMRI neuroimage showing regions of heightened brain activity for a single participant as they read a work of fiction. The lighter areas appearing in white indicate increased activity for close reading; regions appearing dark gray and black indicate increased activity for pleasure reading.

⁵ Stanislas Dehaene, *Reading in the Brain: The New Science of How We Read* (London: Penguin Books, 2009).

Brain images like Figure 6.1 show us where, when, and how much neural activity occurs, in this case, in regions active for one person reading Austen. At the simplest level, fMRI maps blood flow in the brain. When certain areas of the brain are more active, those regions require more oxygen and food (glucose), and thus more blood. Because blood contains iron, and because iron atoms create small distortions in the magnetic field around them, the magnet in the scanner is able to pick up changes in the magnetic field as blood ebbs and flows through various brain regions. fMRI thus allows us to track which areas receive higher amounts of blood over time and, by implication, which areas are more active. So when this participant was close reading, we were able to see (and were surprised to see) that regions including the somatosensory cortex and the motor cortex were activated—areas involved in processing touch, placing ourselves in space, and moving through the world. Hypothetically, this could point to the heightened cognitive demands of close reading, suggesting it requires us to engage more senses and neural networks. Yet this is just one person, one brain image.

Only by looking at a large group of people reading—that is, multiple brain images—can we even begin to generalize about cognitive processes involved in fiction reading. In our study, looking at neuroimages from the entire group of participants reveals the diversity and breadth of how we neurologically respond to literature. Each participant's scans showed different areas of activation. Yet almost all had widespread, near global activation across the brain. The two brain images presented in Figure 6.2, each from a different reader of Austen's novel, help illustrate the profound variation across individuals.

One participant, for instance, showed more activity in the occipital lobe (the region responsible for visual processing) when analyzing Austen's prose. For another, literary analysis created widespread activity across the brain as a whole. For both, brain activity increased significantly for close reading compared to

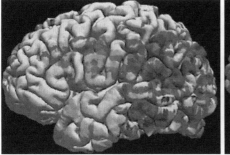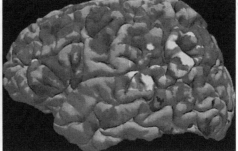

Figure 6.2 Brain scans from two of the eighteen participants in the fMRI study of literary attention conducted by Dr. Natalie Phillips and collaborators in 2012 (Stanford University). Brain images from Participant 3 (left) and Participant 9 (right) not only show different areas highly active during literary reading, but also highlight the unique shape and wrinkles of each person's brain, further emphasizing cognitive diversity.

pleasure reading, pointing toward the cognitive complexity and value of this core skill in the liberal arts. But what's truly fascinating here is that the areas "lighting up" for close reading vary so remarkably from individual to individual. Clearly, no two readers read the same book in the same way. Indeed, as the essays students wrote after leaving the scanner revealed, different readers focus on different things. For example, one student's essay explored how Austen juxtaposes characters and depicts emotions; a second gravitated toward feminist critique and class analysis. Where the first wave of neuroscientific studies sought to find commonality in brain activity for reading in general, this new work not only allows for, but intentionally explores, these variations and individual differences in how we engage fiction. Through this work, we ultimately hope to develop tools that can appreciate both the cognitive similarities in how we respond to—and get lost in—a fictional world *and* how each person's brain responds uniquely to what they read.

While these brain images offer rich insights into the individual and collective reading experience that have heretofore been inaccessible, they are still *static* images of a dynamic process. Fortunately, techniques and methods in neuroimaging are becoming more sophisticated, allowing us to appreciate how brain activity changes over time. One experiment in the Hasson Lab at Princeton took advantage of these technological advances to explore how we tell and listen to stories. In that study, researchers recorded students as they told stories—in one case, an off-the-cuff anecdote about going to prom—inside a brain scanner and collected brain data about how their cognitive activity changed as the stories unfolded. Then they had people *listen* to the story inside the scanner, recording how *their* brain activity changed over time as they listened. The study revealed that as people listened to the story, their brain activity aligned with that of the storyteller, demonstrating a phenomenon known as *neurocoupling*.[6] With a slight delay for the actual communication to occur, both the speaker and the listener experienced rhythmic brain activations, oscillating in tandem. Surprisingly, although creating a story and listening to one pose radically distinct cognitive demands, the story itself invites a deep level of shared cognitive experience. Essentially, when we communicate with one another, our brains reflect this by shifting and changing in unison over time. Literally, two people in conversation are on the same wavelength. We can start to imagine just how earth-shattering this was in cognitive circles if we imagine discovering that the brain activity of a writer composing a work of fiction *mirrored* that of their readers as they read it for the first time.

This study shifted the scope of what we thought fMRI was capable of doing. Rather than simply identifying specific brain regions involved in various tasks and activities, fMRI became a tool that could be used for exploring how whole-brain activity changes dynamically over *time*. As a result, it became possible to

---

[6] Greg J. Stephens, Lauren J. Silbert, and Uri Hasson, "Speaker–Listener Neural Coupling Underlies Successful Communication," *Proceedings of the National Academy of Sciences* 107.32 (2010): 14425–30.

conceptualize how fMRI could uncover new nuances in how we engage with reading literature.

This recognition not only inspired the Austen study of novel reading described above, but also led to a new experiment looking at real-time responses to poetry. In collaboration with Gabrielle Starr, we designed a study that could capture readers' aesthetic responses to poems and measure how their pleasure shifted *as* they read. Participants, reading sixteen sample sonnets from the eighteenth to the twenty-first centuries, highlighted moments they found aesthetically pleasing (i.e., powerful, profound, or moving) and displeasing (i.e., annoying, clichéd, or dull). One might think that we decide whether we like or dislike a poem—or any work—*after* reading it. Yet, as our study has begun to reveal, these large-scale judgments emerge from moments of pleasure and displeasure that accumulate (and shift) as we read each new word, phrase, and section. And, soon, this study will move inside the scanner, and participants will be able to view their own aesthetic responses to poems in real-time on a screen.

Rather than simply comparing poems people love to those they hate, this approach lets us dig into the ebb and flow of pleasure and enjoyment in literary reading, recognizing that our final impressions—the fiction, literature, and poems that we love, remember, and claim shape us the most—always emerge from a complex mixture of fleeting emotions, gut reactions, and in-the-moment judgments. Our early research on the pleasures of poetry reading suggests that, while individual tastes clearly differ, there are fascinating similarities in moments we collectively find moving. In McKay's sonnet, "Dawn in New York," for example, 60 per cent of participants single out the description of people wandering the streets of Manhattan with "wine-weakened" eyes as particularly positive and powerful. At this point, pleasure aligned across readers, revealing an unexpected moment of cognitive and emotional unison. While feelings split over phrases like "tramping tramping feet" or the "grotesques" invoked "beneath the strong electric lights," readers came back together at the poem's end, finding pleasure in the final cryptic phrase: "I go *darkly-rebel* to my work."[7] (See Figure 6.3.)

Over sixteen sonnets, clear patterns of convergence and divergence emerge, revealing complex patterns—or, one could say, rhythms—of emotional response, both personally and collectively. For instance, readers seem to be captivated by the poetics of figurative language (i.e., metaphors, similes, personification, etc.) and find it particularly pleasing, even if that moment describes something quite negative. Students take delight in the "cheerless domes" of McKay's New York and the moment where "rage and wonder battle cruel, and strange," in Michael Ferris' "The Catskill Eagle," as well as in positive topics like love, happiness, or the beauties of nature. As we map these in-the-moment responses to poetry in the fMRI study (begun in Spring 2018), it will mark our first foray into exploring how these ever-changing

---

[7] Claude McKay, *Harlem Shadows* (New York: Harcourt, Brace and Company, 1922), 43.

The Dawn! **The Dawn!** The crimson-tinted, comes

Out of the low still skies, over the hills,

Manhattan's roofs and spires and cheerless domes!

The Dawn! My spirit to its spirit thrills.

Almost **the mighty city is asleep,**

No pushing crowd, no tramping, tramping feet.

But here and there **a few cars groaning creep**

Along, above, and underneath the stret,

Bearing their strangely-ghostly burdens by,

The women and the men of garish nights,

Their eyes **wine-weakened and their clothes awry,**

Grotesques beneath the strong electric lights.

The shadows wane. **The Dawn comes to New York.**

And I go darkly-rebel to my work.

Figure 6.3 One participant's real-time responses to "Dawn in New York" by Claude McKay. Participants were asked to highlight poetic moments that they found aesthetically pleasing in green, and those that were displeasing in red, here marked with underlining (pleasing) and bolding (displeasing). This individual joined most others in liking the phrase "darkly-rebel," but diverged from the majority in disliking "wine-weakened."

feelings—a mixture of engagement, boredom, annoyance, surprise, and delight—shape our cognitive engagement with any literary work.

Neuroimaging: The Curious Case of Reading in a Scanner

While neuroscience and fMRI experiments can provide new insights into the processes of reading, this interdisciplinary approach has a number of limitations. One might expect an interdisciplinary study of reading and the brain to focus on reading as it happens in normal, everyday experience. To a certain extent, our study does this by allowing readers to read a novel at their own speed: a radical departure from traditional fMRI study design. However, in trying to approximate something close to "natural reading," there are many things that MRI simply cannot do—such as offer a truly natural reading environment. A brain scanner is a strange place to read. The magnet that allows us to track blood flow makes loud, erratic noises that are distracting even with protective earplugs. The person being scanned is asked to lie as still as possible inside a small, circular tube, keeping their head in the same place as best they can (Figure 6.4). Such a setting is a far cry from one's favorite nook, bookstore, library, park, or other idyllic reading spot. As a result, the limitations of the scanner raise the question of whether it is truly possible to analyze

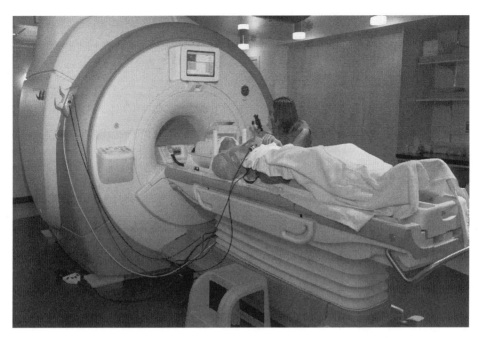

Figure 6.4 Dr. Natalie Phillips walking a research participant through the reading task they will be completing inside the scanner. Photo Credit: Linda A. Cicero/Stanford News Service.

"natural" reading at all. Can we read normally in the strange settings of labs and brain scanners that enable scientific observation? Or do those spaces and practices render reading fundamentally different, and skew the results away from everyday practice?

Of course, reading inside a brain scanner—or simply under observation—is a radically different experience from reading in general. Yet the very limitations imposed by scientific technologies also invite us to reexamine our assumptions about reading, and even redefine how we think about the reading experience. When we first imagined doing a study of novel reading using fMRI, the dream was that people would see a page-like image of Jane Austen's novel, *Mansfield Park*, in the scanner. The primary concerns were about replicating the experience of reading the physical, paperback copy they first engaged outside of the scanner. We focused on editions, fonts, and the perfect back-color for the page that might make the digital rendering seem as similar as possible to the print version.

But lying inside the scanner, these concerns became moot. Not a single page of the novel—or even a long paragraph—was readable when presented in full on the screen at the back of the scanner. Working with these realities forced us away from our biases toward print media and natural reading, and quickly took the study in a different direction entirely, raising a new and exciting set of questions. One of the goals of the study was to examine the "natural" reading of a long literary text such as a novel—something quite different from previous scientific studies that relied on tightly controlled stimuli of words, phrases, or sentences at most. Yet given the limited range of vision achievable within the scanner, pragmatic concerns about sizing, spacing, pacing the text, and participant comfort took priority. The study required a text that subjects could move through at their own pace, one that balanced the need for legibility with narrative continuity. For every block of text, we confronted questions about style and presentation: how much context, for example, did readers need to correctly interpret untagged dialogue between the hero and heroine in *Mansfield Park*? Even in our poetry study, we had to persuade collaborators in radiology that breaking up a sonnet in a study of aesthetic pleasure for the sake of easy visibility would be like splitting the *Mona Lisa* in half and asking people how much they liked it. What were the right compromises to make to handle these technological challenges and yet allow readers to experience the literary work as a whole?

The practice of reading in a scanner reveals ongoing similarities between our engagement with digital texts and print. Digital reading remains heavily influenced by print: e-readers and digital renderings continue to rely on page-based structures, using each device's rectangular screen to simulate a single page and replicate the illusion of page-turning as the reader clicks or swipes. All this implies that texts remain "constant"—something to be replicated as they are printed, copied, or downloaded to new mediums. In this way, the ideal of the print book continues to define and haunt contemporary reading practices, even as digital reading proliferates and we find ourselves reading in strange places like MRI scanners that alter and challenge the hegemony of the codex.

Navigating these practicalities of reading within the scanner points us to how strongly reading is defined by a text's frames, gaps, and presentation. For example, the material constraints of reading in an MRI construct a very different reading experience. Lying on their backs in the scanner, subjects actually read a copy of the text that is reflected on the mirror above their eyes, not one inked on a page or rendered in pixels. This reflection is possible only because of a number of breaks, translations, and mediations of the text: first the text is digitally encoded, then broken into sections and organized by software, and displayed and reflected to the participant in the scanner. Participants interact with the text using a basic clicker that lets them progress to the next piece of text. These mediations thus allow and limit the reader's interaction with the text, and many breaks in the text, ironically, make it more legible to the reader in this context. While this is to some extent universally true of all reading, it is a truth that is always inflected by particular contexts and forms of reading in different situations. And that's exciting—it means that reading is adaptable, variable, and resilient.

Unexpectedly, the MRI scanner makes it possible to reimagine what constitutes reading and adjust to its changing practices and contexts. In an age in which we read text as ink on paper and increasingly as encoded symbols on a screen, or even as reflections in a scanner, we are expanding what we think of as a reading surface.

And now we can read not only on pages and screens, but on the surface of the brain itself. N. Katherine Hayles has urged humanists to respond to these new spaces for reading, declaring: "Now it is time to rethink what reading is, and how it works in the rich mixtures of words and images, sounds and animations, graphics and letters that constitute the environments of twenty-first century literacies."[8] Reading practices are becoming increasingly ubiquitous, expansive, and diverse as technological developments make it possible to read in new spaces. Like other forms of digital reading, reading in a scanner urges us to "rethink what reading is" and opens up new possibilities for such rethinking. In the neuroscience of reading, it turns out, listening to a book—or story—is actually *easier*, methodologically speaking, than letting people read at their own speed. This calls our attention to the need to expand our definition of reading beyond the visual, including audiobooks and braille. As our current study, "The Stories We Tell About Music" is exploring, people hear stories when listening to a piece of orchestral music, urging us to reconsider yet again the line between reading and storytelling. Literary neuroscience is not magic, objective brain science that will solve once and for all how we read and why reading matters. However, the more we understand about how reading functions, the more we can envision how it works in different environments, for diverse readers, and across mediums in the twenty-first century.

Interdisciplinarity: Bridging the Gap

The work of understanding how reading happens and what we can do with reading processes requires interdisciplinary collaboration that defies traditional boundaries, much as digital reading has challenged our knowledge based only on paper texts. In his interview with Neil deGrasse Tyson, Salman Rushdie admitted that he "was supposed to be a scientist."[9] Imagining the famous novelist having to "jump ship" from the sciences to pursue history and the classics caused Tyson to imagine an alternate universe where Rushdie took another path, spending his life becoming an equally astounding, award-winning physicist. Yet this imagining also caught him in the ultimate quandary: it would erase Rushdie's novels. This very conflict—the implicit opposition between humanities and sciences—that forced Rushdie to pick one side or the other also inspired Tyson to come up with a different solution that doesn't mean choosing: "maybe there's a pathway where you could've done both."

This idea—imagining forms of work and knowledge that do both—is what motivates and inspires our ongoing work in literature, neuroscience, and digital

---

[8] N. Katherine Hayles, *How We Think: Digital Media and Contemporary Technogenesis* (Chicago: University of Chicago Press, 2012).

[9] "Salman Rushdie," *StarTalk*, hosted by Neil deGrasse Tyson, season 4, episode 11, *National Geographic*, December 10, 2017.

humanities. Yet for many, the question still remains: why should literary scholars care about brain imaging at all? We want to rephrase the question: why *wouldn't* the neuroscience of reading matter to us as literary scholars? If we truly want to understand the shifting realities of modern reading, we have to authentically bridge C. P. Snow's oft-cited "gap" between the humanities and sciences in a way that resists the mere importation of culturally and academically prioritized models from STEM.[10] Rather, we need to grapple with the interdisciplinary power and productive dissonance of integrating cognitive studies and traditional humanistic inquiry. In this interdisciplinarity, we can start to create truly reciprocal spaces where people can share ideas and collaborate on projects across disciplines. Literary questions can advance neuroscience, expanding traditional methods for studying reading and placing new demands on existing technology and scientific study design. Likewise, engaging in neuroscience provides new perspectives on literary reading, encouraging us to explore the cognitive complexity and diversity of how we engage with art, music, and literature from Oscar Wilde's multisensory parlor to Claude McKay's Manhattan streets.

A true blending of disciplines across the sciences and humanities can help us better understand the reading brain. This effort brings together radical interdisciplinarity and creativity to understand how, as Rushdie put it, literature "changes readers, one reader at a time, but neither the writer nor the reader knows when it's going to happen." Only through broadening our disciplinary lenses are we able to begin finding answers, looking not only at when literature moves us, but at *how*: one reader at a time.

FURTHER READING

Dehaene, Stanislas. *Consciousness and the Brain: Deciphering How the Brain Codes Our Thoughts*. New York: Viking, 2014.

Desai, Rutvik H., et al. "Toward Semantics in the Wild: Activation to Manipulable Nouns in Naturalistic Reading." *Journal of Neuroscience* 36:14 (2016): 4050–5.

Herman, David. *Storytelling and the Sciences of Mind*. Cambridge, MA: MIT Press, 2013.

Phillips, Natalie M., et al. "Patterns of Attention and Memory in Jane Austen." *Jane Austen and Sciences of the Mind*, ed. Beth Lau. New York: Routledge, 2017.

Price, Cathy. "Current Themes in Neuroimaging Studies of Reading." *Brain and Language* 125.2 (2013): 131–3.

Sanford, A. J., and Catherine Emmott. *Mind, Brain and Narrative*. Cambridge: Cambridge University Press, 2012.

---

[10] Charles Percy Snow, *The Two Cultures and the Scientific Revolution* (Cambridge: Cambridge University Press, 1959), 31.

Thompson, Helen, and Shankar Vedantam. "A Lively Mind: Your Brain on Jane Austen." *NPR*, October 9, 2012 (http://www.npr.org/sections/health-shots/2012/10/09/162401053/a-lively- mind-your-brain-on-jane-austen).

Vervaeck, Bart, Lars Bernaerts, Dirk de Geest, and Luc Herman. *Stories and Minds: Cognitive Approaches to Literary Narrative*. Lincoln: University of Nebraska Press, 2013.

Bortolussi, Marisa, and Peter Dixon. *Psychonarratology: Foundations for the Empirical Study of Literary Response*. Cambridge: Cambridge University Press, 2003.

STYLES

7

DISTANT

ELAINE TREHARNE

This chapter draws on the conception and depiction of the book in key examples of medieval manuscripts in Britain to trace the evolution of reading strategies over the *longue durée* of the medieval, from the sixth century to the fifteenth. This period extends from a time when the ability to read was rare and the ability to write yet rarer, to a time when education was available to many, and perhaps up to a third of men and a smaller fraction of women could access books for themselves.

Many assumptions about reading practices in the medieval period depend either on models inherited from postprint scholarship or on an unhelpful emphasis on the difference between the postmedieval and the medieval itself. One imagines the exegetically inclined monastic reader piously contemplating the homilies in a manuscript such as Cambridge, Corpus Christi College 162;[1] the lay person reading aloud to an assembled household the multigeneric devotional and romantic texts in compilations like Oxford, Bodleian Library, Digby 86;[2] the individual's pursuit of proximity to Christ through contemplative engagement with daily hours in such books as London, British Library, Additional Manuscript 49,622 (the Gorleston Psalter)[3] richly adorned with often inexplicable ribald, grotesque, or secular marginalia.

What I shall call the "phenomenal book" involves three components of the legible. Principal among these will be a common mode of textual reception that persisted into the Early Modern period: *literally* distant reading. Positioned far away from the book itself, as it was read out by another individual, for the listener-viewer, what might it have meant to watch something being read? To have experienced the object only ever in a physically and spatially mediated mode (especially if one's visual or auditory senses were differently abled)? The second and related focus is the depiction in manuscripts of the act of delivery of text. Images of books within manuscript art

---

[1] Fully digitized at "Parker Library on the Web" (https://parker.stanford.edu/).

[2] J. Tschann and M. B. Parkes, eds., *Facsimile of Oxford, Bodleian Library, MS Digby 86*, Early English Text Society supplementary series 16 (Oxford: Oxford University Press, 1996).

[3] Digitized at the British Library's "Digitised Manuscripts" (https://www.bl.uk/manuscripts/).

(and other forms of art including wall-paintings, sculpture, and precious objects) have the dominant attributes of completeness and a focus on hapticity—the requirement of books to be *handled* in order to function. The depicted books demonstrate a desire, anthropomorphized, for intimacy with the user that undercuts the phenomenological encounter of the distant hearer-viewer. But what happens when, for the majority of experiencers of the text, there is no intimacy; there is only the transcendental, the perspectival? The third, brief element of my discussion is the inherent spirituality of the book. Here, it can be argued that some complex medieval manuscripts draw the reader-user into an intimate experience only to distance them with a scriptibility that is deliberately resistant to interpretation.

My interdisciplinary methods of reading this evidence vary from the literal (letter-by-letter) analysis of graphs; to the literary; to the analysis of images and what they can reveal about the codicological representation of the medieval book *within* the medieval book. This work is underpinned by a phenomenological approach that is derived from Maurice Merleau-Ponty's effort to understand the embodied experience of being in the world.[4] The object "body"—the object of investigation—is both the user-viewer-reader of the medieval book and the medieval book itself.

Using Books

In the Anglo-Saxon period, and later, what did it mean to have access to a book? Irrespective of subject matter—medical, legal, historical, partly secular, wholly religious—the book was an extraordinary, and yet seen, known, and familiar, object. Carried by Christ and the apostles in contemporary images, used by saints to ward off enemies, worn around the necks of priests, and kissed by kings, the book was totemic, shamanistic, and always apotropaic. It was a container of knowledge, an archive of memories, a repository of lives. It was fetishized, reviled, and venerated.

It is possible to reconstruct the ways in which medieval manuscripts were viewed within their own intellectual and social milieu using the multidisciplinary sources of lexical, literary, artistic, and historical evidence. The manuscript's intentionality, materiality, functionality, and cultural value—the four core attributes of any textual object—demonstrate the significance of every aspect of book production in this early period. The later tenth-century Exeter Book (Exeter Cathedral Library, 150), recently added to the UNESCO Memory of the World Register, is a case in point.[5]

---

[4] See, *inter alia*, Maurice Merleau-Ponty, *Le visible et l'invisible* (Paris: Gallimard, 1964), trans. Alphonso Lingis, *The Visible and the Invisible* (Evanston: Northwestern University Press, 1968).

[5] https://www.unesco.org.uk/portfolio/memory-of-the-world/.

This manuscript was created perhaps at Exeter, or at Glastonbury, in *c.* 960, and it is one of five poetic codices within the overall Old English literary corpus.[6]

The Exeter Book is a large anthology of diverse poems, measuring *c.*318mm by 160mm, and written by one scribe over 131 folios, in a calligraphically expert hand.[7] It may have been a presentation or ceremonial codex used for multiple functions that involved the community and visiting members of the institution to which it belonged.[8] It is certainly an expensive and resource-consuming product, a prestige book, whose own making and potential uses are reflected in texts within the manuscript itself that are focused upon the making of a manuscript book, such as Riddle 26, which is a step-by-step prosopopaeic description of the creation of a religious book.[9] In Riddle 26, the subject itself envisages its readers as those who are to use or *enjoy* (Old English "brucan") the book; those who will be "the safer, the more sure of victory" as a result of their interaction with the spiritual text. This Riddle demonstrates that for its Anglo-Saxon audience the book is conceived of as an embodied phenomenon, with solidity and location (*this* very book), with a power for its readers that is transformational. Just as animal skin, ink, and wooden boards are transformed into a means of salvation through the production of a book, so the recipients of its written text are transformed in this Riddle from simply "children of men" to children of God; from imperfect sinners to the eternal saved.

The Riddle's lack of specificity beyond "using" or "enjoying" suggests that salvation is open to all who can access the book with an open heart. Moreover, the Exeter Book itself is relatively free of marginalia or obvious signs of interaction by contemporary or later readers, beyond some drypoint glosses and indications of later medieval misuse, but does the lack of marking indicate that a book has not been read? Dustin Illingworth's review of Stephen Orgel's *The Reader in the Book* begins with a reflection on what it means to "use" a book:[10]

> the motto of Geoffrey Whitney's *Choice of Emblemes* (1586), the very first English emblem book [is]: *Usus libri, non lectio prudentes facit.* Roughly: "Using a book, not reading it, makes us wise."…A couplet from the emblem's accompanying poem may clarify Whitney's meaning:

---

[6] On the Exeter Book, see, especially, Patrick Conner, *Anglo-Saxon Exeter: A Tenth-Century Cultural History* (Woodbridge: Boydell and Brewer, 1993).

[7] The texts are edited by Bernard J. Muir in *Exeter Anthology of Old English Poetry: An Edition of Exeter Dean and Chapter MS 3501*, 2 vols. (Exeter: University of Exeter Press, 2000).

[8] Patrick W. Conner, "Parish Guilds and the Production of Old English Literature in the Public Sphere," in *Intertexts: Studies in Early Insular Culture Presented to Paul E. Szarmach*, ed. Virginia Blanton and Helen Scheck (Tempe, AZ: Medieval and Renaissance Texts and Studies, 2008), 255–71.

[9] See also Riddles 51 and 45, typically solved as Quill and Bookworm. See Patrick J. Murphy, *Unriddling the Exeter Book Riddles* (Pennsylvania: Penn State Press, 2011); and Craig Williamson, *The Old English Riddles of the Exeter Book* (Chapel Hill: University of North Carolina Press, 1977).

[10] Dustin Illingworth, "An Incomplete Eloquence" (https://lareviewofbooks.org/article/an-incomplete-eloquence/). See also Stephen Orgel, *The Reader in the Book: A Study of Spaces and Traces* (Oxford: Oxford University Press, 2016).

> First reade, then marke, then practise that is good,
>
> For without vse, we drink but LETHE (*leethee*) flood.
>
> Mere reading, he says, is not enough; rather, we must mark our texts lest we forget the wisdom so recently acquired. Inscription is a critical part of "use."

This Early Modern meaning here of "use" to indicate a range of activities from "marking up," to "benefitting from," to "being spiritually and intellectually enhanced by," to "being nourished by" are all potentially implicit in the Old English semantically dense verb, "brucan." A book does not have to be physically marked in order to demonstrate that a reader or browser had passed through the folios. The intellectual and spiritual nourishment resulting from the reading of books was well-understood in early medieval literature, even if its traces are all but invisible.

The Bookmoth Riddle, for example, which forms the subject of Exeter Book Riddle 45, reinforces the significance of this metaphor of consumption and physical engagement with a book's contents; however, it shows that simple ingestion—in this case of language made material—is a parody of the process of "using" or "enjoying" the book:

> Moððe word fræt. Me þæt þuhte
> wrætlicu wyrd þa ic þæt wundor gefrægn,
> þæt se wyrm forswealg wera gied sumes,
> þeof in þystro, þrymfæstne cwide
> ond þæs strangan staþol. Stælgiest ne wæs
> wihte þy gleawra þe he þam wordum swealg.

> A moth consumed words. That seemed to me
> a miraculous fate when I heard about that wonder,
> that worm swallowed the speech of a certain man,
> a thief in the darkness stealing a glorious saying
> and the strong foundation. This thievish guest was not
> any the wiser for the words he swallowed.

If the Bookmoth is the antithesis of the good user-consumer of the book—ingesting the words, but acquiring no nourishment from them—then it is sharply contrasted with the book in Riddle 26, which itself represents and exemplifies the consumed "glorious sayings" ("þrymfæstne cwide"), "strong foundations" ("strangan staþol"), and site of wisdom-yielding words upon which the bookworm feasts.

These two Riddles, and most explicitly Riddle 26, go a considerable way to providing insight into what "the book" as a phenomenon—an experience—meant to some early medieval people who had access to literate communities. These insights are not necessarily about the act of *reading* at all, unless reading is simply ingestion. Wisdom, happiness, friendships, virtue, and love all derive from an appreciation of the salvific book, even though for the majority of early medieval audiences, this might well mean an appreciation of a manuscript or textual object from a physical distance. In sermons and other texts, it is clear that many congregations or other groups of listener-viewers witnessed books and bore testimony to learning only through public experience. During the course of the oral delivery of the saint's life or the homily, the preacher/mediator usually comments on the very occasion itself, as these examples from the Wulfstan-circle corpus and Ælfrician *oeuvre* show:

> Men ða leofestan, gehyrað hwæt us halige bec beodað, þæt we for godes lufan and for his ege ure lif rihtlice libban and mid eaðmedum urum drihtne hyron and urne cristendom and ure fulluht wel healdon, þæt ure dæda beon gode gecweme.[11]

> Dearest people, hear what this holy book commands—that for God's love and in fear of him we should live our lives justly and hear our lord humbly, and hold well to our Christianity and baptism, so that our deeds might be considered good.

> Ac uton þencan georne þonne we þyllic gehyrað, þæt we þe beteran beon, þurh þa boclican lare.[12]

> Let us think keenly when we hear such things that we shall be the better through bookly learning.

In these examples, the implication of the phrase and its variants, "hear what this book says" ("geherað hwæt þeos boc segþ"), is that there is a book present at the time of the text's delivery.[13] This may not seem notable to us, but from it we can infer that far more books must have existed than present numbers could possibly attest, if each preacher, each parish church, had one or a combination of a homiliary or a gospelbook or *libellus* with extracts or small numbers of homilies. The deictic pronoun—*this*—in the nominal phrase "þeos boc" suggests a specificity that imbues the book, or every book, with a presence, a speaking voice, not unlike the anthropomorphic Riddle 26. The personified book can speak, command, remind, lead, and reveal:

> Gehyrað nu, men þa leofestan, hu þas halgan bec eow myngiað and eow þone weg ætywiað and eac in gelædað to heofena rice…[14]

> Hear now, dearest men/people, how this holy book reminds you about the way, and makes it visible to you and also leads you into the heavenly kingdom…

Here the book, seemingly autonomously, inspires and directs, and produces the most spiritually positive consequences for those who remember what has been read

---

[11] My edition and translation, but see also Homily 29 in A. S. Napier, ed., *Wulfstan*, Sammlung englischer Denkmäler 4 (Berlin); repr. with appendix by K. Ostheeren, 1967 (HomU 26, B3.4.26).

[12] W. W. Skeat, ed., *Ælfric's Lives of Saints*, EETS original series 76, 82, 94, 114 (London: Oxford University Press, 1881–1900), I: 336–62.

[13] And there are *very* many others; see, for example, P. A. M. Clemoes, ed., *Ælfric's Catholic Homilies: The First Series, Text,* EETS supplementary series 17 (Oxford: Oxford University Press, 1997); J. C. Pope, ed., *Homilies of Ælfric: A Supplementary Collection,* 2 vols., EETS 259, 260 (London: Oxford University Press, 1967); and Donald Scragg, ed., *The Vercelli Homilies and Related Texts,* EETS os 300 (Oxford: Oxford University Press, 1992).

[14] Homily for the Third Sunday in Lent; see B. Assmann, ed., *Angelsächsische Homilien und Heiligenleben,* Bib. ags. Prosa 3 (Kassel, 1889); repr. with intro. by P. Clemoes (Darmstadt 1964), 138–43 (HomS 13, B3.2.13).

out from it. For these audiences and congregations, their reading is indirect; it is auditory. Through the gospels quoted in sermons—as all scholars of literary history know—clearly, the book is the voice of God. The religious book, whether comprised of sermons, poetry, or legal or liturgical sequences, is thus a metonymic representation of the whole of Christian salvation. But, again, for most, the book as a material artefact would be accessed from a distance, its wisdom indirectly absorbed through the cipher of the reader. It is, perhaps, akin to "reading" an audiobook today, research on which has shown no major distinction in comprehension whether the reader-listener accessed the text via physical, electronic, or audio book format.[15] Certainly, the expectations of medieval preachers and teachers were that their words were heard, understood, and acted on. As such, communities of readers were far greater in earlier centuries than could ever be suggested by the numbers of surviving books or the interventions made in books by readers themselves.

What, then, does the book signify and how is it represented in the early medieval period? Palaeographers, codicologists, and literary historians tend, with discipline-specific reason, to discuss the book as an archaeological object, divisible into its strata that ultimately reveal an origin. It has long been accepted that medieval texts circulated as textual items or as booklets of anything from a single to a handful of quires.[16] This deconstructive appraisal has a physical truth—that the book is a technology engineered through multiple components—but that this is how the book might have been *conceived of*, or depicted imaginatively, is not borne out by the period's illustrative evidence. Indeed, other research perspectives can tell us more about the medieval conception of the book: the representation of the book in illustrations within manuscripts, for instance, or the scriptible presentation of the book, deliberately obfuscating legibility.

Moving through the Book

Whether in Roman mosaics, metal plaques, sculpture, or illustrations within manuscripts, the early book is seldom shown as being read. It is created and written upon—a common image of the book, especially in evangelist portraits, like those in

---

[15] B. A. Rogowsky, Barbara Calhoun, and Paula Tallal, "Does Modality Matter? The Effects of Reading, Listening and Dual Modality on Comprehension," SAGE open (2016): 1–9 (doi/abs/10.1177/2158244016669550).

[16] The majority of catalogs break a book into its textual items and quiring structure; for example, Neil Ker, *Catalogue of Manuscripts Containing Anglo-Saxon* (Oxford: Clarendon Press, 1957; repr. with Supplement, 1991). See also J. P. Gumbert, "Codicological Units: Towards a Terminology for the Stratigraphy of the Non-Homogenous Codex," *Il codice miscellaneo. Tipologie e funzioni. Atti del Convegno internazionale, Cassino, 14–17 Maggio 2003, Segno e testo*, ed. Edoardo Crisci and Oronzo Pecere, 2 (2003): 17–42.

the eighth-century Lindisfarne Gospels;[17] it is closed and demonstrated as containing all that has yet to be revealed, as in the inhabited initial "D" at the bottom left of folio 6r of Cambridge, Trinity College, B. 11. 4, a thirteenth-century Psalter;[18] it is open and displayed, revealed but not usually being read, as is the case with the famous frontispiece of London, British Library, Additional 33,241, the *Encomium Emmae Reginae*, dating from the 1040s.[19] What do these images suggest about the book's function and status? The book is an object that demands a kinaesthetic response and full sensory engagement, as is evident in the three images (as in thousands of others) mentioned above; it is the hand that connects the user and the object, holding the book open, or carrying the book, emphasizing that the book cannot function as intended without an interactor. Moreover, the act of opening a book has the potential to be aesthetically compelling, or visually startling, or intellectually transformative. The opening of a book provides a frame for experience and is always a revelation. It is the case, too, that the unit of meaning in a book is never the page: it is always the opening, where readers are impelled to make connections across the gutter of the inner margins.[20]

Readers know that they must at least touch the book to make it function as a text technology. In order to access the contents, pages must be turned, and users of the codex format engage proprioceptively, in a way that seems natural and obvious to a modern audience. But these only seem to be natural muscular movements because a bookish environment is a highly familiar one, from the experience of a baby's cloth book to the digital Turn-the-Pages technology installed in many libraries and museums. YouTube presents a reminder of the physical and technological *un*familiarity of the book in the comedy skit, "Medieval Help Desk," where a monk requires the assistance of an IT guy (dressed as a lay person) in order to use the book. He has two concerns: how to open and work through the manuscript; and whether or not the information stored in the manuscript will be retained and saved when the manuscript is closed.[21]

The monk shows, hilariously, that not all accessors of book learning—"boclare" in Old English—have this environmental conditioning. In the medieval period, being able to read was a specialized skill, and writing an even more expert accomplishment. When images of books, like the *Encomium Emma Reginae*, are depicted within the book itself, readers and viewers effectively see the volume as self-represented, and

---

[17] See, for example, Matthew's portrait at folio 25v, where he is writing in a complete and extensive manuscript with his quill: London, British Library, Cotton Nero D. iv, digitized at the British Library website (http://www.bl.uk/manuscripts/FullDisplay.aspx?index=11&ref=Cotton_MS_Nero_D_IV).

[18] Digitized at the *James Catalogue of Western Manuscripts* website of Trinity College Library, Cambridge (https://www.trin.cam.ac.uk/library/wren-digital-library/).

[19] Digitized at the British Library website (http://www.bl.uk/manuscripts/FullDisplay.aspx?ref=Add_MS_33241&index=3).

[20] All of these elements of the book will be discussed in my forthcoming volume, *The Sensual Book*.

[21] "Medieval Helpdesk," YouTube, 2007 (https://www.youtube.com/watch?v=pQHX-SjgQvQ).

thus self-authenticating. Distant readers, physically distant from the object containing information, might never have held or kinaesthetically engaged with a book. What difference did this indirect relationship with books have? Books demand hapticity and a proprioceptive response. To see and hear the book, as so many viewer-listeners did, gave access to the mediated text, but not to the fullest interpretative potential of the textual object. It might be argued that the tactile and the optical work together to yield the most genuinely profound apprehension. Touch and vision together provide what Merleau-Ponty called "the first dimension"—depth.[22] The voluminous, which leads to an understanding of depth or heft of the object, is central to any complete understanding of the object in the world. This idea of heft or voluminousness, in addition, insists that as readers we engage with the whole book, not just the images, and not just the text.

For the book, specifically, this holistic approach might make us rethink our relationship to the producers and users of the artifacts upon which we gaze. A book, with its edifice-like structure, invites us to participate in an embodied experience. With a medieval book, we are directly connected to the people who conceived and produced the objects; we engage in sensual contact with other libric visitors, seeing what they saw—even if from a distance; the potential to access what earlier audiences felt, or heard, or smelled is always present; the ability to participate in the movement of the book is there for those who are permitted to handle the object. More, though, the viewer-listener of the medieval religious book (the basis for the discussion here) is invited to discover the spirituality inherent in the book—particularly when, as *readers*, we are reminded to participate with *oculi mentis*, the eyes of the mind.[23]

There is no doubt that the eyes of the mind are essential for accessing many books that have survived from Anglo-Saxon England and later, a significant number of which might be deemed remarkable, *de luxe* volumes that were treasured and venerated throughout the centuries. One such book is Stockholm, National Library, of Sweden, A. 135, a gospelbook written in the mid-eighth-century, possibly at Christ Church, Canterbury, and known as the Stockholm Codex Aureus. At folio 11 is one of the most famous images from Anglo-Saxon England.[24] Here, the opening of the Gospel of St. Matthew proper, monumental square capitals are illuminated in an elaborate design, carefully framed like a stone memorial; the imperial script with its complex ligatures obfuscates reading. The page is initially meant to be looked at,

---

[22] M. C. Dillon, *Merleau-Ponty Vivant* (Albany: SUNY Press, 1991), 3.

[23] *De Genesi ad litteram*, Book xii 6, 15; *On Genesis*, trans. Edmund Hill (New York: NYCity Press, 2002), 470: "When you read 'you shall love your neighbor as yourself', three kinds of vision take place; one with the eyes, when you see the actual letters; another with the human spirit, by which you think of your neighbor even though he isn't there; a third with the attention of the mind, by which you understand and look at love."

[24] A complete digital representation is available (https://archive.org/details/urn-nbn-se-kb-digark-4890092).

and contemplated, rather than read, it seems, and demonstrates the imperative of a moral reading, a reading that is not about ease of legibility (it is *resistant* rather than distant reading) but the demands of the action of reading itself. At the top of the leaf is the inscription of Ælfred, Ealdorman of Surrey, and his wife, Werburg, who "begetan ðas bec æt hæðenum herge" ("ransomed the book from the heathen army") and gave it (back?) to Christ Church, Canterbury in the late ninth century. They seem determined to let us know that it was purchased piously, with "clean money" ("clæne golde"), and to have the book *they* ransomed become, effectively, ransom for their souls.

Upon this folio, it is possible to witness the ritual of the book enacted both at the behest, and on the spiritual part, of the pious Anglo-Saxon, in this case, Ælfred and Werburg. Their inscription into the book is both a ritualistic deed to record details about the saving of the book by these donors and an act of salvation for the very souls of those inscribed (like a *Liber vitae* itself) in its ritualized, liturgical function. This folio, then, becomes not just visually akin to a monument, but also a monumental memorial for Ælfred and Werburg and Alhðryð, their daughter. The family group is saved by their intervention in, and on behalf of, the book: through performative piety and visible gesture of participation these witnesses to the significance of the Word are inscribed—*had themselves inscribed*—into the Book of Life, effectively. This physical proximity of Anglo-Saxon donor with spiritual intercessors in Matthew 1:18 connects the owner of the book with salvation spatially and through representation. It's clear that this folio—and not the opening of the manuscript as a whole—was very carefully chosen for the Old English text outlining the book's history and this family's pious deed. The spaces on the folio, as is the case with modern books' margins, invite careful readers to participate in the performance of the book, but the inscriber of the Codex Aureus also read the page meticulously, choosing the folio with the greatest decorative opulence to make the display of this leaf obvious—inviting onlookers to read and, more, to gaze on the names of Ælfred, Werburg, and Alhðryð. The *de luxe* nature and religious quality and content of the codex also makes its long-term preservation more assured, the eternity of the names' visibility guaranteed.

Equally indicative of the relationship of the individual to the material with which she had contact is the work of an intervener in the Bury Bible, Cambridge Corpus Christi College, 2, part 1. This half-metre high bible, now in three parts, is, as Christopher de Hamel comments, "one of the noblest and most sublime of all English Romanesque manuscripts." Designed and executed at Bury, with illuminations by the professional artist Master Hugo, it has been suggested that the manuscript was intended for use in the refectory for holy readings.[25] It was almost certainly

---

[25] Christopher de Hamel, "The Bury Bible," in *The Cambridge Illuminations: Ten Centuries of Book Production in the Medieval West*, ed. Paul Binski and Stella Panayotova (London: Harvey Miller, 2005), 81–3. It is digitized at "Parker Library on the Web" (https://parker.stanford.edu/parker/(002I) [Part I of Manuscript 2].

displayed, given its exceptional size and use of resources, from the number of animal skins used to make it to the richness of its pigments and expertise of script. It is certain that it was read, and not only read, but interpreted and annotated, which might indicate its use, additionally, in a setting more contemplative than the refectory. On folio 94r, at the opening of Deuteronomy, a later hand, possibly late twelfth-century, has written the words "Moyses" and "Moysen" with a pointed implement, and possibly plummet, into the extensive field of the lower register's blue and green pigment; plus there are a couple of other marks and half-words. That titular label-ling of Moses is relevant and helpful once but arguably akin to minor vandalism twice! The upper register shows Moses and Aaron reading the book of the covenant.[26] In this image the imagined book is clearly bound with boards in order to be held up as Moses does. Significantly, the two open folios are written upon (with the words "Hec dicit Dominus Deus" on the verso)—not by Master Hugo, who produced the book, nor by the contemporary scribe, but by the later title-writer: an intruder who has read the book's images carefully and sought to label the figures clearly for other readers.

The semi-*horror vacui* on the part of the grafitto artist of the book is interesting. On the verso, he has written with pen over a lead inscription; on the recto, there is writing produced with a sharp point—perhaps plummet. The intervener has carefully (despite the intrusive and untidy nature of the act) written words using practiced abbreviations that suggest a scribe trained professionally in cursive writing. For this book-user, a book is represented not by an image alone but by the words that it carries. This is a moment not only of temporary ownership of the book, then, but also of pedagogic compulsion—a desire to recognize the needs of other readers.

Res Significativae

What might this rapid survey of a small number of medieval books signify? It is conscious recognition, first of all, that—in the words of the twelfth-century intellec-tual and theologian, Richard of St Victor: "*non solum voces, sed et res significativae sint,*" "*not only the sound of words, but things carry meaning*"; that is, it is through both an appreciation of the textual artefact, the physical book, and its being *used* that fuller interpretative potential can be attained.[27] Medieval books are inhabited objects, replete with the actions seen and unseen of multiple audiences. In this way, these codices, conceived of as complete artefacts by their contemporary illustrators,

---

[26] Deuteronomy 1:1 and 1:6 "Haec verba sunt" and "Dominus Deus" (see http://www.drbo.org/chapter/05001.htm).

[27] *De sacramentis christianae fidei* (PL 176:185A-B). See also Roy J. Deferrari, *Hugh of St Victor on the Sacraments of the Christian Faith* (Cambridge, MA: Medieval Academy of America, 1951).

are living phenomena that change through time, especially as generations of readers move through the folios, leaving traces of their encounters, even if such encounters are, occasionally, only from a distance.

FURTHER READING

Breen, Katharine. *Imagining an English Reading Public, 1150–1400*. Cambridge: Cambridge University Press, 2010.

Boyarin, Nicholas, ed. *The Ethnography of Reading*. Berkeley, CA: University of California Press, 1993.

Classen, Albrecht, ed. *The Book and the Magic of Reading in the Middle Ages*. Medieval Casebooks. London: Routledge, 1999.

Parkes, M. B. *Their Hands before Our Eyes: A Closer Look at Scribes; The Lyell Lectures delivered in the University of Oxford 1999*. Aldershot: Ashgate, 2008.

Webber, Teresa. "Books and their Use across the Conquest." *Bury St Edmunds and the Norman Conquest*, ed. Tom Licence. Woodbridge: Boydell and Brewer, 2014, 160–89.

8

ASSIGNED

DEIDRE LYNCH

Infringing on Readers' Liberties

In 2018 a rumor arose that Oprah Winfrey—actress, publisher, talk-show host, and, in her guise as book-club impresario, literacy crusader—might run for the presidency of the United States. The satirist Andy Borowitz envisioned how the incumbent president might rally his supporters against a Winfrey candidacy: "Donald J. Trump issued a stark warning to the nation…that, if elected President, Oprah Winfrey would force Americans to read." More specifically, Borowitz pictured Trump warning that

> 'if [Oprah] were President, you better believe that she would make every single American join that book club…People were worried about Obama coming to their homes and taking away their guns…Oprah will come to your homes and leave books there, which is far, far worse.'[1]

You don't go to "The Borowitz Report" for civics lessons. But Borowitz's joke points to the notion that citizens might need to protect from book-boosters like Oprah their constitutional right to booklessness—their right not to read.

Most modern discussions of the meanings and value of reading link that pastime with the individual's self-determination. They associate bookishness with the rights-bearing, independent subject who stands at the center of the liberal political tradition. They also tend to propose that the kind of social interaction that our reading matter sponsors—the interaction with distant authors, separated from us by space and time—releases readers from the constraints they experience in the everyday social realm with other people. The mediated solidarities of reading have, since the Enlightenment, been central to accounts of how civic freedom is obtained by the individual. This is because *these* solidarities, unlike their real-world equivalents,

---

[1] Andy Borowitz, "Trump Warns that President Oprah Would Force Americans to Read," *newyorker.com*, January 8, 2018.

can readily be represented as experiences of mental liberty and freedom from social influence. "The good or ill accidents of life are very little at our disposal; but we are pretty much masters what books we shall read," wrote the philosopher David Hume in a 1742 essay promoting the cultivation of a taste for "the polite arts," "poetry" and "eloquence" among them.[2] In Hume's essay, intercourse with objects of art is valued precisely for enlarging the sphere of the individual's autonomy.

Oprah's Book Club has long affirmed such links between literary reading and empowerment. Despite promoting reading through an up-to-date idiom of self-help and self-actualization, the Club also recalls an older, African-American tradition of uplift that equated education with collective betterment.

But such discussions often falter when they broach the possibility that reading might not (indeed, cannot always) be an arena for free choice—as when, for instance, they treat the nitty-gritty of the process by which literacy itself is acquired. Child readers, whose books are usually chosen and purchased by others, don't conform well to the profile these discussions assume of the reader as an independent consumer, someone who voluntarily acquires and selects the texts with which she develops a relationship. More generally, these discussions stumble over the question of *assigned reading*: of the book that is consumed under circumstances in which the reader has submitted to the supervision and direction of others; the book that has been set by a teacher as homework, for instance, rather than freely chosen; as well as the book that (like a nosy social worker or power-drunk policeman, the usual bugbears of the conservative nightmares Borowitz burlesques) shows up uninvited on her doorstep.

Paradoxically, as we'll see, book-boosters have often attempted to present *real* reading, reading they deem worthy of the name, as an activity that unfolds in their absence. In their representations the character-building projects that reading sponsors are identified more consistently with textual activities that take place in people's free time and in their homes than they are with the textual activities that people undertake at and for work. (This is the case even though competing, more instrumentalist, accounts of reading pivot on the labor market success foretold for those who stay in school and stick to their books. But to be able to read, to possess the capacity to comprehend written texts, is not sufficient, as we'll see, to be *a reader*.)

And though book-boosters are often by profession educators who oversee the acculturation of the young, they themselves have often intimated that real readers don't come into being in the classroom but on the playground or in the clubhouse instead. That intimation has of course the perverse effect of making their own labor invisible. Within the Anglo-American literary tradition, book-love has been identified with truancy and escape more often than it has been identified with the docile

[2] David Hume, "Of the Delicacy of Taste and Passion," *Selected Essays*, ed. Stephen Copley and Andrew Edgar (Oxford: Oxford University Press, 1993), 11–12.

completion of a teacher's instructions. Even in the school story, assigned reading gets sidelined.

To trace the motives and mechanisms of that sidelining, this chapter begins with some of Oprah Winfrey's eighteenth-century forerunners, Enlightenment advocates for children's literature and theorists of education, before considering some late-Victorian and early-twentieth-century architects of the modern-day discipline of literary studies. It teases out in their writings a conflicted acknowledgement that the lived experience of reading is shaped by obligation and coercion as well as independence and escape, by work as well as play, by pain as well as pleasure. I aim to bring to the fore the moments when, sometimes despite themselves, these writers anticipate Deborah Brandt's suggestion that those of us who assist individuals in the "pursuit of literacy" should acknowledge how literacy is also "in pursuit of them."[3]

Enlightenment Literacy, Property, and Book Love

Assign and *assignment* enter English late as terms associated with classroom tasks. (At present, too, they remain more associated with North American educational settings than with their British counterparts.) Early usage associates these terms with property law: the *Oxford English Dictionary* has *assignment* designating in the first instance the transfer of personal property or the allotting of a share, portion, or an allowance from some valuable whole. Of course, for centuries much has been invested in the proposition that ownership should shape the terms in which persons first meet up with reading matter. The book was pretty much the first consumer object to be advertised and marketed particularly to children: three centuries ago, publishers, authors, and booksellers began, with an eye on their sales figures, to acknowledge how much it would be in their interest to link juvenile reading (also juvenile piety) with juvenile owning. Hence the motivational scheme for spurring on young readers that the hymn writer Isaac Watts outlines to parents and guardians when he prefaces his *Divine Songs* (1715). To convert young folks' "duty" into "a reward . . . giv[e] them," Watts says, "the privilege of learning one of these songs every week; if they fulfill the business of the week well, . . . promis[e] them the book itself when they have learnt ten or twenty songs out of it."[4] (The later eighteenth-century preacher Rowland Hill remembered how as a boy he delighted in the *Divine Songs* purely "from the idea that I read them out of my own book.")[5]

Studying the inscriptions deposited in surviving copies of children's books from eighteenth- and nineteenth-century England and America, the flyleaves on which

[3] Deborah Brandt, "Sponsors of Literacy," *College Composition and Communication* 49.2 (1998), 165–85; 183.

[4] Isaac Watts, *Divine Songs* (London: M. Lawrence, 1715), xviii.

[5] Hill is cited in M. O. Grenby, *The Child Reader, 1700–1840* (Cambridge: Cambridge University Press, 2011), 275.

the child reader steps forth as child writer—"Alice Comfort, Jr., her book"—Patricia Crain senses how often the child's demonstration of her developing literacy was made to do double duty as an assertion of the rights of private property. "The Property of Abiah Chapin"; "Grace Comforts Book wherein/ she ought to look not/ only look but understand/ that learning is before/ house and land when/ land is gone, and money spent/ good learning is most exlent [sic]."[6]

Matthew Grenby sums up one lesson that historians of reading can derive from these readers' marks when he observes that "[l]iteracy was understood to be the only proper foundation of ownership: I read and write and therefore I own."[7] He also draws on the evidence of such marginalia to make a different point: a discrepancy between the particular understanding of books to which those owner's marks testify and the contrasting understanding that was mobilized by book purchasers, the parents and guardians who bestowed the books as gifts. Eighteenth-century "adults largely understood children's books as *texts* by which the child could profit," and valued juvenile reading as key to the child's future welfare, whether spiritual or (increasingly) temporal, Grenby explains. (Work hard *now* to improve your reading and you too, like Little Goody Two Shoes, will ride in a coach-and-six.) For their children, on the other hand, books were less evidently valued as the means of accessing future good: for these children, books may quite possibly have represented in the main "material objects offering immediate gratifications to the owner (as opposed to the reader), the possession of which was just as important as the absorption."[8] The disjunction between these viewpoints is indicative of the sorts of complexity and friction that book-boosterism often conceals.

Indeed there are multiple signs of strain when eighteenth-century writers speculate about how children might best be inducted into literacy, speculation that evolves in tandem with the development of children's literature. When Grenby proposes that the notion of private property helped frame the way eighteenth-century children were brought into relationship with books, he evokes the same concept of possessive individualism—I own, therefore I am—that in the liberal political tradition also explains the way human beings are brought into relationship with one another. Foundational for that tradition is the conjectural history that the political philosopher John Locke set out in his influential *Second Treatise of Civil Government* (1689): there, the beginnings of modern civic society and citizenship lie in the social contract that is entered into by property-owners who have sought to secure their property rights, and who, to that end, have freely consented to cede some natural liberties in exchange for that security. However, when in his equally influential *Some Thoughts Concerning Education* (1693), Locke turns from citizens in their

---

[6] These examples derive from Patricia Crain, *Reading Children: Literacy, Property, and the Dilemmas of Childhood in Nineteenth-Century America* (Philadelphia: University of Pennsylvania Press, 2016), 113–20.

[7] Grenby, *The Child Reader*, 29.   [8] Grenby, *The Child Reader*, 274.

relationship to government to children in their relationship to literacy, he struggles to keep the spotlight on the act of consent.

Because Locke is eager to downplay the role that authority and compulsion, discipline and obedience, play within the scene of instruction, he proposes that children be encouraged to think of learning to read as continuous with, rather than distinct from, play. When "your son [sic] is of age to learn to read," "a great care is to be taken, that it be never made as a Business to him, nor he look on it as a task."[9] Sparing the rod is the first principle of this scheme (though corporal punishment continued to define everyday classroom life in Anglo-American culture well into the twentieth century, Locke warns pedagogues against establishing in pupils' minds associations that would link the idea of learning to memories of pain and adult tyranny). But the great care Locke mentions encompasses, as well, some deceit on the part of the pedagogue. Thus Locke mentions in particular how the use of a die painted with letters on each of its sides, rolled to form syllables and words, can "cheat" a boy into learning reading "without knowing how he did so."[10] Your son thinks he is playing at dice; you know he is being taught. (John Newberry's *A Little Lottery Book for Children Containing a New Method for Playing Them into a Knowledge of Letters*, which went through many editions after 1756, monetizes Locke's idea.) Should you follow this method, Locke affirms, your young learner will "never have any chiding or trouble about it; nor fall out with Books, because of the hard usage and vexation they caused him." "[C]hildren have a mind to show that they are free":[11] the scene of instruction ought not to involve, or *seem* to involve, a captive audience.

Locke's book commences accordingly by declaring that the end of education is to bring the child "to be in love with his Book."[12] "My Book and Heart/ Shall never part," as one verse in *The New-England Primer* has it, putting words in the mouth of the child reader it addresses and thereby interpellating this reader as one whose Lockean education has been a success.[13] The acquisition of literacy involves more in this account than the mastery of a technical competence. It involves the formation of a particular kind of affective identity—the making of *readers*, a population defined by their capacity for affection as well as cognitive skills. This book-love helps veil the child readers' submission both to parental authority and to the discipline of letters. The exercise of literacy comes to represent the realization of a desire that defines and expresses the self rather than an instance of compliance with an external authority. Love's alchemy makes it seem to the child as though she is choosing for herself what has already been chosen for her.

[9] John Locke, *Some Thoughts Concerning Education* (London: A. J. Churchill, 1693), 175.
[10] Locke, *Some Thoughts*, 175–6.   [11] Locke, *Some Thoughts*, 76.
[12] Locke, "The Epistle Dedicatory," *Some Thoughts*, n.p.
[13] *The New-England Primer, Enlarged* (Boston: S. Kneeland and T. Green, 1727), n.p.

The voluntarism that governs Locke's account of literacy training in *Some Thoughts Concerning Education* recurs in the 1742 essay of David Hume's, cited earlier, about the advantages of organizing one's identity around the exercise of taste. Sustaining that vantage point on literacy and preserving the alliance between book-boosterism and liberal accounts of self-determination involves, though, some selective memory about the actualities of individuals' reading experiences. For instance, *contra* Hume and his sanguine reference to how "we" exercise mastery in choosing what books to read, historically much of the population in the West—not just the captive audience that children represent but also servants, workers, and colonial subjects—has had reading matter foisted upon it. The origins of the many modern institutions that have enabled printed matter to be distributed "at the expense of someone other than its end users" date to Hume's eighteenth-century lifetime. By the nineteenth century, as Leah Price observes, missionaries, distributors of evangelical tracts, and advertisers sending circulars through the mail would all have figured out how to force reading matter into the hands of people who had never consented to have it.[14] The Enlightenment account of bookish self-determination also depends—sometimes overtly—on amnesia about the frustrations and shamings that have to be endured before the strings of letters in front of the would-be reader resolve themselves into comprehended words, before the child is transported from the inert page to the livelier, if virtual, scene to which her book is supposed to serve as portal. One of the period's most ecstatic celebrations of the sovereignty to be claimed through books may be found in the writings of William Godwin, who in his 1797 "Of an Early Taste for Reading" proposes, "He that loves reading has everything within his reach. He has but to desire and he may possess himself of every species of wisdom to judge and power to perform." But in a later passage the philosopher (who would subsequently become a publisher of children's literature) betrays his awareness that such autonomy is generally hard won. He proposes that children ought to begin to read at so early an age that later they will be unable to remember having learned.[15] Where books' lovability is concerned, timing is everything.

In *Northanger Abbey* (composed around the same time as Godwin's essay), Jane Austen's Catherine Morland emphasizes the pains rather than pleasures that are the lot of the early reader—pains that Catherine herself has evidently been able to put behind her, given her role within the novel as a quixotic heroine who loves books too much. Expressing pity for writers of history books, Catherine remarks in conversation on the "hard fate" that sees them supplying the assigned reading of the eighteenth-century school room and so "labouring only for the torment of little

---

[14] Leah Price, *How to Do Things with Books in Victorian Britain* (Princeton: Princeton University Press, 2012), 135.

[15] William Godwin, *The Enquirer* (London: G.G. and J. Robinson, 1797), 31; 34.

boys and girls."[16] Beneath the dialogue, one perhaps hears Austen herself, figuring out that even if her chosen genre, the novel, has less prestige than history, it is by the same token spared the association with discipline that burdens the books that *are* on the curriculum. When Catherine's companion laughingly disputes her mention of boys' and girls' "tormenting," she counters with her everyday experience as the eldest daughter in a family of ten children:

> You think me foolish to call instruction a torment, but if you had been as much used as myself to hear poor little children first learning their letters and then learning to spell, if you had ever seen how stupid they can be for a whole morning together…as I am in the habit of seeing almost every day of my life at home, you would allow that to *torment* and to *instruct* might sometimes be used as synonimous words.[17]

Torment is a word that seems to belong to the lawless, violent world of Gothic fiction—the literary mode that Catherine will ultimately renounce as an inadequate guide to contemporary reality: "in the central part of England," she will conclude, "there was surely some security for the existence even of a wife not beloved, in the laws of the land, and the manners of the age."[18] But if *Northanger Abbey* affirms civil society's progress out of medieval tyranny, this earlier dialogue intimates that the school-room might represent a refuge for illiberal barbarity in the midst of liberal modernity. As new enterprises of compulsory schooling on both sides of the Atlantic extended reading's reach, book-boosters found themselves having to overlook—or having to contest—how literacy training had become an experience of rote learning, regimentation, and examination. By the eighteenth century's end, there could be only the most uneasy commerce between the legacy of Locke and participation in the new, self-consciously modern classroom management practices that, so as to engage numerous pupils at minimum expense, often made schoolrooms resemble factory floors.[19]

Extracurricular Activities

In the eighteenth-century children's book *The Friendly Instructor*, we can see some effects of that Lockean legacy, its prioritization of bookish affections over bookish discipline especially. A character called Charlotte is set up from the start as the bad reader of the story. Charlotte occupies this role not because of her ineptitude at

---

[16] Jane Austen, *Northanger Abbey* and *Persuasion*, vol. 5 of *The Novels of Jane Austen*, 3rd ed. (Oxford: Oxford University Press, 1933), 109.

[17] Austen, *Northanger Abbey*, 109–10.   [18] Austen, *Northanger Abbey*, 200.

[19] For instance, the monitorial method for literacy training that was set out in the competing schemes of Andrew Bell, author of *An Experiment in Education Made at the Male Asylum of Madras* (London: Cadell and Davies, 1797) and Joseph Lancaster, author of *Improvements in Education, as it respects the Industrious Classes of the Community* (London: Darton, Harvey, Mathews, and Hatchard, 1803).

decoding but because of her assumption that her friend Olivia would be unavailable for play since she had a book in her hand: "I was afraid you have got a task to learn." But Charlotte, it emerges, was judging from her own case, and wrongly: her mistake was to assume that Olivia was like her in not *loving* (in Olivia's words now) "the word of God enough to read it both at school and at home."[20]

Odds are good that for a twenty-first-century secular audience, Charlotte will appear to have the better read on the situation, a clear-eyed sense of literacy's links to social control. Indeed, *we* might say that, in arranging for her reading to traverse the boundary between school time and free time, Olivia is merely consenting to her own indoctrination. My point now, though, involves the repeatability of this move to decouple real reading from classroom tasks—how often the move gets reiterated even within the vastly altered landscapes of print that come into being in later periods, when, for instance, religious reading represents only one exercise of literacy among many others. (This shift was gradual, as the *Oxford English Dictionary* indicates when it documents the length of time required for the sense of *primer* that designates *prayer book* to be detached from the sense of *primer* that designates a *book for teaching reading*. Publishing history dates to the late-eighteenth-century reprint editions of secular authors "for the use of schools.") One recent example of how naturalized the association of real reading with free time has become may be found in "Reading at Risk," a report published by the National Endowment for the Arts in 2004. When its authors documented the decreasing amount of time that Americans were devoting to reading, they omitted from the totals any reading done for work or school. The devotion to what the report called "voluntary reading" and the decision that assigned reading wouldn't count helped overdetermine the report's seemingly paradoxical conclusion that, in an era in which increasing numbers of Americans spent more and more years reading in classrooms, *readers* per se had become an endangered species—and therefore objects of nostalgia.[21]

In "The ethical practice of modernity," John Guillory describes how, in the West, reading came gradually to be separated from collectively-oriented religious practice and assimilated into the emergent domains of leisure and entertainment. Around the mid-eighteenth century, the pursuit of pleasure in reading became a legitimate end of the activity, an "end in itself," no longer justifiable only "as the sweet shell" from which the text's wholesome moral kernel would be extricated. "Reading is universally allowed to be one of the most improving as well as agreeable amusements,"

---

[20] Anon., *The Friendly Instructor; or, A Companion to Young Ladies and Young Gentlemen* (1740; 6th edn; London: Buckland, 1770), 3–4.

[21] See Leah Price, "You Are What You Read," *New York Times Book Review*, December 23, 2007. A 2012 study from the United Kingdom likewise worries over a decline in "reading that we do of our own free will...that having begun at some one else's request, we continue because we are interested." United Kingdom Department for Education Education Standards Research Team, "Research evidence on reading for pleasure," May 15, 2012 (https://www.gov.uk/government/publications/research-evidence-on-reading-for-pleasure).

wrote Eliza Haywood in the opening of her 1744 essay series *The Female Spectator*. In this example of a writer's (self-interested) book-boosterism, Guillory finds an indication that "the pleasure experienced in the exercise of judgment has become in some measure detached from the process by which the moral lesson is extracted from the literary work."[22] Of course, at this same time, the ability to read was becoming both necessary in new ways to individuals' incorporation into the capitalist economy and the fulcrum for new forms of social exclusion. The rise of reading "as an ethical practice of self-improvement" that Guillory describes is, as he would be the first to acknowledge, counterpointed by the rise in the nineteenth century of mandatory public schooling—an institutional context for literacy that over time became geared increasingly to the notion that reading and writing represented a duty to economic productivity, not to God, to Enlightenment, or to oneself. It is also counterpointed by the growing centrality to reading instruction of mechanisms for skills assessment that have increasingly made that instruction serve—as testing separates the college-bound from the unskilled—as a motor of social stratification as well as social inclusion.

The frictions between these developments contribute to a phenomenon described by Patricia Crain, who notices how the "schoolhouse literacy that anyone can get in a public classroom" has never quite made the grade as an instantiation of real reading. Instead, that is emblematized, she suggests, in the nineteenth-century image of a *solitary* child, cradled in a window seat or perched in a tree, with book in hand, dreamily absorbed by the pleasures of the text. "To put the myth the image refers to succinctly: a certain kind of child naturally reads. Such a seemingly immersive, dreamy, self-forgetting, soft, childlike reading relies on deep pockets of cultural and social capital, and plain cash."[23]

To a surprising extent, however, the writers who sought to win English literature a central place within the school curriculum—and so within the apparatus of examining and credentializing—appear awfully preoccupied themselves with this mythologized child. That preoccupation bespeaks in part the cultural afterglow of British Romanticism and the continuing influence especially of William Wordsworth, whose poetry sanctified childhood as a state of imaginative liberty all too often checked by schooling. In his genealogy of English studies, Ian Hunter traces a through line from a key pedagogical innovation of the 1830s—the reformer David Stow's emphasis on play as an occasion of pedagogical development and his proposal that schools for the urban poor should incorporate playgrounds—to the concepts of literary pedagogy that gave English studies a central role in modern notions of a liberal education. Stow proposed in 1834 that the "covered school room" must be supplemented by an "uncovered school room," the better to foster

---

[22] John Guillory, "The Ethical Practice of Modernity: The Example of Reading," in *The Turn to Ethics*, ed. Marjorie Garber et al. (New York: Routledge, 2000), 41.
[23] Crain, *Reading Children*, 3.

the free play in which children independently develop their characters and the better to give teachers opportunities to subject that development to constant moral superintendence. (Tellingly enough, he prefaced his outline of this scheme with an epigraph from Wordsworth's "Intimations of Immortality.") By the early twentieth century, the literary text, Hunter contends, was the privileged support for a comparable pedagogy centered on self-discovery; exercises like the character appreciation or the close reading would become the character-building zones of free play gently supervised by a sympathetic teacher.[24] It is crucial to Stow's playground pedagogy that the adult teacher gets out of the way of children so that they can get on with their playing. And thus the parallel in the 1921 report by the English Association that helped secure literature curricular centrality in Britain: while citing Wordsworth in their turn, the authors develop the somewhat self-sabotaging argument that "the real teachers of Literature are the great writers themselves...[which] leads to the conclusion that for teachers we must have those who will not come between their pupils and the author they are reading."[25]

One can also see traces of that preoccupation with the solitary child, withdrawn from the social world of peers and family and lost in a book, in the moments when these particular architects of English, who are aiming to secure literary reading's status as assigned reading, also contrive to associate it with playing hooky. (That association also short-circuits the anxieties about undue pedagogic influence that also beset these authors.) The English Association's Report, though it advocates for the value of English to modern schooling, is punctuated by asides that glamorize the time when classics dominated the scene of instruction and vernacular literature was *not yet taught*, when it retained, at least for boys from the upper classes, the charm of reading matter that was engaged exclusively for pleasure. The Report thus cites Robert Lowe, the politician who spearheaded education reforms under Britain's Gladstone government, reminiscing in 1868 about the "stolen hours" in which he had strayed from his Latin and Greek with the assistance of a "bookcase in the corner of the study which was full of standard and sterling English books": "I felt like a truant and ashamed," and yet "I owe my success in life to those stolen hours." (The authors editorialize on this as follows: "this quotation...points out emphatically and yet unconsciously the test to which educational theory and practice must constantly be put, the test of application to life.")[26]

There was through the nineteenth and early twentieth centuries real perplexity about how to couple literature's lovability with its teachability. Thus the English Association also worries in this Report, wistfully, that "the very atmosphere of the class-room, with its paraphernalia of study, is one in which the wings of poetry

---

[24] David Stow, *The Training System, Moral Training School, and Normal Seminary* (10th edn, London: Longman, Brown, Green, and Longmans, 1854), 29; Ian Hunter, *Culture and Government: The Emergence of Literary Education* (Basingstoke: Macmillan, 1988), 21.

[25] *The Teaching of English in England* (London: H. M. Stationery Office, 1921), 24.

[26] *The Teaching of English in England*, 55.

cannot readily beat."[27] There was also—and indeed, as films like Peter Weir's *Dead Poets Society* (1989) suggest, continues to be—a persisting association of English literature with what is outside (the playground), beyond, or before the school—and a persisting ambiguity about when and where it is that English teachers actually teach (given their need to avoid "coming between" their pupils and the great authors who are the *real* teachers). An episode in Edward Eggleston's novel *The Hoosier Schoolmaster* (1871) captures Anglo-American culture's tacit investment in the notion that the literary experience that kindles imaginations should somehow be extracurricular for teachers and students alike, an occasion for truancy by both parties. Somehow, some element in the job description of Ralph, the eponymous schoolmaster hero of Eggleston's novel, dictates that the literary part of his curriculum will come to be associated with his day of rest. So on a rainy Sunday, on the eve of his first day in the classroom that will be his new workspace, he wins over the hard-bitten backwoods Indiana family with whom he boards, as he recounts to them "story after story out of all the books he had ever read":

> And "old man Means," and "old Miss Means," and Bud Means, and Bill Means, and Sis Means listened with great eyes while he told of Sinbad's adventures, of the Old Man of the Sea, of Robinson Crusoe, of Captain Gulliver's experiences in Liliput, and of Baron Munchausen's exploits.[28]

Is Ralph on the clock then or not? Is this day off really a work day? *The Hoosier Schoolmaster* anticipates the modern worry that to *assign* the reading of imaginative narrative is to spoil it, that it means killing rather than nurturing the love of books, that it infringes on the self-actualization that is the very reason for reading. It does seem sometimes that the people most prone to fretting about these possibilities are those who as part of their professional lives do that assigning. In *Dead Poets Society* the newly hired English teacher Mr. Keating begins by having the boys in his English literature class rip an essay out of the anthology they have been assigned; he then marches the students *out* of their classroom and into the fresh air.

School stories' ways of framing the literary encounter as secret, sentimental tryst suggests a pedagogical dilemma that appears to be part and parcel of English teaching. As editor for the last decade and a half of much assigned reading, I myself find much to muse on in the rumor circulated among his publishers that M. H. Abrams, the founding editor in 1962 of *The Norton Anthology of English Literature*, wanted that textbook to be a book the student would take outside and read under a tree. If this account is true, the textbook it describes must do something paradoxical; it must leave the space of the curriculum and of required reading, and enter the zone of extracurricular activities. The literary discipline at large might sometimes prefer

[27] *The Teaching of English in England*, 150.
[28] *The Hoosier Schoolmaster: A Story of Backwoods Life in Indiana* (New York: Grosset and Dunlap, 1871), chapter 1 (http://www.schooltales.net/hoosierschoolmaster/).

that sort of pastoral space to academic space and the playground—or uncovered schoolroom—to the schoolroom proper. Reading among the trees is certainly more charismatic than reading for standardized tests. The danger is that the charm of the former distracts us from the challenges we should be mounting to the realities of the latter.

FURTHER READING

Crain, Patricia. *The Story of A: The Alphabetization of America from* The New England Primer *to* The Scarlet Letter. Stanford: Stanford University Press, 2000.

Foakes, R. A. "'Thriving Prisoners': Coleridge, Wordsworth, and the Child at School." *Studies in Romanticism* 28.2 (1989): 187–206.

Lynch, Deidre Shauna. *Loving Literature: A Cultural History*. Chicago: University of Chicago Press, 2015.

Paul, Lissa. "Learning to be Literate." In *The Cambridge Companion to Children's Literature*, ed. M. O. Grenby. Cambridge: Cambridge University Press, 2010, 127–42.

Plotz, John. "Mediated Involvement: John Stuart Mill's Antisocial Sociability." In *The Feeling of Reading: Affective Experience and Victorian Literature*, ed. Rachel Ablow. Ann Arbor: University of Michigan Press, 2010, 69–92.

Rose, Jacqueline. *The Case of Peter Pan: or, The Impossibility of Children's Literature*. Rev. edn. Basingstoke: Macmillan, 1994.

9

ACTUAL

GARRETT STEWART

When the assignments for contributors were divvied up at the proposal stage of this collection, I filed my earmarked "actual reading" away in mind as "simply reading" or "just reading"—as opposed to all the other things you can do with books or pages, or they for you. And *ear*-marked, in my mind, it certainly was. Not least in this age of debate among "distant" versus "surface" versus "too-close" versus "deep" reading—respectively, computerized statistical scanning versus affective first-responding versus quasi-obsessional intensity versus formative sounding—the modifier "actual" (which, for me, could only be an intensifier, like "*really* reading") came to seem more a gauntlet thrown down than familiar territory staked out for revisiting.[1]

"Actual" reading? As distinct from other textual or book practices? Or as anchoring them, at least as norm if not as sine qua non? "Actual" in contrast to abstract or theoretical? Or as a thing to be theorized in itself, whether cleansed of agenda or not? In any case, to turn this anthology remit into anything like a renewed position paper, the modifier "actual" would have to close in, if not down, on where, in literary reception, the *action* really is. When considering standard reading practices, rather than the enhanced deciphering methods of people who are deaf or blind, "actual" reading is best understood as the *actualization* of text on the proverbial "inner ear." But how inward and how anatomical, at that, is such a site? In the scalar basis of linguistic processing—according to the very structuring of the language act—so-called double articulation involves, first, the piecing out of phonemes into morphemes, then of morphemes into lexemes. Articulate(d)ness, at this level, is grounded not in speech acts but only in word sounds. Submerged in silence but immersed in the conditions of utterance, its operations more than merely retinal or

---

[1] I here skim, in my own turn, the methodologies associated, respectively, with Franco Moretti, *Distant Reading* (London: Verso, 2013); Stephen Best and Sharon Marcus, "Surface Reading: An Introduction," *Representations* 108.1 (Fall 2009): 1–21; D. A. Miller, *Hidden Hitchcock* (Chicago: University of Chicago Press, 2016); and my own "formative" rather than formalist emphasis on literature's linguistic substrate in *The Deed of Reading: Literature • Writing • Language • Philosophy* (Ithaca, NY: Cornell University Press, 2015).

cognitive, "actual" reading is the realization of any such potential for speech, as potential only, on the near side of the audible. Churning at the somatic threshold of enunciation, to read is to feel the *possibility* of such speech happening in you: a possibility suspended (suppressed or "inhibited," as neurobiology has it) in the coursing flow of its own discourse. This is a speech "voiced" even *when never, or regardless of whenever*, sounded out—as in the simultaneously seen and heard difference, right there, in that handful, that earful, of shunted word sounds. Such are the accidents and skids of enunciation that make for what James Joyce called "an earsighted view" of textual succession: the very myoptics of the "phonemanon."[2]

Since I had already written several books more or less about the theoretical parameters and analytic flashpoints of this premise, as manifested in the phonetic densities of both poetry and "prose *friction*," I took my new mandate here, under the rubric of "further reading," as a call to do some "actual" further reading, theory to the side at first, in a recent, stingingly satiric, and linguistically astute short story by the young American novelist Bennett Sims. His sardonic purpose, and my heuristic one in turn, is to rethink the "actual" nature of reading from within a wry lampoon of its misapplication to another medium—and then to follow Sims' own allusive lead into screen theory. What turns up there is a more recent work by the film critic cited in Sims' story that offers, by contrast with strictly visual data on screen, one of the more lucid accounts of verbal reading from the phonic, not just graphic, ground up: a film commentary by Michel Chion more attuned to the formative impress of phonemics as the key to alphabetic textuality than are many—make that most— recent books in the self-announced vein of "neoformalist" literary studies.

But Sims first. Whatever the story's particular satiric animus against bad academic reading, animated new writing like his helps spotlight the ways literature has always, if it can be put this way, worked to elicit *its* best from *us*. Such is the inverted vector of sub-vocal response this chapter is out to trace. Literature, of course, may teach us how to read, even across media—and, by the same token, how *not to*. In this respect, the title story of Sims' *White Dialogues* triangulates with the audiophile term "white noise" (a blanketing but indeterminate background sound) in ways that contrast with the literary-theoretical notion of "white voice" (a silent phonetic enunciation) recently advanced by Steven Connor—for whom even the question of *where* reading happens, let alone *how*, is rightly (and, more to the point, resonantly) indeterminate. Connor is glossing "what is called sub-vocalization," as I had done over two decades back in *Reading Voices*: four syllables proffered as an intransitive clause, not a noun phrase, turning on the gerund form of "reading."[3] In his own terms, Connor stresses how literature "does not silence sound: it auditises the field of the visible."[4] This is

---

[2] James Joyce, *Finnegans Wake* (New York: Penguin, 1999), 143, 258.
[3] Steven Connor, *Beckett, Modernism, and the Material Imagination* (Cambridge: Cambridge University Press, 2014), 106. See also Garrett Stewart, *Reading Voices: Literature and the Phonotext* (Berkeley, CA: University of California Press, 1990).
[4] Connor, *Beckett, Modernism, and the Material Imagination*, 113.

because "one who reads silently...is suffused by his or her inner sonority, if inside is exactly where it is, if sonorous is exactly what it is."[5] Energized there is what I have more recently termed, varying Walter Ong's influential notion of "secondary orality" since the phonograph, a "secondary vocality" endemic to the functions of literacy long before machine recording.[6] For it is a simple fact of morphophonemic language that syllables are not herded into wording until heard—somewhere, if heard is the word or place its locus (Connor's sense of equivocation again)—as formative syllabic entities and increments.

Words of Mouth

Such is the premise of literary language so bizarrely inverted and hollowed out by Sims' story about a misjudged lip-reading of silent screen zones: mobile glyphic cysts, so to say, in the audiovisual system of "talking film," little irrelevant pockets of muteness, invisible speech bubbles, bursts of pertinence-free facial motion. Here is the plot of "White Dialogues," such as it is: a present-tense act of witness stretched on the rack of the narrator's intermittent tortured responses, in a university base-ment screening room, to a lecture about such sensorial non-sense in Alfred Hitchcock's *Vertigo*. The response is wrung from a paranoid and increasingly hallucinatory (and nameless) narrator, who has been denied tenure on the basis of his own lone article on Hitchcock and is now being aggravated gradually out of his mind by hearing the claptrap dished out, to departmental acclaim, by the hotshot young postdoc replacing him: a cardiganed preppy identified only by surname as the oddly spelled and (by us) elusively pronounced Bereyter, whose entire research project is based on lip-reading the silent background extras in Hitchcock's *Vertigo*. In a narration about the thresholds of the said, the first clue thus arrives with the first sentence: "Listen to her, Bereyter says, as together we watch the mute woman mouthing something on the screen."[7] Provocation, not vocalization: the deranged claim of what one might call *vocularity*—eyed but unheard speech. It is no accident that the screen on which the looped evidence of such a silent locutionary act is so confidently projected by Bereyter is called, from here out, the "canvas" of his trivial revelations. For it is upon the plane of this representational blank slate that he must

    [5] Connor, *Beckett, Modernism, and the Material Imagination*, 106.
    [6] In contrast to "secondary orality" in Walter Ong, *Orality and Literacy: The Technologizing of the Word* (London: Methuen, 1982), see chapter 2, "Secondary Vocality," in Stewart, *The Deed of Reading*, 41–75.
    [7] Bennett Sims, *White Dialogues* (Columbus, OH: Two Dollar Radio, 2017), 171. Subsequent cit-ations will be cited parenthetically.

de-pict (vocally motorize) what can't, on the other hand, be actually heard—as if in a travesty of Voltaire's remark that "writing is the painting of the voice."[8]

The initially deadpan tonalities of this story's academic satire are as familiar as they are, in this case, deliciously confected and relentless. Compared to the lecture in progress, the narrator's purportedly fantastical claim, in the one article he managed to publish from his dissertation, seems the soul of cogency. By his lights, *Rear Window* and *Vertigo* are in fact two halves of one four-hour movie starring James Stewart—with Jeff from the one, fallen from his titular window at the end, popping up newly injured from an equivalent fall as Scottie at the start of the next. Compared to such an imputed continuity, Bereyter's arcane and maddeningly lauded initiative respects no narrative arcs in its attempt to read, in one disjunct scene from *Vertigo* after another, a pointless "message in a bottle" corked up until now in its vacuum of silence: namely, what uncredited "extras," when mouthing arbitrary word forms in the background of shops and restaurants, can somehow (though with no microphones in earshot) be de-ciphered to be saying from mere facial motion (174). As if in an inverted travesty of computer-assisted "distant reading," such is the infuriating nugatory reading-*in* of this particular *lecture*.

Our vanguard scholarly entrepreneur has, we're informed, combed the film for all such moments of background facial activity. In pursuit of what the narrator dismisses as "chitchat exegesis," Bereyter has then sent his selected clips to an expert in lip-reading, who decodes the snippets phrase by phrase (177). The results are brandished now by Bereyter, while looped in permanent obscurity on the "canvas" behind him, even though the actual content of the educed remarks is admittedly inconsequential. Against his better judgment, it is up to the paranoid narrator gradually more and more frenetically to fixate, to overinvest, to make them mean—so that, toward the story's climax, the detected "We see you" (supposedly legible, without any adduced narrative import, on the lips of a patron at Ernie's restaurant) breaks through the film's fourth wall as a negative revelation. Via the narrator's own recoil from such lackluster contingencies, its accusative collective address ("we...you") ends up, we're told, speaking for all the silent extras in the 1958 film, now dead, who stare through time into the grave-robbing gaze of the lecturer, bent as he is—and I paraphrase and condense the narrator's furious lunatic diatribe—on raiding the silence of the celluloid tombs for some piecemeal resurrection of their mummified and dummy vocables.

In the story's own insidious hermeneutic ecology, however, the lecturer is skewered in the end for his slackness rather than his pointless overexertion. Clueless even when he strikes gold, the feckless pedant claims that a woman at Ernie's restaurant bar is seen to say, as repeated dozens of times in his illustrative loop, "Read my lips...It's Jeff"—without Bereyter apprehending the power of such a find (and its unacknowledged confirmation of the narrator's own published findings). For these

---

[8] Oeuvres Complètes de Voltaire, *Dictionnaire Philosophique* (Paris: Garnier Frères, 1879), 4: 157.

five unearthed words (which of course bear no relation to the swift optic mumble in the actual scene—if one races off to check, as I did) prove, to the satisfaction of Sims' narrative persona, that the woman is asking her male companion (or us, over his shoulder) to recognize exactly that residual character (L. B. "Jeff" Jeffries) from the previous movie, now reborn as Scottie in the continued person of James Stewart. Yet it's not only balked and frustrated self-interest that sets the narrator's teeth on edge, not entirely Bereyter's failure to recognize this ratifying clincher in regard to his predecessor's thesis. At least in the narrator's earlier responses at the back of the screening room, he has objected strenuously to any such violating of the mere "scenery of speech" with faux precision (173). Ambiguity in such matters has an almost absolute sway, since what is written on those faces "in invisible ink" will not plausibly submit to any "crackpot cryptology" (174, 177).

Invisible Links

The narrator's leading case in point makes this abundantly clear. "All right" has been the first snatch of dialogue dredged from silence and oblivion, but it could never pass the necessary test of the unmistakable. Proof positive right there, as if we needed it, that Bereyter's methodology "is not even (if I may put it this way) *sound*" (178). Sims' story now spells this out in ways that bear directly on the deceptive simplicity of just reading—of actual reading—even in alphabetic display rather than screen pantomime. As the narrator asks in high dudgeon: how is one, when "lacking any semantic context," ever "supposed to distinguish between two homophones (two and too, for instance)?" Or "even resolve an ambiguous viseme?" (178) His informed rant deploys there the technical term for those variations in facial signage (the visible semes of motor speech, as it were) that accompany enunciation and, for people with hearing impairments, facilitate the reading of faces (lips, teeth, tongue) in the piecing out of syllabic language. How, then, he asks combatively, is the lip-reader able to tell that "the florist is mouthing *all right*, rather than *all ride* or *hall write* or something else altogether?"—as, say (in silence), for instance, *holler it*? Such are the invisible links of this "invisible ink" (178). Aside from any literary valence in the useless punning thereby evoked and marginalized, the technical hurdles (to sematic disambiguation) are further itemized in confident linguistic terms: "How does she distinguish one bilabial stop from another? One alveolar stop from another? One mid-front vowel from another?" (178). She doesn't, she can't.

A lingering implication here: nor can we either, even in the "actual reading" of already transcribed and encoded syllables. We remain unable in our own right to keep certain phantom phonemes at bay. And if all is a nest of mere differential traces up for phonic grabs and whatever semantic grip they might provide, what about the odd trisyllabic name Bereyter itself on the story's pages, with its open-mouthed diphthong "ey" as another node—or black hole—of uncertainty? It is up to us alone to wonder; the narrator is otherwise convulsed. Is this new junior luminary, his name slurred or purified to two syllables, the Breyter ("brighter") one after all? Or the "be-writer," imposing his own script on the aleatory Hitchcockian place-holders? Or the "be-righter" who (as opposed, say, to besmircher) is out to set things straight? Or, instead, the "be-rator" of cinematic coherence itself, denigrating in his audio autopsies all that gives film its spatial depth and conviction as a feasibly receding soundscape?

None of this syllabic wavering matters to the explicit satire, finally, but it certainly is "material to" the story's metalinguistics. Indeed, any such enfeebled readerly confidence in the syllabic matter of pronunciation serves to ratchet implication one further notch beyond anything implicit in the story's discourse. For in the wake of the narrator's repulsion and outrage, abated only in his late attachment to the corroborative "it's Jeff," what the story (accidentally? connivingly?) leaves us to intuit—not to audit but to perform somatically on our own recognizance—is a digressive logical and then somatic byplay that takes us (me at least, when I tried it) beyond inscription altogether. In the phonetic freefall thus induced, one begins by realizing that the putative miming of an epiphanic "Read my lips...It's Jeff" would not, with any likelihood, have been spoken in this form to the woman's male partner at the bar (189). Even above the ambient noise, he ought to have heard her well enough without resorting to visual decryption. If credibly phonetic at all, which of course it isn't, such a remark would be addressed sardonically to the lecturer and us instead (according to the paranoid logic of the narrator's sense of apostrophe and mute appeal elsewhere) so as to expose, from within its nonsensical premise, the futile phonic excavation underway. By visemic rather than phonemic translation, that is, a potential vocalic implosion of Bereyter's whole procedure is at play here: "Read my lips: it's chaff." Not "without semantic context," but overdetermined in its satire, who is to be sure, that is, from only looking, that the unvoiced velar fricative (j)—if I may momentarily inhabit the narrator's once skeptical technical groove—isn't in fact the voiced palatal fricative (the digraph ch)?

As extraneous dross, as the last straw in all this sheer "chaff," the whole "absurd" method of textual sounding (from *surdus*, for "deaf" or "dull") would thus be *written off* by objecting lips other than the narrator's—but this only through an enhanced itch for the heuristic shaping of sound in a puzzle-solving hermeneutic furor of our own. We don't know, can't know, whether the story "intends" that we play its own game long enough to see (more than hear) this strictly visual acoustic. All we know is that the narrative's insistence on such eyed (or eye-eared) ambiguities as those knotted up in the likes of the name Bereyter have teased us over a further edge (I speak again for myself) into this enacted facial play, this projected test-case mirage, of a non-acoustic match between "Jeff" and "chaff": performed, if so, only visemically—facially, not phonemically—in a non-homophonic sight pun never available to "actual" reading at all.

Filmic Sound Defects

Among the sparse notes on Bereyter's blackboard, preliminary to the paucity of evidence on his looped "canvas," is an aphorism from sound theorist Michel Chion about silent film being "deaf film"—unable even to hear itself (173). The acoustic false bottoms that Bereyter's method pursues amount to vestigial sedimentations of that primal deafness, that horizoning silence. There is no mention, naturally, of Chion's more recent work, published in the same year as Sims' volume: namely, *Words on Screen*.[9] But filaments of connection there are. Instead of the focus on pointless mouthings, asks Sims' narrator, "Why not close read the billboards, or the shop window signage?" (178). The sarcastic question actually points to Chion's latest screen concerns but with a crucial difference: the difference in cinema between simply seeing word forms, foregrounded or not, and the process of "actually reading" them. Reprinting a litany of cinematic inscriptions from corporate logos to street signs, including Carlotta Valdez's inscribed gravestone in *Vertigo*, Chion's point is that writing on screen operates within a separate order of visibility, and of legibility, from the surrounding optic text of its encompassing *mise en scène*. This is precisely because of such script's necessary silent sounding, an internalization (or "endophasia") cognate with Connor's "white voice" or my "evocalization"—as ultimately derived from the "acoustic image" of traditional linguistics.[10]

Chion slots all this into the broader spectrum intended by his coinage "athory-bus": the image without its inferred noise.[11] Though placing no emphasis on out-of-earshot dialogue, Chion does link all lettering on screen with a wide array of other soundless manifestations that would, at a nearer acoustic distance, be audible—as with a locomotive whose chugging smokestack is glimpsed on the other side of a forest, say, or an airliner gaining altitude in the urban distance, that sort of thing. Particular to silent signage, however, is the deciphering somatic apparatus of the viewer/reader, whom we might thus term by portmanteau the *viewereader*. This is the engaged agency through whose phonetic performance, according to Chion, wording exceeds the regime of the visual without becoming part of the soundtrack, though nonetheless tracked aurally in the mind's ear. Connor's phrase comes back to mind, transferred to screen as well as page, where writing "auditises the field of the visual." In contrast, Bereyter's program, though indebted to Chion on the idea

---

[9] Michel Chion, *Words on Screen*, trans. Claudia Gorbman (New York: Columbia University Press, 2017).

[10] Chion, *Words on Screen*, 59; Stewart, *Reading Voices*, 192–231.

[11] Chion, *Words on Screen*, 60.

of "deaf film," is nonetheless—with its privileging of viseme over phoneme—the structural opposite of any such claims about visualized writing in screen projection. Chion's is in fact a para-literary emphasis on "actual" reading as alphabetically cued and silently activated. Here, then, in this latest trajectory of his influential work, is a new version of "off-screen" sound: in this case, however, located *before* the screen, not behind or beside it, where it is operable only in us. Epitomized in isolation when pitted against sheer pictorial manifestation, such is the *passage* of writing— on the way to any subsidiary meaning or depiction—through just that *secondary vocality* that is intimately sprung from lettered impress.

Inscription's *Songrams*

If film theory, concerned with the time-based medium of projection, can thus help precipitate out, from its own flow, the disclosed structure of "actual reading" as another unique order of time-based activity, a separate realm of "word processing," then so might a landmark debate in poststructuralist literary circles be usefully brought (back) to bear here. It is fair to assume that reader-response theorist Michael Riffaterre would rule out any usable pun on the comparable mouth forma- tions of "Jeff" and "chaff," for instance, as not rising (with their different soundings of *e* and *a*) to the standard of phenomenal manifestation in alphabetic text. This follows from the way he vetoes another critic's offered play on "gold" in Poe when dependent on the mere graphic trace of a silent *g* in "right holding."[12] Such retrench- ment against free association is, according to Paul de Man's critique, a typifying conservative move in Riffaterre's semiotics. For here is precisely what de Man drills down on as the normalizing nature of Riffaterre's method, which has chastened the piecemeal chaos of Ferdinand de Saussure's notorious anagram studies into tenable lexical units.

"Up till very recently, French critics never bothered to read at all," de Man quips.[13] Unimpacted by the Anglo-American protocols of close reading, French scholars wrote about literature from the top down. Not so the French-born American expatriate Riffaterre, de Man is quick to acknowledge, while still insisting on a deep and abiding blind spot. For after the painstaking process of moving from anomalies at the mimetic level of poetic discourse to reconciliations at the hermeneutic level, Riffaterre's admittedly exemplary "interpretations" are exposed by de Man as seeking premature closure in a descriptive system of figuration—rather than in its further dismantling, its deconstruction. One of Riffaterre's own litmus test poems, a short text by Victor Hugo, celebrates the tonalities of a Flemish carillon as they generate

---

[12] This is an early pressure point in Paul de Man, "Hypogram and Inscription: Michael Riffaterre's Poetics of Reading," *Diacritics* 11.4 (1981): 22, the rest of whose critique is summarized in what follows.

[13] de Man, "Hypogram and Inscription," 21.

audiovisual figures for the abstraction that is time itself in affective comprehension by the mind. Yet this choreography of proliferating tropes spun from that of a Spanish dancer in performance up and down a crystalline staircase, explicitly invisible, is turned against Riffaterre's own method by a complex argument on de Man's part captured most succinctly in his noting that Riffaterre fails to consider the poem's very title, "Lines Written on the Pane of a Flemish Window"—and precisely in association with the resonant "crystal invisible" of the staircase trope. For the whole exfoliated analogy of time's dance is only actualized in reading, upon such a transparent support, once it has been etched into opacity by script. All is materially written, not phenomenally perceived: all made possible only, as it were, from scratch. For the poem to exist, as the title's own allegory suggests, the window must be deciphered, not seen through. It is the rectangular frame only of differential marks: a page *manqué*.

Lines on the window—and a line drawn in the sand. Riffaterre's figural hermeneutics, charges de Man, forgets that all is at base inscription, sheer symbol in the linguistic sense. And not just in poetry. Time is conjured as a Spanish dancer because it has no content otherwise as a noun; it is merely our word for an immaterial *a priori*. Even if named in the poem, rather than openly figured, it would remain a sheer figure of speech: four letters (five in French) for what no one can actually perceive. Exhaustive in its way and supposedly devastating, this critique. But in our terms, de Man hasn't bothered to read the poem either, barely a line of it, which he treats for the most part in the primal paraphrase of translation, phrase by intermittent phrase. The closest he comes to actually reading what does strike the senses, in any immediate experience of the verse lines, is to register time's counterpart, the equally empty abstraction of "mind" (or "l'esprit"), figured problematically as a "bizarre waking monster," a watchman "made of ears and eyes": a grotesque catachresis for which (as with the unsaid "time") there is no literal tenor.[14] However, de Man highlights this without noting the contradicted privilege etymologically accorded to sight in "surveilleur" ("watchman") when followed first by "d'oreilles" rather than "d'yeux" (ears rather than eyes) in a poem that is first of all about the conversion of sound to image, the peals of the carillon translated to personified figuration. For such is the auditory focal point (of the surveillant ear) stressed—in its phonic rather than sonic traction—neither by Riffaterre's commentary nor by de Man's. Such is this point of *lexical* audition—via the ringing steps of the imagined dancer's chiming footwork, and here via the capping and grammatically inverted last metrical line—from which "de march en marche" (from step to step) is heard "to wander her resonant foot."

Certainly "errer son pied sonore"—if enunciated into meaning in the moment rather than just remembered afterward for comment—"actuates" that moment not by inscription alone, nor merely by description, but by the sounded sense of the

---

[14] de Man, "Hypogram and Inscription," 34.

"pied metrique," the poetic "foot" itself, chiastically set off by an extra homophonic play. Extra, but hardly extraneous, since the poem lands in conclusion upon the ur-pun of all internal echo, call it the arche-homophone: an echo entirely outplaying description, exceeding even inscription, in the *son*-ic chiasm that turns grammatical possession (*son*) into the reverberant dance of belled time, "*son* pied *sonore*"—a phrasing immanently re-son-ant in the beat of its own evocalization. Here then, in reading, *pace* de Man, is where the mind's time becomes, rather than a tenuous abstraction, "actual" after all.

Synched Speech/Lips Inked

Not, perhaps, until Virginia Woolf's paean to sounded time, a century after Hugo, is temporality to be found again so musically figured in the tread (and potential dread) of its stylistic as well as sonic demarcations. Though scarcely healing all wounds in Woolf, time is sealed in the expectancy of sounds spanning the embedded repetitions of "en" en route across Mrs. Dalloway's felt "susp*en*se before Big B*en* strikes"—until, at last, "There! Out it boomed. First a warning, musical; then the hour, irrevocable. The leaden circles dissolved in the air."[15] Before that last transferred epithet from the metal belling, the wavelengths' figured concentricity has opened the final syllable "cal" of "musical" not just to the "cable" of the next adjective but to a further muted inclusion of the reflexive "vocable" in the very pace of this terraced wording. Then, too, in the phonic mean-time, the word "ear" itself has laid its claim on the first syllable of "*ir*revocable"—followed by another cross-word bridge in the thinning dissipation of "there" into "the air." One proof of the ear in actual reading is indeed its occasional disrespect of the eyed word edge. Borders become in this sense linguistic limit tests, with soundings elusive, elisional, given frequent leave and leeway.

In the voice of a later female persona—less sanguine about temporal immersion, a psyche torn asunder more exhaustingly by time's competing demands, her expression thus bent out of shape into a more aggressive wordplay—we hear the way in which phonetics may mark a schism in the very "I am" of female pro/creation. Pulled between the roles of woman as mother, drained of energy, and woman as poet, robbed of time for writing, the first two words of Adrienne Rich's "To a Poet," in figuring the winter of this conflicted discontent, are actually—across the sibilant shiver—three: "I/ce splits."[16] The unforgiving "play" between I's plural and their alternately frozen options splinters the verse itself, as it does for Emily Dickinson's persona when confronting a more metaphysical divide between mortal and

---

[15] Virginia Woolf, *Mrs. Dalloway* (New York: Harcourt, 1990), 4.
[16] Adrienne Rich, "To a Poet," in *Collected Poems: 1950–2012* (New York: W. W. Norton, 2016), 454–5; 454.

transcendental states. Traversing a purgatorial interspace across a flickering phonetic interstice—a borderland figured by metonymic association with trees carved into coffins as the "forest of the dead" (where "before were cities")—the soul is heard bordering, lexically as well as spiritually, on the "fore-rest" of resurrection.[17]

And when auditing the likes of Dickinson's alphabetic densities, we are never far, however seldom noted, from the post-Romantic sonorities of Dickensian prose *friction*, where the strategically frayed phrase may offer its own phonic leverage on the imagined scene. In and beyond de Man's terms, once again description is rooted in the gaps of inscription itself—and then floated there as well on the white noise that can sometimes flood such typographic blanks. Listen to the haunting prison reverb, as italicized here, when the eponymous heroine of *Little Dorrit* is found perched on the

> high fender in the lodge, looking up at the sky through the barred window, until, when she *turned her eyes* away, bars of light *would arise* between her and her friend, and she would see him through a grating, too. (emphasis added on the parallel predicates and their dovetailed phonetic substrates)[18]

Bracketed by the near-anagrammatic switch from "fender" to "friend" (indeed the further phonetic thickening of "her and her friend"), the striated retinal imprint and after-image from the prison bars is figured by a kind of phonic scrim matched to the residual distortion of what she sees, by superimposition, when turning from the window. This perceptual fallout is virtually enacted, that is, upon the reader's ear rather than eye through the uncanny cross-word shadow cast, from cause to effect, across the audited d/rift from the transitive, three-syllabled "turn*ed her eyes*" to its aural remapping in "woul*d arise*." This is what I meant early on by a prose that, reversing the normal vectors of educed response, invites us to bring out the best *in it*.

With my "further" reading of Sims' prose very much in mind, including those parodied mute excavations of facial silence on screen as counter-case, I'm ready to risk a further paradox in the name of a subliminal transference. In the energized circuits of textual response, literature may often seem engaged in reading our own implicit lips for us. Only virtually, of course—but no less palpably. What I've been calling actual reading, by any other name, honors this potential interchange, hews to it, whenever literary writing hones it into the open.

FURTHER READING

Leighton, Angela. *Hearing Things: The Work of Sound in Literature*. Cambridge, MA: Harvard University Press, 2018.

---

[17] Emily Dickinson, "Our Journey had advanced," in *The Complete Poems of Emily Dickinson* (Boston: Little, Brown, and Company, 1927), 213–14; 214.

[18] Charles Dickens, *Little Dorrit*, ed. Stephen Wall and Helen Small (London: Penguin, 1998), 84.

Levinson, Marjorie. "What Is New Formalism?" *PMLA* 122:2 (2007): 558–69.

Stewart, Garrett. *Novel Violence: A Narratography of Victorian Fiction*. Chicago: University of Chicago Press, 2009.

Tyler, Daniel, ed. *Dickens's Style*. Cambridge: Cambridge University Press, 2013.

Wolfson, Susan J. *Formal Charges: The Shaping of Poetry in British Romanticism*. Palo Alto: Stanford University Press, 1997.

Wolfson, Susan J., and Marshall Brown, eds. *Reading for Form*. Seattle: University of Washington Press, 2006.

10

TECHNICAL

ELAINE FREEDGOOD AND CANNON SCHMITT

Technical language excludes. *Enclitics* if we are not linguists, *fetch* if we don't study waves, *covalent bonds* if we've forgotten our high school chemistry, *shoe shining* if we don't box: drawn from highly specialized lexicons, these terms keep us on the outside. Although they are in English, most Anglophones can't understand them. Developed to allow thought to be pursued or work to be done, technical language, willy nilly, divides us from each other. If in some cases its exclusionary force arises as a byproduct, in others that force is precisely the point: inaccessible terminology can so easily be brought to bear in the service of policing the boundaries of a club, whether elite or marginal. How many anecdotes about medicine hinge on doctors consolidating their authority with recourse to words their patients can't define? But the clubs constituted by mastery of technical languages are not entirely closed off; nor, as a consequence, is their membership inevitably static. In principle, if not always in practice, anyone can move from outside to inside by learning the language in question. We may not be able to talk with our gardener about dicots or our neurologist about the occipital lobe today; given time and sufficient interest, however, we could be taught or teach ourselves to do so. Technical language excludes, but not necessarily or permanently.

The exclusiveness of technical language may account for the frequency of its literary appearance as an object of scorn. Comically or infuriatingly opaque, a lexicon that we (whoever "we" might be) can't read makes for an easy and enjoyable target. The *Oxford English Dictionary* (*OED*) tells this story in the terse confines of lexicography, defining "jargon," a synonym for technical language, as "unintelligible or meaningless talk or writing; nonsense, gibberish. (Often a term of contempt for something the speaker does not understand.)"[1] But the *OED* also provides the original sense of "jargon," namely "the inarticulate utterance of birds." Opacity cuts both ways. It may be gibberish, but it may also be birdsong. As one of us has written elsewhere, "From the outside, technical language is poetry."[2]

---

[1] *OED Online*, s.v. "jargon."
[2] Cannon Schmitt, "Technical Maturity in Robert Louis Stevenson," *Representations* 125 (Winter 2014): 58.

To explain why, we could look to Viktor Shklovsky, who extols the estranging effects of words we don't recognize, effects that call attention to those words and, in doing so, enable the heightened state of perception that the Russian Formalists saw as the aim of art. Literary language, Shklovsky points out, "is often actually foreign: the Sumerian used by the Assyrians, the Latin of Europe during the Middle Ages, the Arabisms of the Persians, the Old Bulgarian of Russian literature, or the elevated…language of folk songs."[3] It is also, and for the same reason, often actually technical: the language of law in the novels of Walter Scott; of mining, the theater, or the racetrack in the novels of Émile Zola; of computer science or soap manufacture in Richard Powers's novels of work; of psychoanalysis and mortuary science in Alison Bechdel's graphic memoirs. If one function of technical language in literature is defamiliarization, however, that isn't its only function—or, we'll argue, its most important one. It can be poetry from the inside, too, as Joseph Conrad testifies when he writes that nautical terminology possesses "the clearness, precision, and beauty of perfected speech."[4]

"Perfected speech": a possible definition of technical language, one that imagines it to be purged of the ambiguity in ordinary, everyday language—as well as the ambiguity of not-so-ordinary, literary language to the degree that perfection implies eliminating the drift of the figurative and connotative. For this reason, in spite of its defamiliarizing effects and poetic resonance, technical language frequently stands in for literature's opposite. Words in a novel, we're told, don't work the same way as words in a car repair manual. A different and equally valid first sentence for this chapter would have been: Technical language is unliterary. Perhaps this is why extant protocols for reading technical language in literary texts, to the degree that there are any, treat it as an incursion from another realm. Sometimes it appears as a problem to be solved by trimming, glossing, or footnoting. Sometimes it figures as epaulets in prose, establishing the authority of the narrator and thus the plausibility of what is narrated. This is how H. G. Wells accounted for the use of technical language in his scientific romances: "For the writer of fantastic stories to help the reader to play the game properly, he must help him in every possible unobtrusive way to *domesticate* the impossible hypothesis.…It occurred to me that instead of the usual interview with the devil or a magician, an ingenious use of scientific patter might with advantage be substituted."[5] Of the essence here is the assumption that readers need not grasp technical language. Of the essence, that is, is the assumption that technical language need not really be *read*. In fact, Wells suggests that it works better if readers don't pay too much attention to it, since its purpose is to sound convincing to those not in the know.

---

[3] Viktor Shklovsky, "Art as Technique," in *Russian Formalist Criticism: Four Essays*, ed. and trans. Lee T. Lemon and Marion J. Reis (Lincoln: University of Nebraska Press, 1965), 22.

[4] Joseph Conrad, *The Mirror of the Sea*, in *The Mirror of the Sea and A Personal Record*, ed. Zdzisław Najder (Oxford: Oxford University Press, 1988), 13.

[5] H. G. Wells, *Seven Famous Novels* (New York: Knopf, 1934), viii; emphasis in the original here and throughout.

In this chapter, however, we propose that literary instances of technical language are best approached neither as problems in need of solutions nor as tokens of narratorial authority most effective when not inquired into too closely—nor signs of the real, nor symbols, nor metaphors. We propose that technical language functions *as* technical language: a specialized vocabulary necessary in a particular field that can be translated out of that literal or figurative space. The references above to Scott, Zola, Powers, Bechdel, Wells, and Conrad provide the beginnings of a sense of the scope of such an investigation. All of them, however, depend on a narrow account of the technical as pertaining to a profession (law, psychoanalysis, undertaking) or bound up in specific technologies (for mining, computing, sailing, or time travel). But once you begin looking for the technical in literary texts, for highly specialized language that sits amongst other, more accessible languages, that scope opens out still further. Far from being un- or extraliterary, the technical begins to seem characteristic of literature—maybe even constitutive of it.

Sometimes the field of technical language is literally fields, or housing projects, dells, or divisions. Technical language involves precise knowledge of place and practice, which means that dialect is or might usefully be considered such a language. In what follows, we think about technical language, and dialect as a technical language, in the work of Thomas Hardy, his work both as author and as editor of the Dorset dialect poet William Barnes. Like technical language more traditionally conceived, dialect foregrounds questions of denotation—What does *x* mean? Or, when and where and to whom did *x* mean something?—where *x* could be a linhay or a speäker, two dialect words in Hardy's *The Return of the Native*, the novel we'll spend the most time with. And so of necessity demonstrating how to read dialect as a technical language will involve us in vernacular architecture, archaic technologies, and local varieties of apple. Vladimir Propp objected to such a procedure as classist, as witness this scathing use of "allegedly": "But when one is dealing with the peasantry, the structure of old stoves and the rhythm of lyric songs can allegedly be studied together."[6] Defending his own, countervailing methodology in *Theory and History of Folklore*, he writes: "We know that the closest connection exists between material and spiritual culture, but we separate the material and the spiritual, just as it is done for the culture of the upper classes."[7] For Hardy the pre-structuralist folklorist and regionalist, however, both technical language and dialect are crucial precisely for the link they provide to the material, the proof they give of the inseparability of language and materiality, of language as a kind of materiality. Reading technically, which is not a technical mode of reading but a mode of reading technical language in literary texts, also entails reading the things and techniques and places that that language denotes.

---

[6] Vladimir Propp, *Theory and History of Folklore*, trans. Ariadna Y. Martin, Richard P. Martin, et al. (Minneapolis, MN: University of Minnesota Press, 1984), 4.

[7] Propp, *Theory and History of Folklore*, 4.

Excavations

Hardy's fiction is full of technical terms drawn from an assortment of fields but perhaps most frequently from geology, paleontology, and archeology. In *Two on a Tower*, amongst the equatorial mounts, achromatic lenses, and variable stars (one of the protagonists is an astronomer), we encounter sentences like this one: "Lady Constantine might have felt a nameless fear in thus sitting aloft on a lonely column, with a forest groaning under her feet, and palæolithic dead men feeding its roots."[8] Thanks to John Lubbock, who coined the term "paleolithic" in *Pre-historic Times*, Hardy can conjure not simply the dead but the dead from a past in which humans hunted mammoths and had not yet invented agriculture.[9] In *A Pair of Blue Eyes*, when a character named Knight clings precariously to a cliff face, the danger is heightened because he rests his feet on a "block of quartz" that was "originally an igneous protrusion into the enormous masses of black strata, which had since been worn away from the sides of the alien fragment by centuries of frost and rain."[10] Strata reappear in a figurative register in *Jude the Obscure*: the narrator describes a crossroads in Christminster called Fourways as "teeming, stratified, with the shades of human groups, who had met there for tragedy, comedy, farce," and then, in a pocket *tour de force*, relates two millennia of Britain's history in reverse chronological order, as though excavating layer after layer: "men had stood and talked of Napoleon, the loss of America, the execution of King Charles, the burning of the Martyrs, the Crusades, the Norman Conquest, possibly of the arrival of Caesar."[11] Paleolithic, quartz, igneous protrusion, strata, stratified: each fulfills its task in the local context of a phrase, sentence, or paragraph, but taken together all convey Hardy's intensely felt conviction that mere "historicity" cannot capture the temporality of human existence—his requirement that readers see the lives of his characters as vanishingly brief moments in a *durée* so *longue* that it requires an archaeological or geological scale of measurement.

As these instances show, technical language is a necessity for Hardy, not an affectation or an ornament. His fiction would hardly be possible without it. If sheer content were at issue, or the only thing at issue, lay synonyms or circumlocutions would do just as well. Because it isn't, they wouldn't. Beyond its ability to specify quartz or distinguish paleo- from neolithic, technical language brings with it a vision of the world. To refer to a loose piece of rock as an igneous protrusion into surrounding sedimentary strata is to write from within and ask readers to inhabit an understanding of the planet informed by uniformitarianism, the rock cycle, and deep

[8] Thomas Hardy, *Two on a Tower* (1882; London: Macmillan, 1975), 127.

[9] James Lubbock, *Pre-historic Times: As Illustrated by Ancient Remains, and the Manners and Customs of Modern Savages* (London and Edinburgh: Williams and Norgate, 1865), 2.

[10] Thomas Hardy, *A Pair of Blue Eyes* (1873; London: Macmillan, 1975), 219.

[11] Thomas Hardy, *Jude the Obscure* (1895; Oxford: Oxford University Press, 2008), 111.

time—as well as the dwarfing of the human they all imply. Turning to the *OED* again, we find the following under the entry for "technical" as an adjective: "Of a writer, book, etc.: using or dealing with terms that belong to a particular subject or field; treating a subject in a specialist way; requiring specialist knowledge to be understood."[12] In all three senses Hardy is a technical writer, and his novels technical books.

That this is so becomes still clearer in instances where Hardy, like other technical writers, inducts readers into new lexical and conceptual worlds by defining his terms. At one point in *The Return of the Native*, Clym Yeobright, the native of the title, takes refuge in a corner of Egdon Heath after arguing with his mother about his involvement with Eustacia Vye, who will herself soon join him. "The scene," the narrator relates, "seemed to belong to the ancient world of the carboniferous period, when the forms of plants were few, and of the fern kind; when there was neither bud nor blossom, nothing but a monotonous extent of leafage amid which no bird sang."[13] Like "stratified" in *Jude*, "carboniferous" functions in part figuratively, along the lines of an analogy or simile. Clym and Eustacia are not time travelers, nor have they stumbled on some miraculously preserved remnant of "the eighty-million-year period which began 350 million years ago" ("carboniferous period" per Nancy Barrineau, who compiled the notes for the Oxford Classics edition of *Return* (408n)). Rather, they find themselves in a lush, flowerless, ferny, and silent hollow. The completeness of that description may seem to render "carboniferous" redundant. But the word, first used by W. D. Conybeare and William Phillips in their *Outlines of the Geology of England and Wales* (1822), provides something the description alone cannot: a frame for Clym and Eustacia's romance measured in hundreds of millions of years and including evolutionary changes so dramatic, so barely conceivable, as the advent of flowering plants and birds.[14] George Levine writes that in such moments in Hardy's works the "narrative drive itself gives way to the world that is the condition for the story's unfolding."[15] Here, as so often, that world is a technical one, signaled by a single word. Every technical term derives from a more or less elaborate system of nomenclature—a system that itself corresponds to and instantiates a more or less elaborate set of practices and concepts. Thus every technical term figures both as itself and as a synecdoche for the whole of which it forms a part, carrying that whole along with it.

So, too, every dialect term. Consider the two from *The Return of the Native* mentioned earlier, both deployed by the narrator: "With a speäker, or stake, he tossed the outlying scraps of fuel into the conflagration"; "To dissipate in some measure her abiding sense of the murkiness of human life she went to the 'linhay'

[12] *OED Online*, s.v. "technical."

[13] Thomas Hardy, *The Return of the Native* (1878; Oxford: Oxford University Press, 2008), 200. Subsequent references cited parenthetically in the text.

[14] W. D. Conybeare and William Phillips, *Outlines of the Geology of England and Wales* (London: William Phillips, 1822).

[15] George Levine, *Reading Thomas Hardy* (Cambridge: Cambridge University Press, 2017), 116.

or lean-to shed, which formed the root-store of their dwelling" (21, 121). In context, neither "speäker" nor "linhay" seems necessary; the synonyms "stake" and "lean-to shed," given immediately, provide a clear picture of action and setting. But like "carboniferous," these dialect words give evidence of a congeries of distinct knowledges and practices that, taken together, amount to something like a worldview. If it is more difficult to say than in the case of terms drawn from a profession or a science what that worldview might consist of, the necessity for conveying it via a specialized lexicon may thereby be increased rather than lessened. Hardy needs the things themselves, but he also, and possibly more urgently, needs his characters' words for those things.

Those words much more frequently occur in character speech than as part of the narration, and when they do they go undefined. For readers who do not themselves speak the dialect in question, and in the absence of editorial annotations or a dialect dictionary, such words incarnate jargon as birdsong. Just listen: heling, slittering, fess, strawmote, stunpoll, weasand, kex, outstep, mandy, withywind, scroff, scammish, mollyhorning, ooser, twanky, bruckle. Peppering the speech of the uneducated Wessex characters in *The Return of the Native*, these dialect terms collapse the distinction between two kinds of work that technical language performs: their sensuous appeal or "earworthiness," to borrow Seamus Heaney's tribute to Barnes's Dorset dialect poems, itself guarantees verisimilitude.[16] Thus Grandfer Cantle, who wields the speäker, says about Clym's mother: "I don't care for her, be jowned if I do, and so I told her" (23). To render this sort of character on the page convincingly requires rendering his distinctive speech, in this instance including both the dialect term "jowned" and inverted word order ("and so I told her"). Readers can guess what "jowned" might mean; nothing, however, requires them to know for certain, and the exclusion produced by not knowing is also a form of inclusion, realizing the novel's distinctions between us and them, here and there, now and then.

That the narrator belongs to both worlds establishes and undermines those binaries all at once. The narration takes place in standard English, which presumes "our" world as the default, measured against which the world of Wessex dialect stands revealed as narrow and benighted. Eustacia's tragedy inheres precisely in her experience of that contrast as concentrated with full force on her alone: her sense of entrapment by the local, by the locale. She longs for Paris but also and more tellingly for the fictional seaside resort of Budmouth where she grew up—depicted on Hardy's maps of Wessex as scarcely 20 miles distant from Egdon Heath. Her *bovarysme*, which leads to her death just as it leads to the death of the Flaubert character memorialized in its name, pits modernity and freedom against the heath, the oppressive beliefs and customs of the people who live there, and the dialect they speak. But dialect in *The Return of the Native* does not feature only as a figure for

---

[16] Seamus Heaney quoted in T. L. Burton and K. K. Ruthven, "Dialect Poetry, William Barnes and the Literary Canon," *ELH* 76.2 (2009): 309–41; 312.

imprisonment. Clym, having returned from a place where people do not say jowned, kex, or mollyhorning, no longer speaks like a native, but he is one. Like the narrator, like Hardy himself, he moves across barriers others find impenetrable (by virtue of class, education, or gender). In the same way as the language of geology or paleontology, dialect can expand rather than diminish—at least for those not confined to it and so by it.

The Places of Dialect

Dialect belongs to a group of people by virtue of where (and when) they happen to live, but it was, in the eighteenth century, treated as similar to technical language: Samuel Johnson, writing in the *Rambler* in 1751, declined to use "the dialect of grammarians" in favor of plain speech.[17] A century on, in another nicely ironic example, Henry Reed writes in *Lectures on the British Poets* (1857) that Chaucer and Gower "lay aside the learned dialect and reveal the unknown powers of common speech."[18] Dialect seems to harden into exclusively regional, geographically specific language only toward the second half of the nineteenth century, "the golden age of English dialectology," according to T. L. Burton and K. K. Ruthven, "thanks to an English Dialect Society which by 1896 had published seventy-six books on regional speech in preparation for Joseph Wright's monumental *English Dialect Dictionary* (1898–1905)."[19] If a language is a dialect with an army and a navy (an adage popularized by the Yiddishist Max Weinreich, who overheard it at a lecture he was giving), then a dialect might be described as a defenseless language, and Hardy's work, as a novelist but also as an editor, is a good place to begin exploring its vulnerability.

Hardy took on only one editorial project, and that was his edition of *The Select Poems of William Barnes* published in 1908. He liberally edited the poems but left no ellipses, asterisks, brackets, or other typographical indicators to mark his interventions. It seems that he particularly minded explanations and narrative, especially of a religious variety. He asked his publisher, Walter Raleigh, if it "would be possible to curtail a poem occasionally, so as to be able to include it?" Raleigh's answer: "You should have perfect freedom to omit stanzas."[20] In the event, Hardy cut material from nearly half of Barnes's poems, thirty-five of which were reduced by between one-quarter and one-half.[21]

Such severe pruning comports oddly with Hardy's lament in the obituary he wrote for Barnes: "with his death was lost probably the most interesting link between

---

[17] Samuel Johnson, *The Rambler* 86 (January 12, 1751): 60.

[18] *OED Online*, s.v. "dialect."   [19] Burton and Ruthven, "Dialect Poetry," 310.

[20] W. J. Keith, "Thomas Hardy's Edition of William Barnes," *Victorian Poetry* 15.2 (Summer 1977): 121–31; 126.

[21] Keith, "Thomas Hardy's Edition," 126.

present and past forms of rural life that England possess'd."[22] But "interesting links" perhaps require missing links to make them useful to a canonical English novelist who is also heavily identified with the use of dialect. "In canonical Victorian literature, regional speech is acceptable only when it is embedded in a standard English narration," write Burton and Ruthven; we see this not only in Hardy but also in writers as various as Scott, Emily Brontë, and Elizabeth Gaskell.[23] Standard English surrounds "dialect," keeping it safely within its confines. And because the author of the dialect is identical to the author of the standard English in the text, the differences in class and education associated with "regional" as measured against "standard" are implicitly addressed. Annotated editions of Hardy's novels (and of course other novels too) often include footnotes explaining allusions to Milton or the Wandering Jew, with a sub-set that assigns the label "dialect" to out-of-the-way words followed by a colon and a "standard" definition. In *The Return of the Native*, for instance, we find "reddle" identified as dialect and defined (in the *Norton Critical Edition*, at any rate). But compare the *Sunday Telegraph* for February 1, 2004, the house and garden section of which notes: "The rusty red of the Calico House's decoration comes from a pigment known as reddle, which is derived from iron ore." The word is not identified as a dialect term, and there is no reference to Hardy. "Reddle" lives on outside of Wessex, Dorset, and *The Return of the Native*. It often seems almost random when a word is assigned to "dialect" and when a word is simply defined because it is obscure. In fact, it probably is random.

And yet dialect has to do with knowing a place. In the introduction to his edition of Barnes's poetry, Hardy writes, with a distinct note of melancholy: "Since [Barnes's] death education in the West of England has gone on with its silent and inevitable effacements, reducing the speech of this country to uniformity, and obliterating every year many a fine old local word."[24] "Effacements" and "obliterating" trope dialect words as monumental or concrete, as though they were of a piece with the architecture and landscape to which they pertain. Local words make local worlds: Elizabeth Carolyn Miller describes language as providing a "bioregional ethic, one that imagines human characters, the environment in which they live, and the complex, reciprocal relations between them."[25] A bioregional ethic requires a specialized language, and although dialect is often imagined as simply a transcription of speech (as if there could be such a thing), Patrick Joyce reminds us to be suspicious of positing "a realm of 'real' or 'authentic'...experience anterior to its verbal significations,

[22] Hardy quoted in Martin Dubois, "William Barnes's Economy," *Cambridge Quarterly* 41.3 (September 2012): 301–71; 303.

[23] Burton and Ruthven, "Dialect Poetry," 311.

[24] William Barnes, *Select Poems of William Barnes, Chosen and Edited with a Preface and Glossarial Notes by Thomas Hardy* (London: Henry Frowde, 1908), iii.

[25] Elizabeth Carolyn Miller, "Dendrographic Realism," *Victorian Studies* 58:4 (Summer 2016): 696–718; 710.

rather than seeing that language itself is constitutive of experience."[26] Joyce conveys both the impossibility and the consequentiality of attempts to render dialect on the page.

Dialect, both in and outside of novels, is itself a fiction. Hardy and Barnes were middle-class, educated writers using a connection to local speech to educate and preserve as well as to prove their authenticity and connection to a non-literary, even non-literate milieu. Such projects are deeply technical at every level, from spellings and rhymes to notes and glossaries. Barnes "makes up" Dorset in a language he hears in a particular way and transcribes according to his own lights (his own ears) as well as via existing conventions. In the process, place is concealed as much as revealed. Nadia Nurhussein points out that "dialect strains the intimacy between the writer and his or her audience. The loss of intimacy is the result of the intense focus—of reader and writer—on an unusual printed text."[27] So dialect, like technical language, can serve to exclude those who do not speak it, confirming a competency and a belonging to those who do. And like reading the technical, reading dialect takes on added dimensions and demands added labor: the medium is both the message and the scrim that suggests that you can't actually get there from here. Just as Hardy's maps of Wessex float above an actual Dorset, dialect floats above a spoken language and is redrawn again and again.

In *The World, the Text and the Critic*, Edward Said notes that writing "takes place."[28] We are regularly caught in the medium of languages not our own, and need to come up with a language to make that language more meaningful, more resonant, more, for lack of a better word (and there is always a lack of a better word), real. It is such restoration work that technical reading undertakes. Hardy, a restorer of various kinds himself, may or may not have approved.

The Work of Language

Using one of the geological terms Hardy found indispensable, Mikhail Bakhtin writes that

> language is stratified not only into linguistic dialects in the strict sense of the word...but also—and for us this is the essential point—languages that are socio-ideological: languages of social groups, "professional" and "generic" languages, languages of generations and so forth.[29]

---

[26] Patrick Joyce, *Visions of the People: Industrial England and the Question of Class, 1848–1914* (Cambridge: Cambridge University Press, 1991), 267.

[27] Nadia Nurhussein, *Rhetorics of Literacy: The Cultivation of American Dialect Poetry* (Columbus, OH: Ohio State University Press, 2013), 17.

[28] Edward W. Said, *The World, the Text, and the Critic* (Cambridge, MA: Harvard University Press, 1983), 129.

[29] Mikhail M. Bakhtin, *The Dialogic Imagination: Four Essays*, trans. Caryl Emerson and Michael Holquist (1934–35; Austin: University of Texas Press, 1981), 271–2.

The technical term for this conception of language is heteroglossia, and the Bakhtinian reading of the novel as the literary space for dialogized heteroglossia, which is to say of different socio-ideological languages put into conversation with one another, helps us grasp the work of technical language and dialect as a technical language in literature. As we've argued above, and despite the fact that Bakhtin distinguishes between "linguistic dialects in the strict sense of the word" and "languages that are socio-ideological," dialect words must themselves be understood as shot through with a particular perspective on the world, so that simultaneous with dialect's subordination to standard English in Hardy's fiction (and elsewhere) is its implicit and sometimes explicit challenge to the values of the "standard." As Gillian Beer has written in her searching essay on *Return*: "The reader...enacts all the diverse phases of cultural experience within the span of Hardy's language, not in sequence only but alongside and in contestation with each other."[30] If the concept of dialect distinguishes regional from standard by subordinating the former to the latter, it nonetheless in the same gesture proliferates alternatives, cross-hatching the synchronic with the diachronic, bending the two axes into nearly parallel lines.

But the potential challenge posed by these alternatives may seem foreclosed at the outset insofar as for nineteenth-century regionalists, Hardy among them, the existence of "regions" as such testifies to an asynchronous synchronicity. In *The Return of the Native*, speäkers and linhays, like Propp's stoves, are archaic. Dialect may resemble technical language, that is, but if so it comes closer to the language of alchemy than quantum physics. Or, better, the language of sailing: for although the age of sail has come and gone, small groups of people here and there still communicate using words like tack, wing-and-wing, kedge, and even fothering. We could describe such words as "survivals," in Victorian anthropologist E. B. Tylor's coinage: "processes, customs, opinions, and so forth, which have been carried on by force of habit into a new state of society different from that in which they had their original home."[31] In one of the most technical moments in *The Return of the Native*, Hardy himself invokes "survival" in the Tylorean sense, in the process parsing its difference from "revival": "while in the revival all is excitement and fervor, the survival is carried on with a stolidity and absence of stir which sets one wondering why a thing that is done so perfunctorily should be kept up at all" (120). The survival in question is the mummers' performance of the play of St. George, in which Eustacia Vye becomes an unlikely, passionate, and nervous actor with the goal of entering the Yeobright home, a place that has been off-limits to her because of her class and because she is not native to this Wessex hamlet. Dialect may also provide readers who are not local with a kind of excitement, an entrée into another world or the pretense of one. Dialect takes on the lineaments of a survival as soon as it gets called

---

[30] Gillian Beer, "Can the Native Return?," in *Open Fields: Science in Cultural Encounter* (Oxford: Oxford University Press, 1996), 53.

[31] Edward B. Tylor, *Primitive Culture: Researches into the Development of Mythology, Philosophy, Religion, Art, and Custom*, 2 vols. (London: John Murray, 1871), 1: 15.

dialect. All technical languages, too, live in the shadow of superannuation, the moment when they will be excluded rather than excluding. Meanwhile, they do their appointed work—in literature as well as out.

FURTHER READING

Cohen, Margaret. *The Novel and the Sea*. Princeton: Princeton University Press, 2010.
Freedgood, Elaine. *The Ideas in Things: Fugitive Meaning in the Victorian Novel*. Chicago: University of Chicago Press, 2006.
Freedgood, Elaine, and Cannon Schmitt, eds. *Denotatively, Technically, Literally*. Special issue of *Representations* 125.1 (Winter 2014).
McDowell, Paula. *The Invention of the Oral: Print Commerce and Fugitive Voices in Eighteenth-Century Britain*. Chicago: University of Chicago Press, 2016.
Schmitt, Cannon. "Tidal Conrad (Literally)." *Victorian Studies* 55.1 (Autumn 2012): 8–29.
Sorenson, Janet. *Strange Vernaculars: How Eighteenth-Century Slang, Cant, Provincial Languages, and Nautical Jargon Became English*. Princeton: Princeton University Press, 2017.

11

POSTCRITICAL

RITA FELSKI

What is the relationship between academic reading and reading for pleasure? Between the furrowed brow of the scholar deciphering an intractable subtext and the blissful mien of the subway rider devouring a bestseller? These scenes of reading are usually felt to have little in common; literary critics define their own *modus operandi against* the enthusiasms and effusions of non-expert readers. What I call "postcritical reading" slices across this dichotomy of skeptical detachment versus naïve attachment. It is not so much a specific method—an interpretative technique akin to deconstruction or symptomatic reading—as it is an orientation, or rather a reorientation: a rethinking of how we read and why reading matters.

George Steiner offers a detailed gloss on the figures of the critic versus the reader. He contrasts the judicial authority of the former, who steps back from the text in order to decipher it more closely, to what he calls the "dynamic passivity" of the latter, who wants to be taken over by the text and to merge with it. For critics, the text is an object to be appraised; for readers, it is an encounter based on closeness and vulnerability.[1] The perceived chasm between professional and lay readers has only widened in recent decades; literary scholarship has become increasingly specialized, its language ever more knotty and forbidding. Publication-for-tenure is heavily skewed toward exercises in contextual explanation and historical argument. It is also likely to involve forays into political or philosophical critique: either interrogating a text's complicity with taken-for-granted assumptions or elucidating how it cannily subverts those same assumptions. The prevailing ethos of literary criticism is one of knowingness, wariness, and skepticism: its preferred techniques those of defamiliarizing and denaturalizing. That such methods seem distant from everyday reading is precisely the point—not only because they serve as a means of academic credentialing but because the professed aim of much work in literary studies is to challenge the tyranny of the commonsensical and commonplace.

---

[1] George Steiner, "'Critic'/'Reader,'" *New Literary History* 10.3 (1979): 423–52; 438.

What I call postcritical reading takes a different tack. It pivots on the idea of attachment as much as detachment, grapples with the intricacies of feeling as well as thought, and acknowledges the lively agency of artworks rather than treating them as objects to be deciphered, diagnosed, and dispatched to their proper context. It is not a replication or continuation of lay reading—which would render it worthless in an academic milieu—nor an excuse for anti-intellectualism: figuring out why literature matters raises a formidable array of questions. It does not scorn or suspend standard techniques of literary analysis (close attention to genre, narrative, metaphor, point of view, irony...) but deploys them to differing ends. Rather than looking critically at what a text represents or fails to represent, it asks other questions: What does a text do? What does it set in motion? What ties a text to its readers? How does it affect those readers? Such questions can do better justice to the work of literature—the specific *work* that literature does, whether in the classroom or the world—while also leaving room for contingency and surprise.

Meanwhile, the postcritical, as the word indicates, is shaped by the legacy of critique: literary studies has been transformed—largely for the better—by its decades-long engagement with Sigmund Freud and Michel Foucault, Edward Said and Gayatri Spivak. Yet it is time to reassess aspects of this legacy, including its *epistemological asymmetry*: the promptness to explain what other people want and do (but never one's own desires and actions!) in terms of hidden structures they fail to understand. Joli Jensen puts it well:

> to reduce what other people do to dysfunction or class position or psychic needs or socioeconomic status is to reduce others to uninteresting pawns in a game of outside forces and to glorify ourselves as somehow off the playing field, observing and describing what is really going on.[2]

In literary studies this asymmetry is given a specific spin. Whether their stance is celebratory or censorious, critics tend to read literary works closely, with due attention to textual detail. Yet lay *responses* to these works are often held at arm's length; dismissed; patronized; derided as naïve. To be schooled in literary analysis is to leave such responses behind, to undergo an intellectual and a sentimental education, to swap emotional entrancement for hard-nosed argument. And yet, not only is ordinary reading more varied and multi-faceted than critics have acknowledged; it is also less remote from academic interpretation than they have assumed.

Some scholars, to be sure, have treated non-elite readers and "ordinary" forms of response with respect—see a significant body of work on the history of the book and the history of reading. My own thinking, meanwhile, owes a debt to British cultural studies, which has long insisted that consumers of popular culture are neither dupes nor dopes. Yet a singular strength of cultural studies also turns out to

---

[2] Joli Jensen, "Fandom as Pathology: The Consequences of Characterization," in *The Adoring Audience: Fan Culture and Popular Media* (London: Routledge, 1992), 9–26; 26.

be a weakness; its focus on specific audiences and demographics—Harlequin romance readers or heavy metal fans—has also curtailed its impact. The very framing of such responses as "other"—as the property of a group that is not one's own—lets literary critics off the hook. It allows them to keep these responses at arm's length or to ignore them completely; to dismiss audience studies as being of purely sociological interest; to evade, in short, their normative implications and their challenge to a certain academic self-image. What Deidre Lynch writes about the study of English holds true for the humanities generally: opposition between a specialized guild of interpreters concerned with knowledge and meaning, and a broader public driven by feeling and pleasure, creates a very partial and limited picture of both.[3]

In recent books, I've made the case for a criticism that is more fully attuned to the reasons why people read literature and to the force of aesthetic attachments. Not only have experiences of identification and recognition, immersion and absorption not yet received their academic due, but they shape both popular *and* scholarly response in ways we have failed to acknowledge. My account of enchantment, for example, juxtaposes a queer theorist poring over the words of James Joyce and Virginia Woolf with a working-class woman entranced by a Hollywood movie (Mia Farrow in *The Purple Rose of Cairo*). In spite of their obvious differences (the meticulous parsing of language and style versus the immersion in a fictional world), the scenarios are linked by a shared experience of intense and enigmatic pleasure.[4] These and other forms of response need to be grappled with in all their phenomenological complexity and social variety. They are distinctively aesthetic insofar as they involve engagement with fiction and form, language and mood; and yet such aesthetic affinities cannot be quarantined from audiences' ethical concerns or worldly affiliations.

In searching for a vocabulary to capture this engagement, I am drawn to the language of *attachment*. The idea of "aesthetic experience" is weighed down by a certain intellectual legacy that makes it less than helpful for my purposes. Not only is it commonly conjugated in the singular—as if literature and art afforded only one kind of appropriate response—but it tends to conjure up the picture of a purely subjective drama played out in individual minds. And yet our feelings about a novel, for example, are colored by multiple factors: a trenchant or effusive review; its presence on a college syllabus; whether it's admired by our friends or our foes; scraps of knowledge about a specific author. "Literary evaluation," remarks James Wood, cannot be separated from "the general messiness of being alive... Your love of Chekhov might be influenced by the knowledge that he named one of his dachshunds Quinine."[5] The experience of reading is not dictated by an all-powerful text, nor orchestrated by the devious agencies of an all-embracing "historical

---

[3] Deidre Lynch, *Loving Literature: A Cultural History* (Chicago: University of Chicago Press, 2015).
[4] Rita Felski, *Uses of Literature* (Oxford: Wiley-Blackwell, 2008).
[5] James Wood, *The Nearest Thing to Life* (Waltham, MA: Brandeis University Press, 2015), 75.

context." Rather, it is a matter of specific things coming together; the singular qualities of Chekhov's writings, to be sure, but also, perhaps, a battered biography unearthed in a secondhand bookstore; a course on Russian literature taken in college; a friend's account of an off-Broadway performance of *Uncle Vanya*.

What kind of entailments does the word "attachment" bring? To be attached is to be hooked or tied, but also to be affected or moved. We often associate stickiness with being stuck in place; as something that constrains our freedom and impedes our mobility. Yet things move, and we move with them; we travel, and our attachments come along for the ride. We are talking about Velcro rather than superglue; parts that connect but also rub against each other; that can be unhooked and rehooked. Stickiness is not something to be regretted or repudiated, the condition of all those unable to slide through the world with sufficient dexterity and ease. It is, rather, a non-negotiable aspect of our being in the world. Literary scholars may extol the merits of unbinding and unraveling, negativity and non-identity, but our practices—of reading, writing, teaching, talking—tell a different story, relying on myriad ties to persons, texts, things, and institutions.

Attachment, as I use it here, has little to do with "attachment theory": the school of psychological thought that focuses on emotional bonds between infant and parent. It is not about being diagnostic, being therapeutic, or explaining reading via the psychic dramas of early childhood. Rather than shifting from the objective to the subjective, the move is from bifurcation (literature versus society) to relation. This means zeroing in on differing *kinds* of attachment as they shape the experience of reading. Attachments, after all, can be physical—the dog-eared book I carry around with me; institutional—the novel that crops up every year on my syllabus; cognitive—the essay that gave me a new intellectual vocabulary; ethical or political— the commitments that inform my response to a work of fiction.

The focus of postcritique, in short, is on *what carries weight*. Its key concept— attachment—invites us to re-evaluate the significance and salience of ties. How does a novel entice or enlist us, how does a song surprise or seduce us? Why do we bridle when a friend belittles a book we admire or fall into a funk when a favored TV series comes to an end? Why do we care? The default in literary studies is to see ties as synonymous with coercion and control, regulation and discipline. Literature is thus prized for its potential to break bonds and rupture connections. The line of thought I take here (drawn from actor-network theory) sees things differently; ties are not just forms of restraint or encroachment but inescapable conditions of being. As Bruno Latour remarks, the choice is not between attached or emancipated, but between being well or poorly bound.[6] The language of attachment, moreover, speaks directly to the topic of this volume; whatever else it may be, reading is undeniably a tie between readers and texts. Let us briefly look at three aspects of the tie of reading: affective attachment; ethical and political attachment; and attachment as co-making.

---

[6] Bruno Latour, "From the Concept of Network to the Concept of Attachment," *Res* 36 (1999): 20–31; 22.

Literary critics are starting to register the limits of purely cognitive approaches to art and to chafe at an exclusive focus on language and interpretation. Reading a novel, for example, may involve a thick swirl of emotions, moods, and sensations that standard techniques of deciphering or deconstructing are poorly equipped to address. While critics are turning to affect, however, they rarely own up to their own. Feelings are theorized, historicized, contextualized but not taken on board as part of one's own response. And yet emotions are hardly absent in literary studies, where we find widespread devotion to specific authors; pleasure at teaching a favorite novel; and irritation at seeing it dragged through the mud by obtuse critics or greeted with apathy by students. This avoidance stems, without a doubt, from anxiety about being seen as overly emotive, lacking in rigor and sophistication—and focusing on oneself at the expense of the text. How might these concerns be mitigated?

Here a turn to the language of mood may prove helpful. Mood bridges the gap between thought and feeling; not just Gothic novels and lyric poetry but ironic works of postmodern metafiction convey a mood. It also cuts across divisions of subject and object; we do not have a mood but are in a mood that may emanate from elsewhere. Think, for example, of Austrian writer Thomas Bernhard: master of the tirade, the diatribe, the rant. A typical Bernhard novel consists of a single unbroken paragraph of insults, invectives, and exaggerations spewing from the mouth of a monomaniacal narrator. The defining mood of Bernhard's work, we might say, is *irritation*: what are his narrators if not the quintessential bad-mouthers and fault-finders? Thanks to their endless hectoring and haranguing, sound take precedence over sense; selfhood sags and sways under the torrential force of words gone wild. The reader is bludgeoned by repetition heaped on repetition, by a flood of verbal tics and manic twitches. Attending to mood does not take one away from the text, but deeper into it, to figure out the formal and aesthetic means by which it achieves its effects as well as its attraction. What is the draw of irritation? Why is Bernhard one of the most admired and widely imitated of European novelists? And as we see here, readers can be deeply attached to the vicious and the venomous; nothing about attachment implies a restriction to positive emotions.

The claim that attachment is affective is likely to meet with nods of assent; that it is normative may well inspire a horrified recoil. The language of norms and values has been cast under a cloud in recent decades, widely hailed as hierarchical, exclusionary, authoritarian, coercive. And yet castigating value does not remove one from the field of value. Excoriations of bourgeois hypocrisy or of structural racism carry their own normative force; ethical as well as political criteria are in play, even if they are not fully spelled out. It is impossible to escape value frameworks; we cannot help orienting ourselves to what we take to be the better rather than the worse. The language of attachment allows us to approach these issues from another angle. Norms and values are things we act on but also that act on us. These actions are not simply coercive; they also energize, galvanize, motivate, give weight to our words. Words like justice and freedom have inspired rumblings of discontent, utopian visions, militant manifestos, marches, sit-ins, revolutions large and small.

Such attachments, meanwhile, cannot help but influence our reading, filtering what we perceive and respond to, shaping assessments of narrative, character, and situation. We do not leave our core commitments at the door, like a pair of muddy boots, when we enter the pages of a book. Of course, literary works may also spur us to rethink these commitments or to reconfigure them in ways we did not anticipate. I've talked elsewhere about how Eva Hoffman's remarkable memoir of migration, *Lost in Translation*, pushes back against prevailing ideals of cosmopolitanism, rootlessness, and cultural hybridity. Relocated to Canada and then to the United States, highly literate and schooled at Harvard, Hoffman embodies many aspects of these ideas; and yet her memoir is also a poignant love letter to her native country of Poland and a grieving for all that she has lost. "Nostalgia has often had a bad press in contemporary theory," I wrote. "*Lost in Translation* offers a rich and multifaceted description of what it means to be affectively tied to another country, or to the past, as being far more than an intellectual error or a 'myth of origin.'"[7] After reading Hoffman's book, I'm less quick to dismiss all expressions of cultural nationalism and love of home; more attuned to the potential force of what she calls a geography of emotion.[8] A realignment of perception has taken place. As Paul Ricoeur points out, aesthetics is tangled up with ethics; literature and art serve as an ethical laboratory that allows for unique forms of experimentation with values.[9] Striving to purify acts of reading—insisting that to read literature "as literature" is to excise all traces of our ethical or political concerns—is an exercise in futility. We are *animated* by values in the reading of literature as well as in life.

That sociopolitical identities are not natural, unified, or self-evident, for example, is a point that certainly needs to be made. Yet the deconstruction of such categories has become a rote activity among academics that tells us nothing about why they continue to matter—why certain ideas serve as symbolic glue, why specific images of selfhood stick. Here again, a reorientation—from the language of identity to attachment—opens up new ways of thinking. The latter term conveys that bonds are forged, not found; that they can be made and unmade, but that they will not be magicked into non-existence by theoretical critiques and intellectual sleights-of-hand. Identity, meanwhile, is limited to persons, whereas attachments can be to many other things: objects, places, ideas, styles, moods, memories, dreams, words.

One reason literary critics are sometimes leery of standard forms of social explanations is that reading can often feel like a turn away from the social; an act of refusal or withdrawal, a spurning or renunciation of communal bonds; an experience

---

[7] Rita Felski, "Comparison and Translation: A View from Actor-Network Theory," *Comparative Literature Studies* 53.4 (2016): 747–65; 758.

[8] Eva Hoffman, *Lost in Translation: A Life in a New Language* (New York: Penguin, 1980).

[9] Paul Ricoeur, *Time and Narrative*, trans. Kathleen McLaughlin and David Pellauer, 3 vols. (Chicago: University of Chicago Press, 1984), 1: 59.

of solitude or introspection. We might think here of Orhan Pamuk's novel *The New Life*: one of the most dramatic literary descriptions of what such an experience can feel like. "I read a book one day and my whole life was changed. Even on the first page, I was so affected by the book's intensity I felt my body sever itself and pull away from the chair... What if I raised my eyes from the book and looked around at my room, my wardrobe, my bed, or glanced out of the window, but did not find the world as I knew it?"[10] And yet, while reading may sever certain connections to the world, it also forges other ties: to the intricacies of a style or the architecture of a literary world; to incandescent ideas or half-buried memories; to the smell and feel of books or the endless promise of an untouched archive. Many of our attachments have nothing to do with persons.

Pamuk's description might cause us to assume that the book is the sole agent: the reader, nothing but a helpless victim. Yet things are not so straightforward. The question of agency—who does what to whom in the act of reading—has been taken up repeatedly in literary studies, from wildly different perspectives. Literary works are sometimes seen as all-powerful artefacts, manipulating and disciplining their readers, schooling them in imperialism or neo-liberalism. Conversely, they are also depicted as hollow and insubstantial entities, their meanings created entirely by the communities of readers who interpret them, as in the work of Stanley Fish.[11] Literature is neither all-powerful nor powerless, neither a sovereign nor a slave. It is distinctive; its existence makes a difference; it has undeniable and sometimes far-reaching effects. And yet these effects would not be possible without the help of numerous participants, including readers who submit to being seized by a literary work, in a complex dynamic that blends activity and passivity.

A view of reading as co-creation may bring the tradition of hermeneutics to mind—a philosophy of interpretation that emphasizes reading as an act of co-making and dynamic interaction. We cannot help but bring our selves, with their assumptions and pre-judgments, to the act of reading; and yet reading may also modify our assumptions, shock us into new forms of recognition, and alter our understanding. As Rebecca Solnit writes:

> The object we call a book is not the real book, but its potential, like a musical score or seed. It exists fully only in the act of being read; and its...home is inside the head of the reader, where the symphony resounds, the seed germinates.[12]

Literature must be actualized by its readers in order to exist. And yet this actualization does not only take place "inside the head," as Solnit suggests. While hermeneutics often focuses on a solitary reader facing a solitary text, the approach I'm arguing for allows for a wider range of actors and attachments. Our perception, after all, is also

---

[10] Orhan Pamuk, *The New Life* (New York: Vintage, 1998), 3–4.

[11] Stanley Fish, "What Makes an Interpretation Acceptable?" in *Is There a Text in This Class? The Authority of Interpretive Communities* (Cambridge, MA: Harvard University Press, 1980), 338–55.

[12] Rebecca Solnit, *The Faraway Nearby* (New York: Penguin, 2013), 63.

shaped by the input of friends, teachers, syllabi, online reviews, such that the question of what comes from the work, the self, or the world can be hard to disentangle.

And yet, even as attachments are co-produced in this way, the specific object of attachment *matters*. This mattering is built into the meaning of attachment: that we care about one thing and not another; that we resist the reduction of this thing (e.g., literature) to something else (e.g., psychological, political, or economic explanation). That literature is mediated, in short, does not diminish or devalue its power; rather, the reverse is true. It is via a forging of connections—the acquisition of know-how, relevant vocabularies, accumulation of examples, honed attention to detail—that literary works become more vividly present to their readers. To the Shakespeare scholar, there is a world of difference between *Henry IV*, *Part 1* and *Part 2*; the Stephen King fan will wax indignant if you confuse *Cujo* and *Christine*. And here the work also plays an indispensable part—it enlists us in ways that we may not anticipate. It orients us in certain ways and draws us down interpretative or perceptual paths. Literary works are not just markers of social status; mirrors of identity; minions of pre-existing linguistic schemes. That they can surprise us, discomfit us, tip us toward affinities or obsessions that we did not anticipate reveals the flimsiness of such claims.

In this context, I'm currently rethinking the much-maligned category of identification. In literary studies, identification is often felt to be slightly shameful: something that "other people" do (the naïve; the uneducated; the simple-minded; the sentimental). Within a leftist tradition stretching back to Bertolt Brecht, it is also targeted as a key mechanism of political conformism and collusion. In identifying with works of fiction, readers are no longer able to read them critically, to skeptically assess their claims. Identification is how readers are "sutured" or sewn into an acceptance of the status quo.

This line of thinking is ripe for reassessment. Tackling the academic disdain for identification as a naïve or "bad" reading practice, Faye Halpern points out that "sophisticated literary critics read to identify as well. The difference comes not from the practice of identification but from the differing *grounds* of identification."[13] While lay readers or undergraduates may talk about identifying with fictional characters, literary critics identify with other elements of literary works, their critique of neo-liberalism or their subversion of Western metaphysics. In the latter case identification is a matter of theoretical or political affinities rather than character-based empathy. It involves, nevertheless, a felt attachment to a literary work, a reading grounded in a perception of salient commonalities.

Identifying, in short, is more commonplace yet also more varied than it is often taken to be. It brings into play ideas and values as well as persons; may confound or remake a sense of self rather than confirming it; and is practiced by skeptical

---

[13] Faye Halpern, "In Defense of Reading Badly: The Politics of Identification in *Benito Cereno*, *Uncle Tom's Cabin*, and Our Classrooms," *College English* 70.6 (2008): 551–77; 556.

scholars as well as wide-eyed enthusiasts. I'm interested in a response I call ironic identification, where a sense of estrangement is the connecting tissue binding character and reader. What is held in common is an experience of having nothing in common, of feeling at a second remove from the mainstream of social life. Quite a few protagonists of modern fiction—solitary, adrift, sardonic, or melancholic—solicit such forms of affiliation: *Nausea, The Stranger, Invisible Man.* And here the vectors of causality are hard to pin down; are readers drawn to fictional figures who crystallize their own feelings of anomie; or are they schooled in feelings of estrangement and ennui by reading works of modernist literature? The result, in either case, is what we might call an alliance of strangers: fictional and real persons connected by a shared sense of disassociation. Identification and irony are often assumed to be mutually exclusive: where one is, the other cannot be. And yet irony turns out to be a surprisingly common mechanism of identification—one that is increasingly pervasive in the academic culture of the humanities. It is not that naïve readers identify and that dispassionate critics don't, but that they find different points of connection—affective, ethical, stylistic, political, or some mix of all these. And if everyone reads to identify, then students' search for moments of affinity turns out to be not so radically different from that of literary critics.

A prizing of detachment has been the boundary condition of literary studies in recent decades, undergirded by diverse philosophical or literary justifications. (We might be tempted to call it a fetish except that such a comparison would be unfair to fetishes.) A postcritical perspective invites us to rethink this view of detachment as an ultimate good-in-itself. Rather, it proposes that we detach from something because we are more attached to something else: specific ideas or beliefs; individual authors or a much-loved novel; an image of the critic as skeptical or dissident figure. Such a reorientation, I believe, gives us a more accurate sense of how criticism functions, while also building bridges between academic and lay reading.

Over the last few years, for example, my students have written remarkable essays on their aesthetic attachments: linking textual analysis to the phenomenological, affective, and political complexities of recognition; the urgency and uncertainty of empathy; art's capacity to enchant and absorb as well as to inspire shock or disgust; fan culture and forms of collective identification. In developing these arguments, they engage in acts of analysis, reflection, and judgment to specific ends. They seek to honor the works they care about and the different reasons why they matter, while offering forceful rebuttals of the view that scholarly reading is irredeemably estranged from, or hostile to, reading for pleasure. Of course, criticism and lay reading are not the same, nor can they be—they serve quite different purposes and functions. A postcritical perspective, however, affords a deeper understanding of not just their differences but also their messy entanglement.[14]

---

[14] The writing of this essay was supported by the Danish National Research Foundation (DNRF 127).

FURTHER READING

Citton, Yves. "Fictional Attachments and Literary Weavings in the Anthropocene." *New Literary History* 47.2–3 (2016): 309–29.

Felski, Rita. *The Limits of Critique*. Chicago: University of Chicago Press, 1995.

Felski, Rita. *Uses of Literature*. Oxford: Wiley-Blackwell, 2008.

Hennion, Antoine. "Attachments, You Say? How a Concept Collectively Emerges in One Research Group." *Journal of Cultural Economy* 10.1 (2017): 112–21.

ENUMERATIVE

ANDREW PIPER

Quantity has always been important to debates about reading. Since antiquity, advice manuals have warned against reading too much. Today, we worry about reading too little. Learning how to read the *right amount* is a venerable tradition in bibliotherapy. Numerology, or the study of the meaningfulness of quantity, has also been integral to textual interpretation since at least late antiquity. Augustine tells us that Peter caught 153 fish because it is the sum of 1 through 17, and seventeen equals ten (the number of commandments) plus seven (the number for the Holy Ghost). Lest one see this as a relic of a more superstitious age, Victor Hugo's epic of modern urban life, *Les Misérables*, contains 365 chapters, one for every day of the year, just as twelve-tone music provided the edifice upon which Thomas Mann would rewrite *Faust* to capture the horrors of the twentieth century. Quantity is a commonplace in books, not just in the content we read but also surrounding it: page numbers, chapter headings, volume numbers, publication dates, series numbers, call numbers, and ISBNs.

Enumerative reading is the attempt to account for quantity when we read, to bring together the sign systems of letters and numbers into a more integrated whole (as in *integer*, to make indivisible). It entails a wide variety of practices that can range from the significance of numbers within texts (why are there 1,001 nights?), to the sheer number of texts (what happens when Latin declines as a share of the European book market?), to the numbers of words or entities that populate texts (why do nineteenth-century novels share a predilection for a vocabulary of prevarication?). Sometimes the latter approach goes by the name distant reading, but this is a moniker that makes little sense in practice. Enumerative reading involves observing the most granular elements (periods, letters, words, phonemes, characters, syntax, numbers, sentences) as well as their most synoptic representation. It is deeply circular, or better yet, elliptical.

To enumerate means to count something out, to establish the number of something; in short, to *tally*. According to the *Oxford English Dictionary* (OED), *tally* derives from the Latin for rod or stick, often notched (in French we get *tailleur* or tailor). Tallying was used as a measure for taxation, or counting one's obligations. Quantity implies accountability—visibility and duration. We may love language, but quantity is more primordially related to inscription. Numbers have typically been more important to write down than words. Interestingly, the word tally is not thought to be etymologically related to the Germanic *tale*, which derives from the word for number (eventually becoming *Zahl* in modern German) and one of whose definitions is "to enumerate." As in numerous languages, there is a deep connection between the idea for counting and that of narration. When we read we are experiencing a recount.

Beginning in about the ninth century, it became common practice to tabulate the gospels by verse. "Canon tables," as they came to be known, provided a navigation tool to the New Testament, offering lists of which verses appeared in which gospels (all four, three, two, one). They were commonly illustrated surrounded by Byzantine archways. Quantity was the portal to theological understanding. By the twentieth century, counting the number of books in print would constitute the foundations of the new *Annales* school of social history. The number of readable things mattered.

One of the earliest ways that the quantity of words, rather than the quantity of books, was thought to be significant was in the work of Rudolf Flesch. Flesch was a Viennese immigrant who fled Austria from the Nazis and came to the US in 1933. He ended up as a student in Lyman Bryson's Readability Lab at Columbia University. The study of "readability" emerged as a full-fledged science in the 1930s, during the Great Depression, when the US government began to invest more heavily in adult education. Flesch's insight, which was based on numerous surveys and studies of adult readers, was simple. While there are many factors behind what makes a book or story comprehensible (i.e., "readable"), the two most powerful predictors are a combination of sentence length and word length. The longer a book's sentences and the longer its words, the more difficult readers will likely find it. Flesch reduced this insight into a single predictive, and somewhat bizarre, formula:

$$206.835 - 1.015 \times \frac{W}{St} - 84.6 \times \frac{Sy}{W}$$

W = number of words
St = number of sentences
Sy = number of syllables

According to Flesch's measure, Rudyard Kipling's *The Jungle Book* has a higher readability score (87.5) than James Joyce's *Ulysses* (81.0). Presidential inaugural speeches have been getting more readable over time. So too have novels. Ann Radcliffe's *Sicilian Romance* (63.5) is considerably more difficult than your average novel today. While there will always be exceptions—Hemingway's short sentences and pared-down vocabulary in *To Have and Have Not* is a good example of a text whose difficulty is not tied to its readability score—Flesch's measure is a remarkably successful way of assessing how difficult a piece of writing is. There are now well over thirty such measures, and the list continues to grow.

While Flesch's work went on to become highly influential within advertising and corporate communication, his greatest contribution lay in his best-selling book, *Why Johnny Can't Read*. It advocated the importance of phonics for developing readers. Flesch's book would become the inspiration for one of the most influential writers of the twentieth century: Dr. Seuss. For English speakers of my generation, quantitative knowledge lurks in the shadows of our most formative reading material.

Beginning in the 1980s with the rise of the field known as "natural language processing," and the subsequent dramatic increase in computing power in the 2000s, quantity would become increasingly important for our understanding of how we read. Premised on the single, straightforward idea of "distributional semantics," this work begins with the idea that language's meaning depends on the frequency of the contextual cues that surround it. Meaning, whether a single word, phrase, or an entire document, can be modeled, according to this view, as a probability distribution of co-occurring words (or sounds or any other kind of feature).

For example, my understanding of the word *bread* depends on the contexts in which I encounter it. Sometimes it will be framed as a food item, sometimes as a religious symbol, and from these "events" I develop a mental model of the word's various meanings. When *bread* is meant to convey a religious sense, it is more likely the case—though by no means guaranteed—that I will find some other theologically inflected language. Meaning is never deterministic. When I read the word *bread* in a new context, I activate this model and test it against the context that I am observing in that moment (just as I am also simultaneously updating my mental model to incorporate this new information). I do this at the document level, as well. When I read a work of fiction, I have a set of expectations about the signs I should encounter based on what I have already read. There can be deviations from my expectations, but overall I have a general sense of what I might expect to find. The more I read, the more sophisticated my model becomes and the more sensitive I am to the significance of variations. This is why in order to train people to be more analytical when they read, we do so in part by asking them to read *more*. Quantity is an essential foundation to interpretation.

This process that I have just described is similar to how we now train machines to read. We enumerate, or tally, the "events" of features within a set of documents and then build a model that tries to approximate the category or ideas that we think they represent. It is important that, at least for now, we call this "reading," or perhaps *reading with*. Machines aren't reading by themselves, or achieving some kind of understanding of what they are reading. We are modeling the way that we think human minds model meaning. Enumerative reading is models all the way down.

Again, there is nothing new about this process. We have always used technology to help us read. The material structure of documents helps us know things in certain ways. The codex allows for random access (à la Augustine). The unadorned page that became more common around the turn of the nineteenth century allows for more immersive reading. The index allows for more non-sequential reading.

And the birth of the critical edition allows for more genealogical reading, a better understanding of where a text comes from. Computational models are in this sense no different. They help us know things in certain ways (and not know other things). Despite their macrocosmic claims, computational models are perspectival.

So what are these perspectives? What are the *dispositions* of enumerative reading? I see three primary ones, though others may find more. The first is the way enumerative reading is highly self-reflexive. It turns my mind towards the units or elements from which my understanding of or attachment to a text is made. We might call this an awareness of the "lexical unconscious" after Walter Benjamin, who spoke of the optical unconscious with respect to photography.[1] Enumerative reading is very literal. When I engage in it, I explain how many books I have "read," how many features I have looked at, and how many things I have tested. There is a transparency to the machine's learnedness.

On the other hand, in many cases we cannot fully reconstruct how an algorithm arrives at the judgments it makes. As Michael Polanyi has argued, there remains a tacit dimension to knowledge, whether computational or bibliographic.[2] While we have spent a great deal of time worrying over the opacity of algorithms, we have spent far too little time reflecting on the obscurity of critical judgment. Enumerative reading gives us recourse to this self-reflexive knowledge of our judgments, even if necessarily incomplete. Enumerative reading allows me to try to know what I know.

Take for example the semantics of reading. One way to understand the history of reading is to model the semantic context of the word *read* in its various forms (*read, reads, reading, reader, readers*) and observe how these contexts have, or have not, changed over time.[3] What is it that people talk about when they talk about readers and reading? In the accompanying figure you can see a timeline of the words most commonly associated with these different forms of "read" when they appear in novels since the beginning of the nineteenth century down to the present (see Figure 12.1). The first thing you will notice is the remarkable stability of the semantics of reading. When people read in novels, not much has changed. Those small changes, however, tell an interesting story. We can see an approximate moment towards the end of the nineteenth century when "letters" were no longer the most common thing that people read in novels. Books were. And they have stayed that way ever since, despite our imagined digitalness. The Bible too was also displaced, in this case by novels. Paper gains in significance as a medium, quite possibly as "the paper" (i.e., news). It has since been replaced in the present by "text." At the same time, "aloud" surprisingly remains one of the most common words associated with

---

[1] Walter Benjamin, "A Small History of Photography," in *One-Way Street and Other Writings*, trans. Edmund Jephcott and Kingsley Shorter (London: Verso, 1985), 225–39.

[2] "I shall reconsider human knowledge," writes Polanyi, "by starting from the fact that *we can know more than we can tell.*" Michael Polanyi, *The Tacit Dimension* (Chicago: University of Chicago Press, 1966), 14.

[3] The code and data related to this project are located here: https://doi.org/10.7910/DVN/NGGAQ5.

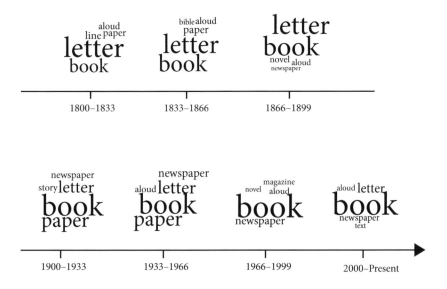

Figure 12.1 Most common words associated with forms of the word "read" in a collection of ~6,500 English-language novels. Image Credit: Eve Kraicer-Melamed.

reading. Contrary to popular wisdom, silent reading is not the only or even the most common way reading is framed in fiction.

There are a host of other stories buried further down in these tables of words, which unfortunately I cannot show here but that are included in the supplementary data. For example, reading becomes considerably more religiously inflected during the mid-nineteenth century, while there is a new emphasis on "poetry" at the beginning of the twentieth. Today, in addition to "bedtime reading," a variety of manuscriptural objects, like diaries and journals, orbit around reading, suggesting the imaginary allure of handwriting in our electronic times.

These insights depend on how context is measured and, of course, which books and how many we take into consideration. Different data will tell a different story. But the process offers an opportunity to reflect on the infrastructures of our knowledge. Through quantity, we take into account the conditions of what we know and how we know it.

The second way enumerative reading disposes us towards our reading material is in its translational nature. Enumeration asks us to move between two different sign systems. In this, I see it as part of the long history of Humanism, which was in many ways founded upon the notion of linguistic and material difference. Humanism was about developing a set of reading practices that fostered the ability to understand the ways in which texts differ between times and places. Translation would emerge as one of its core practices as well as ideals. The knowledge gained in moving between languages, historical epochs, and systems of writing was seen as the highest form of knowledge. Crossing the divide of textual and linguistic difference was a means of potentially crossing the divide to something more spiritually transcendent. Erasmus's bilingual New Testament, which was initially called a new "instrument," might be considered one of this tradition's most important founding documents.

Today, translating texts into quantities has emerged as the overwhelming feature of our cultural moment. Rather than see this as a kind of fallen state, I think we would do well to reposition it within this longer tradition of translational human-ism, to see it as an ongoing attempt to understand the act of commensuration, of making different sign systems compatible with one another. Seen in this way, the literate and the numerate are not agons engaged in a duel, but two components of a more holistic understanding of human mentality.

Finally, enumerative reading disposes us towards our reading material in far more synoptic ways than other forms of reading. It is evident that when examining numerous texts we will move away from more particular observations. What has not been pointed out is that this happens even when we engage with just a few texts. Synoptic statements, not to mention titles, are woven into the fabric of critical dis-course. They too are part of the infrastructure of our knowledge. According to Friedrich Schleiermacher, the so-called father of hermeneutics, these types of state-ments are not aberrant—illicit secretions on the discursive path towards knowledge of particularity—but essential indices of our understanding. As Schleiermacher consistently reminded us, knowledge of the part requires knowledge of the whole. We cannot *not* make such synoptic judgments. Even if we don't explicitly state them in our writing, they are informing our judgments. Enumerative reading foregrounds this process of generalization and subjects it to analysis. It models the conditions through which we arrive at synoptic statements about our reading material.

In his late novel, *Wilhelm Meister's Travels*, Goethe gives us an example of a new kind of modeler, the anatomical sculptor. Instead of being a dissector of dead things (called a *Prosektor* in Goethe's time), he envisions the idea of a *Proplastiker*, some-one who makes in advance, who constructs for the future. In the paradox of the anatomical sculptor, Goethe combines the figure of the dissector, the analyst, with that of the builder, the synthesist. Rather than take individual bodies apart in a kind of second death, the modeler approximates analytical things to come. Analysis, the act of taking apart, and synthesis, the act of piecing together, are imagined to go hand in hand. According to Goethe, we cannot have one without a robust form of the other. This is enumerative reading's ellipse.

For Erasmus, one of Goethe's key predecessors, there was a crucially ethical dimension to synoptic reading. Paraphrase would emerge, perhaps surprisingly, as a vital practice in Erasmus' late output. It was designed, he said, to counter the intel-lectual partisanship of his age. As he wrote in the preface to his *Paraphrase on Acts*, comparing warring humanists to Europe's belligerent kings, "These chaotic enmi-ties between one monarch and another, so fraught with disaster, so implacable, so long-continued, so far beyond all cure—are they not like some desperate sickness of the whole body? Can we discern any part of the world that is immune from the infection of this dread disease? But even more destructive than that is this pestilence, which with its astounding and insoluble conflict of convictions has overmastered all men's minds."[4] The intellectual body politic for Erasmus was being taken apart by too much scholarly particularism. Paraphrase was to be the means through which the overly dissected text could be put back together, and in the process restore a sense of intellectual community. Beginning in 1517, Erasmus, who had already translated and edited the gospels, now turned to paraphrasing them, producing the longest running portion of his entire corpus.

Enumerative reading is the latest inheritor of this humanistic project. With its synoptic aims, it seeks to achieve a sense of community, a "common sense," to the act of interpretation. Through condensation it seeks consensus. Like the anatomical sculptor, it moves past the dissective literalism of the citation towards the synthetic ethos of the model. There is, and has always been, a distinct politics encoded in the act of enumeration.

Enumerative reading thus traverses two imaginary poles in the universe of reading. On the one hand, there is the Pythagorean dream of cosmic order that number signifies. We can find this, for example, in Dante's *Divine Comedy*, where, as Ernst Robert Curtius tells us, "100 cantos take us through three realms (33+33+33+1), the last of which contains 10 heavens. Triads and decads intertwine into unity."[5] When we think about and with numbers, order, form, and beauty are never far from view. On the other hand, there is also the diminutive *model* that number makes visible. We can see this, for example, on display in Goethe's "New Melusina," who lives in a traveling bookcase, or W. G. Sebald's Thomas Abrams, who builds a model of the Temple of Jerusalem for his whole life. Models are childish—playful, quixotic, but also a little bit subversive. Mischief is never far from play. Models tend to mock those who take their own pronouncements too seriously. They undo the certainty and rigidity of divine order.

But Sebald also wanted to remind us of the pain inherent in approximation as well as the potential joy of discovery that such pain entailed. The unreality of models can paralyze us if we get lost in them and never find our way out. But they can also open new worlds. "Now, as the edges of my field of vision darken," says Thomas Abrams, "I sometimes wonder if I will ever finish the Temple and whether all I have done so far has not been a wretched waste of time." After including an image of the Temple that covers both recto and verso and draws the reader's eye into the vanishing point of the book's spine, Sebald continues:

> But on other days, when the evening light streams in through this window and I allow myself to be taken in by the overall view, then I see for a moment the Temple...as if everything were already completed and as if I were gazing into eternity.[6]

---

[4] Desiderius Erasmus, *The Collected Works of Erasmus*, vols. 89 (Toronto: Toronto University Press, 1975), 50: 2–3.

[5] E. R. Curtius, "Numerical Composition," in *European Literature and the Latin Middle Ages* (Princeton: Princeton University Press, 1953), 501–509; 501.

[6] W. G. Sebald, *The Rings of Saturn*, trans. Michael Hulse (New York: New Directions, 1995), 238.

FURTHER READING

Bode, Katherine. *A World of Fiction: Digital Collections and the Future of Literary Study*. Ann Arbor: University of Michigan Press, 2018.

Hammond, Adam. *Literature in the Digital Age: An Introduction*. Cambridge: Cambridge University Press, 2016.

Jockers, Matthew L. *Macroanalysis: Digital Methods and Literary History*. Urbana: University of Illinois Press, 2017.

Moretti, Franco. *Distant Reading*. London: Verso, 2013.

Piper, Andrew. *Enumerations: Data and Literary Study*. Chicago: University of Chicago Press, 2018.

Risam, Roopika, *New Digital Worlds: Postcolonial Digital Humanities in Theory, Praxis, and Pedagogy*. Evanston: Northwestern University Press, 2018.

Shore, Daniel. *Cyberformalism: Histories of Linguistic Forms in the Digital Archive*. Baltimore: Johns Hopkins University Press, 2018.

Turney, Peter D., and Patrick Pantel. "From Frequency to Meaning: Vector Space Models of Semantics." *Journal of Artificial Intelligence Research* 37 (2010): 141–188.

Underwood, Ted. *Distant Horizons: Digital Evidence and Literary Change*. Chicago: University of Chicago Press, 2019.

13

REPEAT

CHRISTINA LUPTON

Proust, Once Again

In honor of this essay, I have started rereading Proust. What a trope, rereading Proust. Julian Barnes recollects Anita Brookner saying that she had just finished a novel and was doing, for a while, exactly as she liked. Teasingly he says: "Well, in your case that probably means rereading Proust." How did he know, she wonders?[1] Still, it's a trope that works. Like the memories Proust conjures to life, mine come rushing back through that keyhole of contact with the first volume of the paperback edition on our shelves. The pink and orange cover transports me back to the heady days of meeting my first great love, when we read Proust aloud to each other in the evenings. All six volumes. Twenty years ago. French names, stumbled over forgivingly. I even find a slip of paper, the user's manual for a digital alarm clock, which we'd used as a bookmark. Rereading takes me right there; leaves me wondering if I can read Proust now. Again? Or for the first time?

Repeat reading happens all the time, of course. As a teacher who returns regularly to a set of books each year or two for class preparation, and a parent entering my second round of reading *Swallows and Amazons* and *Little House on the Prairie* at bedtime, I don't have to go out of my way to engage in it. But repeat reading is also hard to describe. It can be as easily associated with thoroughness as with the dimming down of thought; with populist sentiment, as with the kind of elitism that makes it seem as if some people were just born on their second or third reading of the classics. In 1745, at a time when literate women were supposedly being swept off their feet by the pleasures of fiction, Catherine Talbot wrote to her friend after a day spent reading Milton and Dante:

---

[1] Julian Barnes, "Diary: People Will Hate Us Again," *London Review of Books* 39.8 (April 20, 2017): 41–3; 41.

> Not a new book has showed its head this century, but the comfort is, old ones will bear reading over very often, and I think there is full as much pleasure in reading a very excellent book the fifth or sixth time, as if one had it from the press.[2]

Talbot's friend, Elizabeth Carter, a scholar of classical texts and copious rereader of the texts she was translating from Greek, writes back in enthusiastic agreement: between bookish friends, there is nothing quite like the fifth or sixth reading of the right thing.

Yet repeat readings aren't always compliments to a text or to the reader's discrimination. A twentieth-century steelworker characterizes the bulk of his reading as voracious and hasty until "slowly out of this welter of reading I began to discover the few books which I could go on reading and re-reading."[3] Samuel Johnson describes the merits of Goldsmith's prose lying in the fact that "his plain narrative will please again and again," and E. M. Forster writes affirmatively of his friend's text that "the second time I read it, I enjoyed it more."[4] Certainly, Carter and Talbot's terms—and perhaps Brookner's too—cast rereading as a way to consolidate one's relationship with the right sort of text. In rereading Proust, I hope to become the sort of reader who can claim to know him.

The repeat reader can also be full of anxiety, conscious that a first untutored attempt to internalize a text might have failed. Thomas Hardy despaired for this reason of reading texts a single time as a futile kind of labor:

> I have been led to think again of this by looking over some notes of reading that I took years ago, and finding I had forgotten them entirely. To stick to a few books and read these over and over again is the only way.[5]

Patrick Süskind deems his "amnesia in litteris" a problem so severe that not even a second reading helps: enthusing over a book drawn from his shelves, he encounters his own scrawlings in the margins of a book as those of a stranger whose reactions align mysteriously with his own, struggling to recall the details of even passages he remembers in outline with affection.[6] In this perspective, people reread partly out of fear that class or status or age reduces their mind again to a state of blankness. Without the matrix of prior knowledge and cultural capital, a first reading may not stick. Geoff Dyer, making such self-deprecating representations of his own scholarship the mainstay of essays, describes himself returning, like Süskind, to a familiar copy

---

[2] Elizabeth Carter and Catherine Talbot, *A Series of Letters Between Mrs. Elizabeth Carter and Miss Catherine Talbot, From the Year 1741 to 1770* (London: J. Rivington, 1809), 101.

[3] Quoted in Jonathan Rose, *The Intellectual Life of the British Working Classes* (New Haven: Yale University Press, 2001), 371.

[4] For Johnson, see: James Boswell, *Life of Johnson*, ed. R. W. Chapman (Oxford: Oxford University Press, 1998), 528. For Forster: E. M. Forster, *Selected Letters of E. M. Forster*, ed. Mary Lago and P. N. Furbank, 2 vols. (London: Arena, 1983), 1: 207.

[5] Thomas Hardy to Florence Henniker, *The Collected Letters of Thomas Hardy: 1893–1901*, ed. Richard Little Purdy and Michael Millgate (Oxford: Clarendon Press, 1980), 87.

[6] Patrick Süskind, "Amnesia in Litteris: The Books I Have Read (I Think)," *Harper's* (March 1987): 71–3.

of a D. H. Lawrence novel to find that he has forgotten reading it: "When I re-read *The Rainbow* I thought I might discover, like a flower pressed between the pages, the dried remains of my younger self preserved within it." Despite finding the annotations he made as a student, "there was nothing, no traces of my earlier self, no memories released by the act of re-reading the same page that I had read years before one particular afternoon wherever and whenever that was."[7]

There's also the possibility that repeat reading induces rather than cures amnesia. All kinds of repeat reading make the non-event of our encounter with a familiar text a virtue. Rereadings of the Bible and favorite songs, recipes, forms we've filled in before, and brand names on the toothpaste tube work like this. Gabriel Betteredge, the butler in Wilkie Collins's *The Moonstone*, treats his seventh copy of *Robinson Crusoe* as fetish and talisman, a text to be taken like tonic in times of need and uncertainty. But rather than stirring up emotions, opening the overly familiar novel helps Betteredge return things to their place and resume his position of devoted servitude. Young children sometimes want a certain book read to them so often that a carer learns to recite it without even really seeing the words. Repeat readings can be like the instructions for emergency landings given out on airplanes—we know what they say but have stopped hearing them. At worst this state of repetition approaches the cultural condition Nietzsche described in 1873 as rumination, that of active forgetting and sublimation by which one blithely absorbs the knowledge that might otherwise awaken us to history.[8]

But this kind of textual repetition is not necessarily dull-witted. The association between rereading and affection can be distinguished both from the mindless and the scholarly relations to a text that are forged through rereading. Deidre Lynch argues that literature is born at this juncture, describing it as an approach to books that from the late-eighteenth century onwards seems to "*bear iteration* and also *mandate* it." Reading, she argues, emerges as an activity laced with love precisely at the point where it describes "literature as that which we are always rereading and never reading for the first time."[9] Under these conditions, her readers close in on their object through rituals of re-visitation, with John Clare reading the *Vicar of Wakefield* every winter and Benjamin Disraeli having read *Pride and Prejudice* seventeen times. Through loving the canon, the literary reader becomes in Lynch's terms part of the beat of daily and seasonal time. He may not ruminate, exactly, but he holds a world in balance through habit, partaking of a modern temporal economy in which the circular is restorative and as powerful as the linear.

The avid rereaders of the canon in Lynch's *Loving Literature* are overwhelmingly men of a certain privilege and class. Ownership of books is not essential, but

---

[7] Geoff Dyer, *Out of Sheer Rage: Wrestling with D. H. Lawrence* (New York: Picador, 1997), 104.

[8] Friedrich Nietzsche, "On the Use and Abuse of History for Life," *The Complete Works of Friedrich Nietzsche*, vol. 2, trans. Richard Gray (Palo Alto: Stanford University Press), 87.

[9] Deidre Lynch, *Loving Literature: A Cultural History* (Chicago: University of Chicago Press, 2014), 150.

it's conducive to rereading favorite texts. In his sonnet "On Sitting Down to Read King Lear Once Again," Keats is faced with the choice between two kinds of rereading on a wintry day: Romance or Shakespeare. In choosing *King Lear*, a play he already knows well, he immerses himself anew in the play while shutting up other books that he also possesses: "Shut up thine olden pages, and be mute," he tells the Romances:

> Adieu! for once again the fierce dispute,
> Betwixt damnation and impassion'd clay
> Must I burn through; once more humbly assay
> The bitter-sweet of this Shakespearian fruit.[10]

While this sonnet can and has been read as suggesting a move in Keats's own literary development, the scene also suggests the more literal prerogative that permanent library access bestows upon the reader, to move between and return to texts. Karl Ove Knausgård nails the equation simply when he singles out his relation as a child to *The Children of the New Forest*, "which I loved and read again and again as I had been given it and didn't borrow it."[11] This privilege is not only male. Alberto Manguel introduces Colette as a reader of few books who "rereads the same ones over and over again. She loves *Les Misérables* with what she'll later call 'a reasoning passion'; she feels she can nestle in its pages 'like a dog in its kennel.'"[12] My teenage daughter likes to pack for any trip both a book she is reading and a novel she is rereading, not confusing the different pleasures they bring.

But it is not through either the comforts of repetition or the intensities of possession that most working-class readers have felt their love of reading. This is a corollary to Lynch's argument, which suggests some of the ways connecting literary reading with love has allowed the humanities to become suspiciously disinvested in as a legitimate field of work. For less privileged readers, daily life has quite enough equilibrium anyway: reading is an escape from repetition. Here is Lavena Saltonstall, a nineteenth-century tailoress, describing the world offset by her use of books:

> I am supposed to make myself generally useless by ignoring things that matter—literature, music, art, history, economics....In my native place, the women, as a general rule, wash every Monday, iron on Tuesday, court on Wednesdays, bake on Thursdays, clean on Fridays, go to market or go courting again on Saturdays, and to church on Sundays...The exceptions are considered unwomanly and eccentric people.[13]

The genres of literature addressed to working-class readers, if we follow Richard Hoggart's indictment of the dailies and magazines in *The Uses of Literacy*, are themselves formulaic and predictable. But reading of the kind Saltonstall goes on to celebrate disrupts the routines of work and plot. The pace and the interest with

---

[10] John Keats, *Collected Poems*, ed. John Barnard (London: Penguin, 1998), 220.
[11] Karl Ove Knausgård, *Boyhood Island*, trans. Don Bartlett (London: Harvill Secker, 2014), 306.
[12] Quoted in Alberto Manguel, *A History of Reading* (London: HarperCollins, 1996), 149.
[13] Quoted in Rose, *The Intellectual Life*, 278.

which she devours "literature" is not a sign of commitment, or "steadiness" as Lynch describes it, but of greed for the unknown; for that vast field of novelty there will not be time to cross even once in a lifetime. And I am, in this sense, of Saltonstall's camp. I read fiction quickly and promiscuously, to my detriment as a lover of literature. Her novels are fine but, no, I do not want to spend time reading Ferrante again.

Reusable Plots

The genre of the novel, which Lynch points out is so well-suited to being read cyclically, and loved faithfully and routinely, is generally theorized as a single-use object. If literature can be defined as something we are always rereading, narrative has often been understood as something we are always reading for the first time. Frank Kermode's *The Sense of an Ending* insists on the way in which novels model not the spatial arrangements in which we actually live, but unrealistic temporal ones in which we are propelled by the idea of an ending, the forward-sloping organization of fiction precluding disorder and contingency.[14] In *Reading for the Plot*, Peter Brooks writes with similar conviction of the dynamism of plot as "that which moves us forward as readers of the narrative text, that which makes us...want and need plotting, seeking through the narrative text as it unfurls before us a precipitation of shape and meaning."[15] Readers by these calculations are committed to movement and expectant of resolution. They are like the readers in metafictional novels, from Laurence Sterne's *Tristram Shandy* to John Fowles' *The French Lieutenant's Woman*, who, spurred on by curiosity and suspense, are fictionalized and sent up in their own first, breathless encounter with this narrative suspense.

Another recent account of the novel, Viv Soni's *Mourning Happiness*, suggests that before the arrival of novels, we treated narrative very differently, as a process in which meaning accrued and could make itself felt only once all the parts of a puzzle were in place. Call no man happy before he is dead, warned Aristotle.[16] In Soni's account, the moral importance of waiting-to-see was lost to eighteenth-century novel readers, who bought into the causality of narratives, accepting challenge and hardship as obstacles to be overcome if characters—and readers—were to be rewarded by a satisfying ending. Novels never really represent the happiness they promise, but the allure of reading them is the comfort of knowing that their last pages will deliver us from struggle. Knausgård's childhood of reading has taught him that "you must never give in, never give up, because if you have been resolute, upright, brave and honest, however lonely it has made you and however alone you

---

[14] Frank Kermode, *The Sense of an Ending: Studies in the Theory of Fiction* (Oxford: Oxford University Press, 1967).

[15] Peter Brooks, *Reading for the Plot: Design and Intention in Narrative* (Oxford: Oxford University Press, 1984), 35.

[16] Vivasvan Soni, *Mourning Happiness: Narrative and the Politics of Modernity* (Ithaca, NY: Cornell University Press, 2010), 7.

stand, in the end you are rewarded."[17] This positions him, despite his special relation to *The Children of the New Forest*, less as a reiterative worshiper of literature and more as a consumer of narrative anxious to know how things turn out, a turner of pages who pursues a plot through its twists and turns as a journey justified by its outcome.

Reader-response theory assumes readers like Knausgård. But what can it make of the reader who knows how the journey will turn out? (Not the reader like Süskind, who only dimly remembers its previous iteration, but the reader who anticipates what is coming next). What of the reader who goes back to the erotic scenes of a novel or uses the index to return/revisit as quickly as possible the sentimental ones she remembers best? What of Proust, whose teenage self reads very differently from Knausgård's, with deep devotion to the novels of the fictive writer, Bergotte:

> And so I would read, or rather sing his sentences in my mind, with rather more *dolce*, rather more *lento* than he himself had perhaps intended, and his simplest phrase would strike my ears with something peculiarly gentle and loving in its intonation. More than anything else I cherished his philosophy, and had pledged myself to it in lifelong devotion.[18]

Bergotte is a composite of Anatole France, John Ruskin, and other writers Proust admired. His prose, imagined and hinted at in *In Search of Lost Time* (1913), enters Proust's narrative as a medium in which the narrator will permanently immerse himself. Does this kind of reader have the same motivation to move quickly towards happiness as resolution, the same sense of an ending assumed by Kermode, Brooks, and Soni?

How Rereading Counts

One way to parse this question would be to suggest that critique of any text has always involved a second and third reading. "First reading and critique," argues Stephen Best, "are viewed largely as anathema; second thoughts inspire us to relinquish first impressions, in a process of questioning and revision infused with a skepticism and doubt."[19] Best is participating here in a debate among literary critics about whether critical reading is something to celebrate at all. Perhaps, various theorists of reading have suggested, there's a framework in which other kinds of affective and even superficial or first-time encounters with a text might be valued as much as deep and critical reading has been in the past. Rita Felski's *The Limits of*

---

[17] Knausgård, *Boyhood Island*, 307.

[18] Marcel Proust, *In Search of Lost Time*, vol. 1, trans. C. K. Scott Moncrieff and Terence Kilmartin (London: Vintage, 1996), 134.

[19] Stephen Best, "*La Foi Postcritique*, on Second Thought," *PMLA* 132.2 (2017), 337–43; 337.

Critique comes out strongly in favor of this possibility, emphasizing the way that the reception of literature is enmeshed in what Bruno Latour describes as an actor-network, a spatially and temporally diffuse chain of events and encounters connecting objects and people without being structured by forces like agency or history. Without fully getting into this debate, it is worth pointing out some of the problems that arise when we try to look at repeat reading as an event in this model's terms.

Whatever the problems with critical or deep reading, one advantage is that it justifies the significance of repeat reading. Read the text once through, then read it again as you analyze it: this is what we tell our students. If teenage Proust loves Bergotte, reading him again as an adult adds something to that infatuation. Repetition is part of that trajectory of intellectual growth. In contrast, a sociological account of reading that sticks more closely to the flat description of its occurrence makes the phenomenon of repeat reading a problem. Does an affective encounter with a book hold steady with each new reading, or does the tenor and weight of the experience change with repetition? Perhaps rereading a book makes it more powerful in actor-network terms—but there's no reason why this should be so. Eating an apple or driving a car on a daily basis arguably has the opposite effect, as the action becomes less significant each time we do it. Is Bergotte more or less moving to Proust as he rereads him?

This problem becomes more concrete if we look at the challenges facing scholars researching the history of reading today—with databases of book sales and lending records at their disposal. The records of the small lending library at Innerpeffray have, for instance, enabled an almost complete digital record of the books borrowed from the collection in the last 300 years. Such information offers new opportunities to trace what one might call different actor-networks. We can map out connections between various members of the Scottish community who read the same book, and between those books and the gender of their readers, or the seasons in which they were read. The push of a button reveals how often a book was borrowed, displaying its infectious power quantitively without relying on evidence of its quality. With a bit more effort, it is possible to visualize this activity through graphs or diagrams, where visual representation might show a book's history as a series of readings.

But the case where a borrower takes out an item more than once is difficult to parse further in these terms. Mary Ewing is just one of the many repeat borrowers who shows up in the Innerpeffray database. In 1898, she borrows Edna Lyall's *Their Happiest Christmas* twice, once on the May 2nd and once on August 13th.[20] But what weight should we give to this? The book is a trite piece of juvenile fiction. Did she like it so much that she wanted to reread it? Or so little that she didn't finish it the first time she borrowed it? Did rereading it (if she reread it) make

---

[20] I am using Katie Halsey's unpublished database, which is based on the information contained in the Innerpeffray Library Borrowers' Registers and has been edited by Jill Dye. Mary Ewing appears here under borrower ID No. 2041.

Mary Ewing more critical or more adoring of Lyall's fiction? Perhaps she was a Proust, keen to immerse herself in the narrative, or a Knausgård, wanting to survive the moral tale's challenges, or perhaps she just liked the book's fancy frontispiece. The more descriptive work that Felski advocates might help us understand the positive effects of reading, but it doesn't help much in distinguishing Ewing's second loan from her first. Even if we were to encode repeat encounters with a book so that they were doubly or trebly stressed in a network, it's hard to know exactly what we'd be coding for as we tracked repetition.

The British Library holds the notebooks of a reader who tried explicitly to track his own activity as a rereader. William Grenville was a prominent politician in the late eighteenth and early nineteenth centuries. He served as home secretary and foreign secretary and very briefly as prime minister for a year in 1806, before ending his working life in 1817 as leader of the opposition party. But during the 1790s, when he was in his late 30s and his political work was at a low, he retired briefly to Dropmore, the country estate to which he had moved his reading and writing materials. Grenville had an Oxford degree in classics, and he remained a regular reader of classical literature in the decade after he graduated in 1780. The program of reading he devised during his early retirement involved deepening his acquaintance with the authors he was already in the habit of reading: Aristotle, Cicero, Demosthenes, Homer, Plutarch.

For the purpose of this dedicated period of study, Grenville started a series of notebooks, the pages of which he folded distinctively so as to form two columns. When reading Aristotle and Demosthenes, Grenville writes his notes only in the right-hand columns of his folded pages. His notes recording what he reads each day indicate careful loops of repetition. Tackling a new translation of Aristotle's *Ethics and Politics* in February 1799, he reads pages 39–52; then on February 6th he reads these pages again before continuing to page 86 the next day.[21] But the format he's designed for his pages record another kind of repetition, too. When he begins *The Life of Pericles* in February 1797, he records doubts in the left-hand column of the page about details he thinks might be missing from the translated text. Then, as the image below shows, in December 1798 he uses the left-hand column to write: "In reading this passage again, I feel more confident that the omission of these words is the right emendation of the text" (Figure 13.1).

The left-hand columns in all three of Grenville's repurposed notebooks are surely if sparsely populated in this way with records of repeat readings; their blank spaces left open to the many that Grenville hoped were still to come.

Overall, Grenville charts rereading as something that happens along both a vertical and a horizontal axis. The two-column format of his notebooks allows him to go back in time and show how a second reading corrects, amends, and supplements

---

[21] William Grenville, "Notes on Reading of Gilles' translation of Aristotle" (BL Dropmore Papers, Add MSS 59429), unpublished manuscript, ff.17.

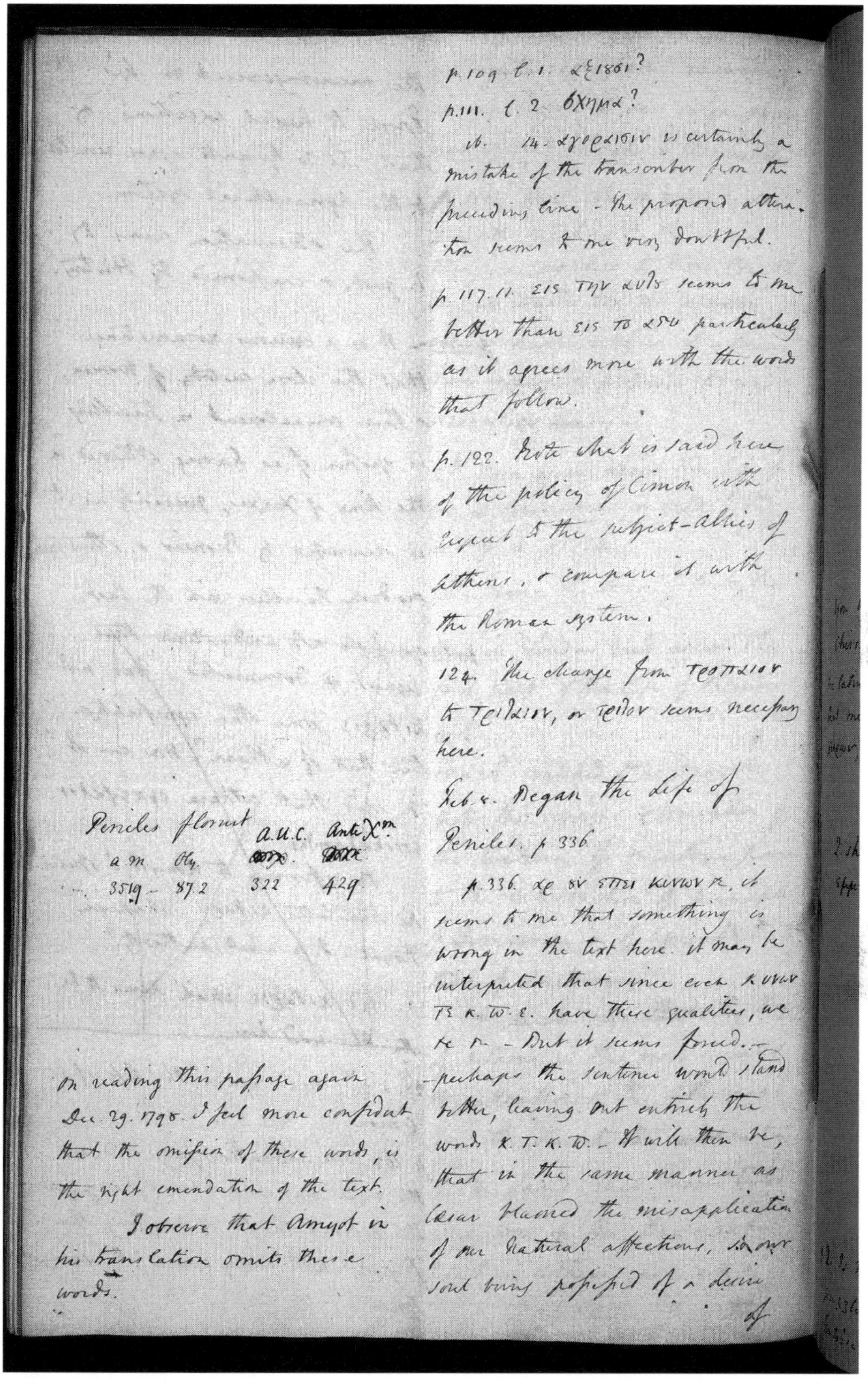

Figure 13.1 William Grenville, BL Dropmore Papers, Add MS 59429 (Dropmore Papers), ff. 17. © The British Library Board.

the event of the first reading, changing the way we encounter it for the first time on the page. Represented properly, Proust's encounters with Bergotte would have to look something like this. They are not distinct points in a network, but events whose repetition gives the network another temporal dimension from the outset. Whether or not this involves Proust becoming more critical, it means that the nature of the repeat encounter with books differs, both from the one we have every day with forks or cars, and from the one we have with a narrative churned through in pursuit of an ending.

Repetitive or Repeating?

Based on what I've suggested so far, repeat readings add up to something more than the sum of their parts. But maybe this is a special case, as Lynch suggests, of literary reading being iterative, and less true of our engagement with other kinds of texts and other media interfaces. Repeatedly listening to a song, playing a computer game, or watching a video clip can seem like an impasse to development. So perhaps there are two kinds of repetition that can be associated with reading: repeat reading and repetitive reading. This seems to be what Ali Smith suggests in *How to Be Both*, a novel invested in the ethics of looking long and digesting deeply various scenes and images. At one point we encounter Smith's keenly observant teenage protagonist, George, watching a violent pornographic video clip on a loop. Her motivation, she explains to her father, is not erotic:

> *This* really happened, George said. To *this* girl. And anyone can watch it just, like, happening, any time he or she likes. And it happens for the first time, over and over again, every time someone who hasn't seen it before clicks on it and watches it. So I want to watch it for a completely different reason. Because my completely different watching of it goes some way to acknowledging all of that to this girl. Do you still not understand?[22]

George suggests that her obsessive replaying of the scene can go some way to rescuing the girl from the violence inflicted on her. It's not that the scene isn't made to be viewed repeatedly—it is repetitive and productive of repetition in a number of ways—but this kind of erotic, mindless repetition is different from the thoughtful kind of reiteration that George advocates. Although the scene isn't art, isn't *iterative* in the sense Lynch argues literature is by the nineteenth century, George is perversely determined to treat it as if it were. By revisiting the scene as *a repeat reader* bent on recognizing the girl in the video, she protests against that other pornographic register in which an image can be played and replayed without the viewer ever reading it more deeply.

---

[22] Ali Smith, *How to Be Both* (London: Hamish Hamilton/Penguin, 2014), 224.

Arguably, new media work against the ethical possibilities of this kind of rereading at the level of materiality, and not just by favoring the superficial at the level of content. Because the formats in which we now encounter digital texts are themselves unstable, going back to them may involve habitual movement on the reader's part without deepening a relationship of any kind to a text's content. I pick up a tablet or phone again and again and again. But I do so mostly in the hope that a page has been refreshed. A document edited. A status updated. In these terms, the repetitive nature of reading online is premised on the possibility of textual change; continuity rarely motivates me to look at the text interfaces I carry around. While we might look back at an article or email on our phone in recollection, it's much harder to find our way back to something online than to stumble onto something new. And if it were continuity we were after, we would often be disappointed: electronic files, even of Kindle books, change and disappear.

Thus, ironically, at a moment when reading seems to have made certain repetitive movements a haptic commonplace, the benefits of returning to the same object have become harder to achieve. In an age when distant readers of data, searchers and scanners of screens, and seekers of new paths through even the oldest of texts proliferate, we may have to acknowledge that repeat reading, for better or for worse, is less likely than it once was to involve following materially worn grooves. The pleasure and surprise associated by Keats with reading his old copy of *King Lear* yet again differ from the ones that we get from returning habitually to a favorite website to check the day's postings.

And yet I want to end here with another recent kind of text, a graphic novel that pays homage to repeat reading. Alison Bechdel's *Fun Home* explores a complex relationship between a father and daughter, honing in on the opportunities that a writer has to play with and reverse historical sequences as she represents them. In the last image of the novel, through "the trick reverse narration that impels our entwined stories," the dead father is able to catch his adult daughter, Alison.[23] But *Fun Home* is also a narrative about reading that is non-linear. Reading is an occupation with which the father of the story is obsessed—so obsessed that he's vicariously followed Alison's progress through a course on *Ulysses* at college, trying to force his own copy of the novel into her hands in order to make her experience a literal retracing of his own. Reluctant to take the gift, Alison asks if she can write in this copy, and then struggles with the course because of her own lackluster engagement with the novel. But *Fun Home* nevertheless takes *Ulysses* as its inter-text. Clearly Bechdel has eventually reread and loved Joyce on her own terms, and it's that second, successful reading of the novel that underpins her telling of the story of her relationship with her father. As a re-writing of *Ulysses* that is premised on this rereading—this second take on her first dismissal of the novel—Bechdel's story diverges from and converges with her father's reading of it in complicated ways. But

---

[23] Alison Bechdel, *Fun Home: A Family Tragicomic* (London: Jonathan Cape, 2006), 232.

it also suggests more simply that reading the same thing again remains a cornerstone of the most creative enterprises as well as our more critical ones.

FURTHER READING

Best, Stephen. "*La Foi Postcritique*, on Second Thought." *PMLA* 132.2 (2017): 337–43.

Bronstein, Michaela. "How Not to Re-Read Novels: The Critical Value of First Reading." *Journal of Modern Literature* 39.3 (2016): 76–94.

Hoggart, Richard. *The Uses of Literacy: Aspects of Working Class Life*. London: Penguin, 2009 [1957].

Lynch, Deidre. *Loving Literature*. Chicago: University of Chicago Press, 2014.

Rose, Jonathan. *The Intellectual Life of the British Working Classes*. New Haven: Yale University Press, 2001.

Süskind, Patrick. "Amnesia in Litteris: The Books I Have Read (I Think)." *Harper's* (March 1987): 71–3.

Soni, Vivasvan. *Mourning Happiness: Narrative and the Politics of Modernity*. Ithaca, NY: Cornell University Press, 2010.

SENSES

14

SIGHT

JOHANNA DRUCKER

Stand on a busy street corner in a city and begin to list the textual instances in view, including those displayed on the device in your hand. Texts of all kinds are present: graffiti, printed matter, and incidental signs, markings on buses, taxis, cars, t-shirts, and screens. The number and types of these written forms can be enumerated and classified according to aspects such as purpose, medium, location, scale, temporal aspects, graphical features, textual tone, voice, authority, and enunciative force. In other words, we can (and will below) come up with a full set of descriptive parameters for the material, linguistic, and social dimensions of writing in the world. These various parameters can be roughly categorized by their relation to substance, site, and effect.

Remarkably, however, in making sense of the textual world, we access this set of descriptive parameters instantly and intuitively by sight. We use a whole variety of reference frames to identify and read texts in accord with protocols that shape their meaning and effect. Many of these are *performative* frameworks rather than *formal* ones. They allow us to process the textual signs in such a way that the *how* of their meaning production is integrated into the *what* of the meaning they produce. Performative dimensions contain instructions for reading—they give us a frame-work within which the authority and effect of a text are dynamically factored into its semantic value. An example that makes this vividly clear is the familiar STOP sign. Its material properties and location tell us as much as the word about what it means. If a version of the sign were hand-drawn with a crayon on paper and taped to a tree, its "meaning" would change dramatically. We read the substance, site, and effect of the features of the *sign* before we read the meaning of the *word*. So a typological approach that classifies the formal properties of textual instances can go only part of the way towards understanding the cultural production of meaning and effect. We need to enumerate the performative dimensions of texts within their sites (actual, physical, or digital) in order to understand the co-dependence of these three categories—substance (language and material), site (position and location), and effect (performance and enunciation). In other words, what texts *do* and how they *work* is not determined simply by what they say and how they look, but *where* and under what *conditions* they perform their work.

Our ability to sight-read in accordance with implicit instructions generally out-strips our conscious capacity to enumerate these frameworks explicitly. We have only to imagine the transposition of a text from one formal, material, spatial expression to another (as in the example of the STOP sign above) to recognize how completely our expectations are already formed in advance of reading. If a familiar feature of the digital environment, like the "delete" button on a keyboard, appeared in a streetscape in some strange, futuristic innovation, it would be deeply disturbing. The question of what it would "mean" is inextricably bound to the equally complicated question of what it would "do" in that situation. Take out buildings? The sky? Air? Traffic? Likewise, if a bit of spray-painted graffiti appeared one morning suddenly sprawled across your laptop screen, as if it were the trace of a random vandal passing through your computer in the night, it would raise an alarm. These instances of defamiliarization immediately demonstrate the extent to which conventions of spatial location are integrated with our reading of texts.

When reading takes place in complex screen or physical environments, with their multiply mediated modes all operating simultaneously, our cognitive load is increased dramatically. Still, within milliseconds, we sort texts into categories. Even before reading them, we recognize that they *are* linguistic expressions meant for communicative purposes; then we determine our reading response according to the many codes that affect their impact. I know before stepping into the street that I can ignore the text on a bicyclist's t-shirt, the ad banner on a bus, but not the "Police Barrier: Do Not Cross" ribbon. We read the list of instructions about times and prohibitions on a city parking sign within a perceptual frame that already recognizes its authority as an expression of a civil code. We are subject to its regulations in every sense—as subjects of a civil order and civic regime and as individuals positioning ourselves in relation to the street, the space, the law, the temporal framework dictated by the information on the sign, and so on. Similar, but different, processes occur in relation to language experienced in a digital environment. Warning messages, error alerts, clickbait, and embedded links offer opportunities for frustration or distraction down one rabbit hole after another in every zone of the screen.

Some written signs cross the boundary between analog and digital worlds, such as the text on a GPS, with its overlays and signals, instructions that project our reading of a landscape from a graphical interface onto a physical environment in real time, in a way that extends older uses of maps and navigational devices. Augmented reality displays further confuse spatial boundaries, deliberately collapsing distinctions between actual and virtual environments. We read site into language but do not always have an explicit understanding of how this occurs, and what features and processes are at work.[1]

---

[1] I have taken up this topic several times, beginning with "Close Reading: A Billboard," *Poetics Journal* 1.2 (1982): 82–4; "Language in the Landscape," *Landscape Magazine* 28.1 (1984): 7–13; "Signs

We see, therefore, that long before we get the specific semantic value, or decode the syntactic structures, we process many aspects of textual semiotics through what the American philosopher, Charles Morris, termed *pragmatics*.[2] Interestingly, neither the renowned semiotician Charles Peirce nor foundational structural linguist Ferdinand de Saussure concerned themselves with these actualities, and the philosophy of language has had to borrow from cultural anthropology, urban studies, graphic design, media history, and other fields to synthesize an adequate foundation for the study of situated textual meaning. As for literary studies, the peculiar notion that a work is not affected by the *circumstances* of its reading is an odd blindspot (especially given the emphasis that networks and processes of literary, editorial, social, and material production are given in bibliography and critical studies). We supposedly read a poem as if it floats outside of the circumstances of viewing. As the study of reading practices makes clear, the conditions of textual production are generative, not passive, and a text is not received, but produced.

Texts are always site-specific works, utterances situated within contexts that structure their meaning through the features that inflect their reception. This page (or screen), here, now, before your eyes, is written somewhere else, far from where you read it, but it participates in the illusion that the space of the page begins and ends at its own boundaries. Texts are neither insular nor autonomous. They are contingent and entangled. We read them from a position and are structured by their modes of address, which involve visual rhetoric and graphical codes as well as social, cultural, and linguistic ones. For literary scholars, textual critics, and people reading in the daily business of life, these codes register but are rarely taken into account. A chapter title, a page header, the arrangement of text to paratext, the placement of text on a page, typography, and other features are all spatial codes taken largely for granted but also factored into meaning. Sometimes such visual features are "read" as a conspicuous part of the text—when we note the stylistic features of a fine press book or a medieval manuscript or a Dada poem using ransom note typography. But unless the treatment is deviant or disruptive, we generally accept and ignore graphical aspects of language.

But to return to the point made above, how should we understand the site of reading? Many texts are not actually written into or onto a landscape, but are *read in the landscape*, an environment whose specific qualities are also, arguably, integrated

---

of Life/Spaces of Art: From Standard Brands to Integrated Circuits," in *Graphic Design and Reading*, ed. Gunnar Swanson (New York: Allworth Press: 2000), 31–49; "Reading Riding at Sears," *OEI* 31–2 (2007): 45–6; "Introduction" to Judy Natal, *Neon Boneyard* (Santa Fe: Center for American Places, 2006); "Species of *Espaces* and Other Spurious Concepts Addressed to Reading the Invisible Features of Signs within Systems of Relations," *Design and Culture: The Journal of Design Studies Forum* 2.2 (July 2010): 135–54; and "Reading Interface," *PMLA* 128.1 (January 2013): 213–220 (http://www.mlajournals.org/doi/abs/10.1632/pmla.2013.128.1.213).

[2] Charles Morris, "Foundations of the Theory of Signs," in *International Encyclopedia of Unified Science*, ed. Otto Neurath, Rudolf Carnap, and Charles Morris (Chicago: University of Chicago Press, 1938).

into the productive reading of the work. Imagine starting a literature class by asking students *where* they read their assignments and seeing how this inflects their responses. If I read *Wuthering Heights* by a pool in a Miami Beach resort, is it a different book than when I read it at a drafty old house in the countryside near Peniston Crag where Heathcliff and Cathy have their assignations? Does the bright sunshine wash out the dark corners of the text, flush the ghosts into the light, and recast the ill-fated passion as an anachronism that has been superseded? Is where we read as important in constituting a text as what we read? If we read site into language when we encounter it, does site also seep into a text when we absorb it on a plane, a subway, or a waiting room? Does my cat's grooming activity on the table next to me become part of the text I am writing? Do my words brighten as the mood in the room shifts from fog-bound morning to sunlit day? These are questions one might answer through lab experiments. But separating the individual factors affecting a reader (mood, attitude, bad breakfast, time pressure, sick child) from the environment of a reading experience (light, dark, warm, cold, windy, wet, unsafe) might be a challenge.

In addition to noting texts written in and on the world, and texts that circulate through it, one final site-specific issue ought to be acknowledged: the ways in which texts *make* the world, shape it by the functions of naming, pointing, signing, identifying, demarcating, and so forth. Marks and signs in the landscape make navigation and orientation meaningful, render the world legible in many cases, and order our experience of space and through it. The human world is written by lines of inscription that perform many specific functions. But the fundamental act of inscription, of marking and signing, positions us in a system that imposes itself on the raw material of the phenomenal world and remakes it as a semiotic one. The very fundamental act of inscription, of making a line, the first act of textual production and semiotic formation, creates the world. Inscription determines how and where we live, walk, drive, direct our gaze and our attention, where we turn away, move forward, and where we feel welcome, safe, or frightened. Writing makes the world.[3] We live in the written world, or, in a more affected turn of phrase, we might even say that we *live* the written world. This fact is so fundamental that it largely goes unnoticed, and this essay only hints at the kind of primary markings that forms the study of anthropologists and animal behaviorists. But noting that foundation means that the discussion of reading as a site-specific activity already assumes the start point of primary semiosis. It takes for granted the initial acts of writing a world and marking it into zones according to which we are then enunciated as subjects of our semiotic practices as well as enunciators of them.

With these preliminary remarks in place, we can sketch the situatedness of texts, the site specificity of language in regard to writing that is in the world, of the world,

---

[3] Tim Ingold, *Lines: A Brief History* (New York: Routledge, 2016).

and moving around the world, to create a typology to describe and analyze the performative dimensions of language.

Go back to the street corner again, any ordinary place—such as a Sunday morning farmers' market—to bring specific examples into the discussion. The activity of the vendors takes over the street; their stalls occupy what on business days is an active thoroughfare. The large stenciled traffic signs on the asphalt, writing on the curbs, and other markings are temporarily ignored. These official texts are semi-permanent signs and words, meant to endure many seasons and to direct traffic flow and activity. They are almost entirely performative, since the meaning of "SLOW" or "RIGHT TURN ONLY" is subsumed by the directing effect. These are instructions for action and behavior, and they carry the force of the civil code. A violation of their directives would be registered against the regulations they are meant to enforce. The material form of these stenciled signs is deceptive—they appear very differently to a driver than they would in a bird's-eye view. They are meant to be seen anamorphically, so that their full extent is compressed—their actual measure is always much greater than one expects; in fact, the stencils are the height of a grown man. Their design inscribes a subject position, a place from which they are speaking and in which they will be received. Sight and site are intertwined in their specificity. In terms of substance, the white reflective paint, the scale and shape of the elongated letters, and the declarative and imperative tones of direct address all play a role in their effect. The spatial and temporal dimensions of their location are also active elements, and the speed and direction at which they will be experienced as well as the expectation of their relative permanence is also evident. The effect is immediate; we barely pause to think about these complexities in slowing to make a turn at the street corner.

On market day, none of this matters. We walk through the zone where printed banners, such as "Fresh Figs," bid for our attention. Their performance is based on a combination of declarative information, seduction, and direction. The words are not just saying something but doing something. Other signs on easel boards announce the day's special, directing us to a stand to the right or left, spatially located and highly performative. They function only in situ. Half of the pedestrians are holding phones, looking at the world while keeping up a conversation or a text, filtering choices about what to buy, what to bring home, in an exchange with a partner who is connected to another space entirely, looking to see if there are, indeed, still onions on the shopping list. We are reading the landscape in relation to other landscapes to which we are connected in real time. But we also read in anticipation of not being present, already recollecting the landscape even as we move through it. What will we realize we have forgotten to buy once we are home? The signs about the food stuffs are identification labels—simple naming devices that also function as asynchronous mnemonics—prompting us to remember what we will need ahead. But even they depend on location, placed in immediate proximity so that we can tell the Thai basil from the regular and reach for the right bunch. Even simple labels are performative. Some are ephemeral, hand-written. One chalkboard announces, "Apples all the way from Sebastopol." These signs are present only for the duration of the market, for a few hours of operation. Peeking above them, behind the stall tents, are the storefront signs—for a Yoga studio, a 99¢ store, and, higher, raised above the roofline, that of a new bar. These are signs meant as signals in a neighborhood. They are part of the block's street-level experience and direct us towards goods and services within a modest range. The elevated bar sign is a mark of change and more ambitious reach, calling out through the neighborhood. On the major through street half a block away, signs are even bigger, more visible, because they have to be seen by motorists. Above all of these, high in the skyline of downtown and the business corridor, the brand signs of mega-corporations are emblazoned against the sky, in vivid multistory letters, some lit, some reflective. These dominate the cityscape, their scale declares their position in the hierarchy of money and power, and they are built to look indestructible and to last until absorbed by merger or acquisition. All of these temporalities and spatialities are interwoven in the physical space, in which ads on bags and texts on shirts and signs move at the rates of gait and stride, meandering or hurrying, glimpsed in passing. Writing is everywhere, acting, speaking, positioning us.

On the phone, the password screen gives way to the grid of apps' icons, and a message, a plan. Where is the spot for a later rendezvous, the address a bright pin on a small map—nearby? Punching in the request for a ride service punctures a hole in the physical world with a virtual one. The screen becomes the focal point of anticipation. The ride and the service display on the screen are part of systems and networks. They are in turn linked to supply chains of fuel, instructions, labor contracts, and other screens that communicate in various cycles of temporal refresh. The screen's interface changes constantly, offering headlines, reviews, messages, and emails, information relevant to the task at hand, or one planned for later, and all of this absorbs attention. As we navigate we simultaneously read the street signs, the app tracking our ride's approach on a labeled map, the moving marquee of a billboard atop a local business, a "lost cat" sign on a pole, a discarded receipt, the claims for organic produce, prices. We have no trouble whatsoever figuring out at any moment how to read each one and what sense to make of its language.

In another complex scenario, imagine the scene at an airport. There you are surrounded by signs and screens that are part of wayfinding, advertising, essential travel information, and a host of small-scale, mini-textual environments—newsstands, restaurant and food service outlets, gates, signs leading to ground transportation, baggage, customs, border control, and security. Again, we have no difficulty sorting the signs by sight. The scene is different in specifics, and in some ways in scale, given the trajectory that each option about navigation and wayfinding projects across time and space. But the airport is a more deliberately and holistically designed environment than the farmer's market, whose temporary signs and structures, imposed on an already richly articulated streetscape, function briefly within a purpose-driven situation. Find this, here, now—the immediacy of the market—is contrasted with the many now-then, here-there transits among origin points and destinations orchestrated by the sign boards and postings in the airport. Traveling in a foreign land, where the language is unfamiliar, we can still figure out which signs we need to read and pay attention to, by virtue of their site and graphical features.

We read the signs, not their words, and much navigation can be done without reading their content. The formal and spatial features of these signs can be mapped onto axes of near and far, monumentally formal and casually informal, and so on. The range of production methods and means adds attributes: electric, plastic, illuminated, printed, digital, analog, etc. The variety of roles adds another set of attributes: wayfinding, information, advertisement, prohibition, naming, branding, pointing, and so on. Tone and mode of address add yet another facet: direct address, indirect statement, interrogative tone, and so on. Scale and distance are crucial features of signs in space, and the view lines for perception are also cones of enunciation—how much space does a sign control by its position? From where can it be viewed, and how does its position command public space? All of these formal and linguistic features are part of the signs' site- and sight-specific meaning.

The temporal refresh rate of signs and screens in the airport is as highly varied as its spatial features. We can identify a typology of time frames for signage as well as spatial positions and roles: *infrastructural* time (linked to the structure's architecture and designed to last as long as the physical space endures unmodified—such as restroom signs, exit and restricted area notices, and some wayfinding signs to locations within the terminal, airport, or transportation systems); *contract* time (mainly commercial, determined by the contract providing space on a hoarding or in a shop or other commercial zone); *synchronous* time (the update of gate information, flight delays, travel information, and messages); and *ephemeral* time (the rapidly changing, temporary installation of signage for a bathroom being cleaned, a door closed, a "Be right back!" or other message). This typology could be nuanced, and subdivided, but the point is that all signage has temporal dimensions as well as spatial and functional ones. Now add textually replete mobile devices into the picture: many small screens, moving through the space, picking up signals and messages constantly. Their displays are all operating on their own time scales: screens within screens play video clips with their own time codes while they also connect real-time video calls and conferencing streams. The same screens display news feeds produced on a range of time schedules, but most stamped with the day's date. And email, sent in one moment to arrive at another, might be delayed by hours, even days, depending on server conditions or back logs, and yet appear in a time-stamped sequence in the inbox chronology. The number of intersecting temporalities is mind-boggling.

Again, these observations could be nuanced, and the categories multiplied across a wide range of specifics. But the fundamental principle remains: that the *where and when* is integral to the *what* of reading and meaning. Spatial dimensions and temporal dimensions are crucial to establishing a systematic framework for a description of the features at work in textual objects.

With all of these considerations in play, can we distinguish between the way language performs in the analog and the digital realms? The two modes interpenetrate to a great degree, and yet, they maintain some distinctions. Language has many roles in the analog realm. These are site-specific in two ways—they can alter a site and they can depend on a site, or both. The tasks of identification, demarcation, prohibition, permission, announcement, and so on are an essential part of the role of language in situ. The effect of their formal, material qualities is evident. These help code language as official or not, and to identify the liabilities and benefits associated with compliance or violation of the implicit or explicit commands. A text is not a word-object set into the world as a gem in a setting. Rather, a text is always a *con-text*, a *with-text*. In this co-dependent relation of viewing, conditions are integral to meaning. These co-dependencies become obvious when we see language outside of these conditions, as in the case of the "Neon boneyard," that vast lot of cast-off signs in the Nevada desert, blinking their "Hotel" and "Parking" messages into the unresponsive night air, or lying silent and unlit, mere skeletons of words that once laid proud, bold claim to space.[4]

The marked and signed features of the analog world have related, if not-quite-parallel, counterparts in the digital realm. Consider the multiplicity of ways signage works in the artifactual construction of the onscreen environments we navigate constantly. Spatiality is governed by very different metrics when its literal and virtual dimensions are not the same, when the screen real estate can be subdivided into a nearly infinite number of smaller spaces. Multiple temporalities are also constantly operating in screen spaces. These are governed by the workings of processors and computational capacities, networked connections and systems. Our perceptual experience of them is not radically different from that of temporality in analog environments, where we already experience multiple, asynchronous, temporal phenomena. We have become used to processing the rapid-fire assault of quickly changing screens, fictional times and discursive ones, multiple modes of representation and manipulation of temporal experience. Looking forward through the rows of seats in an airplane where passengers are absorbed into separate fictional worlds or mental spaces, with films and television unfolding in front of them, one is aware of the externalized interiority of thought space, and the strange view into the many individual psychoses produced by commercial entertainment. Times and spaces of escape, distraction, brutality, affective satisfaction, and engagement or negation—all are graphically visible, distinct, and part of one shared space of individually discrete experiences. We can read all of these, and the newsfeed crawlers on the bottom of the screen, icons and instructions on header and sidebar, and instantly know what to attend to and what to ignore.

---

[4] Natal, *Neon Boneyard.*

The history of interface shows how quickly conventions transfer and modify. When we read a screen we often delimit it at the boundary, looking at it and into it, letting the edge of the device define the limit of our reading. The screen's capacity for absorption scales into multiple granularities, and each of these has its own temporality as well. The inserted media, video clips, slow and fast scrolling, swipes and touches, actions and unfoldings can all operate within the same frame. And we "read" these each according to their own requirements, along the real-time axis of a linear medium, the random access of links and search results, and into the excessively districted realms of social media screen real estate, where each frame-within-a-frame demarcates another function—post, friend, contact, read, note, look, respond, message, and so on. The real estate of interface structures behavior, by design, and in this way the conventions matter more than in an analog world— where I can look beyond, behind, around in a space, not just at it—and they are more codified. We can tell an advertisement from a news story, commercial from editorial content, in most cases, but we cannot tell "where" we are in the multiple intersecting spaces of open windows of our multiple devices except by believing the peculiar fiction of "home" as a place to which we can return. No single spatial system provides the ground for the multiple sub-spaces of a screen. It has no unifying "ground" in that sense.

How is it that we make order of all of this, and perform our reading in accord with the specifics required to make the right sense of a text? The where (location and position) of a text is as much a part of its substance as the what (semantics). This was true in print. Take the numbers or words of a chapter title, "Chapter One" or "Two," and stick them into the body of the text (e.g., "She began one chapter of her life two months later.") The words, obviously, do not perform in the same way, their effect is radically altered. Our reading habits blinded us in many ways to the physical and spatial aspects of reading, to basic considerations like scale, embodied in the artifact so that it can be read comfortably. In the physical environment, the view cones are enormous, and the amount of space commanded by urban signage and highway signs means that the sheer size of "subject" space they enunciate becomes a factor that shapes the world as we navigate. Urban signs, the "public lettering" so wonderfully described by Armando Petrucci in his classic study of Rome, made equally articulate interventions, enunciating civic spaces through position and location.[5] But now the infinitely divisible space of screens adds another set of dimensions to the whole, ones that bring attention back to the overlooked axes of temporal and spatial articulation. Much user experience literature is focused on efficiency, eye-tracking, good design within formal, visual parameters. But almost none of it addresses these performative dimensions of interface.

---

[5] Armando Petrucci, *Public Lettering* (Chicago: University of Chicago Press, 1993).

The situated and embedded richness of texts will always exceed any systematic classification for their study, but nonetheless, an exercise in typology seems in order. Other ways of organizing this could work equally well, no doubt, but the categories used throughout this chapter will be used in making this summary: substance, site, and effect. They allow the many dimensions of materiality and physicality, temporality and spatiality, degrees and variety of performativity in social and cultural realms all to be taken into account. The typology is not explanatory, it does not provide a key to the ways in which meaning is produced, or effect created, but it offers a set of features for assessing and evaluating any instance of textual practice.

Substance: Substance is to be understood as both linguistic substance, that is, the semantic and syntactic features that produce meaning, and material substance, those elements of production that give text its visible form in the world. The linguistic elements include inflection, tone, all of the elements of "person" in the speaker position and spoken subject, of passive and active voice, of mood, style, and so on. The material elements include graphic style—typographic font and its associations, color, texture, conventions of layout, format, and composition, materials of production (wood, metal, glass, neon, LED, mirrored surface, and so on), and, in addition, size, both literal and perceived, and scale. The temporal dimensions of substance involve the properties of a medium—its time of unfolding and viewing, as well as its time of duration on a scale from fleeting to permanent. The social features of language borrow elements of material substance but encode a degree of authority. Who speaks, and with what power in a text? Is it a legally binding statement, part of a civil code, or a bit of commercial advertising? Is it language in the public interest or merely that of an interested party? Who sanctions the language and gives it guarantee or warrant? Though features of syntax may support the particular social features, they are not in themselves sufficient; the extra semantic elements of social function are added by the way the language is embedded in the discourses of cultural groups and networks.

Site: The features of site build on those of substance, adding the view cone, the relative and absolute positions of seeing, the status and zone of the location (upscale and down, official and unofficial, regulated or private). The relative stability and rate of change in a text, mostly unmarked in print and manuscript culture, are present nonetheless as a relatively slow rate of refresh, in striking contrast to the rapid refresh rate of screen temporality. Temporality and spatiality are features of all sites and sights. In print, books and other artifacts are highly coherent and orchestrated sites, and the specificity of location within their structures is also, as already noted, highly coded. The physical environment is far less coherent, and its spaces are criss-crossed with many interlocking textual systems. Utility markings sprayed on the street are a specialized set of glyphs, largely ignored except by the workers for whom they signal important information. To the average viewer, they are indecipherable graffiti, the sign of work being done or planned, or of infrastructure hidden from view. Handmade advertisements for a garage sale simply state the fact, date, address, and yet are implicitly directional, hailing the viewer with a "you, go here" message in the second person. Billboards, advertising hoardings, posted notices, "for rent" signs, and apartment building names—all elements of other networks and systems in which they are one node in a shifting landscape that is constantly being remade, renamed, reordered, and restructured. All are subject to rules and regulations that constrain their appearance. Screen spaces are orchestrated by algorithms, settings, competing agendas, and personal patterns and preferences. Each of these environments is governed by a different set of rules for reading, and they also intersect with each other, framed to remain coherent within their individual spaces and protocols.

Effect: Finally, all of these elements combine in the performative, in the *effect* that a text has or impact to which it aspires: prohibition, seduction, attention, information, navigation, orientation, narration, control. Again, the list could proliferate, but the performative dimension of texts is also site- and sight-specific, produced at the intersections of spatial and temporal locations, dimensions, features of substance, and social position. The brand name "Nike" on one t-shirt and the Latin word "Veritas" on another circulate through the streets. Each speaks from a place and within a whole array of others. The words are meant to be read from a distance that defines a public relation to personal space. Intimacy would be a violation, and an up-close encounter would be an unwelcome, or, at least, unsought engagement with the text. Place and position perform much of the effect of these mobile texts. It signals outwards as a declaration, not an invitation.

Our imaginations can easily spin out here, taking the observations of the current world into a set of possibilities for a not-very-distant future one, in which the message boards of media flash across the sky, our personal communications appear in a fleeting moment of public view, but aimed towards our eye-line and location, and the navigation of the world designed in customized anticipation of wants and needs shapes the world by habit. I will find my way in accord with my past habits of reading, my textual practices, and be blind again in a different way to the possibilities of its many phenomenal spaces because I am stuck in a socially engineered semiotic web. The boundaries of the physical and the virtual are fictive, but the lines between actual and fictional are not. Reading the writing of the world requires critical skills of some discernment if we are not simply to be performed by and as the texts of others.

In conclusion, then, that the semantic value of a text, its *what*, is intimately bound to its circumstances of viewing, its *where*, should be clear. That the many features of site-specificity in our complex multimodal world, with its many systems of inscription and mediation, are always in play is evident. That we are able to decode and make sense of all of these many dimensions is a testament to the adaptability and complexity of the human cognitive system.

FURTHER READING

Drucker, Johanna. "Language in the Landscape." *Landscape Magazine* 28.1 (1984): 7–13.

Drucker, Johanna. "Species of *Espaces* and Other Spurious Concepts Addressed to Reading the Invisible Features of Signs within Systems of Relations." *Design and Culture: The Journal of Design Studies Forum* 2.2 (2010): 135–54.

Garrett, Jesse James. *The Elements of User Experience*, 2nd edn. San Francisco: New Riders, 2010 (www.jjg.net/elements/pdf/elements_ch02.pdf).

Krug, Steve. *Don't Make Me Think: A Common Sense Approach to Web Usability.* Berkeley, CA: New Riders, 2005.

Matz, Kevin. "The Gestalt Laws of Perception and How to Use Them in UI Design." *Architecting Usability*, May 26, 2007 (http://architectingusability.com/2011/05/26/using-the-gestalt-laws-of-perception-in-ui-design/).

Shneiderman, Ben, and Catherine Plaisant, Maxine Cohen, and Steven Jacobs. *Designing the User Interface: Strategies for Effective Human-Computer Interaction*, 5th edn. New York: Pearson, 2009.

15

SOUND

CHRISTOPHER GROBE

Potential Sound

> Each day and at every moment, in fact, we talk about sound…but the second it becomes a topic in itself, suddenly we no longer know what it is.
>
> Michel Chion, *Sound: An Acoulogical Treatise*[1]

People talk of printed literature as having a *sound*, but I confess I'm unsure what they mean. It's pretty clear they're not thinking about the sounds of silent reading: how pages rustle, pencils scratch, and books thud shut. Nor are they thinking, in most cases, of the sounds that *people* make while speaking texts. These, they protest, are the sounds not of literature but of performance—not of words but of lungs and vocal cords. No, in truth, they are thinking of something weirder: the sound that literature *would* make if it could sound itself out somehow. They are thinking, in other words, of a *potential* for sound that lies buried in the silent page.

This view of sound, as silent potential, fascinated the composer John Cage throughout his life. In *4'33"*, his most infamous composition, a pianist sits, fingers arched over the keys but never playing. There is by now a standard line on *4'33"*: this silent piece *does* offer us music, just not the kind we were expecting. By withholding what it seemed to promise us, *4'33"* helps us hear—with all the clarity and attention we bring to music—the many sounds that fill a so-called silence: the creaks, murmurs, and coughs in the concert hall; a voice in the lobby, a siren on the street, and a subway rumbling by beneath our feet. But Daniel Sack, in his book *After Live: Possibility, Potentiality, and the Future of Performance*, turns this common interpretation on its head. Instead of helping us hear music we didn't expect, *4'33"* tunes our ears to expectation itself, Sack says. A pianist who "waits at the open piano

---

[1] Michel Chion, *Sound: An Acoulogical Treatise*, trans. James A. Steintrager (Durham, NC: Duke University Press, 2016), 16.

and chooses not to play…thickens the air with much more than simple silence."[2] What "thickens the air" is not the music of disregarded noise, as other critics have suggested, but a *potential* for music we'll never hear—the music that this pianist seemed to promise but then tactfully withheld.

Tact runs hot and tact runs cold; it means touch, but also refraining from touch—fingers on the keys, but never applying any pressure. Silent readers, like frozen pianists, are tactful creatures. The pianist "chooses not to play," the reader chooses not to speak. This is no mere metaphor; it's a scientific fact. For the last century or so, we've known that people "sub-vocalize" as they read. That is, they activate the muscles and nerves involved in speaking, if only to an imperceptible degree. From this premise, Garrett Stewart has concluded that silent reading "is a kind of blocked or inhibited speaking."[3] It is a vocal performance that we suppress. But just like the pianist's restraint in *4'33"*, the reader's repression leads not to silence but instead to a different kind of sound. Refusing to speak, the reader "thickens the air."

Poetry scholars never put it precisely this way, but they're obsessed with silent reading's potential for sound. This comes out whenever they argue, as they often do, against the practice of giving poetry readings. In *Poetry and the Fate of the Senses*, Susan Stewart observes that "the sound of poetry is heard in the way a promise is heard."[4] She has just finished airing her suspicion that, at readings, poets don't *sound out* their poems so much as they *replace* their poems with sound; or, as she puts it, they turn poetry into a mere "artifact of performance." So, when Stewart compares a poem's sound to a promise, she has in mind the sort of promise that lingers, unfulfilled. Of course the promise *can* be fulfilled—say, in a perfect vocal rendering—but often it isn't, and when it isn't the promise endures. "Whether you, the one who receives the promise, continue to exist or not," Stewart says, "the promise exists. Others may discontinue making and fulfilling promises, the word *promise* might disappear, you or others may no longer remember, or deserve, or make sense of that promise—nevertheless, the promise exists."[5] The potential for sound, in other words, outlasts the faintest echo of sound itself.

At some point, though—likely, before "the word *promise*…disappear[s]"—we'll have to admit that the promise has been broken, that these sounds have been lost irrevocably. Once broken, the promise "cannot be mended," Stewart says, only "regretted or used to establish new grounds of demand or indifference."[6] In a way, that's what this essay is about: the promises a printed poem makes with regard to sound, the reader's power to hold a poem to such promises, and what happens when we admit that a poem has broken its promises, when we must look for "new

[2] Daniel Sack, *After Live: Possibility, Potentiality, and the Future of Performance* (Ann Arbor: University of Michigan Press, 2015), 55.

[3] Garrett Stewart, *Reading Voices: Literature and the Phonotext* (Berkeley, CA: University of California Press, 1990), 129.

[4] Susan Stewart, *Poetry and the Fate of the Senses* (Chicago: University of Chicago Press, 2002), 104.

[5] Stewart, *Poetry*, 104.   [6] Stewart, *Poetry*, 104.

grounds of demand or indifference." Along the way, I'll wind up giving you a brief and personal essay on *O*, a basic atom of vocal culture—and one that, across centuries and cultures, has captivated all sorts of writers, but poets most of all.

"Oh! Oh! Oh!"

What would you give to learn what Mrs. Siddons did with those "Oh! Oh! Oh!'s"? They say that people used to faint when she did it; we don't know.

—Richard Boleslavsky, *Acting: The First Six Lessons*[7]

Olivier's famous 'Oh! Oh!'…must still be resounding in some high recess of the New Theatre's dome: some stick of wood must still, I feel, be throbbing from it.

—Kenneth Tynan, *A View of the English Stage*[8]

Let's begin with a man known for promising too much—more, in truth, than any poet could deliver: Robert Frost. "To be perfectly frank with you," he once confided to an aspiring writer, "I am one of the most notable craftsmen of my time.…I alone of English writers have consciously set myself to make music out of what I may call the sound of sense."[9] This silent music, he went on to explain, carries its own vocal cadence so clearly within that, as you read, you should practically hear the words singing. To show what he means, Frost dashes off three dialogues—scenes of two or three people speaking three or four lines. To Frost's credit, two of these dialogues still work. A century later these two scenes are so vivid, their intonations so obvious, I simply know I could perform them well without rehearsal. The third dialogue, however, leaves me baffled. Frost cautions his correspondent: "The reader must be at no loss to give his voice the posture proper to the sentence."[10] But, tasked with striking these poses, my own voice goes gangly—mortified, but trying to play it cool.

> He says it's too late
> Oh, say!
> Damn an Ingersoll watch anyway[11]

Do *you* know how to say this? I don't. With some effort, I guess I can suss out the context. Our two speakers (*or are there three?*) are running late (*but for what?*), and they blame a bad watch (*is that right?*) for their troubles. But *oh, say*? Does that phrase fit in anyone's mouth? If it did, *when* it did, what did it sound like? And if I knew

---

[7] Richard Boleslavsky, *Acting: The First Six Lessons* [1933], ed. Rhonda Blair (Abingdon: Routledge, 2013), 23.

[8] Kenneth Tynan, *A View of the English Stage, 1944–63* (London: Davis-Poynter, 1975), 27.

[9] Robert Frost, *Robert Frost: Collected Poems, Prose, and Plays*, ed. Richard Poirier and Mark Richardson (New York: Library of America, 1995), 664.

[10] Frost, *Robert Frost*, 665.   [11] Frost, *Robert Frost*, 665.

how it used to be said, would I suddenly know how to force my voice into this pose? After sharing this third dialogue, Frost crows, "Those sounds are summoned by the audile imagination . . . unmistakably indicated by the context."[12] But vocal culture is fleeting—and history can be cruel to those who think they've preserved it in print.

That I stumble on a phrase that starts with "oh" is unsurprising. "Oh" belongs to a special class of words. Rich in significance but poor in meaning, these words start to decay the moment anyone buries them in print. As Ludwig Wittgenstein observes in his *Philosophical Grammar*, "the words 'fine,' 'oh,' and also 'perhaps'" are nothing but "pegs to hang intonations on."[13] Richard Poirier—a man whose ear was trained on Frost but whose mind was always playing Wittgensteinian "language games"— makes the very same point about expletives:

> Obviously, "son of a bitch" is a phrase used all the time to mean anything except what it says, anything from "you're terrific" to "how about that!" Persons who use this phrase are not identifying themselves with the words, but wholly with the performance, with the tonal pitch that can be given to the words.[14]

Poirier thrills to the variety in a "performance" whose "tonal pitch" is only tethered temporarily to particular words. *Fine! Oh, perhaps. Son of a bitch!* These phrases don't encode an intonation; they invite us to play.

And play we do: YouTube is full of videos that collect this kind of performance. Someone has gathered every "Oh!" from *The Sopranos*, each "Oh, geez!" found in *Fargo* (take your pick: film or series), and a steady stream of "Oh my gosh!" from movies, TV shows, and amateur videos posted online. When scattered throughout a film, within a series, or across the web, this sort of phrase might sound rote—if it catches your attention at all. Gathered together, they're like a wall full of paint chips at the hardware store: eggshell and cream next to ivory and bone. Screenwriters know this: when they want to make a showcase for actors, they sometimes write a scene with only one word, which the actors repeat in different tones and with varying intent. In a celebrated four-minute scene from *The Wire*, for instance, two detectives piece together clues on a crime scene, conversing only in variations on a single word: "fuck."[15] In fact, this kind of verbal play—where the words stay the same, even as their significance changes—is foundational to the Meisner technique, an influential approach to realist acting today. In Sanford Meisner's famous "repetition game," actors pass words back and forth until they all turn into conduits for some- thing else: not only intonation, but bodily impulse and social action. "An ounce of

---

[12]   Frost, *Robert Frost*, 665.

[13]   Ludwig Wittgenstein, *Philosophical Grammar* (Berkeley, CA: University of California Press, 1978), 66.

[14]   Richard Poirier, *Poetry and Pragmatism* (Cambridge, MA: Harvard University Press, 1992), 141–2.

[15]   "Old Cases," *The Wire* (HBO, June 23, 2002).

behavior is worth a pound of words," Meisner always said.[16] Through repetition, actors make good on this maxim. They keep repeating until, as Poirier says of people who curse, they identify not "with the words, but wholly with the performance."

Scenes like these do more than prove the vocal prowess or charismatic presence of actors; they also flatter (and train) an audience's ear. *See how well you hear the subtlest variations in vocal performance?* If this is true of one-word scenes or repetition games, then supercuts—where words are stripped of the scene that explains them—are like training at altitude. *See how surely you dive into a dozen scenarios? You don't need a narrative run-up to know what you hear!* Yet even as supercuts highlight the variety in these *oh*'s, they also teach us to see the gesture behind them all. If words like *oh* are just "pegs to hang intonations on," then we learn a lot by paying attention to what gets hung—which intonations seem always ready to hand. The frequent "Oh!" of *The Sopranos* is a word of wounded surprise—and of instinctual aggression in response.[17] As such, it neatly sums up the world of this show: dominated by men who are fearsome (as we expect mobsters to be), but fearsome precisely because they're so fragile, rarely in control of themselves or their surroundings. If, as Wittgenstein argues, understanding a word like "oh" means "being able to use it on certain occasions in a special tone of voice," then supercuts help us feel we understand—one "occasion" or "tone of voice" at a time.[18]

Sonic Texture

It is permissible, and can be very effective, to use the word *oh* as an extreme expression of a particular emotion....

—Ayn Rand, *The Art of Fiction*[19]

...what a phrase like "O for a vanished hand" cannot do is tell us how this "O" should be expressed. It catches the moment between a voice emerging and that same voice disintegrating into empty cries or whispers.

—Robert Douglas-Fairhurst, "Address"[20]

It's not just on YouTube that words like *oh* crowd together for the purpose of training or play. It happens all the time in poetry. Take, for instance, this poem by Alfred

---

[16] Sanford Meisner and Dennis Longwell, *Sanford Meisner on Acting* (New York: Vintage, 1987), 4, 22ff.

[17] "The Sopranos Ohs and Hos!" *YouTube*, TheMotherFarquhar, September 19, 2009 (https://www.youtube.com/watch?v=sRkE_Gv6ALM) (accessed January 11, 2017).

[18] Wittgenstein, *Philosophical Grammar*, 66.

[19] Ayn Rand, *The Art of Fiction: A Guide for Writers and Readers* (New York: Penguin, 2000), 108.

[20] Robert Douglas-Fairhurst, "Address," in *The Oxford Handbook of Victorian Poetry*, ed. Matthew Bevis (Oxford: Oxford University Press, 2013), 67–68.

Lord Tennyson, a poet obsessed with *potential voice* in poems—or, as Yopie Prins puts it, with "voice inverse":

> Break, break, break
>> On thy cold gray stones, O Sea!
> And I would that my tongue could utter
>> The thoughts that arise in me.
> O well for the fisherman's boy,
>> That he shouts with his sister at play!
> O well for the sailor lad,
>> That he sings in his boat on the bay!
> And the stately ships go on
>> To their haven under the hill;
> But O for the touch of a vanish'd hand,
>> And the sound of a voice that is still!
> Break, break, break
>> At the foot of thy crags, O Sea!
> But the tender grace of a day that is dead
>> Will never come back to me.[21]

Persnickety grammarians have long distinguished between "O" (by rule, unpunctuated) and "oh" (followed by a comma or an exclamation mark). "O," they say, signals a word in the vocative case; it tells us someone or something is being addressed. "Oh!," meanwhile, is an interjection; it expresses strong feelings, especially of suffering or surprise. These, however, are silly certainties—the sort that only "eye readers" ever have.[22] Tennyson breaks all these rules one by one. He uses "O" for vocative phrases ("O Sea!") *and* interjections (e.g., "O well…")—and his interjected O's go without punctuation. So, from start to finish, this poem's O's look the same, although surely they are different. The reader's task is therefore clear, if contradictory: as in a YouTube supercut, we're asked to explore their variation while also trying to unite them in a single basic gesture that, together, they all perform.

Their variety is obvious. From the grandeur of "O Sea!" our speaker tumbles into misplaced jealousy. "O well for" the "boy" and the "lad," our speaker exclaims, who shout and sing while he can't "utter" a word! Soon, however, his jealousy melts into longing ("But O for the touch…/And the sound…!") before returning—with a difference?—to where he began: "O Sea!" In his *Philosophical Grammar*, Wittgenstein asks, "Can't I say that the sound 'ha ha' is a laugh and the sound 'oh!' is a sigh?"[23] Well, you can, but that's pretty narrow-minded. If you insist on hearing Tennyson's speaker sigh again and again, then what becomes of his power to thunder or croon ("O Sea!")—or of his power to snap, sniffle, or sneer ("O well for" them!)? In short, what becomes of this poem?

[21] Alfred Lord Tennyson, *Tennyson: A Selected Edition*, ed. Christopher Ricks (Berkeley, CA: University of California Press, 1989), 165.

[22] Frost, *Collected*, 809.   [23] Wittgenstein, *Philosophical Grammar*, 66.

Anytime we say precisely what we hear, it can feel like we're destroying what we silently read—trading a boundless potential for one mere possibility. This is surely what Susan Stewart was thinking when she warned that poetry readings can turn poems into "artifact[s] of performance." But this warning presumes that performance is a one-time event—always definitive and final, never playful and provisional. In actual, literal performances, this is seldom how it goes. Variation from one reading to the next ensures that each poem is filled with unrealized sonic potential. The same goes for variation *within* a poem: many O's clustered together free this word from a single sound (e.g., a sigh) and its conventional significance.

At the same time—like those furious, fragile *oh*'s in the *Sopranos* supercut—Tennyson's O's slowly blur together, too, as in a composite photograph. Heard in composite, the possible O's of "Break, Break, Break" share one potential, which thickens the sonic texture heard in each. "O Sea!" is classic apostrophe: the rhetorical invocation of an impossible listener. "But O for...!" is utterly conventional: an expression of longing for something just out of reach. "O well for...," however, is idiosyncratic. Repeated twice, it is (for me) the crux of this poem. Robert Douglas-Fairhurst hears it as "a smattering of applause" or a "nod of approval," but I can't hear it that way—certainly not in conjunction with the poem's other O's.[24] In isolation, these O's might express any number of things. Together, they vent the same frustrated desire. *O for "a vanish'd hand," "a day that is dead," "a voice that is still!" O for my voice, struck dead and buried in the page! O for the Sea—O for you, whoever you are, if you're listening—O for anyone to hear my unuttered words!* Jonathan Culler once declared apostrophe "embarrassing."[25] Without waiting to hear his reasons, Tennyson would agree: apostrophe indulges in impossible desires, longs for things that are "vanish'd," "still," and "dead." Grandiose passions and weak indignation, the thirst and self-loathing that attend on loss: this embarrassing mixture of feelings is what Tennyson's speaker—what *any* apostrophizing poet—truly deserves.

How to "Hear"

The history of sound is at different moments strangely silent, strangely gory, strangely visual, and always contextual.... If there is no "mere" or innocent description of sound, then there is no "mere" or innocent description of sonic experience.
—Jonathan Sterne, *The Audible Past*[26]

Perhaps you've noticed that I still haven't told you how a single O actually sounds, in "Break, Break, Break" or in any other text. Instead, I've given what film folks call

---

[24] Douglas-Fairhurst, "Address," 67.
[25] Jonathan Culler, *The Pursuit of Signs* (Ithaca, NY: Cornell University Press, 1981), 135.
[26] Jonathan Sterne, *The Audible Past: Cultural Origins of Sound Reproduction* (Durham, NC: Duke University Press, 2003), 13.

the "wrylies": quick annotations of the feeling, tone, or action behind a line. Actors today, on stage or screen, hate "wrylies"—almost as much as they hate directors who dare to give them "line readings." Someone else speaking a line for them to mimic? Intolerable! A line's sound is the result of an actor's work, which goes unseen, unheard by others. That's because language itself, according to the prevailing view, is just the fungible stuff of inner action. To set the melody of any line, as if these words were song lyrics, would be to flout the inner process of actors—to trample on their personal and professional integrity. Well, I'm not trying to give you line readings. I wouldn't dare. Let the hidden work of reading go on—silent, thickening the air—but *do* let the air get thick.

To thicken the sounds you hear in silence, it might help to reconsider what these sorts of "sound" and "hearing" actually are. As Karl Marx famously observed, "The forming of the five senses is a labor of the entire history of the world down to the present."[27] That is, our notions about the senses—that we have five of them, for instance—aren't simple truths about the human body. They're ideological, shaped by millennia of history and a lifetime of culture. The same goes for sensory experience itself. As scholars have argued in sound studies, visual culture, and other sense-specific fields, sensation happens at the crossroads of anatomy, imagination, and technique. That is, techniques that people develop throughout history—and that we individually acquire over the course of our lifetimes—guide how we use whatever anatomy we may have. As soon as this well-trained apparatus picks up a signal, imagination gets involved, shaping what we perceive. Literature, dealing not in sensation but in sensory potential, plays this same game but in reverse. When we say that we "hear sounds" as we read, we mean that we're traveling (with an author's help) from imaginings back to a signal—from signal, perhaps, back to noise.

This movement toward noise may sound chaotic, as if it's sending us away from the meaning of whatever we read; in practice, the opposite is true. When poets write "oh," they find meaning precisely *in* noise—or in a reader's guided journey back to noise. This is nowhere clearer than in all those recent poems where *oh* appears just once—or several times in quick succession—at the climax. The whole poem has been building toward this. All the displaced significance of every other line collects here. So, to "hear" this *oh*—to really know how it "sounds"—becomes the same thing as understanding the poem. That's certainly true in the following prose-poem from Claudia Rankine's *Citizen*, which, like many in that book, recounts an everyday experience of racial animus:

> The new therapist specializes in trauma counseling. You have only ever spoken on the phone. Her house has a side gate that leads to a back entrance she uses for patients. You walk down a path bordered on both sides with deer grass and rosemary to the gate, which turns out to be locked.

---

[27] Quoted in Sterne, *The Audible Past*, 5; Stewart, *Poetry*, 40.

At the front door the bell is a small round disc that you press firmly. When the door finally opens, the woman standing there yells, at the top of her lungs, Get away from my house. What are you doing in my yard?

It's as if a wounded Doberman pinscher or a German shepherd has gained the power of speech. And though you back up a few steps, you manage to tell her you have an appointment. You have an appointment? she spits back. Then she pauses. Everything pauses. Oh, she says, followed by, oh, yes, that's right. I am sorry.

I am so sorry, so, so sorry.[28]

The first "Oh" is a knee-jerk response, and it is clearly the crux of Rankine's poem. This is where two of her book's most persistent subjects, white supremacy and liberal instinct, intersect in this poem. The second "oh" is the sound of social graces returning—but who are we kidding? Niceties can't sound nice anymore, not after the scene that we've just witnessed. The first "oh"—sudden and blunt, muscles seizing—is like a dark moon sliding over an angry sun. "Oh, yes, that's right" does its best to pull us back from guard-dog noises to the lilting cadence of business as usual. Except not quite. *Oh—yes—that's—right.* Like an amateur actor (or a second-rate robot) she takes a pretty poor stab at this line. Of course she fails to paper over the sinkhole that has opened, threatening to swallow Rankine's speaker and us all. No "so, so sorry" will put the lilt back in her voice. No casual cadence will reclaim her innocence. As James Baldwin famously observed, "It is the innocence which constitutes the crime."[29]

White supremacy, in this poem, is itself a problem of the sensory imagination: a force that warps the world by shaping what (white) Americans "see" and "hear." From the moment the speaker tells us that she has "only ever spoken" to the "new therapist…on the phone," we should know where this is heading: a story about "sounding white" and "looking black." But in order to understand the force of this racial imaginary, how it worms its way into our world, you need to hear its inner actions converted back into noise. You need to "hear" the word *oh* just as the therapist blurts it—and, in order to "hear" that, you'll need more than a knowledge of white American vocal culture, more than an ear tuned to *Citizen's* sonic potential. You'll need a mind's ear that's close to your mind's racing heart, and not very far from the pit of its stomach.

Not a Promise, But a Threat

The speech act says more, or says differently, than it means to say.
—Judith Butler, *Excitable Speech*[30]

[28] Claudia Rankine, *Citizen: An American Lyric* (Minneapolis, MN: Graywolf Press, 2014), 18.
[29] James Baldwin, *The Fire Next Time* [1963] (New York: Vintage, 1992), 6.
[30] Judith Butler, *Excitable Speech: A Politics of the Performative* (New York: Routledge, 1997), 10.

> By acknowledging the ways in which our voices are spoken through, we are bound
> to hear more than we meant to say.
>
> —Susan Stewart, *Poetry and the Fate of the Senses*[31]

A poem performed—even, I suggest, one sounded in silence—is never the work of a single person. It's a space around which communities gather, in which whole cultures can be heard. That's the point that Tyler Hoffman makes in *American Poetry in Performance* about certain "sermon poems" by black writers.[32] Some of these poems clearly encode the cadence of black preachers, as if for outside ethnographers to "hear." Others treat true knowledge of this cadence as an aural shibboleth: if you "hear" these poems, it means you know the black church. Literary "hearing" often functions this way. Take, as another example, Frank O'Hara's famous line from *Lunch Poems*, "oh Lana Turner we love you get up."[33] Besides providing yet another example of a climactic, lynchpin *oh* in recent poetry, this line relies on specific aural knowledge—in this case, of a certain gay, male vocal culture. As Doug Mao once suggested to me, you might in fact be able to tell a whole history of campy affection by following this *oh* from midcentury poems like O'Hara's to, say, early twenty-first-century sitcoms. Specifically, he was thinking of the following line from *Will & Grace*: "Ah, Oprah! What are you doing on that horse?"[34] (That he remembered this line as "Oh, Oprah…" proves the point: vocal traditions can alter what we "hear," as can a leading question from a friend.) As soon as he said it, I knew I'd *always* "heard" O'Hara's *oh* that way, without ever knowing why I did. And when Kamran Javadizadeh pointed me toward the "Payne Whitney Poems" of James Schuyler— another gay poet and one-time roommate of O'Hara's—I instantly knew I was hearing this same *oh* in the last line of "Sleep": "Give my love to, oh, anybody."[35]

I wouldn't normally cite cocktail-party chatter in scholarship, but these methods are pertinent to my point. Just as we speak in many voices (not all our own), so we hear with the help of the people who lend us their ears. My ear was tuned to the viral spreading of *O* throughout poems by Deborah Nelson (Walt Whitman's "O Captain, My Captain"), Rhonda Cobham-Sander (Derek Walcott's *Omeros*), Carrie Noland (Saint-John Perse's *Éloges*), and Michael Weinstein (John Berryman's *Dream Songs*). Meanwhile, I heard the recent trend toward lone, climactic *O*'s with the help of Raphael Allison (Tracy K. Smith's "Wade in the Water") and, once more, Kamran Javadizadeh (Donika Kelly's "Love Letter"). That's what I meant when I warned you from the start that this would be a personal essay on *O*: not that I planned to get confessional, but that my argument would reveal my networks, my cultures, my

[31] Stewart, *Poetry*, 143.

[32] Tyler Hoffman, *American Poetry in Performance: From Walt Whitman to Hip Hop* (Ann Arbor: University of Michigan Press, 2013), 94ff.

[33] Frank O'Hara, *Lunch Poems* (San Francisco: City Lights, 2001), 64.

[34] "Heart Like a Wheelchair," *Will & Grace* (NBC, November 6, 2003).

[35] James Schuyler, *The Morning of the Poem* (New York: Farrar, Straus and Giroux, 1981), 51.

social life. It was bound to be personal—not the way a diary is, but the way date books or browser histories are.

Still, no matter how "personal" your hearing may be, what you "hear" while you read can still take you by surprise. Sometimes, it can even take you by force. As an example of this, consider Patti Smith's poem "rape." (The full poem is available in her 1973 book *Witt*, as well as in the Norton edition of her *Early Work: 1970–1979*.[36]) It won't take readers long to notice that this poem gives them the lyrical perspective of an unrepentant rapist. This is clear in many places, but I hear it most of all in his *O*'s: a rapist's crooning pleasure-song ("ohhh that's soft," "ohh yeah that's hard"), which turns orgasmic ("ohhh ahhh") before the poem is through. By the poem's final lines, these *O*'s are everywhere, throbbing through other words, pushing the poem toward its rapturous conclusion: "bobby sock-o let's flow.../let's rock let's roll/ let's whalebone let's go/let's deodorize the night."

No one who hears this poem—even in the mind's ear—can stay clear of its execrable pleasures. For Smith, this was the point. Performed often at concerts in the early 1970s (the heyday of feminist consciousness-raising), "rape" was surely an act of punk transgression—something akin to David Bowie's performance in persona as the Nazi-loving Thin White Duke. On recordings of Smith performing "rape," it's obvious she takes pleasure in slipping into a predator's skin—in having an audience *see her do it*. But on the page the poem works differently—less shock and awe, and more a kind of slow entrapment. With its insistent rhythm and rhyme, much of it cutting against the poem's visible form, this poem hails the reader's ear, loudly demanding to be "heard." This demand can feel violent—straining our tact, dragging our bodies (real or imagined) into a terrible scene of subjection.

By affording us no other place to stand, no chance to stay aloof or to profess our innocence, the poem *involves* us. This involvement can have unforeseen effects. Garrett Stewart suggests that our "principal organs" for silent reading are "the listening throat and mouth of the reading voice."[37] In reading "rape," you may feel as though your "listening throat and mouth" have been hijacked by a rapist. If so, you will feel this power as a violation, planting this man somewhere inside you, like a demon or a disease. But the poem also generates raw vocal power—*Let's flow…let's go*—and this power might be put to other ends. In their strained and stifled silence, your "listening throat and mouth" might more plausibly belong to his victim. If so, then this poem may be a paradox: the words are his, but the voice they empower is hers.

I began this essay by talking about the promise poems make, but this *promise* can be felt as a *threat*. Threats land hard, but they cannot simply *do what they say*—not right away. To say, "I promise" is (in the proper circumstances) to have promised, but, as Judith Butler argues, threats don't work the same way. They merely open

---

[36] Patti Smith, *Witt* (New York: Gotham Book Mart, 1973), 24. Patti Smith, *Early Work: 1970–1979*, 2nd edn (New York: W. W. Norton & Company, 1995), 52.

[37] Stewart, *Reading Voices*, 11.

"a temporal horizon" in which the threatened "act *might* be achieved" (emphasis added). Within that window of time, Butler notes, a threat "may well solicit a response...it never anticipated":

> Instead of obliterating the possibility of response, paralyzing the addressee with fear, the threat may well be countered by a different kind of performative act...turn[ing] one part of that speaking against the other...[38]

Smith's "rape" can inspire this sort of response. Though it stifles its victims, it also gives us a voice. Feel it, there: in your "listening throat and mouth." This is not the rapist's voice, which you can hear but hold at bay. It is the voice of another who speaks through him, who "turn[s] one part of that speaking against the other" and makes the threat say "more, or...differently, than it means to say." *The sound of poetry is heard the way a threat is heard.* There might be power, even freedom, to be found in that.

FURTHER READING

Allison, Raphael. *Bodies on the Line: Performance and the Sixties Poetry Reading.* Iowa City, IA: University of Iowa Press, 2014.

Bernstein, Charles, ed. *Close Listening: Poetry and the Performed Word.* New York: Oxford University Press, 1998.

Eidsheim, Nina Sun. *The Race of Sound.* Durham, NC: Duke University Press, 2019.

Grobe, Christopher. "On Book: The Performance of Reading." *New Literary History* 47.4 (2016): 567–89.

MacArthur, Marit. "Monotony, the Churches of Poetry Reading, and Sound Studies." *PMLA* 131.1 (2016): 38–63.

Perloff, Marjorie, and Craig Dworkin, ed. *The Sound of Poetry/The Poetry of Sound.* Chicago: University of Chicago Press, 2009.

Phelan, Peggy. "'Just Want to Say': Performance and Literature, Jackson and Poirier." *PMLA* 125.4 (2010): 942-7.

Prins, Yopie. "Voice Inverse." *Victorian Poetry* 42.1 (2004): 43–59.

Stewart, Susan. *Poetry and the Fate of the Senses.* Chicago: University of Chicago Press, 2002.

Wheeler, Lesley. *Voicing American Poetry: Sound and Performance from the 1920s to the Present.* Ithaca, NY: Cornell University Press, 2008.

---

[38] Butler, *Excitable Speech*, 11–12.

16

TOUCH

GILLIAN SILVERMAN

Clara Claiborne Park begins her memoir, *The Siege: The First Eight Years of an Autistic Child*, by describing the phenomenon of pointing:

> To point is so simple, so spontaneous, so primary an action that it seems ridiculous to analyze it. All babies point, do they not? To stretch out the arm and the finger is, symbolically and literally, to stretch out the self into the world—in order to remark on an object, to call it to another's attention, perhaps to want it for oneself. From pointing comes the question "What's that?" that unlocks the varied world. To point, to reach, to stretch, to grab, is to make a relation between oneself and the outside.[1]

From pointing, to stretching, to grabbing—the extended arm showcases the subject in relation to her surrounding environment. Following Park, then, to touch is to cross over, to leave the realm of the self, to approach intersubjectivity with other beings or with the object world. In seeing, there is recognition, but in touch, there is the primal experience of contact—the fingers press against that which is foreign and in the process the boundaries between self and other are obscured. All touched objects function briefly as prosthetics, extending the body in new directions, creating, through the erasure of distance, a formal unity.

Reading usually begins with touch, but accounts of literacy tend to downplay this contact with the text, creating a contradictory experience for the reader. On the one hand, books, magazines, Kindles, even 8.5" × 11" paper are sized for our bodies—generally made to be toted, to fit on laps, to be manipulated with fingers. As Thomas A. Volger writes,

> The book is embodied in the form of an intimate portable object.... [It] must be of a middle size in order to embody images of the completeness, simplicity and stability of the ideal of a "self." Its size and production costs must be congruent with private ownership.[2]

---

[1] Clara Claiborne Park, *The Siege: The First Eight Years of an Autistic Child* (Boston, MA: Little, Brown, 1982), 6.

[2] Thomas A. Volger, "When a Book is Not a Book," in *A Book of the Book: Some Works and Projections about the Book and Writing*, ed. Jerome Rothenberg and Steven Clay (New York: Granary Books, 2000), 459.

In a related point, Gary Frost comments on the "primary corporeal nature" of the book, "both as an analogy to human anatomy and as a hand-held object." Books, like bodies, are upright. We speak of their spines, headers, and footnotes. Their recto and verso sides create a "bilateral symmetry and asymmetry" that mirror the left and right handedness of readers.[3] Thus, books are both fashioned after the body and designed for manual manipulation.

On the other hand, books have long been accompanied by proscriptions *against* touching, or at least touching too much. In the nineteenth century, early precursors to braille were rejected precisely because they involved too much fondling. Hebrew scholars still use a *yad*, or pointer, when reading the Torah (even in codex form) to avoid bodily contamination of the Holy Scriptures. Children are socialized out of touching their books, expected, as they age, to trade tactile pleasures (like those found in *Pat the Bunny*) for interpretive ones.

Stated slightly differently, reading is largely theorized as a cognitive activity, despite the holding, grasping, and turning it necessitates. Indeed, for many scholars the physical book disappears the moment its contents are intellectually engaged. As Georges Poulet writes,

> Where is the book I held in my hands? It is still there, and at the same time it is there no longer, it is nowhere. That object wholly object, that thing made of paper, as there are things made of metal or porcelain, that object is no more, or at least it is as if it no longer existed, as long as I read the book. For the book is no longer a material reality. It has become a series of words, of images, of ideas which in their turn begin to exist.[4]

Amazon.com's publicity team reaffirms Poulet's comments in their marketing campaign for the Kindle: "The most elegant feature of a physical book is that it disappears while you're reading. Immersed in the author's world and ideas, you don't notice a book's glue, the stitching, or ink."[5] Perhaps noticing the materiality of books (or e-readers) is frowned upon because it suggests the failure of cognitive work. In any case, proscriptions against touch are made explicit through the tendency to render all activity on the part of the reader passive. We speak not of touching books but of finding them touching, not of moving paper but of being moved by it. If, as stated earlier, touching involves the extended arm reaching out to that which lies outside, in reading that practice is rendered non-material; for Poulet and for the folks at Amazon, we visit other worlds imaginatively, leaving our bodies behind.

---

[3] Gary Frost, "Reading by Hand: The Haptic Evaluation of Artists' Books," *The Bonefolder: An E-Journal for the Bookbinder and Book Artist* 2.1 (2005): 3–4.

[4] Georges Poulet, "Criticism and the Experience of Interiority," in *Reader-Response Criticism: From Formalism to Post-Structuralism*, ed. Jane P. Tompkins (Baltimore: Johns Hopkins University Press, 1980), 41–49; 42.

[5] Quoted in James Mussell, *The Nineteenth-Century Press in the Digital Age* (New York: Palgrave, 2012), 19.

In this context, the invitation to touch a book takes on significance, even an edge of transgression. Consider Marcel Duchamp's soft sculpture *Prière de toucher* (*Please Touch*) created in collaboration with artist Enrico Donati (Figure 16.1). A catalog produced in numbered editions for the 1947 *Exposition Internationale du Surréalisme*, the cover features a reproduction of a breast (putatively modeled on Duchamp's mistress) in foam rubber on black velvet and cardboard. The breast clearly functions as an erotically charged object, but I am emphasizing its specific presence on a book, along with the accompanying command (on the back cover) to "please touch." Here Duchamp invites readers to engage the haptic pleasures of books, making explicit what many of us intuitively know—that books are not simply semantic formulations, that we often delight in their construction, that their material covers offer sensual gratifications (even when not shaped to resemble a breast). Art historians have understood Duchamp's soft sculpture as a playful rejoinder to the ubiquitous "Do Not Touch" signs that usually accompany museum exhibitions, but it is equally a comment on the book-object, which, like the art

Figure 16.1 Marcel Duchamp, *Prière de toucher (Please Touch)*, 1947. Book with collage of foam rubber, pigment, velvet, and cardboard adhered to removable cover. Cover: 9 1/4 x 8 1/16 inches (23.5 x 20.5 cm). © Association Marcel Duchamp/ADAGP, Paris/Artists Rights Society (ARS), New York 2018.

object, is often figured in visual and cognitive terms—as that which gives pleasure through distanced comprehension rather than through handling.

This understanding of reading is partially a result of the systematic downgrading of touch as a sensory function. As historians of tactility have explained, early philosophers, since at least the Renaissance, lauded those senses that operate at a distance—hearing and sight—while treating the proximal senses—taste, smell, touch—with suspicion and disdain, largely because of their more direct connection with the body. According to David Parisi, this begins to change in the late nineteenth century when scientists like Ernst Weber sought to quantify, through experimentation, the sense of touch, portraying it as "rational, predictable, and manageable." The hope, Parisi explains, was to "transform touch into an efficient epistemological instrument, capable of accurately and predictably measuring the external world."[6] Despite these advances, however, touch remains underexplored, a downgraded and repressed sensory mechanism whose role in cognition is largely ignored. It is subordinated, in particular, to the optic, that king of perceptive modes that has reigned since the Enlightenment. While empirical evidence suggests that the act of seeing is an intersensory phenomenon, reliant on proprioception and touch as much as on vision, it is usually conceived as functioning autonomously, allowing us to imagine that seeing is tantamount to knowing. Chantal Faust expresses the implicit connection between the visual and the epistemological in this way: "To see things more clearly, to gain a better perspective over a situation, to give it a good hard look, to eyeball something: all of these sayings about seeing are bound up in forms of knowledge and critique."[7]

Nowhere is this emphasis on sight as the basis for knowledge more explicit than in the practice of reading. "The book is an extension of the eye," Marshall McLuhan wrote famously in explaining how technologies of print contributed to the dominant role of the visual in Western perceptual schemes.[8] According to McLuhan, because typography favors seeing over all other senses, it has systematically contributed to a detached form of linear perception, characterized by fixity and rationalism, in which "the interplay of all the senses in haptic harmony" no longer exists.[9] To read, in other words, is to mobilize the optic in the service of linear continuity and at the expense of more mosaic and intuitive schemes of understanding. Julie Kane extends McLuhan's thesis by suggesting that print literacy is the basis for left hemisphere brain dominance, a phenomenon that has contributed to the enshrinement of analytical thought and the concomitant marginalization of poetry,

---

[6] David P. Parisi, "Tactile Modernity: On the Rationalization of Touch in the Nineteenth Century," in *Media, Technology, and Literature in the Nineteenth Century: Image, Sound, Touch*, ed. Colette Colligan and Margaret Linley (New York: Routledge, 2016), 189–213; 192, 203.

[7] Chantal Faust, "Haptic Aesthetics," *Transimage Conference*, Plymouth, 2016.

[8] Marshall McLuhan and Quentin Fiore, *The Medium is the Massage: An Inventory of Effects* (New York: Random House, 1967), 33–6.

[9] Marshall McLuhan, *Gutenberg Galaxy: The Making of Typographic Man* (Toronto: University of Toronto Press, 2011), 21.

magical thinking, and animism in Western life.[10] In this way, books have been placed at the center of a perceptual scheme allied with vision, lateral sequencing, and rationalism, where touch (and the other proximal senses) seem to play little part despite their necessary role in our encounters with print. Partly as a response, scholars have pointed to the bibliographic elements of texts—including tactile aspects like size, binding, and thickness of paper—along with the extra-semantic work of books, emphasizing, for example, their object status and their uses beyond reading. In this way, touch has been invoked, albeit usually indirectly, as an implicit element of book engagement.

Thinking about reading in relation to touch (alongside vision) is important, for it can partially elide the linearity and rationalism that McLuhan aligns with the book. Touch has the ability to upset the logic of telos or sequentialism because it involves reciprocity, as phenomenologists like Maurice Merleau-Ponty have pointed out. To touch something is always also to *be* touched, to feel the pressure of another object, or even another part of one's own body, pushing back.[11] While other senses may enjoy a similar mutuality (Merleau-Ponty also writes of the reversibility of vision whereby the seer, by virtue of her embodiment, is also capable of being seen), touch perhaps more explicitly destabilizes one's subject position, so that the fiction of our acting on the world independently is more readily exposed. For this reason, Eve Sedgwick has written that "the sense of touch makes nonsense out of any dualistic understanding of agency and passivity."[12] Susan Stewart makes a related claim when she writes (following Emmanuel Levinas) that "touch is nonteleological; it begins and goes forward without anticipating any particular point of arrival."[13] An exploratory touch—more caress than grasp—is partial and incomplete; it never fully anticipates its direction, and in this way it forestalls perceptual mastery.

It is for this reason that some scholars have embraced what Laura Marks calls "haptic criticism." Originally invoked as a way of referencing the perceived tactility of visual art, the phrase now refers to forms of criticism that linger on the materiality of the aesthetic object and its ability to evoke a desire to touch. Such a desire attenuates the distance between spectator and object, bringing the two into more intimate contact, while disabling the instrumentalism usually associated with purely visual critique. Marks describes her own form of haptic criticism as "mov[ing] along the surface of the object, rather than attempting to penetrate or 'interpret' it, as criticism is usually supposed to do."[14] Haptic criticism is thus a species of what Stephen Best and

[10] Julie Kane, "Poetry as Right Hemispheric Language," *PsyArt: A Hyperlink Journal for the Psychological Study of the Arts* (2007), n.p. (http://psyartjournal.com/article/show/kane-poetry_as_ right_hemispheric_language accessed July 2017).

[11] Maurice Merleau-Ponty, *Phenomenology of Perception* (New York: Routledge, 2002), 106–7.

[12] Eve Kosofsky Sedgwick, *Touching Feeling: Affect, Pedagogy, Performativity* (Durham, NC: Duke University Press, 2003), 14.

[13] Susan Stewart, *Poetry and the Fate of the Senses* (Chicago: University of Chicago Press, 2002), 168.

[14] Laura U. Marks, *Touch: Sensuous Theory and Multisensory Media* (Minneapolis, MN: University of Minnesota Press, 2002), xiii.

Sharon Marcus have called "surface reading"—designed to replace deep interpretive plumbing of the text with recognition of the book's voluptuous, non-symbolic immediacy.[15] Recognizing that reading involves touch means integrating the optic and the haptic, so that post-Enlightenment ideals of distanced cognition are tempered by the textured trace of the physical book and its affective role in our lives.

To explore further the role of touch in reading, it is helpful to return to Duchamp's *Prière de toucher* (*Please Touch*). Like his readymades—a series of found objects ranging from a bicycle wheel to a men's urinal—this piece works to resist what Duchamp called "retinal" art, or art that appeals primarily to the eye.[16] But the book is perhaps a more complicated choice for this than is a urinal or wheel. For the book is an object already located halfway between the aesthetic and the functional, the eye and the hand. It demands touch even as it obscures that demand through its alignment with high art—Literature with a capital L. For this reason, the book is particularly useful in destabilizing the boundary between optics and haptics or art and the everyday. Perhaps this explains why so many artists interested in such intersections have chosen the book as their medium. So-called artists' books make use of the codex structure but in ways that exceed the practice of readerly interpretation. Artists' books shut down semantic engagement in favor of beauty, conceptualism, or interactivity, which is why Garrett Stewart calls them forms of "demediation."[17] They draw attention to the materiality of their form, the very "glue, the stitching, or ink" that the Kindle marketers insist disappears as soon as we begin to read. Thus, unlike the mass-produced book—sized for our bodies and constructed for our convenience—that obscures its material features in favor of seamless linguistic transmission, artists' books can be gargantuan or tiny, physically impenetrable or exquisitely fragile, their dysfunctionality as reading material calling attention to their *thingness*.

While most artists' books are visually arresting, I would like to single out a few productions that invite touch, and, in particular, that can be engaged only through hands-on manipulation. Consider, for example, the flexagon, a multidimensional object constructed through folded strips of paper which can be flexed to reveal hidden faces not visible on the original back and front panels (Figure 16.2). Part of what this form does is confuse the distinction between the outside of the book and its inside, since every fold reverses "cover" and "pages" much like how Gilles Deleuze describes the working of origami.[18] In this way, flexagons resist the impulse to privilege the book's semantic interior over its material conveyance; indeed, the two are conflated the moment the book-object is engaged. Moreover, the form demands

[15] Stephen Best and Sharon Marcus, "Surface Reading: An Introduction," *Representations* 108.1 (2009): 1–21.

[16] Calvin Tomkins, *The World of Marcel Duchamp: 1887–1968* (New York: Time-Life Books, 1966), 9.

[17] Garrett Stewart, "Bookwork as Demediation," *Critical Inquiry* 36.3 (2010): 410–57.

[18] Gilles Deleuze, *The Fold: Leibniz and the Baroque*, trans. Tom Conley (Minneapolis, MN: University of Minnesota Press, 1993), 6.

Figure 16.2 Carolyn Shattuck, *The Quilts of Gee's Bend*. Printed to honor the Gee's Bend women. Flexagon, H-3.5 x W-8.5x D-8.5 inches.

active haptic participation, since to "read" a flexagon, one must pick it up and subject it physically to various twists, flips, and inversions. If McLuhan character-izes print literacy as visual, lateral, and linear, then the flexagon actively thwarts these tenets, insisting on manual engagement and yielding meaning only through non-sequential, mosaic movement.

Eve Kosofsky Sedgwick's untitled flexagon offers a case in point. Sedgwick is, of course, best known for her writing on Victorian literature and queer theory, but she also produced an impressive collection of artists' books, many of which comment on her theoretical interests. Her two-dimensional flexagon (technically termed a hexaflexagon for its six faces) is imprinted with rubber-stamped Koi fish sur-rounded by text from Marcel Proust's *In Search of Lost Time* (Figure 16.3). The illustration I've provided captures one static face of the flexagon but not the dynamic movement and continuous finger play it invites when engaged. The object recalls Sedgwick's investment in tactile experience—what her *Dialogue on Love* calls "skin hunger"—as well as her interest in the relationship of text to texture, as explicated in *Touching Feeling*.[19] It also recalls her interest in the preposition "besides" as a way of circumventing critical theory's obsession with hidden origins. In contrast to a surface/depth model of understanding, the word "besides" invokes an anti-dualistic scheme of proximity, since "a number of elements may lie alongside one another."

[19] Eve Kosofsky Sedgwick, *A Dialogue on Love* (New York: Beacon, 2000), 206.

Figure 16.3 Eve Kosofsky Sedgwick, Hexaflexagon, 2008. Folded paper, approx. 7" in diameter. Copyright by H. A. Sedgwick.

Indeed, one might say of the flexagon what Sedgwick has written of the preposition "besides"—that it comprises a wide range of relations including "paralleling, differentiating, rivaling, leaning, twisting, mimicking, withdrawing," and so forth.[20] The flexagon concretizes Sedgwick's material and tactile preoccupations—concerns that are only ever approximated (through words) in her theoretical writing—while disabling questions of origin and telos. It therefore demands that we approach the book-object in a new way.

The accordion book, like the flexagon, also invites manipulation, and its haptic investments are especially evident in Sammy Seung-min Lee's *The Beads in My Hand* (Figure 16.4). Lee's artist's book is constructed through a series of connected panels, each featuring an image of a blurred hand holding a series of colored beads threaded together and surrounded by unreadable text. Smaller movable panels superimposed on the blurred hand create the possibility of dynamic action by suggesting (while also calling forth from the reader) haptic participation. On the back of Lee's piece—against the magnified image of a hand's interior and in undulating lines that cannot be read without manipulating the work—appears Stephen Mitchell's English translation of the poem "Handinneres" or "Palm" by Rainer Maria Rilke. It reads as follows:

---

[20] Sedgwick, *Touching Feeling*, 8.

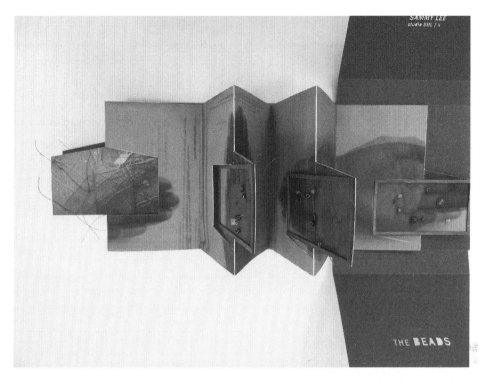

Figure 16.4 Sammy Seung-min Lee, *The Beads in My Hand*, 2009. Double-sided accordion extending from base of box. Cloth-covered boards with inset paper illustration, 6.5" x 6.5" x 1.5".

> Interior of the hand. Sole that has come to walk
> only on feelings. That faces upward
> and in its mirror
> receives heavenly roads, which travel
> along themselves.
> That has learned to walk upon water
> when it scoops,
> that walks upon wells,
> transfiguring every path.
> That steps into other hands,
> changes those that are like it
> into a landscape:
> wanders and arrives within them,
> fills them with arrival.[21]

Invoking the hand as the counterpart of the foot—an appendage that "travels," though through the air rather than on land, face up rather than heel down—Rilke characterizes the palm as more spiritual than functional: it "receives heavenly

[21] Rainer Maria Rilke, *Ahead of All Parting: The Selected Poetry and Prose of Rainer Maria Rilke*, trans. Stephen Mitchell (New York: Random House, 1995), 181.

roads," it can "walk upon water," it "transfigur[es] every path." Perhaps most importantly, unlike its pedial counterpart, the hand "steps into other hands," creating "landscapes" of connection. This understanding of the hand as that which travels and holds, transfigures and joins, is reiterated in Lee's book-object, which depicts a hand both cupping objects and moving, in the company of other hands, not only through its own reproduction in the multiple panels but also through the implied presence of Lee, of Rilke, and of the reader, whose own hands must actively engage the accordion book to glean meaning. As with Sedgwick's flexagon, Lee's work emphasizes the materiality of the art object and its relationship to touch, reminding us both of the sensual aspects of books and of the way these might countervail the linear sequencing and cognitive mastery usually associated with the practice of reading.

One final example: Susan Joy Share is an artist, perhaps best known for her "book performances" in which she mixes bodily movement with the physical object of the book—draping book-like creations on her head and around her body; building accordion structures that she plays with in her hands or wears as costumes (Figure 16.5). In explaining the confluence of her interests, Share has said,

Figure 16.5 Susan Joy Share, *Fog and Flame*, 2000. A folded cardboard quilt worn as head gear. Bookboard, linen cord, acrylic, 57" x 4" x 6" closed, 72" x 57" x 1" open.

I enjoy the physicality of the book, how we relate to it with our bodies. When we move a book, we are manipulating it, and it's that idea of manipulation that has been my focus, how we connect physically, how our bodies relate to the book.[22]

Share is interested not simply in the tactile aspects of books but also in the kinesthetic and proprioceptive aspects of reading—how our bodies and books occupy space together. Brian Massumi has helpfully explained the difference:

Tactility is the sensibility of the skin as surface of contact between the perceiving subject and the perceived object. Proprioception folds tactility into the body, enveloping the skin's contact with the external world in a dimension of medium depth: between epidermis and viscera. The muscles and ligaments register as conditions of movement what the skin internalizes as qualities....Proprioception translates the exertions and ease of the body's encounters with objects into a muscular memory of relationality.[23]

It is partly this "muscular memory of relationality" that Share's performances enact. Rather than processing the book as semantic meaning, she physically records it as a felt and lived experience of intersubjectivity, reminding us of the phenomenal and object-oriented dimensions of reading. Books, for Share, are not, *contra* McLuhan, extensions of the eye but extensions of the body, ways of reaching across distance and heterogeneity to achieve intimacy.

In one of her most intriguing performances, *Unfoldings*, Share occupies the stage with a large box that she pushes around with her head, embraces, sits on, and then begins to unfurl. Inside are reams of textured pages, each one attached to the next through various book-binding techniques. Share moves and dances among these pages, rifling her fingers across those that are particularly rich in tactile sensation, uncoiling others so that they splay from her hands to the floor like flowing water (Figure 16.6). At one point Share boxes her own body in by the pages so that she needs to high-step over the construction to escape. Through it all, one has the sense that Share is unpacking the book in physical terms, literalizing the experience of being immersed in text. At the end of the eight-minute performance, Share reverses her movements, refolding the pages of her "book" so that no sign of the alternative world contained by it is visible. The effect resembles the aftermath of reading, where the closed book remains inscrutable, never betraying the metamorphosis (in its reader and on its pages) occasioned by it. Share has said that a similar performance piece, *Unfolded World*, is about "the transformation of the [book] object and our transformation as we manipulate it."[24] We are used to thinking about reading as a potentially transformative experience, in which we visit other worlds and are altered by them. In her performances, Share corporealizes that experience; it's not narrative that changes us (*Unfoldings* contains no spoken word, and the unfurled book is

---

[22] Susan Joy Share, *Basically Books: The Artwork of Susan Joy Share*, YouTube, December 19, 2012, (https://www.youtube.com/watch?v=n1OrR_0W4p4&t=66s).

[23] Brian Massumi, *Parables for the Virtual: Movement, Affect, Sensation* (Durham, NC: Duke University Press, 2002), 58–9.

[24] Share, *Basically Books*.

Figure 16.6 Susan Joy Share, *Unfoldings*, 1985, a 13" cube that opens out, up, and across the floor. Bookboard, paper, cloth acrylic, cord, photos, 13' cube (closed); 5' (high) x 15' (wide) x 15' (deep) (open).

utterly lacking in semantic elements) but the book-object, which we manipulate and which affects us in turn. By emphasizing bodily touch, then, Share takes reading out of the realm of metaphor, so that we encounter otherness not cognitively but in material and sensual terms.

John Cutrone, Director of the Jaffe Center for Book Arts, has said of Share's performances, "I think of this as the future of the book."[25] Perhaps what he means is that Share's immersive relation to the book resembles virtual reality (VR)—the computer-generated three-dimensional environment that invites physical interaction from its participants. Of course, Share's performances are not oriented towards the digital age; nevertheless, insofar as they imagine book engagement as an immersive full-body experience, they are a helpful springboard from which to think about VR reading, now only in its infancy. The Chimera Reader by Oculus, for example, asks participants to don head gear from which they can access e-books. Enhancements include the reader's ability to set their experience of reading in any environment they choose—from a Victorian study to an Amazon rainforest—but

[25] Quoted in Phillip Valys and South Florida.com, "An Artist with Spine," *South Florida Sun Sentinel*, October 18, 2013 (https://www.sun-sentinel.com/entertainment/theater-and-arts/sf-sh-susan-share-book-art-boca-101813-20131018-story.html).

outside of this and the reproduction of the experience of turning pages, there isn't a lot of tactile or proprioceptive feedback integrated into the system as of yet. A variant of this VR technology developed by MIT's Media Lab invites readers to put on a body suit that allows them to feel the sensations experienced by a book's protagonist, including increased heart rate, temperature changes, and tightness/constriction in the chest.[26] The first book programmed for use with this body suit is James Tiptree Jr.'s *The Girl Who Was Plugged In*, a science fiction novel about a young woman whose bodily movements are controlled by others. Thus, the reader wearing the body suit can combine the semantic pleasures of reading Tiptree's novel with a sense of felt identification with its protagonist.

Other advancements in haptic reading technologies focus more on cutaneous touch. *Strange Rain*, for example, is an app that can be downloaded onto any mobile device. Once activated, it allows users to control with their fingers the amount and frequency of cascading rain falling on the touchscreen, as if on a skylight. When set in different modes, users also manually control music, color, and text. In the "story" mode, for example, users can conjure up lines from the short story "Convertible," written by app creator Erik Loyer. Each tap on the screen triggers a thought from the story's protagonist, Alphonse, who is standing in the rain. Tap quickly and up pop the words, "Now I'm shivering." Tap again after leaving the screen alone for a bit and one triggers the phrase, "notice me notice me." Changes in color and rainfall also accompany these textual snippets. Maria Engberg has written of the app, "*Strange Rain* defamiliarizes the screen that you have become accustomed to handling, so the more you touch the stranger the rain and the skies become."[27] Like the Russian formalists, then, the app works to estrange us from the usual work of our fingers—swiping, typing, clicking—so that we are re-attuned to the motion of our digits and thus to potential experiences of beauty. The problem is that the touchscreen interface is rather homogenous. Whether one taps lightly or with vigor, the feedback is essentially the same; what changes on the screen is the music, color, and text. Which is to say that the aesthetic experience is heightened primarily in relation to other senses (vision, hearing) even as the fingers remain the controlling force.

The limitations of *Strange Rain* speak to the difficulty of using digital technology to create rich experiences of touch. As David Parisi points out,

> One hundred and thirty years after the phonograph recorded sound and one hundred years after cinema replicated the eye, the technological extension of touch remains a nascent project….[T]he culture industry consistently falls short in its attempt to deliver a "data of experience" capable of substituting for experience in its nonmediated form.[28]

[26] Aaron Souppouris, "Sensory Fiction is a Prototype that Lets You Feel a Book's Emotions," *The Verge*, February 2, 2014 (https://www.theverge.com/2014/2/2/5370844/sensory-fiction-mit-media-lab-immersive-storytelling-concept).

[27] Maria Engberg, "Performing Apps: Touch and Gesture as Aesthetic Experience," *Performance Research* 18.5 (2013): 20–27; 22.

[28] David Parisi, "Fingerbombing, or 'Touching is Good': The Cultural Construction of Technologized Touch," *The Senses and Society* 3.3 (2008): 307–28; 315.

Hence commodity culture's endless parade of digital products that promise to appease (but that never can satisfy) what Parisi calls our "touchlust."

A similar conceit is at the center of Courtney Maum's recent novel *Touch* (2017). Maum's protagonist, Sloane Jacobsen, works as a trend forecaster and is famous for having invented "the swipe"—that ubiquitous finger movement that opens up our mobile devices. Convinced that consumer tech culture has reached a new low in alienating its users, Sloane predicts a return to touch. "Simple, physical companionship is going to be the catchword," she prophesies; "services will be offered where you can pay to be held. . . . If our capacity for tenderness and interpersonal connection continues to abate . . . we'll have to go outside of our relationships for affection. Intimacy is going to be outsourced."[29] Pitted against her are not only her boss, the soulless director of a tech company appropriately called Mammoth, but also her longtime boyfriend Roman, a self-proclaimed "neosensualist," who believes that the end of penetrative sex is nigh and who wears a full body Zentai suit that makes skin-to-skin contact impossible.

Sloane begins the novel by imagining tech solutions to the "touch deficit" (52): a wearable that would "let you know how long it's been since you've been touched" (51), "a flesh-colored, textured tablet" (95), "voluntary skin grafts" (160). By the novel's end, however, she no longer believes that touch-hunger can be redressed through advanced technology. "Social interaction is going to take the place of social media," she proclaims at the novel's climax.

> In-personism is going to trump clicktivism. . . . I see dating systems based on phero-mones instead of algorithms. I see daily check-in spots in wellness centers where people can be embraced. I see doctors regulating patients' current levels of human contact as carefully as their blood pressure.   (269, 271)

Sloane sees a new order where independent bookstores thrive, reading makes a comeback, and penmanship is trendy, all part of the new "renaissance in touch" (167). Indeed, it's no surprise that Sloane begins her own rehabilitation from touch deprivation by presenting her sister with a handwritten card that they read together. The card is described as having a material heft to it—"She held it in her palm like something without wings" (279). In a world of disappearing snapchats and short-lived viral videos, Maum suggests, handwritten notes hold the promise of both solidity and solidarity.

Something similar might also be said of the book ("Print will make a comeback too," Sloane insists (227)). As a message from an author to a reader, the book, like the personal card, has an intimacy to it, intensified by the physical object itself. We touch books—we turn pages; our index fingers lodge in the spines of texts as place-holders; the book's weight is felt as pleasure or burden—and our attitudes towards these books turn, in part, on this contact. When we treasure a book from our child-

---

[29] Courtney Maum, *Touch* (New York: Penguin, 2017), 117. Subsequent citations will be included parenthetically in the text.

hood, we treasure not the ideal story but its allographic manifestations—*this* copy read aloud by one's mother; *that* copy stained with juice. And more often than not, it is touch that mediates the specificity of these forms, allowing us to connect with the haptic vestiges of our intimates or of our younger selves. The mass-produced book becomes singular through touch, taking on an auratic quality via proximity, not distance. In reading we generate intersubjective relations; we meet that which lies outside of us. Our hands as much as our eyes are integral to this encounter.[30]

FURTHER READING

Classen, Constance. *The Deepest Sense: A Cultural History of Touch*. Urbana: University of Illinois Press, 2012.

Crary, Jonathan. *Techniques of the Observer: On Vision and Modernity in the Nineteenth Century*. Cambridge, MA: MIT Press, 1992.

Drucker, Johanna. *The Century of Artists' Books*. New York: Granary Books, 2004.

Getzinger, Günter. "Technology and the Loss of the Tactile." *Yearbook 2002 of the Institute for Advanced Studies on Science, Technology, and Society*. Munich: Institute for Advanced Studies on Science, Technology, and Society, 2002, 221–30.

Jay, Martin. *Downcast Eyes: The Denigration of Vision in Twentieth-Century French Thought*. Berkeley, CA: University of California Press, 1993.

Littau, Karin. *Theories of Reading: Books, Bodies, and Bibliomania*. Cambridge: Polity, 2006.

McGann, Jerome. *The Textual Condition*. Princeton: Princeton University Press, 1991.

McKenzie, D. F. *Bibliography and the Sociology of Texts*. Cambridge: Cambridge University Press, 1999.

McLaughlin, Thomas. *Reading and the Body: The Physical Practice of Reading*. New York: Palgrave, 2015.

Mileaf, Janine. *Please Touch: Dada and Surrealist Objects after the Readymade*. Hanover: Dartmouth College Press, 2010.

Patterson, Mark. *The Senses of Touch: Haptics, Affects, and Technologies*. Oxford: Oxford University Press, 2007.

Price, Leah. *How to Do Things with Books in Victorian Britain*. Princeton: Princeton University Press, 2012.

Senchyne, Jonathan. "Vibrant Material Textuality: New Materialism, Book History, and the Archive in Paper." *Studies in Romanticism* 57.1 (Spring 2018): 67–85.

Tilley, Heather. "Introduction: The Victorian Tactile Imagination." *Interdisciplinary Studies in the Long Nineteenth Century* 19 (2014) (https://www.19.bbk.ac.uk/articles/10.16995/ntn.723/).

Warne, Vanessa. "'So that the Sense of Touch May Supply the Want of Sight': Blind Reading and Nineteenth-Century British Culture." *Media, Technology, and Literature in the Nineteenth Century: Image, Sound, Touch*, ed. Colette Colligan and Margaret Linley. New York: Routledge, 2016, 43–64.

---

[30] Thanks to the artists for permission to print and to Katherine Crowe, Curator of Special Collections and Archives at the University of Denver, for access to their artists' books collection.

17

AURALITY

GEORGINA KLEEGE

Sometimes friends tell me that they hear my voice when they read something I've written. This is meant as a compliment, but I confess I can't relate. Whatever I read always comes to me in the same voice. As a legally blind person, I have been reading aurally for almost fifty years now. In fact, because I am a writer and English professor, it can be said that I make a living reading. In addition to reading and rereading my own writing, I read students' papers, class texts, all manner of books, periodicals, emails, and websites, and I do it all almost exclusively with my ears. For many years, I was compelled to defend this practice. Teachers, family members, rehabilitation specialists, classmates, colleagues, and students were skeptical about, even hostile, to the idea that I could gain the same benefit from reading with my ears as others derive from the use of their eyes. More recently, with the growing popularity of audiobooks among sighted people, I feel less judged. But what makes people recoil in horror is my preference for synthesized speech over recordings made by human readers. Worse, I speed it up to a rate of about 400 words a minute—even faster if I am reading at a late stage in the writing process and want merely to skim through a piece one last time before sending to my editor.

Scientists who study reading define it as the active deciphering of symbols, either visible in the case of print or handwriting, or tactile in the case of braille, into language. Listening to a voice reading, whether that voice is human or synthetic, does not involve the same deciphering process and so is understood as merely listening. To this I say, there's listening and then there's *listening*. For the casual and occasional reader—someone who listens to an audiobook to while away the hours on a long road trip—aural reading is a lesser mode of information processing. It is assumed to be passive—in one ear and out the other. But for a long-time and habitual aural reader, it is an active pursuit, an attentive selection and absorption of meaningful sounds.

I'm a good listener. This is a term often applied to people in the "helping professions," to denote empathy and compassion. But good listening can have a more deliberate intensity—listening for, not merely listening to. When my screen reader is set at the highest speed, I am not so much listening to every word, as listening for key words and phrases: the subject and verb of every sentence, for instance. Sometimes I am listening for the rhythm of the sentences as they whiz past me. When the prose is particularly dense, I slow down the voice. When I'm tired or distracted, I speed it up to jolt me into alertness. Part of being a good listener is the ability to tune out extraneous sounds that might distract from the active listening required to process an aural text. I have my screen reader set to read aloud each letter as I type it. Theoretically this allows me to catch typos as I make them, but in reality it creates a protective barrier of sound that helps keep me focused. As I write this, someone is jack-hammering next door, but I am only aware of it when I stop typing. It is this aspect of good listening that allows me to tolerate the artificiality of the synthetic voice perpetually in my ears.

My listening skills are not innate. Contrary to the popular myth about blindness, I do not possess exceptional hearing. Given my age, I expect that my hearing is already or will soon become below average. For now, I turn up the volume; later, I may resort to some other method. When blind people are understood as merely defective—sighted people minus sight—the skills we develop and the ways we use tools and technologies seem supernatural. Computer generated text-to-speech (TTS) technology came into my life only when I had already been blind for twenty years, and the particular ways I use my screen reader developed through trial and error, not because anyone taught me. My history as an aural reader, like most personal histories, is long and convoluted. Before it was shaped by the evolution of phonographic technologies, it was shaped by changes in special education orthodoxy.

When I first became visually impaired at the age of 11, aural reading was not the first option offered to me. At the time, the mid-1960s, the conventional wisdom was that for children who had any residual vision at all, that vision should be used to read print. This was sometimes expressed with a certain use-it-or-lose-it urgency. I was offered large print textbooks and all manner of large and small magnification devices. Under the best circumstances, magnification allowed me to read word by word, though never in the clusters of words that fluent visual readers absorb as their eyes jump in saccades across the line and down the page. More often than not, magnification gave me headaches, made me dizzy or nauseated. Unless I took breaks, I threw up or passed out. When I complained that reading in this way was slow, inefficient, and painful, I was exhorted just to try harder. Talking books, the term used for recorded texts intended specifically for blind people, were offered as a grudging last resort, with unvoiced disapproval. The implicit message was that education was supposed to be hard, and that there was something shameful in asking for it to be made easier. My earliest memories of talking books were of something illicit. So naturally I craved them.

Braille instruction was not offered at all. The orthodoxy at the time regarded braille as a technology of the past made obsolete by modern recordings and high-powered magnification devices. There was also a belief that someone with any degree of residual vision would be inclined to read the pattern of dots visually rather than tactually. Note the contradiction: educators acknowledged that I could not read standard print unless it was substantially magnified, but worried that I would somehow manage to visually decipher patterns of tiny white dots on a white page. Eventually I taught myself braille in my 30s and can attest that reading it visually did not even tempt me. Because I learned braille as an adult, I use it sporadically, and I resent the attitude that deprived me of learning it as a child when it might have become more central to my education and life. Since then, there have been studies showing the benefits of early braille instruction. Perhaps the prejudice against it has diminished. Now, the advent of electro-mechanical refreshable braille displays makes braille a viable option for blind children in the present and future. Still, economic factors often outweigh pedagogical value in special education. Braille instruction requires a braille teacher, an expense at which many school districts balk. I still meet visually impaired students today who are pressed to use one reading modality over another.

During the period when talking books were an illicit pleasure, I was developing my skills as an aural reader even though I had few talking books to read. Since reading visually was such a struggle, I often did not finish reading assignments. I discovered that my teachers tended to repeat or paraphrase the assigned reading the next day in class. They also typically read aloud whatever they were writing on the blackboard. My high school French teacher repeated everything three times, each time using slightly different vocabulary, so that even the student who understood the first time gained from the repetition. I listened to teachers in math and history classes, and sure enough, many essentially did the same thing. In general, I discovered that if I really paid attention, really listened deliberately, I could get by without doing the reading.

By the time I was a university student, and had greater agency over my own education, I abandoned all the magnification devices and became an aural reader. I have used every generation of talking book format—long-playing records, cassette tapes, compact discs, and, finally, digital files. For many years, talking books and the devices that played them were only available from government agencies that serve blind people. The devices all had special features which made them significantly more expensive than the commercial models from which they were adapted.

When the books I needed or wanted were not available from the library services, I hired people to record themselves reading aloud to me. When I began teaching writing, I required my students to record themselves reading their work out loud. Once TTS technology emerged, my array of hardware included flatbed scanners to convert print to text files that I could read on my computer and, later, from handheld devices. I also downloaded books in electronic formats from websites serving people with print disabilities such as Bookshare, and others that serve the general public such as Project Gutenberg.

All the while, I was developing my skills as a good listener. In my many years of listening to human readers, there is much I've learned to tune out. Regional or national accents, mumbling and mispronunciations, coughing, yawning, giggling, sighing—all these things can be disregarded. Back when I hired people to record books, I became a connoisseur of voices. What I was listening for had less to do with tonality and pitch than with enunciation. But with all the reading I had to do as a student and, later, as a writer and professor, speed became the most prized quality. TTS screen readers allow for higher rates of speed than analog recordings of human voices without any loss of enunciation. Initially, this was the major appeal of synthesized speech. Also, with the advent of the Internet, it was the only way to read anything online.

I have narrated my history as an aural reader in terms of one technology replacing another. There was a period of approximately twenty years, however, when I was using multiple technologies at the same time. My desk used to be cluttered with cassettes and players, both the large and small sizes, a flatbed scanner, plus a range of other devices, earphones, microphones, batteries, and chargers along with the cords and cables needed to connect and run them. My cat delighted in unspooling cassettes, which added to the general chaos. Mental clutter paralleled this physical clutter as I worked to remember the format of my current reading material. Was I reading something on tape or on my computer? Which side of that cassette did I leave off reading?

Since the late 1990s I have completely converted from recordings of human readers to TTS technology, on my computer and on a range of portable devices, including my phone. At long last I could clear my desk—and my brain—of all the clutter. I made this switch with some regret and nostalgia, however, for the loss of all those voices—loved ones' and strangers'—who read to me. There are many books that I remember in the voice of a particular reader. When my paid reading assistants delivered their recordings, even their most casual comments often influenced or enhanced my reading. It was especially hard to give up having my students read their work to me. Reading one's work aloud is a valuable editorial exercise, and it was often appealing and telling to hear the emotional qualities that came into students' voices as they read passages that gave them trouble or made them proud. But it had become so easy for students to add background music and sound effects to their recordings, making them more like highly produced radio plays than unadorned reading. Even without these embellishments, some writers are better vocal performers than others. I decided that it was fairer for the same voice to read everyone's work.

What the synthesized voice lacks in affect and pronunciation, it makes up for in tirelessness and absolute malleability. While human readers get tired, bored, or sick, and sometimes add unwanted commentary to texts simply by intonation, the synthesized voice reads whatever I throw at it and will persevere until I tell it to stop. There are things I can demand of a synthesized voice that no human reader would tolerate and no analog playback device would allow. It will read the same paragraph or sentence over and over, at different rates of speed, sometimes word by word, occasionally even letter by letter. When it mispronounces, I make it spell out the word. If I want, it will announce all the punctuation and changes in paragraphs.

The manufacturers of TTS technology often describe these virtues as efficiency. Recently I sampled different voices available to the reading app on my phone. The voices each read a brief text—auditions, so to speak—to allow consumers to comparison shop. The voices are gendered, or at least come in a range of pitches from soprano to bass, and are identified with gendered names: Arthur, Daniel, Catherine, Heather. There are even voices identified as "child-like." The voices come with national accents: British, American, Australian, Indian English, Castilian and North American Spanish, and so forth. A typical sample described the voice as "Efficient, fast and of very high quality, why not try me out with your own words?" Another claimed that it would "make your leisure reading more efficient and enjoyable." Others claimed to have a wider emotional range. "I have good news, you can try me out," one opined pluckily. And another, named Will Happy, says, "I can read text that you want to hear in a cheerful voice." A British male voice named Peter comes in both happy and sad versions. I admit that I have some trouble detecting the difference between the three versions, and I am not sure when or why I would choose a voice to impose this kind of emotional layer to my reading.

Although I appreciate the principle of choice, I seem always to opt for the default voice, even though the newer versions are slightly more humanoid. The voice on my computer is a medium tenor named Reed. In the world of TTS technology, this passes for wit. It also may be an acknowledgment that "read" is one of those verbs that can be pronounced differently depending on the tense, but the screen reader cannot always get the context. So when I read this sentence now, it pronounces the verb in the past tense even though I intend it to be in the present.

Other readers may be happy to have so many choices. They can choose the national accent to match the author's or character's nationality. A friend of mine chooses the voice to coincide with the author's gender. Recently she reported some consternation when the male voice reading a novel by a male author encountered a first-person narrator who was female.

What I value about the synthesized voice is not so much efficiency as an endearing earnestness. It's hard not to anthropomorphize. I know that this voice sometimes shows up in my dreams. What I really mean is that it is predictable. I can anticipate all its quirky foibles and so ignore them. But it is ubiquitous, so constantly in my ears all day and all night that my mind erases its presence. It has become aurally transparent. I am no more conscious of it than a sighted reader is of fonts.

As I mentioned, the rise in popularity of recorded books for the general public since the 1980s may have normalized blind people's aural reading practices. Now, I'm hoping that the ubiquity of synthesized speech in quotidian technologies will continue this work toward greater social inclusion. For instance, the marketing of Siri, the iPhone's TTS and speech-to-text interface, touts the technology as allowing users to read and write eyes- and hands-free. Early advertisements showed people running, driving, cooking, and engaged in other tasks while commanding Siri to read emails, send texts, and look up information on the web. Some of these ads even featured blind people among all the other users in a rare characterization of them as consumers of new technology rather than objects of charity. Many drivers depend on the synthesized voice in their GPS. Public transportation systems around the world feature synthesized voice announcements. There are increasing numbers of household appliances that have some kind of synthesized voice interface so that users, sighted and blind alike, can interact eyes- and hands-free. People are becoming more familiar with synthesized voices, making TTS technology specifically for blind people seem less unusual.

Synthesized voice technologies are not only ubiquitous but are more and more likely to be already loaded into the device's software package, as with the iPhone. Everyone is not aware of this, of course, which is why I often find myself enlisted to show off these features to friends and even strangers who question me about my reading practices. When friends complain about the tiny print on a website they're trying to read on their phone, I show them how to turn on the screen reader. My students often comment on my ability to notice proofreading errors even though I'm reading their work with my ears. I point out that the synthesized voice reads word for word, while visual reading, where the eye jumps in saccades, makes it too easy to engage in wishful seeing, missing small errors and omissions. I encourage them to turn on the screen reader that's probably already built into their computer and try it for themselves. If reading one's work out loud is a good editing trick, hearing it read by a synthetic voice can be equally revelatory.

The more mainstream consumers find uses for these features, the more blind people benefit. Newly blind adults may be less dependent on social service agencies as they adapt to their new condition, using the same electronic devices they already own in different ways. Manufacturers will be less likely to discontinue these features if large numbers of general users find them valuable. As print newspapers, magazines, and books are digitized and become available online, blind people benefit, but only if the digital versions of texts are compatible with their reading technologies. For instance, early versions of Google Books were produced as image rather than text files, which made them inaccessible to screen readers. A text file happens to be easier for anyone to navigate using word search functions, so there are good reasons to produce digital texts this way.

Unfortunately, while digital files of every publication exist, they are not always available to people with print disabilities. This remains a major barrier to educational and professional opportunities for blind people. Once I had to wait over a year for one of the library services to record new books, and they only recorded a fraction of the books I wanted or needed, which meant paying someone to record or scan them instead. The time lag has decreased, but some effort and cajoling are still required to get publishers to provide accessible electronic formats. As I finish any writing project, I still have to wonder when and how I will be able to read it in its published form. Will I be able to read the other articles and chapters in the same volume? This will happen only if sighted people take up the cause and make the demand of their publishers.

For now, I remain optimistic. I have lived long enough to perceive progress. For the first time in my life, blind people stand on the threshold of complete access to information on a par with the sighted majority. There are many who dread the digitization of the world's libraries, who cannot imagine curling up with a computer screen rather than with a traditional book, who shudder at the sound of a synthetic voice, but my history tells me that human beings can and do adapt to all sorts of unlikely situations. The point of reading is the transmission of ideas from one mind to another, and that can happen through the eyes, the fingertips, or the ears, through a printed or embossed page or the simulacrum of a page on a screen. So why not the simulacrum of a voice?

When my sighted friends who enjoy audiobooks rave about a new novel read by a famous actor or its author, I am happy for them. But if I want to hear a great performance, I'll listen to a movie. If I want to know what an author sounds like, I'll find an interview. If I want to read a novel, I'll do it with the same voice that's reading to me now.

FURTHER READING

Hull, John. *Notes on Blindness: A Journey through the Dark*. London: Profile Books, 2017.

Kleege, Georgina. *Sight Unseen*. New Haven: Yale University Press, 1999.

Krug, Rebecca. *Margery Kempe and the Lonely Reader*. Ithaca, NY: Cornell University Press, 2017.

Rubery, Matthew. *The Untold Story of the Talking Book*. Cambridge, MA: Harvard University Press, 2016.

18

DEAFNESS

REBECCA SANCHEZ

"*Reading*," the media and disability studies scholar Mara Mills notes, "has always been a roomy word."[1] Indeed, as the other chapters in this volume attest, far from being confined to the visual scanning of printed words on a page of paper, we now take for granted that reading can involve engagement with a range of materials and practices, all of which, in Mills's words, "encourage[] new bodily habits and forms of attention."[2] Despite this apparent roominess, however, the word "reading" has not, by and large, been perceived as capacious enough to describe the activities of decoding and interpreting signed literatures. The vast majority of work on, for example, American Sign Language (ASL) and reading, including the important collection *Language Acquisition by Eye*, examines the impact of signed language use on written language literacy. The very notion of literacy in signed languages emerged in academic literature only in the 1990s.[3]

The absence of analysis of signed language reading practices can be explained partly by a pervasive failure to recognize signed languages as "real" languages in the first place, even among scholars who study language and literature for a living. Such ideological resistance to the notion of non-normative communicative practice and of languages in modalities that are neither spoken nor written draws on long histories of ableism and, more specifically, audism (the belief that those who can hear or who behave as though they can hear are superior to those who don't) that I won't rehearse here. Even in Deaf spaces, however, "reading" is rarely used to describe the encounter with signed language texts, despite the now fairly frequent use of the words "text," "literacy," and "literature," all of which are similarly etymologically

---

[1] Mara Mills, "What Should We Call Reading?," *Flow* 17.3 (2012) (https://www.flowjournal.org/2012/12/what-should-we-call-reading/). Italics in original.

[2] Mills, "What Should We Call Reading?"

[3] For analysis of ASL literacy in the context of new literacy studies, see Todd A. Czubek, "Blue Listerine, Parochialism, and ASL Literacy," *The Journal of Deaf Studies and Deaf Education* 11.3 (2006): 373–81.

linked to written modalities, to describe engagement with works in ASL.[4] So, for example, Carol Padden and Claire Ramsey's "American Sign Language and Reading Ability in Deaf Children" and Robert J. Hoffmeister's "A Piece of the Puzzle: ASL and Reading Comprehension in Deaf Children" both provide accounts of the effect that "literacy skills in ASL" have on "English reading skills."[5] While it may be technically accurate that when one is reading one is enacting literacy, it is notable that "reading" is carefully avoided in the context of signed languages. We do not, after all, imagine ourselves curling up with a cup of tea to enact literacy on a favorite poem. These distinctions matter to the ways we imagine our relationships to language and, through it, to one another.

This chapter will argue that we can and should discuss the decoding and interpretation of signed language texts as reading, that the pleasures (and frustrations) of reading are available to those who engage with signed texts. Such usage has a variety of benefits: validation of the engagement with signed language literatures and recognition of literacy in non-written modalities, an introduction of the tools developed through the substantial body of work on reading practices in written (and audio) modalities to studies of the ways individuals engage with signed texts, and an enrichment of existing scholarship on reading by the particularities that attend reading practices in signed languages.

I begin with this account of resistance to describing encounters with signed language texts as reading in part to highlight an erasure that has too often itself been rendered invisible, but also by way of explanation of the particular focus of this chapter, which will be on reading signed language literatures (primarily ASL). Given the broadness of the chapter's title ("Deafness"), it is important to note that not all deaf people use signed languages; the analysis offered here is not intended as an exhaustive account of the reading practices of all deaf people in all modalities, or even in all signed languages (of which there are over 200). Nor is this focus intended to suggest that the relationship between physiological and/or cultural deafness and written language literacy is uninteresting or unimportant. Given the imbalance in existing scholarship, however, I want to take this opportunity to focus on aspects of deaf engagement with literature that have been under-analyzed.

My project here is twofold: first, to describe experiences of reading signed languages, either visually or tactilely (as do signing DeafBlind people), in order to introduce vocabularies and frames of reference relevant to manual languages to conversations about what precisely people are doing physically, intellectually, emotionally when they are reading. And second, to explore some of the ways that these

---

[4] "Deaf" is often used to refer to cultural deafness, while "deaf" indicates a physiological condition. While useful in some contexts, this terminology perpetuates a problematic binary perception of "types" of deaf people, so I will be using it sparingly.

[5] Robert J. Hoffmeister, "A Piece of the Puzzle: ASL and Reading Comprehension in Deaf Children," in *Language Acquisition by Eye*, ed. Charlene Chamberlain, Jill P. Morford, and Rachel I. Mayberry (New York: Psychology Press, 1999), 143–63; 143.

practices enable alternative theorizations of reading and its potentials. If it is the case that, as Stephen Best and Sharon Marcus note in their introduction to a special issue of *Representations* on surface reading, "the disasters and triumphs of the last decade have shown that literary criticism alone is not sufficient to effect change," it is also true that the political potentials of relationalities that attend non-normative reading praxis have neither been exhausted nor even fully explored.[6] What happens to our understandings of reading when they are critically deafened? When they encounter the epistemologies and ontologies that attend deaf experience and praxis?

One of the first areas of divergence between reading in signed and written modalities is the temporality through which one encounters a signed text. As philosopher Teresa Blankmeyer Burke notes of her own reading practices,

> I...can read an English text in a fraction of the time that I use watching an ASL video text....with written English (or any language) one can view a page of text at once. That's a big chunk of information. Now, contrast that with a sped-up video. It seems to me that at some point, speeding up the video results in a deterioration of signal (whether auditory or visual), and consequently, impacts comprehension.[7]

Rather than being able to scan back and forth, to seamlessly revisit previously read portions of a sentence or page, readers of signed language texts must retain sections of the text in their memory.

Moreover, in addition to the technological difficulty faced by anyone attempting to rewind to a particular moment, signed languages do not present blank spaces between words in the way that written texts do. One cannot absent one's hands from the signing space between individual signs, so they tend to run together. Even with a text that has been recorded and can be rewatched, then, signed language literatures place different kinds of cognitive demands on readers.[8] One cannot pause to stare at and contemplate an individual sign in the way one can pull out discrete written words even when they are arranged in sentences and paragraphs.

The structural necessity of this focus on transitions—the patterns of handshapes or movement that are used as bridges between the semantic contents of various signs—is linked to the basic fact that signed languages unfold before the viewer in shared time. Viewers read signed texts at the rate at which they are played. The texts can be sped up or slowed down, but the rate of reading will always be the rate at which the human on screen is producing the signs. Signs are never static, and that movement itself often becomes part of the meaning of a work. In Bernard Bragg's

[6] Stephen Best and Sharon Marcus, "Surface Reading: An Introduction," *Representations* 108.1 (2009): 1–21; 2.

[7] Teresa Blankmeyer Burke, "Time, Speedviewing, and Deaf Academics," *Possibilities and Finger Snaps* (blog), 2016.

[8] For information on the cognitive demands of reading a text without spatial separation between words in the context of Western scripts, see Paul Saenger's *Space between Words: The Origins of Silent Reading* (Palo Alto: Stanford University Press, 1997).

"Flowers and Moonlight on Spring Water," for instance, each of the poem's nouns (night, river, flowers, moonlight) is depicted in motion: Night falls upon the flowing water. Flowers bloom. The moonlight rides on the water's ripples, and the stars twinkle on its surface. And these images overlap; Bragg begins signing river while still completing the sign for night, has his flowers bloom while the rippling water is still settling.[9] And this movement and overlap of the poem's elements are part of how the text signifies. Unlike the written equivalent of this scene, which would describe a still life, "Flowers and Moonlight" plays on its transitions and the relationship of ASL to space and time to present an alternative understanding of the natural world, one which is active and interpenetrative. The implications of this environmental ethic are legible only when we read the transitions (i.e., the literary features) of the poem.

As Bragg himself observed, many of the elements we attend to when close reading a signed text have no equivalent in written modalities. "Flowers and Moonlight" illustrates one aspect of the relationship between ASL texts and visual images. Rather than ekphrastically describing what a particular scene looks like, signed texts enact images; they perform translations of images into language. Miriam Lerner's documentary history of ASL poetry *Heart of the Hydrogen Jukebox*, for example, features a series of unattributed image translations in which a poet stands in front of a backdrop of a natural image and interprets it. In one poem, trees whose leaves have changed to orange and yellow stand in the background of an image whose foreground is a lake that spills over into a series of plashing waterfalls.[10] As in Bragg's poem, the images are all in motion, blending into one another; the rustling of the trees' leaves becomes the rippling water which, changing axis, churns over into the falls. Again, the poem presents the natural world as interpenetrative and dynamic. It also highlights a feature of reading skills in manual languages; namely that, for sighted signers, literacy in a signed language brings with it a skill set pertaining to the reading of visual images. Rather than describing what a picture looks like, signers (and particularly literary signers) can interpret that image into language.

The piece also emphasizes the role of what ASL storyteller Ben Bahan describes as the "cinematographic technique" embedded in ASL reading practices.[11] Beyond the basic fact of its motion, elements of the poem overlap with editing techniques to highlight parallels between signed and cinematic grammars. As the text unfolds on the signer's hands, images accumulating over time, new elements are also added

---

[9] Bernard Bragg, "Flowers and Moonlight on the Spring Water," YouTube, updated July 16, 2010, trans. author.

[10] *Heart of the Hydrogen Jukebox,* dir. Miriam Lerner, prod. Miriam Lerner and Don Feigel (Rochester Institute of Technology, 2009), DVD.

[11] Ben Bahan, "Face-to-Face Tradition in the American Deaf Community: Dynamics of the Teller, the Tale, and the Audience," in *Signing the Body Poetic: Essays on American Sign Language Literature,* ed. H-Dirksen L. Bauman, Jennifer L. Nelson, and Heidi M. Rose (Berkeley, CA: University of California Press, 2006), 21–50; 29.

to the photo in the background so that it reflects the images in the text. Emphasizing the relationship between signer and text (and between text and image), the poem ends with a rippling effect being overlaid on the signer's body that mirrors the vertical stripe pattern of the waterfall into which the signer fades.

> The striking resemblance between signed and cinematic grammars was famously observed by William Stokoe, who, along with Dorothy C. Casterline and Carl G. Croneberg, is credited with demonstrating that ASL is a language:…the essence of sign language is to cut from a normal view to a close-up to a distant shot to a close-up again, and so on, even including flashback and flash-forward scenes, exactly as a movie editor works….Not only is signing itself arranged more like edited film than like written narration, but also each signer is placed very much as a camera: the field of vision and angle of view are directed but variable.[12]

Close reading a signed text necessitates attentiveness to techniques like fast forwarding, juxtaposition of images, and manipulation of the length of particular shots that shape the meaning of the text. In the unnamed poem described above, for example, the poet's signs speed up to present the frenetic-ness of the water rushing over the falls. Similarly, in Ian Sanborn's "Caterpillar," variations in sign speed are used to represent the caterpillar's metamorphosis, the sped-up signing suggesting a choppiness that is part of the text's aestheticization and denaturalization of the biological process it presents.[13]

In addition to these temporal effects, the changes in field of vision and camera angle that Stokoe notes shape the experience of reading a signed text by linking narrative perspective (and therefore the reader) to various characters or elements of the environment. This alignment often occurs through a feature of ASL grammar called role shifting, adopting the styles of movement, eye line, and expression of various entities within a text through changes in body position and affect. These entities need not be human or even animate. As I will discuss shortly, role shifting produces ethical effects by embedding the physical inhabitation of the perspectives of others within both literary and quotidian language use. It enables the creation of a scene that unfolds as might a film. This spatial, relational awareness is being read in a text along with grammatical features that have closer equivalents in written languages.

Beyond shared visual grammars, film (or digital footage) as the material medium of signed texts structures the encounters people have with them as artifacts. As Christopher Krentz has noted,

> before the advent of film technology, people had no effective way to record American Sign Language (ASL)….All communication through ASL had to happen live and face to face. The arrival of film technology in the early twentieth century changed this dynamic: it enabled people to capture and preserve what had once seemed transitory…

---

[12] Quoted in Oliver Sacks, *Seeing Voices* (New York: Vintage Books, 1990), 71–2.
[13] Ian Sanborn, "Caterpillar," YouTube, 2014 (https://www.youtube.com/watch?v=MTgGQnxX5Uw).

providing a potential permanence to works in ASL and other signed languages.[14] In the context of written modalities, reading has been conceived as a means of having an encounter out of time with another human. If writing has historically offered the potential to project ourselves beyond our particular moment, reading is the site that stages that encounter between past and present. For signed languages, however, both their youth (ASL celebrated its bicentennial in 2017) and the relative newness of video recording technology means that we are just now moving past living memory of the first preserved ASL texts.

The context in which these texts were produced (as well as their content) is itself significant to the ways we think about the function of ASL literature and how we read it. In the face of an ideological push to eliminate signed languages from deaf education at the beginning of the twentieth century, the National Association of the Deaf (NAD) produced a series of films (twenty-two in total between 1910 and 1930, of which fifteen survive).[15] The best known is a 1913 speech given by then NAD president George W. Veditz arguing for the "Preservation of the Sign Language." Self-consciously situated between the undocumentable and unrecoverable signed languages of the past, which appear only as tantalizing references, Veditz describes not this lost heritage but rather the role of signed languages in the future. "As long as we have deaf people on this earth we will have sign language," he proclaims, "and as long as we have our films we can preserve our beautiful sign language in its olden purity."[16] He exhorts viewers to beware "false prophets" who would ban signed languages, arguing, "enemies of the sign language, they are enemies of the true welfare of the deaf."[17]

If, as Marlon Kuntze argues, ASL texts should be recognized as such because what matters to textuality is not the written modality but rather "content that is recorded and left 'suspended' in time"; if, that is, there cannot be texts without recording, these recordings are the first ASL texts.[18] It is striking, then, that the first ASL text constitutes both a presentation of the capacities of what Veditz refers to as "the sign language" (a documentation of its aesthetic and communicative value) and a plea to save it from eradication. Read today, "Preservation of the Sign Language" constitutes an encounter with the past (the film is on the border of incomprehensibility for contemporary signers) that is just barely past. And its thematic concern with a version of oralism that sought to eradicate signed languages

---

[14] Christopher Krentz, "The Camera as Printing Press: How Film Has Influenced ASL Literature," in *Signing the Body Poetic: Essays on American Sign Language Literature*, ed. H-Dirksen L. Bauman, Jennifer L. Nelson, and Heidi M. Rose (Berkeley, CA: University of California Press, 2006), 51–70; 51.

[15] For an account of this history, see Douglas C. Baynton, *Forbidden Signs: American Culture and the Campaign against Sign Language* (Chicago: University of Chicago Press, 1996).

[16] George W. Veditz, "Preservation of the Sign Language," YouTube , NAD, 2011 (https://www.youtube.com/watch?v=XITbj3NTLUQ).

[17] Carol Padden, "Translating Veditz," *Sign Language Studies* 4.3 (2004): 244–60.

[18] Marlon Kuntze, "Turning Literacy Inside Out," in *Open Your Eyes: Deaf Studies Talking*, ed. H-Dirksen L. Bauman (Washington, DC: Gallaudet University Press, 2002): 146–57; 147.

continues to haunt ASL literature. This explicit use of literary, theatrical sign language to enact the value of sign (and, by extension, the cultures and lives of the people who use it) remains at least implicitly present in all signed literature.[19] Reading ASL texts, then, is always already political. It involves accepting the fact of ASL as a language, of recognizing that it is worthy of the close reading practices more typically thought of as applying to writing. This history, too, is part of what signers read when they encounter an ASL text.

As I mentioned earlier, the ways that animacy operates in signed languages opens up new ways of being with others in language, what we might, following Robert McRuer in *Crip Times*, refer to as "alternative *disabled* ways of being-in-common together" through grammatical features like role shifting.[20] Reading (decoding and interpreting) such features requires the viewer to imagine the embodied experience of entities beyond themselves. In Bernard Bragg's "The Pilot and the Eagle," for instance, the poetic signer (signed texts are not narrated by "speakers") uses role shifting and visual vernacular (an aesthetic form that combines role shifting and mime to create highly visual and theatrical texts) to inhabit the subjectivities of both titular characters in a process that invites readers to reimagine their relationships with the nonhuman. The poem opens with the eagle perched on a branch, turning its head to observe what lies below with a series of syncopated movements. It then takes off, the signer's arms reflecting the rhythm of the wings as it soars and swoops, cutting between a close-up of the eagle and a long shot that suggests what its flapping wings might look like at a distance. A human pilot observes the bird, and the two fly together for a time, before landing.[21]

Like many ASL texts, the poem meditates on the relationship between the human and nonhuman, experimenting with how a human body might capture and express otherness through movement and facial affect. The eagle is obviously mediated through the limitations of human perception and embodiment, but rather than domesticating that alterity through anthropomorphism as we typically understand it, the poem pushes the human signer (and, indeed, the human pilot) toward eagle-ness (or, at least, toward an encounter with a nonhuman other that is viscerally imagined and experienced). As with the troubling of assumptions about the status of the natural world in "Moonlight and Flowers" and the untitled image translation from *Heart of the Hydrogen Jukebox*, "The Pilot and the Eagle" demonstrates the potential inherent in signed grammars to stage questions about what constitutes humanness and how it intersects with other forms of being.

---

[19] For more on the ways literary signing has been used to make the case for the humanity of deaf people, see Jennifer Esmail, "The Power of Deaf Poetry: The Exhibition of Literacy and the Nineteenth-Century Sign Language Debates," *Sign Language Studies* 8.4 (2008): 348–68.

[20] Robert McRuer, *Crip Times: Disability, Globalization, and Resistance* (New York: New York University Press, 2018), 75.

[21] Bernard Bragg, "The Pilot and the Eagle," YouTube, Dawn Sign Press, 2018 (https://www.youtube.com/watch?v=2cCM0Ykre58).

Signed texts also function as a nexus of social interaction for humans through what is perhaps their most obvious feature: embodiment. If part of what a consideration of textual materiality in signed texts calls us to attend to is film, it also, foundationally, directs us to human bodies. While a signed text might "transcend" (in Gérard Genette's sense of the word) the materiality of film, the experience of encountering literature through a human body (in the case of Tactile ASL, having literature produced on one's own flesh) can never be bracketed from the text's semantic content.[22] To receive information, one must either visually or tactilely engage the signer's body, a body that conveys grammatical information through the face, eyes, arms, and torso as well as the hands in ways that inextricably bind text to signer. Translated (transmediated) into printed words or braille, or even signed by a different person, the text is fundamentally altered. Part of what theorizing reading practices in signed languages calls us to consider, then, are the implications of the relationship between bodies, subjects, and language. What does it mean, in place of a history of the book, to have histories of bodies?

Part of the answer to the question has to do with the ways that signed texts stage encounters between humans. To read anything in ASL is to have an encounter with another human, a human enacting their human-ness through language. Emmanuel Levinas has defined "the face of the other man as being the original locus of the meaningful," the place where humans recognize that "no one can stay in himself; the humanity of man, subjectivity, is a responsibility for others, an extreme vulnerability."[23] And it is into this series of recognitions that one throws oneself when reading a signed text. As well as being both an embodied state and a collection of cultural identities, deafness is also, foundationally, a series of modes of interacting with other people and with nonhuman entities. And many of those relationships come into being in the encounters rendered possible through the composition and reading of literary texts.

Beyond the general recognition of the other as (vulnerably) human, signed language texts demand that we read the textual surface that is another's body. As Heidi M. Rose explains, in ASL texts "the poem literally lives in the poet, and the poet gives the poem life through performance"; they are particular poets who inhabit particular bodies, and that particularity is inextricably bound up in the meaning of signed literary works.[24] Humans are not mechanically reproducible. In addition to the grammatical information one reads on the face and body of a signer,

---

[22] Gérard Genette, *The Work of Art: Immanence and Transcendence*, trans. G. M. Goshgarian (Ithaca, NY: Cornell University Press, 1997), 10.

[23] Emmanuel Levinas, *Entre Nous: On Thinking-of-the-Other*, trans. Michael B. Smith and Barbara Harshaw (New York: Columbia University Press, 1998), 145; Emmanuel Levinas, *Humanism of the Other*, trans. Nidra Poller (Urbana: University of Illinois Press, 2006), 67.

[24] Heidi M. Rose, "The Poet in the Poem in the Performance: The Relation of Body, Self, and Text in ASL Literature," in *Signing the Body Poetic: Essays on American Sign Language Literature*, ed. H-Dirksen L. Bauman, Jennifer L. Nelson, and Heidi M. Rose (Berkeley, CA: University of California Press, 2006), 130–46; 136.

that signer's body also conveys extra-linguistic information about the signer including, potentially: age, size, race, ethnicity, disability, and (depending on the fluency, style, diction, and details of grammar and syntax) educational background and region of origin. These messages are read (or mis-read) along with, and as part of, the literary text.

In Ayisha Knight-Shaw's "Until," for instance, which presents the poetic signer seeking to assert agency in a context of intersectional oppression, the signer describes the liberatory moment of moving from "hating the curves of my body" to "finally piercing my belly and reveling in its beauty."[25] The ASL gives readers a specific location on the poetic signer's body, which is, of course, also Knight-Shaw's. It is a body that is materially present in time and space, read as occupying particular racial and gender categories, and of being a particular size and shape. The poem's descriptions of the signer's experience of coming to terms with her body are always interpreted in the context of how this specific signing body (and the signer's subjectivity) are read by viewers.

Some of the implications of this inseparability of author and text, as well as relationships into which readers are drawn through the process of reading, are embedded in the ASL for signed poetry, which differs from the sign for written poetry that is etymologically tied to music. The sign for signed poetry involves the dominant hand moving up and outward from the body as the hand opens from an A to a bent claw handshape. Derived from the sign for self-expression, it dramatizes the taking of something from within and presenting it to the viewer, a kind of offering of the self. This is how ASL defines its poetry. If it remains true that, as with all literature, poetic or narrative signer and authorial perspective cannot be collapsed, it is also the case that the embodied modality of signed texts results in a unique entanglement of the two, and that, as in "Until," the materiality of the poet's body as the medium for textual transmission is always part of how a text is decoded and interpreted.

Moreover, the embodied materiality of signed texts means that there can be no neutral or unaccented performance of language. In viewing signed texts, readers decode a set of questions about linguistic fluency and style. Signed languages, like spoken ones, have regional accents. Different-sized subjects with differently shaped hands produce signs that look or feel different. When reading tactilely, the roughness or smoothness and size of the signer's hands also become part of the text. And cultural and racial identity (as well as class, sexuality, gender) shape not only the ways readers perceive the relationship between the signer's body and the semantic content of a work, but also specific language usage.

As Knight-Shaw explains in an interview, "Black culture, gay and lesbian culture, and Jewish culture are all part of who I am and that affects how I sign, my language."[26]

---

[25] Ayisha Knight-Shaw, "Until," YouTube, 2006 (https://www.youtube.com/watch?v=q3ufVYN3t8M).
[26] Ayisha Knight-Shaw, *Basic Black*, YouTube, WGBH, June 4, 2009 (https://www.youtube.com/watch?v=XISRR5TVYqQ).

Racial segregation in deaf schools; the difficulty of sharing signs across large geographical distances before the advent of the Internet; an individual's access to education; exposure to English, SEE (Signing Exact English; an attempt to produce English "on the hands," the UK equivalent of which is SSE (Sign Supported English)), and PSE (Pidgen Signed English; a contact language that emerges at the intersection of ASL and English), as well as innumerable other linguistic variations that occur as signers navigate multilingual and multimodal spaces, can all play a role in shaping an individual's signs. And all these elements may be legible on a signer's hands, may be decoded and interpreted as part of the experience of reading a text.

To invoke W. B. Yeats, in signed literatures the dancer is the dance. And part of what the textual materialism of signed texts reminds us is that, apart from the idea of written words on a page, or aesthetic language preserved in time, texts are sites where humans encounter other humans (and, indeed, nonhuman entities), where we might begin to fulfill Luce Irigaray's call to "learn how to be with the other."[27] In addition to the cognitive and logistical particularities of reading in signed languages, then, such reading practices also involve ethical engagements. When we are not forced to continually make the case for the status of signed languages as languages, through appeals to the ways in which they mirror other linguistic modalities, we have the opportunity to explore these areas of intriguing difference, areas that have the potential to shape our understanding of reading in all modalities.

FURTHER READING

Bauman, H-Dirksen L., Jennifer Nelson, and Heidi Rose, eds. *Signing the Body Poetic: Essays on American Sign Language Literature*. Berkeley, CA: University of California Press, 2006.

Baynton, Douglas C. *Forbidden Signs: American Culture and the Campaign against Sign Language*. Chicago: University of Chicago Press, 1996.

Chamberlain, Charlene, Jill P. Morford, and Rachel I. Mayberry, eds. *Language Acquisition by Eye*. New York: Psychology Press, 1999.

Chen, Mel. *Animacies: Biopolitics, Racial Mattering, and Queer Affect*. Durham, NC: Duke University Press, 2012.

Esmail, Jennifer. "The Power of Deaf Poetry: The Exhibition of Literacy and the Nineteenth-Century Sign Language Debates." *Sign Language Studies* 8.4 (2008): 348–68.

Harmon, Kristen. "Writing Deaf: Textualizing Deaf Literature." *Sign Language Studies* 7.2 (2007): 200–7.

Saenger, Paul. *Space between Words: The Origins of Silent Reading*. Palo Alto: Stanford University Press, 1997.

[27] Luce Irigaray, "The Path toward the Other," in *Beckett after Beckett*, ed. S. E. Gontarski and Anthony Uhlman (Gainesville, FL: University Press of Florida, 2006), 39–51; 50.

19

ACCESSIBILITY

JONATHAN LAZAR

Accessibility means flexibility. We all read using different lenses. Some of those lenses are metaphorical, and some of us use physical lenses such as reading glasses or bifocals. Some of us use bookmarks. Some of us mark up important passages using highlighters or pens, and others use Post-it® notes. We are all taught to read as children, switching at some point in our primary years, from "learning to read" to "reading to learn." Depending on our post-secondary and graduate education, we may have been taught to read differently, to focus on different aspects of the writing. We may have been taught to evaluate differently, placing more emphasis, for instance, on arguments made in words (e.g., law) versus arguments made in data (e.g., science).

The purpose of reading often depends on our age and stage of life. We may read for pleasure, or we may read for work. We may read fiction, textbooks, instructions on how to build furniture, signs on how to leave a building or airplane in an emergency, or kiosk-based instructions at a transportation hub. When we are planning a great meal, we may read recipes; when we're heading to the supermarket, we may read our GPS device; when we're shopping, we may read the labels on food, and when we're checking out, we may read instructions on a machine. We read exams from the time that we are young to the time that we are entering professions in law, medicine, or teaching. We read text messages from our friends, or widely distributed Amber or Silver alerts that pop up on our smartphones. Access to reading is necessary for all, but, in some cases, such as when we receive alerts about weather conditions, food recalls, or safety hazards on the road, having reading materials in a fully accessible format is the difference between life and death.

In terms of format, some people prefer to read a print book or a newspaper. Other people prefer to read their texts digitally, and other sections of this collection focus primarily on digital reading. Within digital reading, there is a vast quantity of options: standard 18" or 21" monitors. Laptop monitors. Tablet computers. Smart phones. E-readers. Wall-mounted displays. Everyone has their preference for how they digest text. Some people like printing out emails. Some people prefer reading on a screen over a hard copy, unless they need to do lots of markup and comments. Some people prefer using applications such as MS-Word, while others prefer Adobe PDF format. Some Americans may prefer to read content such as news in a language other than English. Others may have low task knowledge (e.g., the average citizen trying to understand their tax forms) and therefore may prefer an easy-to-understand synopsis, or a version written in "plain language." Some people may have low literacy skills and therefore may need assistance with reading. Much of this essay (and this book) will refer to reading in the developed world, but there are entirely different issues related to reading in developing countries.

Increasingly, people expect that they will have the flexibility to read on the device that they want. People often assume that it is their right to read materials in whatever format they want. Changing the font size, or the font face, or the color of text in contrast to the background color on a screen are features that people assume that they have the right to, even without realizing that they are actually accessibility features. Having a website provide the same content in multiple languages, or in multiple file formats, is almost viewed as a right. In some countries which have language requirement laws (e.g., all content on Canadian websites must be in both English and French), it is a legal requirement.

People with disabilities, having been so frequently left out of the world of reading, make no such assumptions about their rights. Even when people with disabilities have the legal right to access reading material in the format that they need and can process, often they must enforce that right when book publishers, content providers, educational systems, and administrators do not provide reading content in appropriate formats. Consider Mark Riccobono, President of the National Federation of the Blind, who reads using either braille or audio output. Or consider famous physicist Stephen Hawking, who could see print but was physically unable to turn the pages of a printed book. They need access to the same reading material as everyone else, just in a different format. Despite the fact that all books are now "born-digital," ready to be transformed into multiple formats, books are nevertheless still frequently turned into inaccessible formats (such as improperly formatted PDFs). People (not only those with disabilities) must often transform a book into the most accessible format for them and their devices, a time-consuming process, meaning that they will not have access to the same book at the same time as everyone else. Additionally, people with disabilities often must fight, argue, and advocate for themselves with the content providers in order to obtain the content in an accessible format.

Notice the contrast between those without disabilities who believe that they have the right to content in any format (but legally do not), and those with disabilities who legally do have that right but often are not given equal access. Accessibility means flexibility. More specifically, it implies having print presented in the format that one wants, with options for larger print, audio, or braille. If you have a reading disability such as dyslexia, accessibility may mean hearing a word in computer-synthesized speech output at the same time that the word is highlighted on the screen. Regardless of the format, accessibility is, at its core, the same technical basis for flexibility that all people want—the flexibility to read material on the device one wants, in the format that one wants.

Accessibility doesn't only mean taking existing printed words and making them available in other formats. Accessibility also means taking a communication, which sometimes was not originally in printed word format, and translating it into printed word format. So, for instance, transcripts of audio and captioning on video mean that audio and video can now be "read." While these features started out as approaches to benefit those who are Deaf and/or hard of hearing, transcripts and captioning are used by everyone, including students doing research studies who need to do textual analysis, people who are in loud or silent places and can't listen to audio, English-language learners, and even nonhuman entities, such as search engines. In addition, video description involves describing the video presentation, the setting, the feel of the scene. Alternative text and extended descriptions for graphics and charts help all people understand the meaning of images.

Accessibility increases the amount of information that can potentially be read. Furthermore, accessibility is really innovation. Technologies that first started out as assistive technologies to fill a specific need for people with disabilities (e.g., captioning, e-books, voice recognition) were then adopted by a much broader population of users once those users realized how useful these new approaches are. For instance: imagine that you are in a new country where you do not know the language. You can use an application such as the KNFB Reader on your smart phone to take a picture of a restaurant menu that is in another language, convert it into computer-synthesized speech, and translate it into your native language. The app is useful for anyone, even though it started out as an assistive technology for blind users.

Legal Foundations of Accessible Reading Material

While everyone wants to have the ability to read materials in the format of their choice, for people with disabilities there are legal requirements for this flexibility in reading format. At an international level, treaties such as the UN Convention on the Rights of Persons with Disabilities (CRPD) focus on equal access to digital content and technologies for people with disabilities. For instance, Article 21 of the CRPD requires governments to "Provid[e] information intended for the general public to persons with disabilities in accessible formats and technologies appropriate to different kinds of disabilities in a timely manner and without additional cost" and encourages "the mass media, including providers of information through the Internet, to make their services accessible to persons with disabilities."[1]

[1] UNCRPD (https://www.un.org/development/desa/disabilities/convention-on-the-rights-of-persons-with-disabilities.html).

The Marrakesh Treaty to Facilitate Access to Published Works for Persons Who Are Blind, Visually Impaired or Otherwise Print Disabled also focuses on accessibility of digital content. There are two key provisions required of signatories to the Marrakesh Treaty: (1) exceptions to national copyright law for providing alternate formats for people with print-related disabilities; and (2) allowing for the export and import of accessible reading materials (so that the same materials in the same language do not need to be uniquely created in each country).[2]

Many countries already have exceptions to copyright law (e.g., the Chafee Amendment to the Copyright Act in the USA, the Copyright (Visually Impaired Persons) Act 2002 in the UK, or the Copyright Amendment Act 2006 in Australia) allowing for the transformation of copyrighted material to alternate reading formats for people with print-related disabilities. This isn't new or groundbreaking. Non-profit organizations such as Bookshare and Learning Ally, along with government-related organizations such as the Royal National Institute of Blind People in the United Kingdom, Canadian National Institute for the Blind, Vision Australia Library, and the USA Library of Congress National Library Service for the Blind and Physically Handicapped help serve the reading needs of those labeled as having "print-related disabilities"—challenges seeing print, physically handling printed materials, or cognitively processing printed materials. The processes in place to ensure that the materials are only utilized by certified people with print disabilities (in accordance with copyright laws and the various exceptions to those laws) are well-established. In addition, primary, secondary, and post-secondary educational institutions are often required to provide reading materials in accessible formats to students with print-related disabilities. In most of the developed world, there is a clear legal framework for ensuring accessibility of reading materials to people with disabilities.

The change over time in reading, from primarily paper-based materials to primarily digital materials, expands what is technically feasible, and what people with disabilities expect. In the past, the three different approaches for creating reading material in alternative formats were audio recordings of books, large print books, and tactile (primarily braille) books. In 1999, in the case of *Doe v. Mutual of Omaha* (a 7th Circuit Court of Appeals case related to insurance, not books), Judge Richard Posner famously said, "it is apparent that a store is not required to alter its inventory in order to stock goods such as Braille books that are especially designed for disabled people."[3] But in 1999, the choice was paper books or braille books. In 2020, most consumers (with or without disabilities) want books in digital format. The same version of those digitally formatted books can then be presented in multiple formats: as standard or larger sized print on a screen, as print on paper, as audio, or as refreshable braille.

---

[2] Marrakesh Treaty to Facilitate Access to Published Works for Persons Who Are Blind, Visually Impaired or Otherwise Print Disabled (http://www.wipo.int/treaties/en/ip/marrakesh/).

[3] *Doe v. Mut. of Omaha Ins. Co., 179 F.3d 557* (7th Circuit, 1999).

Libraries are leading the way in making reading materials available in fully accessible formats. Many public libraries are now evaluating how, given the switch from primarily paper to digital reading resources, they can serve people with print disabilities at their local branch rather than referring them to a Library for the Blind and Physically Handicapped (or equivalent). So, for instance, many public libraries are lending out e-book content as well as e-book devices. Digital libraries (essentially databases of articles) present a great opportunity for public libraries to flex their spending muscle. When public libraries pressure digital libraries that they procure to become accessible, it means that public libraries can then serve additional patrons with print-related disabilities. The Association of Research Libraries has also been leading this trend: their Web Accessibility Toolkit provides guidance for how research libraries can provide fully accessible reading materials.[4] In the landmark *Authors Guild, Inc. v. HathiTrust* (2014) case in the USA, the 2nd Circuit Court of Appeals upheld a lower court ruling protecting the rights of a coalition of university libraries (HathiTrust), under fair use, to digitize books in order to allow for the creation of a full-text database to assist in searching, which, under the Chafee Amendment, at the same time also served the rights of patrons with print disabilities.[5]

Technical Foundations of Accessible Reading Material

Why isn't more reading material in accessible format? It's a puzzling question. The technical standards for accessibility exist, and they are not new. The previous sections described the approaches that were used in the past for creating accessible reading material. However, all reading material, digital content, books, and signs are now born digital. The expensive, time-consuming process of converting reading material into an alternative format is no longer necessary. When digital reading material is prepared today, the simple step of using international technical standards can ensure that the reading material will be accessible to all.

The Web Content Accessibility Guidelines (WCAG), now in version 2.1, provide an international standard developed by the World Wide Web Consortium (W3C) and utilized by nearly every government in the developed world that has a law related to accessibility for digital content. These guidelines are not just for the web; the WCAG2ICT allows developers to utilize the WCAG in non-web contexts. The WCAG 2.1 is built around four key concepts that can be can applied to nearly any type of digital technology or content:

1. *Perceivable*—Information and user interface components must be presentable to users in ways they can perceive;

---

[4] Web Accessibility Tookit (available at http://accessibility.arl.org/).
[5] *Authors Guild, Inc. v. HathiTrust*, 755 F.3d 87 (2nd Circuit, 2014).

2. *Operable*—User interface components and navigation must be operable;
3. *Understandable*—Information and the operation of user interface must be understandable;
4. *Robust*—Content must be robust enough that it can be interpreted reliably by a wide variety of user agents, including assistive technologies.[6]

A technical standard, EPUB3, is designed more specifically for reading material in the form of books. Digital books using the EPUB3 standard adapt to user preferences for how the content is presented, allowing for full accessibility for all types of print-related disabilities. EPUB3 succeeds in allowing for the flexibility (e.g., reflow of text) of presentation lacking in other formats (such as PDF). The EPUB3 format ensures that the navigation features that most readers expect from a print book, for example, page numbers, chapter numbers, indexes, and subheadings, are fully available for all readers, regardless of format. Like everyone else, people with disabilities want the flexibility to jump around in their reading materials, skim, and search for specific headings. From a technical point of view, the accessibility of reading materials is generally easy. Some technical challenges do remain in the creation of accessible versions of complex visual graphs and complex scientific notations, although there are already many existing solutions.

Looking Toward the Future

The technical and legal frameworks for accessible reading material are already in place. Consumers, with and without disabilities, want flexibility in the format of their reading material. So why do book publishers fight against people with disabilities?

There are many examples of publishers and content providers fighting against giving people with disabilities equal access to reading materials in the USA. The Communications and Video Accessibility Act of 2010 requires, among other things, that all e-book devices (the actual hardware) be accessible for people with disabilities, since the devices have Wi-Fi and are therefore classified as communications devices. Yet the Coalition of E-Reader Manufacturers has applied for, and received, multiple waivers from this requirement. As mentioned in previous sections, the Authors Guild fought a lawsuit (*Authors Guild, Inc. v. HathiTrust*) to stop universities from digitizing their books and making them accessible. From 2007 to 2015, Amazon fought making its Kindle e-reader devices accessible, prompting the U.S. Departments of Justice and Education to advise universities that they may not adopt them for classroom usage without providing equivalent alternatives. The U.S. Department of State withdrew a $16.5 million dollar contract for Amazon Kindle e-readers for similar reasons. Groups such as the National Federation of the Blind filed lawsuits

---

[6] Web Content Accessibility Guidelines (https://www.w3.org/TR/WCAG21/).

against public libraries and universities that utilized inaccessible Kindle or Nook e-reader devices. Amazon allows publishers (as per the request of the Authors Guild) to disable the text-to-speech function on Kindle books by request. In 2009, the Association of American Publishers and the Authors Guild went so far as to put out a statement encouraging publishers to negotiate contracts that prohibit books being read aloud using text-to-speech features on the Amazon Kindle, even in the privacy of one's home.

Book publishers and content providers clearly are not working proactively to help individuals with disabilities who want to read their books. Why do publishers do this? Do I think that they hate people with disabilities? No. I think that they view these situations through a strictly economic lens: publishers think that by controlling the flexibility of their formats, they can sell consumers the same book two or three times (one sale in paper format, another in audio format, etc.). I don't think that's a rational argument, but I do think that publishers, like many other industries, are slow to understand the new paradigms of the digital age. No one knows the exact motivation of publishers. However, by their actions, publishers, content providers, and e-book hardware providers are saying that they don't believe that people with disabilities should have equal access to reading materials.

So, within the context of accessibility, what is the future of reading? Perhaps the future of reading is putting together a coalition to hammer home the message that accessible reading benefits all readers, not only readers with disabilities. This can be thought of as the "curb cut" argument. Curb cuts benefit not only wheelchair users but also bikers, Segway users, and people toting strollers, prams, or wheeled luggage. Likewise, whether or not they have a disability, people often want to read in different digital formats. Book publishers and other content providers often seem to want to limit or narrow the scope of reading. They want to dictate the terms of how words are read, in what format and what situations. I suggest ten ideas to push back against publishers and broaden the scope of how one could potentially read:

1. International legal documents such as the CRPD and Marrakesh Treaty (discussed earlier) already require accessibility in reading materials. Yet those documents have not yet influenced many national laws related to reading materials. Perhaps there is an opportunity to educate policymakers and legislators about the need for stronger statutes or codes requiring the accessibility of all reading materials. For common law countries where court cases are binding law, perhaps there are opportunities for disability advocates to test cases related to the accessibility of reading materials. Class action lawsuits (where allowed) on behalf of all readers with print-related disabilities might offer a useful means to advocate through the legal system.

2. Authors, when they sign book contracts, must push publishers to ensure that publishing in "Accessible EPUB3" format is a requirement expressly stated in the book contract. Often, publishers will not publish books in that format unless

required to do so. Perhaps universities who employ many of the people who write and edit books can make this a requirement, or a strong encouragement, as well.

3. The concept of "open access" needs to be broadened to include accessibility. Some governments are now requiring that when research is government-funded, the publications must be freely available to the public, not behind a pay wall. Some universities are doing the same thing. This idea of open access is nice, but how open is the access if it's not accessible to people with disabilities, and if it's not usable by people with different types of reading needs who may simply want flexibility in the presentation of format? The open access movement also needs to include accessibility. Perhaps the open access movement, without accessibility, is still a "closed access" movement. Something interesting to ponder.

4. Universities and libraries (public, special, and university libraries), as large consumers of books, digital content, journals, and other reading materials, can use their formidable buying power to enforce accessibility rules upon their vendors. Some universities and libraries have already started to do this. Given the legal risk that both universities and libraries face in procuring inaccessible reading materials, there is an incentive to force vendors toward improved accessibility. Universities can also place similar rules upon content generated from grant funding.

5. The concept of accessibility of reading content needs to be taught to students in all university programs related to reading, including graphical design, computer science, information studies, and reading education. We cannot expect change if our designers, programmers, and software engineers are not familiar with the concepts of accessibility. Organizations already focusing on increasing accessibility content in curriculum (such as www.teachaccess.org) can help.

6. Advocates can push the major booksellers to make information about the accessibility of their reading materials available online. It's often not immediately obvious when shopping for books online whether or not the materials are accessible (unless they're clearly marked as being in an accessible EPUB3 format). Consumer protection laws (which require the transparency of all terms and details of a transaction) might be used to support these efforts.

7. Advocates can seek publicity for accessible reading. When was the last time that you saw a news article about this topic? A TV program? A protest or rally? As far as I know, a protest (against publishers) on this topic only occurred once, in 2009, in New York City. Perhaps it's time to break out the picket signs and bring attention to this topic again.

8. Governments, national, regional, and local, are all creators of reading content. How accessible is that content? We must hold our governmental agencies to the highest standard of reading accessibility. It would be unreasonable to expect private actors to create accessible content when our government agencies are

not role models. We need reliable data on the accessibility level of reading material provided by various governments, and we need to hold them accountable for following their own laws.

9. It is important not only to look outside of our fields and disciplines but also to look within. How many professional organizations produce only accessible reading materials? How many disciplines include strong policy statements about accessibility? How many disciplines have a code of ethics, and how many of those codes ensure equal access to knowledge within that field?

10. How much research are we doing about the accessibility of reading materials? What gaps are there in the research? What research would help drive this agenda? What tools and/or processes are still needed? We must have a better idea of where research is still needed.

FURTHER READING

Blanck, Peter David. *eQuality: The Struggle for Web Accessibility by Persons with Cognitive Disabilities*. Cambridge: Cambridge University Press, 2014.

Jaeger, Paul T. *Disability and the Internet: Confronting a Digital Divide*. Boulder, CO: Lynne Rienner Publishers, 2012.

Lazar, Jonathan, and Michael Ashley Stein, eds. *Disability, Human Rights, and Information Technology*. Philadelphia: University of Pennsylvania Press, 2017.

Lazar, Jonathan. "The Potential Role of US Consumer Protection Laws in Improving Digital Accessibility for People with Disabilities." *The University of Pennsylvania Journal of Law and Social Change* 22.3 (2019): 185–204.

Lazar, Jonathan, Daniel F. Goldstein, and Anne Taylor. *Ensuring Digital Accessibility through Process and Policy*. Amsterdam: Morgan Kaufmann, 2015.

Wentz, Brian, Paul T. Jaeger, and John Carlo Bertot, eds. *Accessibility for Persons with Disabilities and the Inclusive Future of Libraries*. Bingley: Emerald Group Publishing, 2017.

BRAINS

20

NEUROSCIENCE

PAUL B. ARMSTRONG

What happens in people's brains when they read a literary text, and why should literary critics and theorists care? It's not necessary, after all, to know how the digestive system works or how the liver processes alcohol to enjoy a good meal with a glass of wine. Most physiological and cognitive processes function effectively beneath awareness and, indeed, are not even accessible to consciousness. It is certainly the case that neurons fire when we read and that various cortical processes are set in motion when we have an aesthetic experience, but it is not self-evident that we need to know about these things in order to go about our business as readers, critics, or theorists. What neuro-philosophers call an "explanatory gap" separates what is going on at the neuronal and cortical levels from our experiences with art and literature, and the tools and theories of neuroscience are not necessarily any more helpful for making sense of a poem or a painting than the expertise of a gastroenterologist would be to choosing a dinner menu.

Nevertheless, literary critics typically make assumptions, whether tacitly or explicitly, about how we know and how language works, and if these are inconsistent with the best science about the brain that is a problem we should not ignore. Scientific theories develop and change, and the consensus about some matters is stronger than others (which is why it is wrong to build an argument on the basis of a single experiment or scientific report as some literary theorists do). But just as climate change and Darwinian evolution are not in doubt even though they are historically and socially constructed theories that are subject to ongoing testing and revision, so some of the findings of neuroscience about neuronal and cortical processes are sufficiently well-established that they should be regarded as constraints on what counts as a reasonable hypothesis. The claims literary critics and theorists make, for example, about language, the historicity of reading, and the social and moral powers of literature are based on assumptions about cognition that can and should be tested against the relevant science. Science won't settle all of the disagreements we have about these matters, but some claims turn out to be stronger than others (as I will show), and other claims are just plain wrong.

The brain is a bushy ensemble of anatomical features whose functions are partly fixed by genetic inheritance but are also to a considerable extent plastic and variable. Contemporary brain-imaging technologies have mapped in exquisite detail specific regions of the rear visual cortex, for example, that respond to orientation, motion, and color, but the development of these areas will depend on how they are used. Their receptivity will vary according to the inputs they receive, and if they are deprived of stimulation during certain critical periods, they will atrophy. For example, the fusiform gyrus is an area of the visual cortex dedicated to face recognition, a functionally specific anatomical area that, if damaged, can result in "prosopagnosia," an inability to identify faces. Babies respond to a broad spectrum of faces, including those of other species like monkeys, but this response diminishes over time to kinds of faces to which the infant is not exposed. The lamentable but understandable result is that adults have difficulty distinguishing types of faces they seldom encounter in their communities.

Neuroscience is not phrenology, however, and cognition is not simply a matter of one-to-one correspondence between a stimulus and the response of a particular neuron or cortical region. Fundamental cognitive processes like vision and hearing (both crucial to reading) entail top-down, bottom-up interactions between widely distributed regions of the brain that are reciprocally connected and that get organized in a particular manner for specific tasks and can be realigned (more or less easily, depending on their physiological structure and their history) as the need and opportunity arise. The brain knows the world by forming and dissolving assemblies of neurons, establishing patterns that become habitual through repeated firing. Although the functions associated with a particular cortical location can be disabled if it is damaged, no region works alone, and its role can vary according to how it interacts with other areas. The visual cortex of a blind person, for example, can adapt and become responsive to touch when reading braille, and some sight-deprived people, as well as animals, have been shown to have superior sound localization because the unused parts of their visual cortex are recruited for auditory functions.

These instances of plasticity may seem exceptional, but they are examples of the general rule that the function of any area of the cortex depends on its connections and interactions with other areas. This is why, according to a recent survey of the research on emotions, there is "little evidence that discrete emotion categories can be consistently and specifically localized to distinct brain regions."[1] This review of the experimental evidence shows, for example, that the amygdala is not uniquely and exclusively associated with fear but is also active "in orienting responses to motivationally relevant stimuli" that are "novel," "uncertain," and "unusual."[2]

---

[1] Kristen A. Lindquist, Tor D. Wager, Hedy Kober, Eliza Bliss-Moreau, and Lisa Feldman Barrett, "The Brain Basis of Emotion: A Meta-Analytic Review," *Behavioral and Brain Sciences* 35.3 (2012), 121–43; 121. Also see Lisa Feldman Barrett, *How Emotions are Made: The Secret Life of the Brain* (New York: Houghton Mifflin Harcourt, 2017).

[2] Lindquist et al., "Brain Basis of Emotion," 130.

Various studies have similarly shown that the anterior insula, typically connected with disgust, "is observed in a number of tasks that involve awareness of body states," including "movement," "gastric distention," and even orgasm.[3] This research has cast doubt on the claim, popularized by neuroscientist Paul Ekman, that there are certain basic, universal emotions that all members of our species share because they are based on genetically fixed structures of our neuroanatomy. The neurobiology of emotions is more variable, heterogeneous, and open to change than Ekman's theory assumes.

Brain-body-world interactions can affect the functions of particular cortical regions and the connections between them. The brain is not an orderly structure consisting of rule-governed relations between fixed elements like a computer with hard-wired connections between components that operate according to logical algorithms. The computer analogy has been discredited because the brain is much messier, more fluid, and more open to unpredictable (if not unlimited) developments than this linear, mechanical model assumes. To understand a complex cognitive phenomenon like vision, emotion, or language, it is not enough to identify modularity and structure; it is necessary, rather, to trace the configurative, non-linear, to-and-fro processes through which various components of our dynamic cognitive systems interact and reciprocally constitute each other.

This is one of the reasons why the concept of a "universal grammar" based on a mental organ for language (what Steven Pinker popularized as a "language instinct") has fallen out of favor.[4] Although particular regions of the brain (Broca's and Wernicke's areas) are linked to syntactical and semantic functions that go haywire if they are damaged, there is no single module for language and no discrete, anatomically identifiable set of regions that would constitute the grammar unit predicted by structural linguistics. Brain-scanning studies have repeatedly shown that linguistic abilities like speaking, writing, and reading involve the entire cortex and entail far-flung syntheses of cortical areas and connections between the brain and the body. Correlative evidence is provided by cases of aphasia in different languages, which reveal not an anatomically based, universal grammar system that gets knocked out with the loss of language function but, rather, what neuroscientist Stephen Nadeau calls "graceful degradation."[5] Everything doesn't simply collapse and disappear; instead, some functions are more or less strongly preserved, in different patterns of vulnerability that depend on cross-cerebral connections and redundancies, and that vary between linguistic communities. This evidence is better accounted for by the probabilistic regularities established through cross-cerebral connections developed through experience than by an innate, logically ordered grammar.

[3] Lindquist et al., "Brain Basis of Emotion," 133–4.

[4] Pinker uses the phrase in *The Language Instinct: How the Mind Creates Language* (New York: HarperPerennial, 1995).

[5] Stephen E. Nadeau, *The Neural Architecture of Grammar* (Cambridge, MA: MIT Press, 2012), 88.

One consequence of these findings for literary studies is that we should be careful to evaluate claims for universality against the contradictory fixity and plasticity of our cognitive make-up. The formalist goal of identifying orderly, universal structures of language and mind doesn't match up well with the bushiness of the brain or with how cognitive patterns emerge from our embodied experiences of the world. The legacy of structuralism remains evident in some kinds of cognitive narratology that aim to identify and classify the underlying "frames," "scripts," and "preference rules" that support our ability to tell and understand stories. The dream of developing the ideal, all-encompassing taxonomy dies hard, but proposals for classificatory schemes to explain how we make and construe meaning should be treated skeptically because they reify and oversimplify the interactive cognitive processes through which our inherited neurobiological dispositions get reshaped and reformed.

Language is what neuroscientists call "a bio-cultural hybrid" that develops through the interaction of inherited functions and anatomical structures in the brain with culturally variable experiences of communication and education. Any claims for cognitive or linguistic universality need to square with our bio-cultural hybridity. Whatever transcultural, transhistorical regularities may exist in the ways that we know, act, or communicate are a product of variable but constrained interactions between brain, body, and world. The sources of these regularities are typically both biology and experience. It's not simply that nature is fixed and nurture variable. There are regularities and variations in both domains.

For example, somewhat speculative but highly suggestive evidence about recurrent preferred shapes across different writing systems indicates that the regularities of the world's alphabets are attributable both to the biology of the eye and the visual cortex and to typical patterns of visual experience. According to evolutionary neurobiologist Mark Changizi, visual signs in writing systems "have been culturally selected to match the kinds of conglomeration of contours found in natural scenes because that is what we have evolved to be good at visually processing."[6] Through a statistical analysis of images of naturally occurring shapes as recorded in various photographic databases, Changizi found that objects often form T- or L-like patterns when they are viewed together—whether placed next to or in front of each other, partially blocking one's vision of them. Sometimes, but more rarely, an X-shape occurs, as when one branch of a tree crosses another. Three lines forming a triangle seldom occur in a natural scene. According to Changizi, the frequency with which these shapes occur in nature is, surprisingly and strikingly, closely comparable to the statistical distribution of similar shapes found in the world's written symbol-systems. That is, across the seemingly very different systems of alphabetic signs in use around the world, T- and L-shapes are more common than X's, and

    [6] Mark A. Changizi, Qiong Zhang, Hao Ye, and Shinsuke Shimojo, "The Structures of Letters and Symbols throughout Human History Are Selected to Match Those Found in Objects in Natural Scenes," *American Naturalist* 167.5 (2006), E117–E139; E117.

triangular forms rarely occur. This is not accidental, he postulates, but evidence of the development of written signs that the visual brain could easily recognize because they resembled natural forms to which it was accustomed and which it had evolved to process efficiently.

These findings both confirm and qualify a central dogma of contemporary literary theory, Ferdinand de Saussure's famous claim about the arbitrariness of the sign.[7] The variety of the world's alphabets testifies to the cultural contingency of the sign (any particular written code is no more necessary than any other), but their geometric similarities are evidence of the visual system's evolved, pre-inscribed capacities for registering typical, naturally recurring forms. The alphabetic sign is a bio-cultural hybrid whose range of variation is limited by the visual geometry of familiar shapes which the brain is predisposed to recognize. The sign is arbitrary and can vary because the brain is plastic and adaptable, but its variations are limited because this plasticity is constrained by characteristics of the visual cortex that evolved in response to regularities in perceptual experience.

Our ability to read is similarly a bio-cultural hybrid, with consequences that literary theories of reading need to take into account. The unnatural, culturally acquired capacity to read written texts came about through the repurposing of genetically inherited functionalities in the visual cortex. Reading is a relatively late development in the history of our species that could only emerge by exploiting pre-existing neurological systems. As neuroscientist Stanislas Dehaene points out, we learn to read Shakespeare by adapting cortical capacities that our species acquired on the African savanna. What had to occur is what Dehaene memorably calls "neuronal recycling"—the redeployment of "a cortical territory initially devoted to a different function."[8] This is an instance of what neuroscientists call "neural re-use," the capacity of a cortical region to acquire new functions through interactions with different areas of the brain and the body in response to novel experiences.[9] The ability to read is not something children inherit. Rather, they can only learn to read by adapting genetically inherited circuitry to uses for which it did not originally evolve, and some of the difficulties encountered by beginning readers, as well as some of the differences in how easy this learning is for readers in different languages, can be traced to mismatches between the requirements of decoding written signs and the cortical systems that must be converted to this purpose.

Clinical and experimental evidence suggests that this conversion occurs in a region of the brain devoted to the recognition of visual forms. The first indication of a "visual word form area" (VWFA) dedicated to reading came in the late nineteenth

---

[7] Ferdinand de Saussure, *Course in General Linguistics* [1915], ed. Charles Bally and Albert Sechehaye, trans. Wade Baskin (New York: McGraw Hill, 1966).

[8] Stanislas Dehaene, *Reading in the Brain: The New Science of How We Read* (New York: Penguin, 2009), 147.

[9] See M. L. Anderson, "Neural Re-use: A Fundamental Organizational Principle of the Brain," *Behavioral and Brain Sciences* 33.4 (2010): 245–66.

century when a patient who suffered a minor stroke lost the ability to read while retaining the capacity to speak and even to write (although he could not read his own writing) and to recognize objects other than written words. Brain-imaging research led by Dehaene's laboratory has identified an area of the lower left hemisphere that is activated in response to written signs (but not spoken words), located between regions involved in the recognition of objects and faces. This finding is controversial because the VWFA is not homogeneous and still bears traces of other activity (as one would expect because it is repurposed from other functions), but evidence of its existence and its role in word-recognition is compelling.

Brain-imaging experiments show that the VWFA is activated by all alphabetic systems, by Chinese as well as Roman characters, and by both the Kanji and Kana scripts used by Japanese. These experiments reveal the niche in the brain's architecture that has been redirected to a specific cultural activity that arose too quickly for biological evolution to produce with genetic changes, and this is powerful evidence for the mutual accommodation of nature and culture assumed by the hypothesis of neuronal recycling. The universality of the niche across cultures with different alphabets is evidence of the restrictions of pre-given cortical structures, even as the conversion of a particular region of visual recognition neurons to a learned, culturally variable activity shows the plasticity and adaptability of the brain.

This research suggests that, while reading is historical, it changes on different time-scales. The properties of the visual cortex involved in the construal of written signs are a product first of all of the long evolutionary history of the human brain's development that produced its particular features and abilities different from (and similar to) other mammals whose origins we share. A shorter but still considerable period was then required for these cortical structures and processes to be repurposed through the neuronal recycling that allowed reading to emerge—a reorientation of cortical functionalities that must be repeated again and again as this enduring cultural capacity is handed down through education from generation to generation (reading is an unnatural act; not everyone learns how to do it, and some brains have more trouble with it than others do). On the smallest temporal scale are the individual variations that may occur in the wiring of readers with different personal histories (including their habitual hermeneutic practices as members of distinctive interpretive communities).

Our species' development of the capacity to read illustrates the dual historicity of cognitive functions. Some of our epistemological equipment is based on long-term, evolutionarily stable capacities like the responsiveness of the visual system to edges, orientation, lines, and shapes, but these capacities are open to change depending on learning and experience—they can be recruited, in this case, to identify alphabetic signs—because the function of a cortical region depends on how it interacts with other components of the dynamical system. The brain can be molded by cultural institutions (like literacy) that adapt particular areas and capacities for their purposes, but, as with reading, these capabilities need to be relearned with each generation until or unless the neural reuse through which they are repurposed becomes evolutionarily adapted into the biological makeup of the species. The structures and functions of the brain are historical because they are the products of evolution, but some capacities are more enduring than others and shared by members of our species across time and around the globe (and are "universal," in this sense) even as they get reshaped and repurposed through particular, historical, socially situated experiences of learning (their bio-cultural hybridity).

The conventional wisdom in current American literary criticism is that reading is radically historical, and that it is consequently a mistake to make inferences about how readers in the past processed texts on the basis of our lived experiences as readers today.[10] This assumption oversimplifies the historicity of our cognitive functions. The neuroscientific research suggests that there are fundamental continuities in how the brain reads that extend across the several-thousand-year span during which our species has interpreted written texts. Phenomenological descriptions of the reading experience should consequently not be dismissed as ahistorical and essentialist, as contextualist critics typically do. Recent work on neuroscience and literature suggests that phenomenological models of reading are scientifically justified because their accounts of our embodied cognition are based on long-enduring, species-wide cortical, neuronal processes.[11] The correlations between neurobiological and phenomenological accounts of cognition, perception, and reading in fact help to explain the connections between how we process texts today and how our forebears construed them—connections that demonstrate how meaning-now is related to meaning-then, a crucial (but too often neglected) dimension of reading's historicity. If reading allows us to reach across history to worlds long gone but preserved in the traces they have left behind, this merger of horizons is made possible by transhistorical continuities in the neurobiology of the brain.

Neuroscientists have recently discovered the usefulness of phenomenological descriptions of perception, time, and intersubjectivity because these provide behavioral models that correlate in mutually illuminating ways with what contemporary imaging techniques reveal about neuronal and cortical processes. In a parallel development in literary studies, phenomenological theories of reading, literature, and interpretation (especially the work of Wolfgang Iser and Paul Ricoeur) are similarly enjoying renewed interest because of how they account for basic processes of embodied cognition. For example, just as cognition entails the configurative construction of gestalts on the basis of partial perspectives and incomplete clues, so reading is a to-and-fro process of building consistent patterns and filling in textual indeterminacies. Similarly, just as perception is a temporal process of making

---

[10] See Paul B. Armstrong, "In Defense of Reading: Or, Why Reading Still Matters in a Contextualist Age," *New Literary History* 42.1 (2011): 87–113.

[11] This work is discussed at greater length in Paul B. Armstrong, *How Literature Plays with the Brain: The Neuroscience of Reading and Art* (Baltimore: Johns Hopkins University Press, 2013).

predictions about what lies beyond our immediate horizons, so reading is an anticipatory and retrospective activity of projecting and modifying expectations. Finally, just as knowing other minds involves paradoxical processes of simulating and imagining another's experience on the basis of my own, so reading puts my own thought processes to work in order to animate perhaps new and unfamiliar ways of thinking and feeling held ready by the text. These aspects of embodied cognition are all likely to be common to the experience of readers now and in past generations because they are based on structures and functions of the brain that go back to the African savanna and beyond.

Neuroscientific findings about the paradoxical cognitive processes undergirding intersubjectivity have important implications for the social and moral powers of literature—the capacity of the reading experience to promote prosocial behavior including empathy and mutually beneficial collaboration. The processes of identification entailed in knowing others (as in the experience of reading) are acts of doubling "me" and "not-me" that are inherently unpredictable and open to a wide range of variation. This is why, for example, the effects of empathy are notoriously ambiguous, as the scientific literature on the topic amply attests. It is widely acknowledged, for example, that the fellow-feeling of empathy does not necessarily produce ethically beneficial, prosocial sympathy and compassion. Indeed, as neuroscientists Grit Hein and Tania Singer point out, "empathy can have a dark side" because it can be deployed for Machiavellian purposes "to find the weakest spot of a person to make her or him suffer."[12] Or, as empathy researchers Jean Decety and Claus Lamm point out, feeling another's emotional state may cause "personal distress" and result in aversion from the sufferer rather than sympathetic concern and involvement.[13] The consequences of simulating and identifying with another's experience are not foreordained, and there is good reason to doubt the assertion that reading stories will make us better people or that literature is inherently humanizing.

The doubleness of empathic understanding is evident in the classic definition of identification as *Einfühlung*, in which one "feels oneself into" the experience of another. Theodor Lipps's oft-cited example is the anxiety a spectator may feel while watching a circus acrobat on a high wire, where the thrill of the performance is based on the spectator's vicarious sense of the tightrope walker's danger.[14] What Antonio Damasio calls the "as-if body loop," whereby the brain simulates body states that are not caused by external stimuli, may indeed be set in motion by such

[12] Grit Hein and Tania Singer, "I Feel How You Feel but Not Always: The Empathic Brain and its Modulation," *Current Opinion in Neurobiology* 18.2 (2008): 153–8; 154.

[13] Jean Decety and Claus Lamm, "Empathy versus Personal Distress: Recent Evidence from Social Neuroscience," in *The Social Neuroscience of Empathy*, ed. Jean Decety and William Ickes (Cambridge, MA: MIT Press, 2009), 199–213.

[14] Theodor Lipps, "Einfühlung, Innere Nachahmung und Organempfindungen," in *Archiv für die Gesamte Psychologie* 1 (Leipzig: W. Engelmann, 1903), 185–204.

a participatory experience.[15] But such an "as if" recreation of another's observed behavior may not produce the same kinesethetic sensations she is experiencing. In this case, the cool, calm, and collected professional performer probably does not experience the same fear, anxiety, and excitement as the spectator—otherwise she might become paralyzed and fall—even as the spectator's ability to enjoy the act depends on not being in any real danger. Similarly, when we read about a character's fictionally represented experiences or identify with a narrator's point of view, our self does not simply disappear in a merger of ego and alter ego. Rather, setting in motion a paradoxical doubleness that both joins and separates self and other, readers exercise their own powers of configurative comprehension so that another world, based on perhaps different pattern-making structures, can emerge. The result, as Iser points out, is a paradoxical duplication of subjectivities, an interplay of the "alien me" whose thought patterns I recreate and inhabit, and the "real, virtual me" whose configurative powers of understanding cause this other world to take shape and, in the process, can find themselves transfigured and transformed.[16]

The bodily feelings generated by following a story and vicariously, empathically participating in the actions it represents—whether Aristotle's classic examples of pity and fear or any other of the widely various emotional responses stories can evoke—are consequently double and split. They are "as if" emotions that both are and are not the bodily, kinesthetic sensations we would have in an original experience. The "as if" quality of embodied experiences of identification has been widely documented in experimental studies of an observer's vicarious participation in another's pain or disgust. Experiments have shown that neurons in the insula and the anterior cingulate cortex (ACC) fire not only in response to a pinprick or an electric shock but also at the sight of someone else receiving the same painful stimulus—or even to a report that someone else would be poked or shocked. But the responses of observers are also sensitive to individual differences—more intense, for example, if a loved one is receiving the stimulus, or less intense if the witness is someone (like a nurse or an acupuncturist) conditioned to view pain and regard it as potentially beneficial—and these variations suggest in turn that the "as-if body loop" set in motion by the brain's simulation routines are a doubling of self and other, not a simple, one-to-one match. Similarly, well-known experiments have shown that the anterior insula responds during the experience of disgust prompted by an unpleasant smell as well as during the observation of someone else's disgusted facial expression. But observing another person's disgust is not likely to result in actual vomiting because the experience both is and is not the same bodily sensation as the feeling it duplicates.

[15] Antonio R. Damasio, *Descartes' Error: Emotion, Reason, and the Human Brain* (New York: Putnam, 1994).

[16] Wolfgang Iser, *The Act of Reading: A Theory of Aesthetic Response* (Baltimore: Johns Hopkins University Press, 1978), 152–9.

Feeling with a character depicted in a story or adopting the attitudes suggested by a narrator would similarly entail a doubling process of simulation and inference "as if" we were experiencing embodied, kinesthetically original sensations. The doubling of the "like" and the "not-like" in "as if" simulations helps to explain, for example, the oft-observed paradox that emotions such as fear and terror, which would otherwise cause discomfort or pain, can instead give rise to pleasure in aesthetic reenactments. Our identification with the tragic hero both is and is not the same as her experience, and this makes all the difference. But this doubling also need not result in a purgation of the emotions it simulates because mirroring another's sensations can instead stimulate and spread them contagiously. Aggression is not an automatic response to represented violence, however, because the doubling of "me" and "not-me" in empathic identification is an "as"-relation that can be variously configured and can have different outcomes depending on how the negation in the interplay of "like" and "not-like" is staged and received. The interactions between these patterns of representation and response may transform renderings of aggression and conflict into aesthetic pleasure, moral repulsion, or imitative violence depending on how the "as" is configured in the narrative and on how it is refigured in the listener's or reader's response. None of this is predetermined or foreordained.

Neuroscience cannot predict what the moral and social consequences of reading literature may be, but once again there are experimentally based findings about the brain that suggest constraints about what should count as a legitimate hypothesis in an area of literary inquiry. Anyone who claims that stories make us more sympathetic to other people or that violent movies or video games lead to an increase in social aggression should be met with skepticism. But purely formalist, "art for art's sake" accounts of literature are also dubious because they ignore how reading activates and may reshape and refigure processes of embodied cognition at work in our everyday lives. To repeat, although neuroscience will not settle our controversies— there is no danger that the scourge of scientific positivism will close off inquiry and debate—the acceptance of a few empirically tested postulates about the workings of the brain may at least rule some mistaken views out of bounds. Plenty will remain to argue and theorize about, and disputes that operate within constraints established by scientific consensus are more likely to be rigorous, productive, and interesting than speculation untethered by fact.

FURTHER READING

Armstrong, Paul B. *How Literature Plays with the Brain: The Neuroscience of Reading and Art* (Baltimore: Johns Hopkins University Press, 2013).

Cave, Terence. *Thinking with Literature: Towards a Cognitive Criticism* (Oxford: Oxford University Press, 2016).

Ethington, Philip F. "Sociovisual Perspective: Vision and the Forms of the Human Past." *A Field Guide to a New Meta-field: Bridging the Humanities-Sciences Divide*, ed. Barbara Stafford. Chicago: University of Chicago Press, 2011, 123–52.

Evans, Nicholas, and Stephen C. Levinson. "The Myth of Language Universals: Language Diversity and its Importance for Cognitive Science." *Behavioral and Brain Sciences* 32.5 (2009): 429–92.

Gallagher, Shaun, and Dan Zahavi. *The Phenomenological Mind*, 2nd edn. London: Routledge, 2012.

Garratt, Peter, ed. *The Cognitive Humanities: Embodied Mind in Literature and Culture.* London: Palgrave Macmillan, 2016.

Iser, Wolfgang. *The Act of Reading: A Theory of Aesthetic Response.* Baltimore: Johns Hopkins University Press, 1978.

Kukkonen, Karin. *A Prehistory of Cognitive Poetics: Neoclassicism and the Novel.* Oxford: Oxford University Press, 2017.

Ricoeur, Paul. *A Ricoeur Reader: Reflection and Imagination*, ed. Mario J. Valdés. Toronto: University of Toronto Press, 1991.

21

MENTAL REPRESENTATION

ANDREW ELFENBEIN

The past two decades have witnessed the flowering of book history and media studies. When I started my career, "bibliography" crept along as a relic loved only by pedantic editors. A work's physical state had no role in the modes of criticism then dominating the field. Since then, the turn to historicism in literary scholarship, along with the rise of electronic media and the web, have made what once seemed arcane or uninteresting into matters of urgent importance. Traditional work on familiar distinctions between media (visual, verbal, aural) has joined newer scholarship about the experience of reading works in different forms (on the page, desktop, laptop, phone, or tablet), hearing them (in person, online, on a phone), and seeing them (at a museum, on Instagram, on the television).

Differences between different realizations of a work have become central to certain modes of interpretation because they reveal huge changes in the potential reception of a work. Such questions are now fundamental to the broad field of digital humanities, and they ask scholars to confront long-held assumptions about how they access texts, move through them, remember their place in them, and annotate them. Popular journalism has developed a parallel interest in new media, including quasi-apocalyptic jeremiads about the evils of moving from paper to screen, and sobering meditations on the belief that digitization has broken absolutely, even catastrophically, with previous modes of reading.

Although analyses of the media long antedate Marshall McLuhan, his books about the media environment were so widespread that they became an intellectual origin for media studies, whether they deserved to or not. McLuhan treated developments in media as fundamental shapers of history:

> Until writing was invented, man lived in acoustic space: boundless, directionless, horizonless, in the dark of the mind, in the world of emotion, by primordial intuition, by terror. Speech is a social chart of this bog.
>
> The goose quill put an end to talk. It abolished mystery; it gave architecture and towns; it brought roads and armies, bureaucracy. It was the basic metaphor with which the

cycle of civilization began, the step from the dark into the light of the mind. The hand that filled the parchment page built a city.[1]

For McLuhan, moving from speech to writing had world-altering significance. While most scholars now reject ascribing such causal force to changes in media (a view known as "technological determinism"), at least in the humanities, explicit professions of avoiding this view accompany implicit reliance on it when scholars actually analyze media. A McLuhanesque consensus remains that differences in media have major consequences for transmitting information. Even when McLuhan's actual claims no longer hold sway, his style does: sweeping generalizations and enthusiastic attribution of vast power to media.

None of this is especially new or surprising. And yet, as a teacher, I encounter phenomena every time I teach that point to a different reality. In the classroom, students have difficulty remembering basic distinctions about the medium of what they encounter. When I teach Shakespeare's plays, students refer to them as "novels." When discussing the difference between textual works and film adaptations, students confuse the two. When I emphasize the value of hearing works read aloud, blank indifference greets my exhortations, and I am not surprised. When students do read aloud, they make so little use of the capacities of the voice that they might as well have read silently. In addition, it has become shorthand to comment on what a book "says," as if silent reading and oral speech were indistinguishable. These experiences point to a common issue: to my students, the source of a literary experience does not matter much. Visual, verbal, and aural materials are easily confused, at least to those who have not been told to distinguish among them.

If these differences between media blur, differences within media, such as those between various printed editions or film adaptations, are even less important for my students. I may ask them all to use the same edition of a work based on my sense of the best combination of price, legibility, and scholarly annotation, but students see little reason to respect my preference. Any edition will do: for them, they're all the same. After an assignment in which I ask students to compare and contrast nineteenth-, twentieth-, and twenty-first-century editions of a work, they may understand that different editions can give very different messages about a work. But this realization does not come spontaneously: it takes a full assignment to make visible what they otherwise would not notice. For my students, something about a work divorces itself from the medium, as if the physical embodiment mattered little for their experience.

The result is a binary: on one side, among scholars, massive attention to a work's physical medium; on the other, among my students, utter indifference to it. Both make intuitive sense. As we read, we may create mental images of what we are

---

[1] Marshall McLuhan, Quentin Fiore, and Jerome Agel, *The Medium is the Massage* (New York: Random House, 1967), 46; I attribute the quotation to McLuhan because the words are his, despite the presence of his collaborators on the visual aspects of the book.

reading and hear voices speaking the words, so that in everyday reading, the gap between reading and hearing a work may not seem huge. Likewise, we may have had the experience of seeing a film of something we read and thinking, "That's not how I imagined [fill in blank] at all," or of hearing a performer read a work and noticing an inflection entirely different from the one we had silently heard to ourselves. If our own memories move between different imagined modes of presentation, it may not be surprising that they can be confused.

At the same time, as we experience a work, we may be acutely conscious of its physical medium: a codex, a refrigerator note, a tablet, a phone, the television, the cinema screen, a laptop. For some, the physical medium has a version of what Walter Benjamin called "aura": for Benjamin, aura was the unreproducible magic surrounding an original work of art that was lost in reproduction.[2] A version of aura attaches to certain modes of presentation that feel more authentic than others. Hearing a symphony or rock concert live has an aura that listening to a record does not, as does reading a real codex as opposed to reading a computer screen. Such perceptions of aura stress that media are not interchangeable.

Beyond these perceptions, the physical medium matters not only in itself but also for the ways in which we access, use, talk about, and discard it. The cheap bestseller bought in Target, the rare volume available only in research libraries, the block-buster on Netflix, the avant-garde film seen only once because all copies were later destroyed: issues of access, prestige, class, privilege, leisure, and economics undergird these different media and differentiate their potential effects. Given how distinctively each is embedded in an array of social relations, it seems especially puzzling that they could ever be confused or that mode of presentation could ever seem not to matter.

To make sense of these two seemingly contradictory trends, I introduce a term not often considered in media studies or the history of the book: comprehension. As a term, "comprehension" feels like it belongs in discussion of K-12 (kindergarten through twelfth grade) school education, where it gauges the skill of developing readers, but not in an examination of adult audience response. Many adults may remember having undergone reading comprehension tests in childhood that were used, in possibly dubious ways, to sort students into ability levels. Given such distasteful memories, it is not surprising that scholars in the humanities have left this term to educators.

Yet comprehension highlights aspects of understanding overlooked by scholars in reading, book history, and media studies. In educational psychology, the emphasis on comprehension arose from the need to understand aspects of reading that went beyond decoding (the ability to translate written symbols into words). Students might decode successfully but still not understand what they read. Given this, educators realized that the goal of reading instruction had to go beyond decoding

---

[2] Walter Benjamin, "The Work of Art in the Age of Mechanical Reproduction," in *Illuminations*, ed. Hannah Arendt, trans. Harry Zohn (New York: Schocken, 1969), 217–51; 221.

to include comprehension as well. In education, successful comprehension requires creating a coherent and usable mental representation of a work, whether visual, verbal, or aural. This definition has three terms that need glossing: "coherent," "usable," and "mental representation," and I'll begin with the last. Why bother with this term at all? Isn't it enough to do what literary scholars always do and focus on the work? The concept of mental representation stresses the difference between what is read, heard, or seen and what the reader/listener/viewer makes of it. Psychologists use "mental representation" to describe what remains in memory of a text, in whatever medium, that someone has experienced.

When reading, a reader's mental representation usually bears only a tenuous relationship to the words on the page; this is true, *mutatis mutandis*, for viewing or hearing, although I will focus on reading in this essay. By the time we finish a paragraph of a work, we cannot reproduce its exact words, especially if we are discussing complex, involved literary language or dense, technical expository prose. We may occasionally remember striking words or phrases, but these are rare. At the same time, we infer much not stated overtly in the work, in whatever medium. For example, in Emily Brontë's *Wuthering Heights*, the servant Zillah leads Lockwood to his bedroom:

> While leading the way upstairs, she recommended that I should hide the candle, and not make a noise; for her master had an odd notion about the chamber she would put me in, and never let anybody lodge there willingly.
>
> I asked the reason.
>
> She did not know, she answered; she had only lived there a year or two; and they had so many queer goings on, she could not begin to be curious.[3]

Some of what we infer when reading this passage may seem to be so obvious that it hardly deserves noticing, such as that Zillah wants Lockwood to hide his candle and not make a noise because seeing a candle and making a noise could alert her master (Heathcliff) that someone would be occupying the forbidden chamber. The text as written describes two actions (hiding the candle, not making a noise) and an explanation (Heathcliff does not want anyone in the chamber). But for the passage to make sense, readers have to know that candles are visible in the dark and that noises can alert people to the presence of others. These inferences arise from common knowledge that hardly seems worth mentioning—and yet, without it, the passage does not make sense.

Beyond such low-level inferences, experienced readers may make more sophisticated ones. Having been told that Heathcliff does not want anyone to lodge in this room and that there are "so many queer goings on" at Wuthering Heights, readers may expect that, soon, they will encounter another such going on—and, indeed, they do, when Lockwood has a bizarre, violent nightmare about the Heights' former inhabitants. Such an expectation is a predictive inference, a guess about what will happen later in a work. Whereas the inferences about candles and noises

---

[3] Emily Brontë, *Wuthering Heights* (1847), ed. Ian Jack (Oxford: Oxford University Press, 1976), 17.

come from a reader's everyday experience, inferences about what will happen next are more specific to literature. In life, creepy hints do not necessarily give rise to creepy realities, but they do in literature because readers with enough experience assume them to be pragmatically relevant: if the hints were not relevant, they would not be there. For readers with enough experience of the Gothic, Brontë is dropping clues. While predictive inferences may seem obvious to literary scholars, average readers do not make them as often as literary scholars might assume. Bridging inferences like the ones in the previous paragraph happen relatively automatically, especially if the knowledge to make them is easily accessible; predictive inferences, in contrast, are more often optional and depend on reader knowledge and motivation.

Neither the bridging nor the predictive inference is in the text: it comes from a reader. Such inferences may enter a reader's mental representation, along with emotional reactions, evaluative comments, metacognitive monitoring of how well the reader is understanding, and much else not in the work. Just as little in the verbatim work enters a reader's mental representation, much that is not, does. For anyone interested in the reception of literary works, understanding mental representation is at the heart of knowing what readers do with what they read.

"Mental representation" may imply a more static construct than it should. Readers constantly update their representation, and at each moment, some parts of it grow stronger and others weaker. An element can become stronger for many reasons: a reader thinks it is important, it is repeated, or it has causal significance for later events; an element likewise can become weaker for corresponding reasons (it does not seem important, is not repeated, and does not have causal significance). Once readers have finished, their representations do not disappear: they move into long-term memory. From there, readers may be able to retrieve them when needed, although what they retrieve is not a static block but a dynamic set of traces shaped to fit an occasion. For example, the mental representation of *Wuthering Heights* you may retrieve if you are giving a general plot summary will be quite different from the one you will retrieve if you are describing how Brontë's novel treats dogs.

While all readers construct a mental representation, not all readers comprehend because some mental representations are more successful than others. Psychologists use the concepts of "coherence" and "usability" to define this success. "Coherence" means that the different elements of a mental representation fit together meaningfully. The reader determines what counts as meaningful, so a reader may recognize that a work is filled with paradoxes, ambiguities, and uncertainties without creating an incoherent representation. As soon as a reader can recognize that paradoxes, ambiguities, and uncertainties are intentional, at whatever level of agency intention is understood, representation becomes coherent. For literary scholars, an incoherent representation is more likely when faced with prose from a field about which they know little than when reading a densely postmodern work of fiction.

Psychologists stress usability in relation to comprehension for reasons that humanists often neglect: reading is rarely an endpoint. Readers read with many goals, and their success depends on whether they reach them through reading. These goals can range from straightforwardly utilitarian (reading a cookbook or instruction manual) to subtly self-interested (reading to reinforce one's self-image as belonging to a certain class or sector in society). Reading is a moment in a chain of purposive action that begins before the moment of reading and ends after it is finished. The self-sufficient bubble of reading often assumed by literary scholars is a useful scholarly fantasy, but not one that describes everyday reading practices.

So, if comprehension needs a coherent and usable mental representation, how important is medium to comprehension? As I have mentioned, medium and all that accompanies it are central to the phenomenological experience of a work: the feel of a book; the look of a page or a screen; the timbre, volume, and pitch of a voice. Yet, important as these are, they are not quite as important for a mental representation, especially the one that remains after the actual experience of a work has ended. While different media require medium-specific skills (such as knowing how to read), comprehension as a process uses many skills that cross media. Regardless of media, audiences may recruit relevant background knowledge, make inferences, evaluate information, predict what will happen, undergo emotional reactions, connect different parts of what they experience, and notice how well they comprehend or not. This list is neither complete nor mandatory: the presence of these actions will vary widely depending on factors ranging from the social setting of the event to the individual's working memory capacity. Completeness is not the point. What matters is that general strategies for comprehension exist across media. These strategies work as they do because comprehension belongs to the mind of the experiencer, a medium that remains stable regardless of the media in which the work was experienced.

When psychologists discovered that basic similarities in comprehension processes persisted across media, they posited the existence of "general comprehension skills." Understanding these has been important in education for teaching the prerequisites of successful literacy. If, as I noted above, teaching children to read involves comprehension as well as decoding, then comprehension skills can be strengthened not only through reading books but also through learning to understand in different media. Watching television and even playing computer games do not have to be the enemy of reading. They can be a useful site for developing general comprehension skills that allow children to build better mental representations.

Knowing that so many cognitive processes are shared when comprehending different media may make it less surprising that my students so easily confuse them or assume that the differences are ultimately not important. Mental representations in long-term memory, while not identical across media, are similar enough that distinctions among them can seem secondary. As far as differences within media, such those among different editions of the same text, general comprehension may again drive student indifference. To them, it is not obvious that they will end up with a substantially different mental representation if they read a cheap edition or an expensive one, an edition published hundreds of years ago or one published yesterday, an edition with many footnotes or one with bare text. Given their goals in reading, students may not care about these differences; in this indifference, they certainly do not represent all readers, but they represent tendencies largely ignored by scholarship on media.

For example, Stephen Mailloux attacks the editorial scholar G. Thomas Tanselle for what he calls Tanselle's "textual platonism":

> For Tanselle the work somehow exists in an ideal realm independent of its textual manifestation in a published or unpublished archival document. Moreover, Tanselle goes on to suggest that scholars cannot be certain they have reached this ideal realm of works in the way that, apparently, they can be certain about the material realm of documents. I find this textual platonism difficult to fathom. The common-sense view that different material texts do seem to represent contrasting versions of the same work can be acknowledged without resorting to an ideal realm of the immaterial Work.[4]

Mailloux contrasts Tanselle's supposed platonism with his own hard-headed practicality: there is nothing but a text as physical embodiment. For him, "different material texts" are different, so that they are "contrasting versions of the same work."

But how important are those contrasts? For an editor or bibliographer, they are central. But does that centrality matter for a work's reception? The concept of mental representation provides at least partial support for the textual platonism that Mailloux rejects. Not only across different versions of the same medium but even across different media themselves, critical aspects of building a mental representation remain similar, to the extent that individuals may not remember the source of the experience itself. I am not denying that differences among physical manifestations of a work deserve study. I am arguing that the audiences may care less about those differences than scholars do, and for good reason.

No conclusions about reader response can be drawn from the medium of a work. It is interesting and valuable to analyze what a work's intended audience seems to be, and for this analysis, the medium is central. Works are packaged differently, not only in different media but also within the same medium, so that a cheap paperback edition sends out different signals from an expensive, highly wrought one. Yet no firm conclusions about a work's effect on its experiencers can be drawn from that packaging because the medium of a work may or may not enter a memory representation. Even if it does, it may not have a prominent or easily retrieved place in that representation. Textual platonism is not a naïve fantasy: it is an important aspect of long-term memory for art.

Similarly, the concept of comprehension underscores that nothing about a medium enforces a particular mode of reading. I do not deny that there are important

---

[4] Steven Mailloux, "Reading Typos, Reading Archives," *College English* 61.5 (1999): 584–90; 588.

physical differences between, for example, reading on a page versus on a screen. But those physical differences do not in themselves guarantee different results. What matters more are the processes that go into creating a coherent and usable mental representation. Both in the way that they remember material and in the way they actually read, skilled readers are good at adapting to different goals.

They are helped in part by the mind's organization of memory. Human memory is an umbrella term for several different memory systems; two that are especially relevant for reading are semantic and episodic memory. An episodic memory is memory for an event; in the context of this discussion, it would typically be an auto-biographical memory of encountering a work in some form. For episodic memory, the medium of the encounter may matter greatly, as well as the entire setting of the encounter. The likelihood of remembering the entire physical context of a work (the feel of the page, the sound of a voice, the room in which one reads) probably increases with the length of the event. If you spend many hours and days reading the same edition of Proust or Tolstoy, having picked up the same edition again and again will reinforce your memory trace for that edition. The same is true for other media, such as listening to the same audiobook narrator for a long time: the sheer amount of time spent hearing that voice may help strengthen its retrievability.

Yet the way we remember media has another side apart from the physical circumstances of the encounter. We may remember the plot, characters, aspects of the setting, and even words or phrases from a novel; images, background music, or actors' faces from a movie; or the melody of a song. In all cases, we often can do so apart from our ability to recapture the autobiographical experience of the work. Such memories belong to "semantic memory." Psychologists distinguish episodic from semantic memory by using the distinction between what we remember (an event) versus what we know (items of knowledge). In ordinary language use, the distinction between remembering and knowing is not as strict as psychologists want it to be, but the terms are useful in helping to grasp the difference between episodic and semantic memories. Events experienced by an individual (what I did last night) are remembered in a different way from bits of world knowledge (Paris is the capital of France) that people accumulate during their lives and that exist in the mind apart from an immediate context.

All semantic knowledge begins as episodic. At some moment in one's life, one learns for the first time that Paris is the capital of France. Yet, in what psychologists call "source amnesia," people typically forget where and when they learn such knowledge, unless they have some particular reason for retaining it. This amnesia arises because, after learning that Paris is the capital of France, you are likely to encounter the same fact many subsequent times, in many places, so the memory for the first encounter is likely to fade. Moreover, you often have no need to remember the source of this information, so you do not. Usually, nothing about the event of learning it is salient enough to make it easy to retrieve, such as a strong emotional connection or a frequently repeated encounter with the knowledge source.

If we apply the distinction between episodic and semantic memory to memory for works of art, you may remember quite a bit about a work's content without remembering much, or indeed anything, about the context in which you experienced it. Gertrude dies by poisoning in *Hamlet*, van Gogh's *Starry Night* features blues and yellows, Bach's most famous *Toccata and Fugue* is in D minor. To retrieve such facts, you do not have to have your memory deeply connected to the medium, whether on stage, page, film, digital reader, or audio text. Likewise, if you have encountered a work in different versions of the same medium—if, for example, you have read several editions of *Jane Eyre* or seen different adaptations of *Pride and Prejudice*—your memory for the plot events does not necessarily require you to distinguish among them. The opposite is also true: you may vividly remember the circumstances of reading/listening/hearing a work without remembering much about the actual work at all. For example, you may recall adult care providers reading to you, though you are not sure exactly what they read; impressions of vivid comedians may linger in your mind long after their jokes have faded; the experience of a powerful film may outlast knowledge of exactly what happens in it.

The distinction between episodic and semantic memory reinforces that the medium in which a work is encountered may not matter for how you remember it. Everything depends on the purpose of retrieving the memory; medium is more likely to matter for episodic rather than semantic memory. If you are discussing a novel in a book club, you may draw on your semantic memory to recall finer points of the plot. If you are describing your favorite places to read, you may draw instead on your episodic memory of having read books in a particular place (your bedroom, a coffeeshop, the library) more than the content of any one of those books. The mind never experiences artworks in a vacuum: they are always encountered and remembered for specific, local goals.

Just as medium does not determine memories, so it does not determine actual behavior during reading. Far more important is the purpose of the reading; in terms of the definition of comprehension, usability determines reading behavior. When readers read the same material with the goal of studying it versus the goal of being entertained by it, they use different comprehension strategies. In both cases, they decode the same words on the page, but what they do with the words looks quite different. The reading process of those leafing through a magazine in a dentist's office will differ from that of someone analyzing the same material for a scholarly journal. The reading of someone who barely glances at a website will differ from the reading of someone for whom the website contains vitally important information. Goals may lead readers to choose one medium over another. If you are wanting to be entertained during a long road trip, an audiobook might be the right choice for you; if you want to study a text carefully, you may prefer a codex. However, once that choice has been made, your goal will matter more than the medium itself for your experience. It is possible to study a text carefully on an audiobook and to read a codex for entertainment. The medium itself does not require a particular mode of reading, although certain properties of a medium may lead it to be a good choice for certain goals.

Nevertheless, media scholars, even those who believe that they eschew technological determinism, still speak about reading as if the medium were the key element in it. For example, N. Katherine Hayles writes,

> Given the increase in digital reading, obvious sites for new kinds of reading techniques, pedagogical strategies, and initiatives are the interactions between digital and print literacies. Literary studies has been slow to address these possibilities, however, because it continues to view close reading of print texts as the field's essence. As long as this belief hold sway, digital reading will at best be seen as peripheral to our concerns, pushed to the margins as not "really" reading or at least not compelling or interesting reading.[5]

Such comments divide "digital" reading from "close reading of print texts," as if the medium so determined modes of reading that they can be named for it. Hayles criticizes literary scholars for elevating close reading of print as the only mode of reading and encourages them to acknowledge what she calls "digital" reading. She makes an important point about the problematic exaltation of one mode of reading within literary criticism; valuable as close reading may be as a disciplinary practice, it is of limited use in trying to understand the historical place of literary reading, the reading practices of university students, or the role of long-term memory in shaping readers' memories for what they read. Yet she treats as a difference in medium what is actually a difference in goal: "close," disciplined reading versus what we might call "good enough" reading, reading whose goal is to grab a gist meaning as quickly as possible and that has little interest in attending to finer details of meaning and form. Both kinds of reading are possible in both print and digital media. When it comes to reader preferences, many readers do indeed prefer print when their goal is to study carefully; likewise, it may be true that reading in digital media often accompanies rapid, good enough reading. Consequently, some media may acquire habitual associations with some reading practices, but those associations are loose and subject to individual variation. The medium itself does not determine the reading practice.

The study of reading should declare at least partial independence from the study of media. It already has this status in psychology, but in the humanities, reading is persistently linked with fields such as media studies, book history, and digital humanities. Important as reading is for those fields, they understandably privilege their disciplinary focus: books and media. Much about reading, such as the comprehension and memory processes I have described, becomes visible only after reading acquires its own focus, rather than when it remains an appendage of other areas of interest. Until reading becomes an independent site of study in the humanities,

---

[5] N. Katherine Hayles, *How We Think: Digital Media and Contemporary Technogenesis* (Chicago: University of Chicago Press, 2012), 59–60.

unanswered questions about it will be cloaked by debates that are fundamentally not about reading. The benefit that the psychological study of reading offers to the humanities is not that it answers all the potential questions one might have. Instead, psychology, by studying reading apart from its usual disciplinary accompaniments in the humanities, allows facets of reading usually ignored to become visible.

FURTHER READING

Elfenbein, Andrew. *The Gist of Reading*. Palo Alto: Stanford University Press, 2018.

Goldman, Susan R., Arthur C. Graesser, and Paul van den Broek, eds. *Narrative Comprehension, Causality, and Coherence: Essays in Honor of Tom Trabasso*. Mahwah, NJ: Lawrence Erlbaum, 1999.

Kintsch, Walter. *Cognition: A Paradigm for Cognition*. Cambridge: Cambridge University Press, 1998.

McNamara, Danielle S., and Joe Magliano. "Toward a Comprehensive Model of Comprehension." *Psychology of Learning and Motivation* 51 (2009): 297–384.

Ouellette, Laurie, ed. *The Media Studies Reader*. New York: Routledge, 2013.

Traxler, Matthew, and Morton Ann Gernsbacher, eds. *Handbook of Psycholinguistics*, 2nd edn. London: Elsevier, 2006.

Zwaan, Rolf A. *Aspects of Literary Comprehension: A Cognitive Approach*. Amsterdam: John Benjamins, 1993.

22

MINDREADING AND SOCIAL STATUS

LISA ZUNSHINE

What does it mean for one fictional character to be more complex than another, and why does it matter? One way to define complexity is to look at characters' ability to reflect upon their own and other people's mental states, that is, their ability to *embed* their own and other's thoughts and feelings on a higher, or deeper (pick your metaphor) level. For instance, when Fanny Price, of Jane Austen's *Mansfield Park*, realizes the significance of Edmund Bertram's taking up a newspaper and removing himself from the general conversation, she is embedding mental states on the fourth level. She *realizes* that Edmund *knows* that Henry Crawford *wants* to talk with Fanny privately about her *feelings*:

> [As] Edmund perceived, by [Henry's] drawing in a chair, and sitting down close by her, that it was to be a very thorough attack, that looks and undertones were to be well tried, he sank as quietly as possible into a corner, turned his back, and took up a newspaper, very sincerely wishing that dear little Fanny might be persuaded into explaining away that shake of the head to the satisfaction of her ardent lover.... Fanny ... grieved to the heart to see Edmund's arrangements.[1]

Fanny's capacity for complex embedment contrasts starkly with that of Lady Bertram, seated right next to her, who is constitutionally incapable of embedding thoughts and feelings above the second level, but also, in fact, with everyone else at Mansfield, for Fanny frequently seems to be one mental state above, or ahead of, whichever Bertram or Crawford happens to be at hand. Here, for instance, Edmund is aware of Henry's intentions regarding Fanny, but Fanny does him one better, for she is aware of Edmund's intentions regarding Henry's intentions regarding herself.

---

[1] Jane Austen, *Mansfield Park* (Oxford: Oxford University Press, 1990), 310.

This may seem, at first blush, just a fancy new way to talk about the old distinction between round and flat characters, but it is not.[2] (After all, we wouldn't characterize either Edmund or Henry as flat.) Instead, the focus on the characters' relative capacity for complex embedment captures a distinct dynamic of its own. In exploring this dynamic, students of literature might start out by drawing on research in cognitive science, but they may ultimately use that research to shed new light on issues that have long been of special interest to our own discipline, such as the role of historical contexts and power relations in the production and reception of literary texts. (I emphasize the literary-critical ends of this enterprise to stake out my position in the ongoing debate between cognitive literary scholars, such as myself, and "Literary Darwinists," who think that the goals and methods of literary criticism should be superseded by those of science and whose implementation of this agenda may be more accurately described as scientistic.[3])

Here is a brief overview of my perspective on mindreading and culture. In experiencing fictional characters' actions as caused by their thoughts and feelings (Edmund picks up the newspaper because he *wants* to help Henry), we exercise our cognitive adaptations for mindreading, aka theory of mind. On some level, these adaptations do not fully distinguish between the mental states of real people and of imaginary entities whom we "meet" on page, on screen, or on canvas: as soon as we are faced with behavior, we start attributing intentions to the behaving agents. In modern industrial and postindustrial societies, this eagerness to attribute mental states underwrites a variety of fictional forms and (more broadly) leads to the emergence of "cultures of greedy mindreaders,"[4] characterized by countless modes and niches that continuously satisfy and whet our mindreading appetites.

One aspect of mindreading, which in recent years has received sustained attention from social and developmental psychologists as well as cognitive neuroscientists,[5] has to do with embedded mental states, or as one essay's title has it, "thinking

---

[2] See Natalie M. Phillips, *Distraction: Problems of Attention in Eighteenth-Century Literature* (Baltimore: Johns Hopkins University Press, 2016), 179–80; and Lisa Zunshine, "Bakhtin, Theory of Mind, and Pedagogy: Cognitive Construction of Social Class," *Eighteenth-Century Fiction* 30.1 (2017): 109–26; 118.

[3] See Lisa Zunshine, "Introduction to Cognitive Literary Studies," in *The Oxford Handbook of Cognitive Literary Studies*, ed. Lisa Zunshine (New York: Oxford University Press, 2015), 1–9; and Nancy Easterlin, "Voyages in the Verbal Universe: The Role of Speculation in Darwinian Literary Criticism," *Interdisciplinary Literary Studies* 2.2 (2001): 59–73; 64.

[4] See Lisa Zunshine, *Getting Inside Your Head: What Cognitive Science Can Tell Us About Popular Culture* (Baltimore: Johns Hopkins University Press, 2012).

[5] See Rebecca Saxe, "The Right Temporo-parietal Junction: a Specific Brain Region for Thinking about Thoughts," in *Handbook of Theory of Mind*, ed. Alan Leslie and Tamsin German (New York: Routledge, forthcoming 2021) (http://saxelab.mit.edu/ sites/default/files/publications/Saxe_RTPJChapter.pdf); Saxe and Nancy Kanwisher, "People Thinking about Thinking People: The Role of the Temporo-parietal Junction in 'Theory of Mind,'" *NeuroImage* 19 (2003): 1835–42; Patricia H. Miller, Frank S. Kessel, and John H. Flavell, "Thinking about People Thinking about People Thinking about…: A Study of Social Cognitive Development Child Development," *Child Development* 41.3 (September 1970): 613–23; and Ian Apperly, *The Cognitive Basis of "Theory of Mind"* (New York: Psychology Press, 2011).

about people thinking about people thinking."[6] While cognitive scientists look at embedments structuring our daily social interactions, cognitive literary critics extend this inquiry to cultural representations. Elsewhere, I have discussed patterns of embedment in fiction, such as, for instance, the difference between explicitly spelled out and implied mental states of characters, narrators, and readers.[7] Here I build on that work to look at possible ideological underpinnings of the choices made by writers when they portray some characters as capable of more complex embedment than others. As I see it, ideology enters the picture when writers intuitively invert certain real-life dynamics of mindreading in their allocation of complexity.

The First Model: Reflecting Real-Life Dynamics

Let's start with real-life dynamics. Perhaps because of the unfortunate terminology (both "theory of mind" and "mindreading" imply too much conscious reflection and perspicacity), it is sometimes assumed that some people are better mindreaders than others; that is, that they are more accurate than others in their attribution of mental states. In reality, there is no such thing as an across-the-board good or bad mindreader. It all depends on the social context in which one finds oneself. For instance, one way to immediately improve one's mindreading skills is to take a demotion in one's social hierarchy. Studies have shown that people in weaker social positions engage in more active and perceptive mindreading than people in stronger social positions.[8] It works even when we know that it's just a game: "when one is given the role of subordinate in an experimental situation, one becomes better at assessing the feelings of others, and conversely, when the same person is attributed the role of leader, one becomes less good."[9]

In real life, those in superior social positions may assert and "exert their status precisely by refusing to read mental states of others."[10] Mindreading obtuseness can function similarly to strategic ignorance: "it is the interlocutor who has or pretends to have the *less* broadly knowledgeable understanding of interpretive practice who will define the terms of the exchange."[11] The powerful, Rebecca Solnit writes, "swathe themselves in obliviousness in order to avoid the pain of others and their

---

[6] Miller et al., "Thinking about People Thinking," 613.

[7] Lisa Zunshine, "The Secret Life of Fiction," *PMLA* 130.3 (2015): 724–31.

[8] See Henri Carlo Santos, Igor Grossmann, and Michael E. W. Varnum, "Class, Cognition and Cultural Change in Social Class," *PsyArxiv Preprints*, July 2, 2018 (https://psyarxiv.com/92smf/).

[9] Sara E. Snodgrass, "'Women's Intuition': The Effect of Subordinate Role on Interpersonal Sensitivity," *Journal of Personality and Social Psychology* 49.1 (1985): 146–55.

[10] Simon Stern, email communication, March 8, 2018.

[11] Eve Kosofsky Sedgwick, ed., "Privilege of Unknowing: Diderot's *The Nun*," in *Tendencies* (Durham, NC: Duke University Press, 1993), 23.

own relationship to that pain. There's a large category of acts hidden from people with standing: the more you are, the less you know."[12]

Mansfield Park reflects this dynamic quite accurately, at least in its depiction of its female protagonist. Fanny Price is young (merely a child, when she first arrives), female, and poor—a charity case with no obvious claims to beauty or intelligence. To survive and thrive in social circumstances stacked against her so thoroughly, she has to be particularly attuned to other people's wishes and intentions, and so she is. Again and again, she is placed on the top of the mindreading chain, in direct inversion of her social position vis-à-vis her relatives and acquaintances.

One of several ways in which Austen accomplishes this is to first present us with a seemingly complete scene, outlining everyone's embedded feelings—which seem complex enough, for the time being—and then superimpose Fanny's mind on top of that scene. For instance, when the golden youth of Mansfield Park embark on their ill-conceived theatrical production, we learn that Julia Bertram is jealous of her sister Maria, who is clearly preferred by Henry Crawford; that Maria ignores Julia's feelings; and that Julia hopes that Maria's fiancé, Mr. Rushworth, will become aware of the impropriety of her behavior and expose her to public humiliation:

> [Julia] was not superior to the hope of some distressing end to the attentions which were still carrying on there, some punishment to Maria for conduct so shameful towards herself as well as towards Mr. Rushworth....Maria felt her triumph, and pursued her purpose, careless of Julia; and Julia could never see Maria distinguished by Henry Crawford without trusting that it would create jealousy, and bring a public disturbance at last.

To this mix of second- and third-level embedments Austen then adds Fanny's awareness of Julia's feelings, while also making sure that there is no reciprocal awareness (and hence comparable complexity) on Julia's side:

> Fanny saw and pitied much of this in Julia; but there was no outward fellowship between them. Julia made no communication, and Fanny took no liberties. They were two solitary sufferers, or connected only by Fanny's consciousness.[13]

Fanny's consciousness is indeed the place where various characters get "connected," or, to put it differently, where many of the novel's fourth-level embedments take shape. To spell one of them out (an exercise which typically results in painfully pedestrian prose, for, in the original text, those high-level embedments are often implied rather than laid out in their full propositional glory), we can say that Fanny *knows* that Julia *is miserable* because Julia *knows* that Henry *likes* Maria. We can further say that Fanny *intuits* that Julia *hopes* that Mr. Rushworth *will realize* that Maria's behavior makes people around them *think* that he is a fool and revenge

---

[12] Rebecca Solnit, "Nobody Knows," *Harper's Magazine* (March 2018): 5.
[13] Austen, *Mansfield Park*, 197.

himself upon her, and that, though otherwise compassionate toward Julia, she can't quite find it in herself to empathize with this particular hope of her cousin's.

As Austen is considered, in some quarters, the patron saint of cognitive literary criticism (i.e., someone whose prose is particularly amenable to cognitivist exploration), let us now turn to authors from very different cultural and literary traditions. In the eighteenth-century Chinese classic, Cao Xueqin's *Dream of the Red Chamber*, aka *The Story of the Stone* (ca. 1750), girls and young women typically embed mental states on a higher level than rich men and older rich women.[14] Although beautiful, accomplished, and pampered by their families, these female characters are powerless. Their fates are decided by their elders, who cannot—and will not—read their emotions and, consequently, doom their young charges to lives of misery or to early deaths.

The striking mindreading skills of Cao's young women stand out in the long history of the literary response to social stratification in premodern China. As Haiyan Lee observes,

> [In societies] structured by kinship sociality... theory of mind is certainly present and useful but not always prized in social life and does not animate expressive culture to the same extent [as it does] in modern commercial societies structured by stranger sociality, cosmopolitanism, and social mobility.... The hierarchical structures of [kinship sociality] place a greater premium on theory of mind for subordinates than for the powerful, hence attaching a tinge of opprobrium to its exercise.[15]

When subordination follows the lines of gender, mindreading acumen (configured as cunning) follows closely:

> Women in a patriarchal and patrilineal society, especially young daughters-in-law, are structurally motivated to be inward-looking, to adopt a calculating, fawning, and defensive mentality, and to orient their action around the intentions of the more powerful (senior, male) members of the kin group.[16]

Fawning, defensive, and calculating underlings, female or male, do not make for sympathetic fictional characters, which is why such personages tend to "ply shady trades as go-betweens, procuresses, litigation masters, soothsayers, brokers, and garden-variety hangers-on who prey on the honest and unsuspecting." Yet, as Lee argues brilliantly,

> [In some] exceptional circumstances... mind-reading becomes an asset and the consummate practitioner is admired and celebrated as a cultural hero. Most of these

---

[14] Lisa Zunshine, "From the Social to the Literary: Approaching Cao Xueqin's *The Story of the Stone* (Honglou meng 紅樓夢) from a Cognitive Perspective," in *The Oxford Handbook of Cognitive Literary Studies*, ed. Lisa Zunshine (New York: Oxford University Press, 2015): 176–96.

[15] Haiyan Lee, "Measuring the Stomach of a Gentleman with the Heart-Mind of a Pipsqueak: On the Ubiquity and Utility of Theory of Mind in Literature, Mostly," *Poetics Today* 41.2 (2020), forthcoming. For in-depth discussion of "kinship sociality," see Haiyan Lee, *The Stranger and the Chinese Moral Imagination*. Palo Alto: Stanford University Press, 2014.

[16] Lee, "Measuring the Stomach."

circumstances involve forces of good combatting forces of evil, as in warfare or criminal investigation. More rarely, theory of mind is mobilized to emplot romantic courtship.[17]

In other words, we can read the literary history of premodern China as punctuated by the appearance of works that valorize a character's capacity for complex embedment of mental states. Those works include warfare chronicles (such as Luo Guanzhong's fourteenth-century *The Romance of the Three Kingdoms*) and detective novels (such as the eighteenth-century case studies of Judge Dee), as well as the *bildungs-roman*-courtship-novel extraordinaire *Dream of the Red Chamber*. Although some of the *Dream*'s young women (most obviously, Wang Xi-feng) still come across as defensive and calculating, most are true to the ideal that the middle-aged Cao Xueqin set out to bring back to life, after finding himself one day, in low spirits, "thinking about the female companions" of his youth:

> As I went over them one by one, examining and comparing them in my mind's eye, it suddenly came over me that those slips of girls—which is all they were then—were in every way, both morally and intellectually, superior to the "grave and mustachioed signior" I am now supposed to have become.[18]

And so, in direct contrast to the young women of, for instance, *The Plum in the Golden Vase* (ca. 1590), whose sharpened capacity for high-level embedment of mental states makes them cheats, liars, and hypocrites,[19] the cognitive complexity of the girls from the *Dream* manifests itself in their admirable social sophistication and poetic sensibility. Far from damaging their personalities, their subordinate status lends poignancy to their moral and intellectual superiority.

Let us cross national boundaries again. If we look at Russian literature before the 1760s (that is, before Russian writers became exposed to Western European models, such as sentimental novels, which prized sociocognitive complexity in their protagonists[20]), we see something very similar to what Lee describes as the association of such complexity with "pipsqueaks," that is, with socially insignificant personages who, nevertheless, manage to create problems for "gentlemen."

There is, for instance, Frol, from the anonymous *Tale of Frol Skobeev* (1680–1720), a social nonentity who rises to wealth and nobility by thinking one step (i.e., one mental state) ahead of various aristocratic figures who come his way. Frol is a pettifogger (remember Lee's observation that a social nonentity may use his mindreading skills to become a "litigation master"?), who tricks the only daughter of a

---

[17] Lee, "Measuring the Stomach."

[18] Xueqin Cao, *The Story of the Stone*, Volume 1: *"The Golden Days,"* trans. David Hawkes (London: Penguin, 1973), 20.

[19] For discussion, see Lisa Zunshine, "I Lie Therefore I Am," in *Approaches to Teaching* The Plum in the Golden Vase, ed. Andrew Schonebaum (New York: MLA, forthcoming).

[20] Lisa Zunshine, "'Think What You're Doing, Or You'll Only Make an Ugly Reputation for Yourself': *Chin P'ing Mei* (金瓶梅), Lying, and Literary History," in 认知诗学 [*Cognitive Poetics*] (December 2017): 44–62.

rich courtier into sleeping with him and then elopes with her. When the distraught parents find out what has happened, they first want to prosecute the rogue, but then relent and start showering the young couple with land and money, all the while cursing their "thief" and "knave" of a son-in-law.[21]

They relent because Frol knows how to manipulate their feelings. When they send a servant to inquire about the health of their child, Frol asks his wife to pretend to be sick and tells the servant: "See for yourself, my friend, how she's doing: that's what parental wrath does—they scold and curse her from afar, and here she is, dying."[22] Frol *wants* his parents-in-law to *think* that their *anger* is killing their daughter, a stratagem that quickly cools their wrath and sets Frol on the way to prosperity.

Critics consider the *Tale of Frol Skobeev* an early example of Russian picaresque.[23] Viewed in the context of the present argument, this characterization raises the intriguing possibility of a cognitivist reading of the literary figure of the picaro. From Mateo Alemán's *Guzmán de Alfarache* (1599–1604) to Daniel Defoe's *Moll Flanders* (1724), picaros use their superior mindreading skills to flatter, bully, cheat, and steal their way to economic survival. They are simultaneously a threat—to the extent to which their society still retains traces of "kinship sociality" (and what society does not?—even if just in the form of cultural fantasies about a golden age, when all behavior was transparent and pro-social and no mindreading acumen was called for)—and a treat for readers who follow their double-dealing tricks with guilty delight.

We find the association between characters' low social status (low, that is, in relative rather than absolute terms: always in comparison with someone else in the story) and their heightened capacity for complex embedment, in a broad spectrum of fictional narratives. Some characters embed complex mental states as they mastermind a plot to help their bumbling masters, as do "clever slaves" of ancient Greek and Roman comedies. Some do it as they trick a larger or more violent and dangerous animal in order to save their lives, as do Brer Rabbit of West African folklore and the little mouse of Julia Donaldson's *Gruffalo*. Some seem to lack any agenda and merely display a mastery of innuendo beyond that of their social "betters," as does Algernon's servant Lane in Oscar Wilde's *The Importance of Being Earnest*.[24]

Some have central billing, as does P. G. Wodehouse's Jeeves. Others make only brief appearances in one scene, as does Wilde's Lane. Still others, such as the office cleaners from Rachel Cusk's *Saving Agnes* (1993), are episodic characters who lack

---

[21] Zunshine, "'Think What You're Doing,'" 47.

[22] Translation mine (original at: http://www.drevne.ru/lib/frol.htm).

[23] Marcia A. Morris, *The Literature of Roguery in Seventeenth- and Early Eighteenth-Century Russia* (Chicago: Northwestern University Press, 2000), 51.

[24] See Michael Patrick Gillespie's discussion of the master-manservant dialectic in "From Beau Brummell to Lady Bracknell: Re-viewing the Dandy in *The Importance of Being Earnest*," in Oscar Wilde, *The Importance of Being Earnest*, ed. M. P. Gillespie (New York: Norton, 2006), 179.

any identifying features, and manage to outclass the main protagonist in the business of mindreading while remaining nameless and faceless:

> Agnes slammed into the house in a state of considerable distemper. She had been forced by the nonchalance with which the editorial department was approaching its deadline to stay late in the office, working alone while the cleaners emptied bins and vacuumed floors around her. Watching them sanitize the unsavory detritus of her day she had been besieged by feelings of shame and guilt, and had attempted to engage them in pleasantries. Not beguiled by her condescension, however, they had roundly rebuffed her overtures and left her feeling that a mysterious exchange of power had taken place, the precise maneuvers of which she was not able to fathom.[25]

If we map out this "mysterious exchange of power" in terms of its underlying mental states, we can say that Agnes *wants* to make herself *feel better* by engaging in small talk with the cleaners (second-level embedment). The cleaners, however, *know* that she *wants* to use them to make herself *feel better* (third-level embedment) and refuse her that satisfaction. As Agnes apparently expects that her class privilege will automatically translate into superior social acumen (even though she can't see the cleaners as people with faces and names), when their conversation doesn't follow that scripted path, she is left disoriented and angry.

The Second Model: Inverting Real-Life Dynamics

So far I have considered cases in which the relative sociocognitive complexity[26] of fictional characters tracks the real-life correlation between weaker social positions and more active and perceptive mindreading. I now turn to literary texts which invert this correlation. The way I see it, neither pattern in and of itself says anything about the aesthetic value of the text, but the latter (i.e., the inverted correlation) is an indicator of a particular ideological agenda on the part of the writer, whether she is consciously aware of it or not.

My first example comes from Frances Burney's epistolary novel *Evelina* (1778). Having discussed it elsewhere, I will only say here that the differential capacity for embedment functions in *Evelina* as a form of heteroglossia, complementing other speech markers associated with class difference. Hence Burney's shopkeepers and parvenus with shopkeeper mentality don't rise above the second level in their attribution of mental states, while her ladies and gentlemen of leisure effortlessly weave third-to-fourth level embedments into almost everything they say.[27]

---

[25] Rachel Cusk, *Saving Agnes* (New York: Picador, 1994), 157.
[26] For a definition and discussion of the term, see Zunshine, "The Secret Life," 728.
[27] Zunshine, "Bakhtin," 126.

How does one explain this reversal of the real-life sociocognitive dynamics? We may speculate that it reflects the period's anxiety about the incipient porousness of class boundaries or/and the Burney family's nervousness about their own social standing. Either way, it seeks to naturalize social class, portraying upper-class characters as more aware of their own and other people's feelings, and hence more deserving of readers' sympathy than lower-class characters, with their limited capacity for complex embedment.

Note that by framing *Evelina*'s pattern of embedment as an ideological project, we assume the ready availability of a cultural template according to which mindreading acumen is associated with higher social standing. Inaccurate as this template may be when it comes to real-life communication, it nevertheless took hold in the eighteenth-century popular imagination, informing, in particular, certain genres of polite literature, such as sentimental plays and novels. Developed side by side with such "pipsqueak"-centered genres as the picaresque, they engaged in parallel play with them (pretending, that is, that the other doesn't exist: think of Daniel Defoe's *Moll Flanders* and Richard Steele's *The Conscious Lovers*, or of John Cleland's *Fanny Hill* and Samuel Richardson's *Clarissa*).

To reconstruct the genealogy of this template one may turn to Restoration comedy, in which aristocratic wits, such as Dorimant from George Etherege's *The Man of Mode*, embed mental states on the fourth and even fifth level, while their mistresses and hangers-on can barely keep up with them.[28] Granted, for many a Horner—the upper-class plotter from William Wycherley's *A Country Wife*—there is a Lucy: the clever servant, who steps in at a critical juncture to save her "betters" from catastrophe. Still, after the 1670s, aristocratic high-embedders became a recognizable literary type, paving the way for the letter-writing sophisticates of Richardson and Burney. Restoration plays obviously came with their own political agendas—one of which was to please a series of royal patrons and their friends (who would consider themselves the greatest wits of them all)—which demonstrates yet another way in which ideology can drive the inverse-correlation model in fiction.

Going yet further back, one finds a ruler high on the sociocognitive spectrum in Shakespeare's *Measure for Measure* (1604). Shakespeare's men in power are not generally known for mindreading perspicacity, yet Duke Vincentio seems to derive a peculiar personal satisfaction from reading and scripting the complex emotions of his subjects. Thus he wants Isabella to think that Angelo beheaded her brother, Claudio—even though Claudio is alive—so that, later, when she least expects it, he can reveal to her the true state of affairs and turn her despair into "heavenly comfort":

> Isabella [Within] Peace ho, be here!
> Duke. The tongue of Isabel. She's come to know
> If yet her brother's pardon be come hither:

---

[28] Lisa Zunshine, "Why Jane Austen Was Different, and Why We May Need Cognitive Science to See It," *Style* 41.3 (2007): 287–90.

> But I will keep her ignorant of her good,
> To make her heavenly comforts of despair,
> When it is least expected.[29]

The Duke knows that Isabella will be devastated when she hears of her brother's execution. He also *knows* that she will be happy beyond measure when she learns that he is alive—*happier*, presumably, than she *would have been* had she not first *believed* that he is dead (fourth-level embedment). This is to say that the Duke is angling to put himself in a god-like position in which he will have complete access to Isabella's feelings both now and later (i.e., when the truth is revealed). His mindreading hunger is tinged with sadism, even as he wishes to bring Isabella's happiness to the highest pitch (a literary mindreading dynamic that I dub, elsewhere, "sadistic benefaction"[30]).

Measure for Measure is considered one of Shakespeare's "problem plays." As Steve Vineberg puts it, "the long final scene can strike an audience as sadistic...And when the Duke proposes marriage to Isabella, after all he's put her through, you may wonder what Shakespeare could have been thinking of." Directors deal with this problem differently. Some play up the Duke's emotional cruelty, showing that Isabella can't catch a break in the patriarchal society of Shakespeare's Vienna; others explain the Duke's behavior by his desire to see if Isabella is capable of generosity—of "moving beyond her own injuries to act on another's behalf"[31]—as when she kneels before the Duke to ask for Angelo's life while still believing that Angelo has killed her brother. However charitable toward the Duke, this reading still can't explain away his stated intention to plunge Isabella to the lowest depths of despair in order to render her subsequent joy more intense. He may claim that he does it for her own good, but he gets out of it an intoxicating fantasy of complete access to her feelings.

What I find striking about the ethical problem that the Duke's behavior presents is that it seems to be mainly *our* problem, rooted in our own particularly historically situated sensibility. Shakespeare himself may not have viewed the Duke's actions as objectionable. The reason I say this is that I can't discern even a hint of punishment meted out to this "sadistic benefactor." The Duke remains beloved by his subjects, and, as the play ends, he is on the brink of being rewarded with a marriage to a much younger, beautiful, and virtuous woman. To paraphrase Hamlet, this is hire and salary, not acknowledgment of a problem.

So let us put aside our "ethical" response for a moment. Let's remember instead that real-life rulers stink at mindreading and that Shakespeare didn't need the research of contemporary cognitive psychology to know this, and neither did his

---

[29] William Shakespeare, *Measure for Measure*, in Shakespeare, *The Complete Works*, ed. G. B. Harrison (Fort Worth: Harcourt Brace College Publishers, 1980): IV. iii.110–14.

[30] Zunshine, *Getting Inside*, chapter 3.

[31] Steve Vineberg, "Problem Plays," *The Threepenny Review* 52 (1993): 32–4; 33.

audience.[32] This means that, for them, equating mindreading prowess with higher social standing may have had a different political meaning altogether. The space of the play allowed Shakespeare and his contemporaries to fantasize about their social betters who would care about their underlings' feelings so deeply that they would spend their time figuring out ways of getting inside their heads and scripting their emotions. For, as sadistic as this endeavor strikes us today, an early-modern subject might have actually been flattered by the thought of it and wondered if she might not have deserved more political attention from her rulers than she had been getting.

Is this the only possible reading of the Duke's unexpected sociocognitive complexity? Of course not. I don't aim to supply such a reading. Instead I want to stress that this complexity *is* unexpected—and must have been so for early seventeenth-century audiences—and that, more often than not, the association between the capacity for high-level embedment and high social status has specific political underpinnings.

I also want to show how using insights from contemporary cognitive science (such as the association of better mindreading skills with lower social status) can help us historicize our emotional response to a fictional character, a response that would otherwise seem obvious (as in, "the Duke is sadistic! Poor Isabella! What could Shakespeare have been thinking of?"), and thus be ahistorical. Cognitive historicism[33] has been gaining ground across different fields of literary scholarship; with this essay, I hope to contribute to its growing repertoire of interpretive models.

A Footnote on Cognition and Ideology

When, under oppressive political regimes, literary (and cinematic) production becomes explicitly regulated, mindreading sophistication acquires new ideological meaning. Thus, in fiction published in the Soviet Union under the aegis of Socialist Realism, characters of lower social status would sometimes be portrayed as less sociocognitively complex than characters of higher social status. That is, they do *not* engage in high-level mindreading when confronted with the machinations of high-status characters.

This may seem like an unambiguous example of the second model, but it is not. Although, technically speaking, these low-embedding characters, such as unskilled

[32] For an important discussion of what it means for an author to display an intuitive awareness of various "cognitive" insights that couldn't have been known to the scientific (or natural-philosophic) thought of her day, see Patrick Colm Hogan's *Sexual Identities* (New York: Oxford University Press, 2017).

[33] See Mary Thomas Crane, "Cognitive Historicism: Intuition in Early Modern Thought," in *The Oxford Handbook of Cognitive Literary Studies*, ed. Lisa Zunshine (New York: Oxford University Press, 2015), 18–33.

factory workers, indigent peasants, and orphaned vagrant children, occupy the lowest rung of the socioeconomic ladder, they are not at all the "pipsqueaks" of yesteryear. Instead they are the new aristocracy—aristocracy of the spirit, as it were—even if they are never referred to this way. The future belongs to them. Due to their currently disenfranchised status, they are ultimately guaranteed privileged access to educational, political, economic, and reproductive resources. In contrast, various "old specialists" ("spetsy" in the half-respectful-half-contemptuous jargon of the 1920–30s), who have managed to parlay their education under the tsarist regime into lucrative high-status jobs under the Soviets, are doomed to irrelevancy and extinction. It is those well-heeled characters, as well as their repulsive young protégés, who cheat our low-status protagonists of their rightful share of the socialist paradise, but not for long, never for too long.

For instance, Sania Grigoriev, the protagonist of a widely beloved novel by Veniamin Kaverin, *Two Captains* (1938–45), is shown to be almost completely without guile, and so are his friends and his girlfriend/wife. It is his arch-adversary, a stockbroker under the old regime and school principal/distinguished scholar under the new, N. A. Tatarinov, as well as Tatarinov's favorite disciple, Romashov, who engage in complex mindreading aimed at destroying the hero. When, at the end of the book, Sania, a former-vagrant-child-turned-Arctic-pilot, gains the upper hand, it is because of his determination, courage, and good luck, and not because he has more cunning than his enemies. In 1948–56, Kaverin recreated this mindreading dynamic in another popular (and also repeatedly televised) novel, *The Open Book*, whose upright protagonist, a poor-scullery-maid-turned-famous-microbiologist, ultimately triumphs over her plotting adversaries. Their old-school Machiavellianism is no match for her talent and "open-book" personality.

Call it the first model with a twist. What we have here is our familiar correlation between lower social standing and high-level mindreading skills, except that low-status characters (i.e., the doomed bourgeois elements) may *initially* come across as high-status characters, while the downtrodden workers, peasants, and vagrants may take some time to reveal themselves as the new aristocracy. And this proletarian aristocracy presumably does not need to excel in mindreading, since the revolution of 1917 has already stacked the socioeconomic odds in their favor.

Besides, their enemies may not be that great at mindreading either. In her study of the fate of detective fiction in the People's Republic of China, Lee provides an important insight into a particular historically specific form that the literary association between high social status and low mindreading skills can take under the watchful eye of the Communist Party. As she explains, after 1949,

> [The] hitherto thriving detective fiction was labeled a bourgeois conceit and suppressed. The new society was to be organized as a political communitas in which all were brothers and sisters under the benevolent, paternal care of the Communist Party. Everyone had a designated place in society and everyone was a known quantity. Who

would have any need for mind-reading in such a transparent society?…The only genre fiction permitted to flourish in the socialist period was the spy thriller. Crucially, the mind-game that sustained this genre was directed against "the class enemy," both internal and external. Still, enemy agents were not permitted to truly shine socio-cognitively. Rather, they schemed and connived at a low cognitive level, making laughably naïve assumptions and rudimentary blunders. And it took minimum twists and turns to ensnare them in the vast net of the people's justice.[34]

So while the proletariat had no need to "shine" sociocognitively, their enemies were "not permitted" to do that. Did that result in decades of official literary production with generally lowered levels of mindreading complexity, while works featuring truly sociocognitively complex characters had to find outlets elsewhere: abroad or in the underground/*samizdat*? And did that mean that the sociocognitive complexity of narrators, implied readers, and implied authors had to be dialed down as well?

At least one factor that seems to bear out this conjecture is the suppression, in Soviet fiction, of the style of writing that we now associate with unreliable narration. Ilya Ehrenburg's *Julio Jurenito* (1922), Yuri Olesha's *Envy* (1927), and Konstantin Vaginov's *Works and Days of Svistonov* (1929) still featured unreliable narrators,[35] but, once, in the early 1930s, Socialist Realism became the dominant paradigm, such stylistic experimentation was put paid to. Thus Vsevolod Ivanov's *U* (1932) was not published in the Soviet Union until 1988, while Leonid Dobychin's brilliant *The Town of N* (1935) was singled out for castigation during the 1936 campaign "against formalism and naturalism," driving its author to suicide. With its move away from character-based embedment to embedment emerging almost exclusively from a give-and-take between the implied author and implied reader, *The Town of N* engaged in an experimentation with fictional subjectivity that must have come across as politically subversive. Indeed, as Richard C. Borden observes, it is "something of a mystery how the book was published at all at the height of Stalinism, when dogmatic conservatism, to say nothing of philistinism, ruled the art establishment."[36]

Developing a sustained argument about the repressed sociocognitive complexity of literature under the Soviets is beyond the scope of this essay. I merely pose it here as an open-ended question and a direction for further exploration. What I want to emphasize, with this and other case studies from English, Chinese, and Russian literary traditions, is that cognition and ideology are bound with each other in a

---

[34] Lee, "Measuring the Stomach"; see also Haiyan Lee, "Society Must Be Defended: Chinese Spy Thrillers and the Enchantment of *Arcana Imperii*," unpublished paper.

[35] For a recent discussion of functions of the unreliable narrator in Russian novel of the 1920–30s, see Г. А. Жиличева, "Функции «Ненадежного» Нарратора в Русском Романе 1920–1930-х Годов," Вестник ТГПУ *(TSPU Bulletin)* 11.139 (2013): 32–8.

[36] Richard C. Borden, "Leonid Dobychin's *The Town of N*: Introduction," in Leonid Dobychin, *The Town of N*, trans. (from the Russian) Richard C. Borden with Natalia Belova (Evanston: Northwestern University Press, 1998), viii.

variety of historically specific forms, and that a cognitive-literary inquiry is thus fundamentally a historicist inquiry.

FURTHER READING

Cook, Amy. *Shakespearean Neuroplay: Reinvigorating the Study of Dramatic Texts and Performance through Cognitive Science*. London: Palgrave Macmillan, 2010.

Crane, Mary Thomas. *Shakespeare's Brain: Reading with Cognitive Theory*. Princeton: Princeton University Press, 2001.

Lee, Haiyan. *The Stranger and the Chinese Moral Imagination*. Stanford: Stanford University Press, 2014.

Richardson, Alan. *The Neural Sublime: Cognitive Theories and Romantic Texts*. Baltimore: Johns Hopkins University Press, 2010.

Spolsky, Ellen. *Satisfying Skepticism: Embodied Knowledge in the Early Modern World*. Farnham: Ashgate, 2001.

Tribble, Evelyn B. *Cognition in the Globe: Attention and Memory in Shakespeare's Theatre*. London: Palgrave Macmillan, 2011.

Zunshine, Lisa. *Getting Inside Your Head: What Cognitive Science Can Tell Us About Popular Culture*. Baltimore: Johns Hopkins University Press, 2012.

23

CONSCIOUSNESS

ANEŽKA KUZMIČOVÁ

Speaking about reading is risky, but speaking about reading and consciousness is even riskier. If reading is only beginning to take shape in scholars' minds as a circumscribed phenomenon worthy of concerted research scrutiny, consciousness itself has been disputed for centuries. How does consciousness work? Do people have it in the first place? And how does it relate to reading?

The mechanics of human consciousness—this notional interface between one's brain and the physical world—has wide-ranging interest for various domains of mundane life. In healthy drivers, temporary disruptions can cause fatal accidents. Disputes in criminal court often boil down to the question of whether the accused party, or a witness, actually could perceive a given thing or consciously act in a given situation. Behind the current rise of meditation techniques is the promise that they will make us less oblivious, increase our consciousness. Reading is another such domain, because insight into the workings of consciousness is key to the effectiveness of any script-based education. The buzzwords associated with issues of literacy and learning today—attention, metacognition, self-regulation, and so forth—all relate closely to the phenomenon of consciousness.

These buzzwords emerge at a time when scholars are beginning to accumulate evidence in support of the view that one's general learning ability, as well as one's empathy and personality development, benefit strongly from the habitual reading of stories and novels. For example, psychologists Suzanne Mol and Adriana Bus conducted a meta-analysis of ninety-nine different empirical studies comprising data from over 7,000 participants aged 2 to 21.[1] They found not only that leisure reading increases one's learning ability but also that its positive impact on learning increases with age; the older a person is within the given range, the more it matters for their learning achievement whether they read for leisure or not. Other studies, such as experiments by David Comer Kidd and Emmanuele Castano, show that the

---

[1] Suzanne E. Mol and Adriana G. Bus, "To Read or not to Read: A Meta-analysis of Print Exposure from Infancy to Early Adulthood," *Psychological Bulletin* 137.2 (2011): 267–96.

reading of novels, and especially literary ones, enhances one's empathy skills in the short and long term.[2] Following the warnings of literacy experts, however, there is talk about the momentous decline of these beneficial "deep reading" leisure practices.[3] The "depth" that we are allegedly losing as a side effect of the digital turn refers, again, to nothing less than our consciousness as we read.

But what do we know about the particular state of consciousness of readers absorbed in fictional narratives, whether in print or on screen? We worry about its frailty and importance for sustainable society development, but we know very little about its nature. The following discussion reviews and partly contests three ideas about how consciousness works when we read stories and novels. Each in its own way, these ideas tend to inform how long-form reading is discussed and taught today. First, this chapter revisits the general notion that the reading consciousness is a container of sorts, holding a circumscribed amount of textual stimulus. Second, it argues against the view that readers commonly abstract their personal concerns away in reading literary text, and that they do so with benefit. Third, it proposes that the reading consciousness encompasses rather than excludes the physical situation and environment of reading. For each idea revisited, I will consider practical implications in terms of how reading could be taught, assessed, and staged in educational settings.

Reading as a Way of Being

Simply put, consciousness is what our brain "knows" about a given situation. In relation to non-conscious phenomena (say, the onset of a migraine), consciousness adds a subjective feel of what these phenomena are like (it hurts). One pervasive notion in the field of literacy seems to be that when we read a stretch of narrative, our consciousness is a container of sorts. As we make our way through the text, its contents gradually pour into our consciousness (and to a large part spill out again). Trained readers' minds may also take up various higher-order and formal aspects of the text in addition to the basic gist. The more important information should ideally stick in our mind, the container, for future use. This is how our reading ability is also measured with various instruments, such as the Programme for International Student Assessment (PISA) Test administered by the Organisation for Economic Co-operation and Development (OECD).[4] The more facts we retain in short-term

---

[2] David Comer Kidd and Emmanuele Castano, "Reading Literary Fiction Improves Theory of Mind," *Science* 342.6156 (2013): 377–80.

[3] Maryanne Wolf and Mirit Barzillai, "The Importance of Deep Reading," *Educational Leadership* 66.6 (2009): 32–7.

[4] OECD, *PISA 2015 Results*. Volume I: *Excellence and Equity in Education* (Paris: OECD Publishing, 2016).

memory, and the more comprehension and analysis questions we correctly answer immediately after reading a story, the more conscious and valuable our reading is understood to have been.

The container metaphor is partly fitting; in the instant of testing, some facts about the text can be retrieved from memory (those that stayed in the container) while others simply cannot (those that spilled out). However, it tells us little about how readers experience stories and novels when they are in the midst of reading, especially if undertaken for leisure, outside of any testing situation. Then, the reading consciousness is more like a sieve moving back and forth through a viscous medium, I propose, than like a container taking in a continuous stream.

Individual differences aside, leisure readers do not seem to spontaneously remember much detail of the novels they read: the exact sequence of events, the core of each conflict, names of places or characters, or the name of the author for that matter.[5] Such is the case especially if the novels are lengthy and perused in portions over extended periods of time. Often leisure readers do not even recall these details when explicitly asked to do so. This is not necessarily because these readers' consciousness, their immersion, was not "deep" enough, but because they might largely read novels without a prior view to remembering anything in particular. I will return to this idea shortly; but first, a story in support of the sieve metaphor.

Spontaneous memories of complex narratives tend to be discontinuous and haphazard with respect to what is "objectively" important, though they have been shown to sometimes cluster around nodal story points such as moments of conflict resolution between characters. One type of phenomenon that tends to stick for longer in the reader's mind (in its capacity as container) is mental imagery.[6] For the sake of illustration, let us assume that listening to a story is similar to reading one silently, an argument I have made elsewhere.[7] Many years ago, I heard a lecture elaborately citing a story from an honorable literary source, the author or title of which (appropriately enough for this discussion) I never remembered. In that story, a laundress in the distant past is washing sheets by a river. A priest comes by and delivers a sermon to her while she is working. When the sermon is finished, he asks if she remembers what he said. She replies that she does not, in fact, for the sermon was like the river washing through her sheets; it sieved through her, and her soul is now cleansed nonetheless. While I would fail a test on the further context of this story

[5] Marisa Bortolussi and Peter Dixon, "Minding the Text: Memory for Literary Narrative," in *Stories and Minds: Cognitive Approaches to Literary Narrative*, ed. Lars Bernaerts et al. (Lincoln: University of Nebraska Press, 2013), 23–37.

[6] Karen A. Krasny and Mark Sadoski, "Mental Imagery and Affect in English/French Bilingual Readers: A Cross-linguistic Perspective," *Canadian Modern Language Review/La Revue canadienne des langues vivantes* 64.3 (2008): 399–428.

[7] Anežka Kuzmičová, "Audiobooks and Print Narrative: Similarities in Text Experience," in *Audionarratology: Interfaces of Sound and Narrative*, ed. Jarmila Mildorf and Till Kinzel (Berlin: De Gruyter, 2013), 217–37.

snippet, the image of liquid content washing through the mind was so embodied and powerful that for an instant I felt the repeated impact of cold water in my chest as I listened. This sensation, together with what I have come to consider as the story's true characterization of narrative reception in general, is what makes me remember the snippet after more than a decade.

The mental image froze my consciousness of the story at a particular point in time, preserving some of it for future reference. As my anecdote suggests, mental imagery is a powerful instrument to cognition. Indeed, large-scale surveys by Suzanne Mol and Jelle Jolles have shown that our individual propensity for mental imagery relates closely to reading enjoyment, and to academic success overall.[8] However, much of high-quality reading time can go by without vivid mental images. During this time, it can prove difficult to say what was in our consciousness at any given point. Suppose you are reading a hypothetical novel in which a new minor character has just been introduced. Were you conscious of the three adjectives defining this character a couple of lines back, or did you make your way through them automatically? Which adjectives were they? It might appear that as you read them, you were still reflecting on the main protagonist's philosophical thoughts that were articulated in the preceding paragraph. And yet an indistinct sense of that new person has somehow been added to your story experience. It is in this respect that the reading consciousness is more of a sieve (or a thinned sheet being washed in thrusts) than a container.

My example might seem to suggest that you never were conscious of the descriptive passage in question; that much of long-form story reading actually happens non-consciously and lacks depth at all. Many readers, however, would likely recognize having read a literary descriptive passage if they encountered it verbatim a hundred pages later in the same novel, a phenomenon that puzzled philosopher and literary theorist Roman Ingarden nearly a century ago.[9] How can the passage seem familiar if you do not remember noticing it the first time around? And how come experiments such as those of Kidd and Castano show habitual readers of fiction to be profoundly transformed by reading in the long term despite having access to so little of their text experience, both in the act and in retrospect?

Philosopher and psychologist Susan Blackmore proposes a view of consciousness that is helpful in grasping the paradox. Blackmore is concerned with consciousness in general and does not address the activity of reading. In its unparalleled complexity, however, reading provides a wealth of intriguing examples relevant to her idea. In Blackmore's account, humans typically neither lack consciousness, as some thinkers radically believe, nor have it in the form of a continuous stream of conscious experience, as most other people think. Blackmore argues that what appears like our stream of consciousness—for example, the feeling of text pouring smoothly

[8] Suzanne Mol and Jelle Jolles, "Reading Enjoyment Amongst Non-leisure Readers Can Affect Achievement in Secondary School," *Frontiers in Psychology* 5.1214 (2014): 1–10.

[9] Roman Ingarden, *The Cognition of the Literary Work of Art*, trans. Ruth Ann Crowley and Kenneth R. Olson (Evanston: Northwestern University Press, 1973).

into the notional container of our mind—is an illusion conjured in response to random probes later on. The nature of a probe will necessarily determine how past experience is reconstructed. On this understanding, trying to pinpoint the precise "contents" of one's consciousness in retrospect, as people are expected to do with confidence in court, is misguided. Let me quote one of Blackmore's examples:

> In a noisy room full of people talking you may suddenly switch your attention because someone has said "Guess who I saw with Anya the other day – it was Bernard." You prick up your ears – surely not – you think. At this point you seem to have been aware of the whole sentence as it was spoken. But were you really? The fact is that you would never have noticed it at all if she had concluded the sentence with a name that meant nothing to you.[10]

The problem in reading long-form narrative is that the number of verbal probes that can guide one's grasp of the preceding text—the direction in which the sieve of consciousness will be thrust next—is endlessly higher than in the processing of Blackmore's two-clause utterance. In light of this insight, it seems a mystery how any two people can ever come close to converging in their subjective experience of a story or novel.

Many scholars, such as Philip Davis or Marco Caracciolo,[11] are working toward a better understanding of this mystery. In contrast to what I have tried to convey here, they emphasize the power of literary language to transform one's unruly text experience into a shareable stream, that is, momentarily to halt the sieve of consciousness and turn it into a container. The importance of such research cannot be stressed enough. However, the vast disparity of PISA reading outcomes and other literacy indices, across and within classrooms and countries, suggests that the alleged power of literature might not affect every pupil indiscriminately. Not without a reading pedagogy that takes proper notice of how consciousness works—or does not work. As part of testing and other classroom practice, such pedagogy would introduce probes and questions about texts *prior* to reading rather than afterwards, as PISA and similar measures typically do. It would also integrate systematic training in mental imaging as an aid to both memory and pleasure.

Reading as a Way of Being Yourself

The next idea to be discussed here pervades—especially but not exclusively—the higher tiers of reading education, in literature classes at secondary schools and universities. It is the idea that when you set out to interpret a novel or story, you can

---

[10] Susan Blackmore, "There Is No Stream of Consciousness," *Journal of Consciousness Studies* 9.5–6 (2002): 17–28.

[11] Philip Davis, *Reading and the Reader* (Oxford: Oxford University Press, 2013); Marco Caracciolo, *The Experientiality of Narrative: An Enactivist Approach* (Berlin: De Gruyter, 2014).

and should abstract away from the various contingencies of your current situation. For most of the twentieth century, academic literary studies were dominated by the notion of the so-called "affective fallacy," which derided idiosyncratic responses based on personal life experience.[12] Contemporary research agendas like that of Philip Davis focus precisely on the ability of literary fiction to lift one's mind out of personal concerns in order to reconnect it to existential themes such as mortality, which are equally valid to us all. Less literary reads, in turn, are sometimes dubbed "escapist." They are thought to make readers forget about real life altogether, *including* the fact of their mortality. For both the literary and non-literary cases, there is an assumption that the reader's preexisting self becomes largely overridden in consciousness by interpersonal meanings.

In my view, more credit should be given to the reader's sense of self when we think about how narrative informs our consciousness. Even Blackmore's simple anecdote speaks to the importance of personal relevance as our mind picks out stimuli for conscious processing. Blackmore says, "you would never have noticed…if she had concluded the sentence with a name that meant nothing to you." Evidence from empirical studies of reader response suggests that, in the complex process of story reading, it can be similarly difficult to tease apart the question "What does this mean?" from the question "What does this mean *to me*?" In leisurely book talk, the conversational floor is often divided according to real-life experience and expertise. When discussing a story set in a medical environment, for instance, reading groups tend to be (naturally) most eager to hear the insights of the doctors in their midst.

I would even go further in suggesting that for many leisure readers, the added value of narrative lies not in the invitation to forget oneself (Davis' chosen perspective) but in momentarily becoming conscious of one's self and one's problems in specific ways that may be less readily available otherwise. It is a known fact that outside of academic contexts, people report reading literature in order to identify with characters and their shortcomings, to cope with difficult situations, and to learn new things about life (rather than about literature in some abstract sense). This is what they say about their preferences when filling out surveys, and what they tick in questionnaires *after* being exposed to texts in experimental studies.

But how do these different personal realizations inform consciousness in the very course of reading? Often enough, they may come in the form of propositional thought ("Oh my, this character is acting just like me"). Just as often, however, they may assume the form of mental imagery. My previous example was of a mental image closely adhering to the wording of a given narrative—liquid content sieving through me like the river through a sheet, precisely as the laundress said. Many of the mental images that occur to us in reading may, however, adhere to wording only

---

[12] William K. Wimsatt and Monroe C. Beardsley, "The Affective Fallacy," *The Sewanee Review* 57.1 (1949): 31–55.

loosely. Instead, they feed on our personal memories triggered by the narrative. If my associations to the word "river," say, had made me briefly imagine the chilly swims I used to take with my grandparents in the Elbe river when I was a child. Uffe Seilman and Steen Larsen, two psychologists who studied personal responses to text in the 1980s, coined the term "reminding" for this type of conscious associations.[13] As to format, remindings can be just about anything—word chains, snippets of encyclopedic knowledge, or melodies such as the tune of an old song with the word "river" in it.

Perhaps the most important finding of Seilman and Larsen and their successors is that the remindings of truly affect-laden, personally lived experiences are much more common in literary narrative compared to other types of reading materials, and that their frequency directly affects the pleasure taken in reading. Paradoxically, the latter is especially true for remindings of negative personal experiences. Thus, depending on our situation, a given story or novel will yield—among many other things—a more or less intense parade of conscious thoughts, memories, and images in which our very selves play an active part. It is in this sense that literature affords a unique form of self-consciousness, in which you focus on yourself and yet you do not, because the story you are reading is really about others.

Most scholars of literature and reading, including some of those who study live readers' experiences, would classify remindings such as my Elbe memory as "diversionary" and akin to mind-wandering. Indeed, there is evidence that such memories can divert students' attention from particular poetic devices in a text, thereby hampering literary analysis.[14] But it would be untenable to argue that they are diversionary with respect to one's mindset when opening a book for pure leisure, which is seldom geared to anything so specific.

As for the analogy with mind-wandering, a phenomenon that reportedly takes up as much as a quarter of normal reading time, remindings would again represent a rather special case.[15] According to philosophers of consciousness Zachary Irving and Evan Thompson, the one distinctive feature of mind-wandering is that it is "unguided" thought.[16] This means that when your mind begins to wander, the topic of your thought will be prone to change while there is no regulatory force to

[13] Uffe Seilman and Steen F. Larsen, "Personal Resonance to Literature: A Study of Remindings While Reading," *Poetics* 18.1–2 (1989): 165–77.

[14] Shelley Sikora, Don Kuiken, and David S. Miall, "Expressive Reading: A Phenomenological Study of Readers' Experience of Coleridge's *The Rime of the Ancient Mariner,*" *Psychology of Aesthetics, Creativity, and the Arts* 5.3 (2011): 258–68.

[15] Jonathan W. Schooler, Erik D. Reichle, and David V. Halpern, "Zoning Out While Reading: Evidence for Dissociations between Experience and Metaconsciousness," in *Thinking and Seeing: Visual Metacognition in Adults and Children,* ed. Daniel T. Levin (Cambridge, MA: MIT Press, 2004), 203–26.

[16] Zachary C. Irving and Evan Thompson, "The Philosophy of Mind-Wandering," in *Oxford Handbook of Spontaneous Thought: Mind-Wandering, Creativity, and Dreaming,* ed. Kalina Christoff and Kieran C. R. Fox (Oxford: Oxford University Press, 2018), 87–96.

reinstate the initial topic. In narrative reading, however, there is indeed a regulatory force to keep your remindings in check: the text. As long as the text holds the readers' interest, their consciousness will keep returning to it. At the same time there is proof, as mentioned above, that without the mind being prompted to wander away to personal associations, one's interest in the text will suffer. A feedback loop seems to be at work here. If we accept that remindings are a type of mind-wandering in the first place, then this feedback loop supports another idea put forward by Irving and Thompson, namely that mind-wandering, albeit unguided, can in principle be task-related. The task at hand when reading: letting a narrative wash through one's mind.

PISA and similar projects keep reporting a worrisome link between students' degree of social advantage and their ability to read, especially with pleasure. From a very early age, excellence in literacy seems to be reserved for the socially privileged. The standard explanation is that due to environmental factors, disadvantaged readers lack academic dispositions in a narrow sense: the ability to focus, pursue goals, think critically, and so forth. This is probably true. A complementary question, arising from my view that reading is a particular form of self-consciousness, is whether these low-performing readers might also be lacking in their capacity to think, with depth and pleasure, about *themselves* as they read (and perhaps also in general). A literary and reading pedagogy embracing, rather than deriding, remindings and self-reflection would be a first step toward redressing such imbalance. One of the probes to be introduced prior to reading would then be the question: "What does this remind you of—in your self?"

Reading as a Way of Being in a Place

The last idea that I would like to revisit is that reading transports you—that is, decouples your consciousness—away from your immediate environment. While it is certainly relevant to think about literature as adventurous mental travel, and while the metaphor has great pedagogical interest especially in early reading promotion, it is sometimes taken too literally.

In measuring attention during narrative reading, for instance, researchers widely administer questionnaires such as the Transportation Scale or Narrative Engagement Scale. These questionnaires ask readers to rate, in retrospect, how aware they were of their reading environment. Attention to text is then simply assumed to be *inversely* related to scores given to statements of place awareness, as in the following example: "While I was reading the narrative, activity going on in the room around me was on my mind."[17] The underlying view is that the physical place has little to add, other than distraction, to one's conscious experience of a written narrative.

---

[17] Melanie C. Green and Timothy C. Brock, "The Role of Transportation in the Persuasiveness of Public Narratives," *Journal of Personality and Social Psychology* 79.5 (2000): 701–21.

In some parts of the world, accordingly, silent literary reading is practiced communally in primary and secondary classrooms under the assumption that a controlled environment free from stimuli optimally supports concentration. And to get the most out of reading during their spare time, pupils are advised literally to shut the door on their otherwise stimulating world.

Yet it is a simplification to think that when we read, all things outside the text, or outside our virtual stock of reminders for that matter, are necessarily distracting. Often enough the place where we read is an integral part of our story experience in a positive sense. For instance, think of the places where you typically read for leisure. How do they sound? Most probably they are not absolutely quiet, as such places are hard to find in natural conditions and actually difficult to be in without training. Now let us recall Blackmore's proposal about consciousness. What it implies is that the inconspicuous soundscapes of our mundane life—the hum of traffic outside your building, birds screeching somewhere further away—only *seem* to have been outside your consciousness once you finally look up from the book you have been reading. The reason: they are not as easily remembered in the illusory form of a stream. Nevertheless, they may have been part of your reading experience all the while. Another philosopher of consciousness, Eric Schwitzgebel, has run ingenious experiments in which he asked participants to introspect in response to trigger signals generated at random intervals while carrying out their usual activities. He found that some of the time consciousness indeed appears to encompass unattended phenomena—such as bird screeches in the background—that are unrelated to one's immediate activity.[18]

At less abstract levels, one fact challenging the idea of the reading consciousness being decoupled from physical environment is that readers often have strong opinions about places to read. Some, but by no means all, of these opinions have to do with noise levels and soundscapes.

With a group of collaborators, I have run a study exploring students' reading behaviors from a spatial angle.[19] It yielded a number of insights. For instance, many if not most participants reported seeking out white noise (nature sounds, music, voices in public spaces) to accompany their reading for both leisure and study purposes. Importantly, this was often linked to a preference for sharing their reading space with other people as well as to sensitivity toward what those people were doing. Apparently readers experience reading as a highly situated activity and also as a distinct way of claiming and inhabiting a place. In this light, having pupils read silently in classrooms may seem a good choice from the communal sharing point of view, but less so if the classrooms are too quiet.

---

[18] Eric Schwitzgebel, "Do you Have Constant Tactile Experience of Your Feet in Your Shoes? Or is Experience Limited to What's in Attention?" *Journal of Consciousness Studies* 14.3 (2007): 5–35.

[19] Anežka Kuzmičová, Patrícia Dias, Ana Vogrinčič Čepič, Anne-Mette Albrechtslund, André Casado, Marina Kotrla Topić, Xavier Mínguez López, Skans Kersti Nilsson, and Inês Teixeira-Botelho, "Reading and Company: Embodiment and Social Space in Silent Reading Practices," *Literacy* 52.2 (2018): 70–7.

Elsewhere I have detailed how the physical environment can also inform readers' consciousness by way of reinforcing mental imagery, that is, when one's physical situation somehow corresponds to the setting or contents of the story being experienced.[20] For instance, if I knew where to look for the laundress story in print and read it on the Elbe bank I used to visit as a child, or near any other river for that matter, my mental images of it would likely be even more vivid. This effect would not necessarily depend on me actually hearing the river (in my memories, the Elbe is perfectly still) or seeing it peripherally in the moment of experiencing the story; the sheer sense of its physical proximity would probably suffice to prop my mental imagery. This principle of environmental propping has a wealth of possible applications in reading pedagogy as teachers can evoke story settings through various priming techniques and classroom adjustments. They can also inspire pupils to experiment with different reading environments in their spare time so as to enhance the story experience.

In my hypothetical propping scenario, the serendipitous sense of a nearby river merging in my consciousness with the fictitious river might further reinforce future memories of my physical encounter with the story. But as it happens, although I heard the laundress story nowhere near a water resource, I still remember this encounter fairly well. After many years I still know where, when, and from whom I heard the anecdote. I am not suggesting that all past narrative experiences are as intimately tied in memory to where they took place. But some are, and clearly not only those propped by congruent settings. Perhaps certain life circumstances support such highly situated forms of reading consciousness, a view also held by astute observer of consciousness Marcel Proust:

> what our childhood reading leaves behind in us is above all the image of the *places* and *days* where and when we engaged in it. I have not escaped its sorcery: intending to speak about reading I have spoken of everything but books, because it is not of books that the reading itself has spoken to me.[21]

Proust's observation, then, is where the three strands of this chapter come together. It chimes with evidence of readers looking for "themselves" in literature in sensitive times especially, as a way of coping or identity formation. Childhood and young adulthood, the life period in which the foundations of our reading habits and abilities are laid, happens to be one such sensitive time. Additionally, as young readers are busy tackling literacy acquisition in a technical sense, their reading consciousness is also bound to be the most unruly and the least amenable to the neat container metaphor. Educators may more or less intuit this double exceptionality. The challenge is exploring it to the pupils' benefit—when teaching, designing tests, and

---

[20] Anežka Kuzmičová, "Does it Matter Where You Read? Situating Narrative in Physical Environment," *Communication Theory* 26.3 (2016): 290–308.

[21] Marcel Proust, *On Reading*, trans. Damion Searls (London: Hesperus Press, 2011), 18. Italics mine.

setting the physical stage of their narrative experiences. In digital times, when reading and text are becoming mobile to a degree that would have baffled the sedentary experiencer Proust, we must remember to worry about not only the notorious depth of the mind's container but also the reach and agility of the sieve that is the reading consciousness.

FURTHER READING

Blackmore, Susan. *Consciousness: An Introduction*, 2nd edn. Oxford: Oxford University Press, 2011.

Charlton, Michael, Corinna Pette, and Christina Burbaum. "Reading Strategies in Everyday Life: Different Ways of Reading a Novel Which Make a Distinction." *Poetics Today* 25.2 (2004): 241–63.

Fialho, Olivia, Sonia Zyngier, and David Miall. "Interpretation and Experience: Two Pedagogical Interventions Observed." *English in Education* 45.3 (2011): 236–53.

Hurlburt, Russell T., and Eric Schwitzgebel. *Describing Inner Experience? Proponent Meets Skeptic*. Cambridge, MA: MIT Press, 2007.

Koopman, Eva Maria (Emy), and Frank Hakemulder. "Effects of Literature on Empathy and Self-Reflection: A Theoretical-Empirical Framework." *Journal of Literary Theory* 9.1 (2015): 79–111.

Kuiken, Don, David S. Miall, and Shelley Sikora. "Forms of Self-Implication in Literary Reading." *Poetics Today* 25.2 (2004): 171–203.

Kuzmičová, Anežka. "Literary Narrative and Mental Imagery: A View from Embodied Cognition." *Style* 48.3 (2014): 275–93.

Kuzmičová, Anežka and Katalin Bálint. "Personal Relevance in Story Reading: A Research Review." *Poetics Today* 40.3 (2019): 429–51.

Miall, David S., and Don Kuiken. "Aspects of Literary Response: A New Questionnaire." *Research in the Teaching of English* 29.1 (1995): 37–58.

Wolf, Maryanne. *Tales of Literacy for the 21st Century*. Oxford: Oxford University Press, 2016.

24

PLEASURE

G. GABRIELLE STARR AND AMY M. BELFI

Some pleasures seem unreflective, unbidden, or unasked. Others seem to involve savoring, complexity, distance, and thought. The pleasures of reading are both. However, finding pleasure—or any sensation at all—does not rely on a simple physiological process, even for everyday experiences, like a smile or a sunset. No matter how seemingly unmediated or quick, human experience is complex in both phenomenological and physiological terms. The range of aesthetic experiences rooted in reading far exceeds the reach of pleasure, yet exploring pleasure teaches us something important about how and why literature and other arts matter in life. In this essay, we first look at pleasure and aesthetic pleasures broadly, then focus more closely on the pleasures of poetry as we lay out some key findings—and some speculations—about how pleasure may work in reading.

While pleasure has long been visible in aesthetic criticism, many commentators understand it as a broadly irreducible fundamental against which other affects and feelings are measured. Indeed, for much of the history of canonical aesthetics, pleasure was understood to be, as Edmund Burke described, a "simple idea, incapable of definition."[1] The idea that pleasure is an elementary experience long dominated across disciplines. In behavioral psychology and cognitive neuroscience, the question of irreducibility has been key: "Is pleasure really one thing…or is 'pleasure' just a label for a broad collection of qualitatively different things?"[2] It is worth exploring whether pleasure—much less aesthetic pleasure—is a stable concept or experience. Indeed, while what pleasure *feels like*—the phenomenological and subjective experiences of pleasure—offers clues about how pleasure works, we should also ask about the particular *uses* of pleasures.

As part of a functional account of pleasure, recent work in psychology has posited two different kinds of pleasures, which feel different, and have different behavioral

---

[1] Edmund Burke, *A Philosophical Enquiry into the Origin of Our Ideas of the Sublime and Beautiful* (New York: Oxford University Press, 1990), 30.

[2] James Russell, "Introduction: The Return of Pleasure," *Cognition and Emotion* 17.2 (2003): 161–5; 162.

outcomes. Charles Carver argues that as a group of positive affects, pleasures enable us to focus and refocus attention; pleasure of whatever kind allows for observation of and engagement with environments in important ways. The argument is straight-forward, if counterintuitive. One experiences pleasure in regard to two different physiological systems for motivation: there is the pleasure of attaining what one desires, as well as that of avoiding what one wishes to escape. These two conditions feel subjectively different: there is the thrill that comes with winning, but also some-thing like a queasy satisfaction in having escaped once again (from, e.g., failure or embarrassment). Carver argues, however, that these pleasures differ not just in how they feel, but in the ways they influence our behavior and ability to attend to the world. Pleasures are motivators, and they function at a basic level as a signal that individuals have achieved a goal. Somewhat paradoxically, however, pleasure may signal that people have done things *too* well. If people are hitting the mark, always, nothing needs to change: "positive feelings arise when things are going better than they need to. But they still reflect a discrepancy."[3] We find ourselves pleased that we've succeeded, but, to take Carver's metaphor, when we reach the top of the hill it's time to take the foot off the gas.

This view extrapolates from the core functions of pleasure in motivation to propose a general theory of how pleasure might work beyond a narrower view of goal-oriented behavior. Carver argues that pleasure allows one to repurpose attentional and emotional resources to explore the world more freely: "A pattern in which positive feelings lead to … an openness to shifting focus would minimize … adverse consequences" (e.g., being so lost in pleasure that you ignore the world around you).[4] It is relatively clear how negative emotions and pain narrow our field of vision, narrow attention.[5] Intriguingly, some positive emotions and pleasures may also focus us narrowly on a single goal or turn attention only to the pleasure itself; others send us outward: Barbara Fredrickson first described this as the ability of pleasure to enable one to "broaden and build."[6] Kimberly Chiew and Todd Braver have proposed a mechanism by which this may occur, indicating that positive affect may increase, in a small but measurable way, the ability to control attention proactively and focus on tasks of our choice.[7]

[3] Charles Carver, "Pleasure as a Sign You Can Attend to Something Else: Placing Positive Feelings within a General Model of Affect," *Cognition and Emotion* 17.2 (2003): 241–61; 246.
[4] Carver, "Pleasure as a Sign," 249.
[5] Elaine Scarry, *The Body in Pain: The Making and Unmaking of the World* (Oxford: Oxford University Press, 1985).
[6] Barbara L. Fredrickson, "The Role of Positive Emotions in Positive Psychology: The Broaden-and-Build Theory of Positive Emotions," *The American Psychologist* 56.3 (2001): 218–26.
[7] Kimberly S. Chiew and Todd S. Braver, "Dissociable Influences of Reward Motivation and Positive Emotion on Cognitive Control," *Cognitive, Affective, and Behavioral Neuroscience* 14.2 (2014): 509–29.

Aesthetics and the Uses of Pleasure

What holds about everyday pleasures doesn't necessarily hold, however, for the pleasures of aesthetic life. While some theorists (e.g., Burke and William Hogarth) have sought to link aesthetic pleasures to other kinds, others (like Immanuel Kant or George Santayana) have claimed that aesthetic pleasures are fundamentally distinct. In the *Critique of Judgment*, Kant argues that beauty requires more than mere liking. Liking emerges when we find something agreeable at the moment and for ourselves. Beauty, on the other hand, emerges when we claim that what we find pleasing should be universally so.[8]

One possibility here is that aesthetic pleasure is of a fundamentally different cast than other pleasures. If there are indeed differences, however, where do they arise: do they come in some way from the object (art carries features not found elsewhere in the world around us)? Or, do they emerge from the ways in which we approach art, phenomenologically, culturally, behaviorally, and physiologically? Most probably, yes to both. There are other key questions. Do individuals have recourse to a single, consistent internal standard of aesthetic pleasure? Is the scale continuous or discontinuous? How do experiences generally understood as negative function in aesthetic experience?

Experimental work, both behavioral and in fMRI, offers an intriguing perspective. First, there are probably multiple internal scales and standards for an individual experiencing aesthetic pleasure, and they may vary with artistic genre. Poetry elicits intense pleasures in some people, while novels leave them cold. The peak experiences for a preferred genre may be higher than for another; these differences might be used in behavioral and neural investigations to help differentiate components of aesthetic experience. Second, when it comes to questions of persistent or consistent pleasure, it turns out that on repeated engagements with artworks, test-retest paradigms show individuals tend toward relatively stable levels of pleasure (with variations that may be linked to mood, changing tastes, or new knowledge).[9]

---

[8] See Immanuel Kant, *Critique of Judgment*, trans. Werner S. Pluhar (Indianapolis: Hackett, 1987), part 1, sections 7–9, for description of pleasure, the agreeable, and the universality of the judgment of beauty.

[9] Work on continued pleasure with aging and dementia is particularly compelling: Andrea R. Halpern et al., "'I Know What I Like': Stability of Aesthetic Preference in Alzheimer's Patients," *Brain and Cognition* 66:1 (2008): 65–72; Andrea R. Halpern and Margaret G. O'Connor, "Stability of Art Preference in Frontotemporal Dementia," *Psychology of Aesthetics, Creativity, and the Arts* 7.1 (2013): 95–9; Daniel J. Graham, Simone Stockinger, and Helmut Leder, "An Island of Stability: Art Images and Natural Scenes—but Not Natural Faces—Show Consistent Esthetic Response in Alzheimer's-Related Dementia," *Frontiers in Psychology* 4 (2013), https://doi.org/10.3389/fpsyg.2013.00107.

Third, at least two different neural systems help underpin aesthetic pleasures.[10] One is, broadly speaking, linear and continuous, and involves reward systems.[11] Reward here refers to a pleasure that an individual will work to achieve, and functions very similarly across different domains, from food to sex, money, and aesthetic response. The second system does not respond in a linear way, engaging fully only in the most intense of aesthetic experiences, and involving a set of regions in the brain that are part of the default mode network.[12] The default mode network, first discovered by Marcus Raichle and colleagues, is also active in imagining the future and the past, thinking about others' thoughts, and introspective activity.[13] These neurophysiological systems help integrate pleasure into aesthetic experiences in different ways, and they may correlate with phenomenological and categorical kinds of aesthetic pleasure too: one closer to mere liking (mapping onto reward), and one that only emerges at the limits of the scale (visible in the selective response of parts of the default mode network). Indeed, while some cognitive neuroscientists have claimed that there is a common denominator in the pleasures we take in looking at human faces, landscapes, art, and many of our varying desires, that is not the whole story.[14]

The pleasures of intense aesthetic experience of artwork seem to have distinct physiological signatures. Yet it also seems clear that the object itself shapes one's pleasures. Not only might one feel differently about a sonnet than a landscape, but evidence suggests there are systematic ways in which pleasures function differently when they emerge in engaging artifacts rather than objects that seem more natural. A range of behavioral experiments that ask individuals to indicate how pleasing they find different classes of objects has shown that one may usefully differentiate these classes by measuring how much people agree on their pleasures in engaging them. For example, there is, across cultures and individuals, very high agreement in evaluations of facial beauty; individual disagreement is largely due to differences in experiences.[15] A direct comparison found that private taste accounts for 75 per cent

---

[10] Edward A. Vessel, G. Gabrielle Starr, and Nava Rubin, "Art Reaches Within: Aesthetic Experience, the Self and the Default Mode Network," *Frontiers in Neuroscience* 7 (2013): 258; "The Brain on Art: Intense Aesthetic Experience Activates the Default Mode Network," *Frontiers in Human Neuroscience* 6 (2012), https://doi.org/10.3389/fnhum.2012.00066.

[11] Vessel et al., "The Brain on Art," figures 3 and 4.

[12] Vessel et al., "The Brain on Art," figure 5.

[13] For a recent overview, see Marcus E. Raichle, "The Brain's Default Mode Network," *Annual Review of Neuroscience* 38.1 (2015): 433–47.

[14] Steven Brown, Xiaoqing Gao, Loren Tisdelle, Simon B. Eickhoff, and Mario Liotti, "Naturalizing Aesthetics: Brain Areas for Aesthetic Appraisal across Sensory Modalities," *Neuroimage* 58.1 (2011): 250–8; Tomohiro Ishizu and Semir Zeki, "Toward a Brain-Based Theory of Beauty," *PLoS One* 6.7 (2011): e21852; Teresa K. Pegors, Joseph W. Kable, Anjan Chatterjee, and Russell A. Epstein, "Common and Unique Representations in PFC for Face and Place Attractiveness," *Journal of Cognitive Neuroscience* 27.5 (2015): 949–73.

[15] Laura Germine et al., "Individual Aesthetic Preferences for Faces Are Shaped Mostly by Environments, Not Genes," *Current Biology* 25.20 (2015): 2684–9.

of variance (the degree to which individuals diverge) for pleasure in abstract artwork, and only 40 per cent of variance for pleasure in faces.[16] Indeed, with the shift from overtly natural objects to objects more clearly born of human artifice, the picture looks radically different: photos of real-world scenes shown on their own, for example, lead to high agreement, with pairwise correlations (a measure of convergent preferences) of around .67; yet using similar measures, visual art is much more subject to disagreement, with correlations of around .14.[17] With poetry, the story is much the same. For sonnets, intraclass correlations (another measure of resemblance) show agreements around .13, for haiku of .16, and for sestinas, as we show below, less than .05.[18]

It is worth pausing to recognize how surprising this steep contrast might be. Take the case of landscape and landscape paintings. A number of critics have shown that the concept and practices of landscape appreciation depend partially on artistic practices. In English, the term "landscape" itself emerges from art and comes to be applied to a view that carries the qualities of a painted vista.[19] The selection of viewpoints and the composition of scenes in the artistic canon has had a formative effect on taste in evaluating nature. Equally, as humans shape the world, planting, cultivating, and preserving it, we have done so in accord with principles honed in the arts.[20] Landscapes in general thus have good claim to being, in part, cultural artifacts. René Magritte even sought to remind his viewers that he wasn't offering objects (pipes, clouds, windows) themselves but pictures of them. However, it is still striking that individuals respond to photographs of real-world scenes and paintings of them, as well as to photographs of faces and paintings of them, with such a distinct difference in how much *pleasure* may be generalized or shared.

A further distinction marks the pleasures of beauty: they can be selectively disrupted or diminished, unlike gustatory or tactile pleasures, by adding in taxing cognitive tasks. Aenne Brielmann and Denis Pelli asked individual participants to bring six "movingly beautiful" images into the lab, where they were also shown images with highly positive valence (from the International Affective Picture Scale (IAPS) picture set, one long studied and tested in psychology research), shown plain images (medium valence IAPS and what Brielmann and Pelli identified as

[16] Helmut Leder et al., "Private and Shared Taste in Art and Face Appreciation," *Frontiers in Human Neuroscience* 10 (2016), https://doi.org/10.3389/fnhum.2016.00155.

[17] Edward A. Vessel and Nava Rubin, "Beauty and the Beholder: Highly Individual Taste for Abstract, but Not Real-World Images," *Journal of Vision* 10.2 (2010): 1–14; and Vessel et al., "The Brain on Art."

[18] Amy M. Belfi, Edward A. Vessel, and G. Gabrielle Starr, "Individual Ratings of Vividness Predict Aesthetic Appeal in Poetry," *Psychology of Aesthetics, Creativity, and the Arts* 12.3 (2017): 341–50.

[19] Kenneth Clark, *Landscape into Art* (Boston: Beacon, 1961).

[20] For a good overview, see Selim Kemal and Ivan Gaskell, eds., *Landscape, Natural Beauty and the Arts* (New York: Cambridge University Press, 1993). The introductory essay by Kemal and Gaskell is particularly useful for framing the landscape/nature interpenetration.

plain IKEA furniture), and given two different sensory pleasures (candy and a plush stuffed object).[21] They found that a task that requires working memory and the ability to control attention had no effect on the pleasure individuals took in the IAPS pictures (highly valenced or not), the IKEA photos, the candy, and the object. However, the task radically diminished the pleasure individuals took in what they had previously found beautiful.

The pleasures of beauty are distinctive in that they require additional, and varied, cognitive acts: remembering; imagining; comparing; projecting; evaluating; feeling. (Many of these families of cognition are supported by the default mode network, which is also engaged in powerful aesthetic response.) This is not somehow to verify a Kantian formulation that "free play" of particular cognitive faculties is essential in aesthetic response. Rather, it is to say that there may be ways of understanding more fully the varieties of cognitive processes that are particular to the pleasures of reading, viewing, or listening to works of art, and to affirm that these cognitive processes are in fact essential to the pleasure, not ancillary to it.

Poetic Pleasures

If the cognitive textures of the pleasures of reading are somehow fundamental to those pleasures, it may be because artworks provide a larger range of aesthetic affordances than does, typically, the natural world. The term "affordance" comes from the work of James Gibson, who argued that objects and spaces "afford" certain dominant possibilities for engaging, manipulating, or navigating them: the shape of a handle offers a few primary modes of grasping; a cliff offers only a certain number of handholds; a path offers a given route.[22] We contend that literature (alongside other arts) affords particular, yet truly multiple, primary points of engagement, too, from moments that may evoke particular emotions to words that engage powerful imagery, opportunities for empathy, moral or ethical challenges, etc. If there are dizzyingly multiple possible and primary affordances for pleasure in reading, this may be in part because finding new ways of taking pleasure in the world is fundamentally a creative act.

At a basic level, the difference in the degree to which individuals agree in their pleasures when it comes to artworks may argue for a difference in kind: it becomes

---

[21] Aenne A. Brielmann and Denis G. Pelli, "Beauty Requires Thought," *Current Biology* 27.10 (2017): 1506–13; Peter J. Lang, Margaret M. Bradley, and Bruce N. Cuthbert, "International Affective Picture System (IAPS): Technical Manual and Affective Ratings," *NIMH Center for the Study of Emotion and Attention* (1997): 39–58.

[22] James J. Gibson, *The Ecological Approach to Visual Perception* (New York: Psychology Press, 1986), see 18, 36 ff., and 127.

possible not just that characteristics of individuals (our differences, our experiences) but that characteristics of objects may have *functional distinctions* linked to pleasure. As we have argued, exploring the differences in pleasures across objects enables a new way to differentiate classes of objects from one another. Thus, while there are concepts and generic principles that enable us to class faces together, or landscapes together, and to distinguish them from visual art or poems (we've used the concept of the artifact above; there are others), it appears that pleasures can differentiate them too.

What might be the source of disagreement between our pleasures in a painting and a real scene? The two objects give much of the same conceptual information about distances, vista, objects, and so on. A vision scientist might argue that the data available to the visual system varies in many ways—some subtle, some not—between the two. Yet one further distinction is that one object continually announces its fictiveness, its status as an art object, by a range of formal features, and one of the signs that unifies them might be called something like style. If, as Whitney Davis argues, from the perspective of visual culture, style is a rhetorical concept that sets the stage for the viewer's interaction with the artwork, then from the perspective of our pleasures, style may be in part understood as that which enables us to disagree about the pleasure we take in art.[23] Style, as one element of form, would in this sense be one of the things about which we disagree.

This raises one further (for now) intriguing question. Many thinkers assign a particular canonical value to an aesthetic whole, granting the entirety of the object a different weight than any particular part might have. Older ideas of art that privilege "beauties"—that is, excerpts circulated in letters, conversations, commonplace books, anthologies, etc.—as complete, and even paradigmatic, gave way to Samuel Taylor Coleridge's view of organic form. This view went on to be contested by twentieth-century formalist criticism, in which a work declares its aesthetic shape quite early on.

In research completed at New York University, we selected two subjective features of reading experience that seem particularly likely to involve a more holistic or extended view of a poem: vivid imagery, which may be constructed over several lines or across stanzas, and an individual's emotional response, which may change or build over the course of the poem. We designed an experiment to test the relationship between the strength of emotional reaction, emotional valence, the perceived vividness of imagery, and overall aesthetic pleasure in reading the whole of a poem or increasingly longer parts. As a highly regularized genre that is easily subdividable, sestinas seemed a good test case. We selected twelve poems having stanzas that could stand alone grammatically (occasionally adding final punctuation

---

[23] Whitney Davis, *A General Theory of Visual Culture* (Princeton: Princeton University Press, 2011), chapter 4.

to an individual stanza). The "short" versions were the sestina's first two stanzas (60–134 words), the "medium" versions were the first four stanzas (131–287 words), and, finally, "long" were the complete sestinas (207–461 words). All of the poems were first published in the twentieth or twenty-first century, composed in English, and taken from published anthologies, though we avoided poems frequently taught in literature courses or likely to be recognized (e.g., Elizabeth Bishop's "One Art").[24]

One might think that reading a poem in its entirety, or even increasing the length of engagement—and with it increasing the amount of information or detail—might promote the ability of readers to engage emotionally or to imagine vividly. However, reading both parts and wholes elicited similar levels of pleasure, as well as similar vividness of imagery and strength of feeling. (See the Appendix of this chapter for details of the experiment.) Part of this finding may be linked to the internal cohesion of individual stanzas. While sestinas are generally unrhymed, the formal repetition of end-words from stanza to stanza establishes a pattern that may promote readers' sense that even a pair of stanzas is a complete entity. Importantly, we also found that aesthetic pleasures seem to be constituted in similar ways across both the poem excerpts and the complete poems: the relative contribution to aesthetic pleasure (as measured by individual subject regressions) of vivid imagery, strength of pleasure, or affective valence was unchanged either by length or by reading a part rather than a whole.

These findings contrast slightly with a version of literary formalism that suggests poems have internal signals of closure, but which has held that the final lines of a poem as a whole have particular resonance in signaling aesthetic completion.[25] Individual stanzas may carry such signals as well. Additionally, because both medium and complete versions contained the short one (the first two stanzas), it is also possible that early components of poems have an important influence in determining the degree of aesthetic pleasure overall, consistent with Kenneth Burke's argument that in their opening lines, literary objects train readers in how to read them.[26] While the value of a poem as a whole remains, it is not clear that this value is always indexed by readers' pleasure. We must seek it elsewhere.

What we think is clear, however, is that aesthetic pleasures have a complexity that requires a fulsome understanding of what pleasure actually does. The close connection of aesthetic pleasures to cognitive resources, whether those of emotion or imagery, or particular systems, like the default mode network, is worthy of note in part because it suggests that aesthetic pleasures may be one subset of the kinds of

---

[24] Daniel Nester, ed., *The Incredible Sestina Anthology* (Austin: Write Bloody Publishing, 2013); Carolyn Bear Whitlow and Marilyn Krysl, eds., *Obsession: Sestinas in the Twenty-first Century* (Hanover: Dartmouth University Press, 2014).

[25] Barbara H. Smith, *Poetic Closure: A Study of How Poems End* (Chicago: University of Chicago Press, 1968).

[26] Kenneth Burke, *The Philosophy of Form* (Berkeley, CA: University of California Press, 1973).

pleasures Fredrickson identified as those that "broaden and build." Those pleasures, as we described above, allow a freedom to choose, to redirect attention, to look up, in a sense, from narrow focus on detail to something else. In the case of poetry, that may mean the ability to explore features of form, whether they be rhyme and meter, or, more broadly, formal structures like stanzas and sestinas. Indeed, it may be the case that the pleasure readers take is what helps them take a part for a whole, or see the whole as something new.

The study of aesthetic pleasures as exploratory pleasures, broadening pleasures, may ultimately enable us to learn more about how that family of pleasures functions to help any of us open our minds to explore features of the world, concepts, moral engagements, other people, and social complexity more generally. There is much left to learn.

Appendix

Research was performed at New York University (NYU) under the approval of the NYU Committee on Activities Involving Human Subjects. Participants were recruited online using Amazon's Mechanical Turk (MTurk). We restricted participation to individuals with approval ratings of at least 95 per cent on at least 1,000 previous MTurk tasks. We limited the geographic location of participants to the United States. Participants consisted of 141 adults who were native English speakers (data from eight additional participants was excluded due to incomplete responses). These participants were divided into three groups: those who read short (n=48), medium (n=47), and complete (n=46) versions of the sestina.

Each participant read one version (short, medium, or complete) of each of the twelve sestinas and answered several questions after each (titles/first lines are available upon request). No one read multiple versions of the same poem, and each read one version of every poem. After each item, participants rated what they read on four dimensions in the following order: (1) vividness of imagery; (2) valence of emotions experienced while reading; (3) strength of their emotional arousal; and (4) aesthetic pleasure derived from reading the work. Each rating was made on a continuous scale using a slider bar with values ranging between 0 and 100. Each excerpt or poem and the four questions were presented on one screen. After responding to the questions, participants advanced to the next poem or excerpt.

Analysis and Results

To identify differences between groups (short, medium, and complete) we conducted a MANOVA, with length as the between-subjects variable, and our five characteristics of interest as dependent variables. The overall MANOVA did not show a significant effect of length, [$F(8,270)$=1.62, p=0.11, η^2=0.04]. When examining the post-hoc one-way ANOVAs, we found no significant effects of length on vividness [$F(2,138)$=2.39, p=0.09, η^2=0.03]; valence [$F(2,138)$=1.53, p=0.22, η^2=0.02]; emotional strength [$F(2,138)$=0.12, p=0.88,

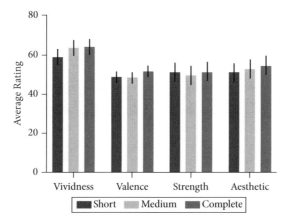

Figure 24.1 Mean ratings for short, medium, and long conditions. Error bars depict 95 per cent confidence intervals.

η^2=0.01]; or aesthetic pleasure [F(2,138)=0.52, p=0.53, η^2=0.01]. See Figure 24.1 for graphical depictions of the means for each rating.

Individual subject regressions were computed to measure how well the factors of vividness, valence, and emotional strength predicted ratings of aesthetic appeal, and whether the predictive ability of these variables differed as a function of length. On average, strength of emotional arousal was the best predictor of aesthetic pleasure (average standardized β: 0.39 for short, 0.43 for medium, 0.45 for long), followed by the valence of felt emotions (average standardized β: 0.30 for short, 0.24 for medium, 0.23 for long) and vividness of imagery (average standardized β: 0.15 for short, 0.20 for poems, 0.21 for poems). Summary statistics of these regressions are plotted in Figure 24.2.

When comparing the regression results between the three lengths, a one-way MANOVA revealed no significant differences in the predictive ability of the three ratings between the three poem lengths [F(6,274)=0.43, p=0.85, η^2=0.01].

We also investigated agreement among the raters for short, medium, and complete conditions. We calculated intraclass correlation coefficients (ICCs) from single measures for each characteristic using the ICC (2,1) "consistency" measure. As assessed by ICC (2,1), participants showed similar patterns of agreement for short, medium, and complete conditions. For all lengths, participants showed the highest agreement for valence, followed by vividness, then arousal and aesthetic pleasure. Overall, agreement was quite low for each rating scale. To compare ICC values between the three lengths, we calculated 95 per cent confidence intervals to assess the degree of overlap between the three lengths.[27] This indicated that there were no significant differences between ICC values for any of the ratings (Figure 24.3).

[27] Margarita Stolarova, Corinna Wolf, Tanja Rinker, and Aenne Brielmann, "How to Assess and Compare Inter-rater Reliability, Agreement and Correlation of Ratings: An Exemplary Analysis of Mother-Father and Parent-Teacher Expressive Vocabulary Rating Pairs," *Frontiers in Psychology* 5 (2014), https://dx.doi.org/10.3389/fpsyg.2014.00509.

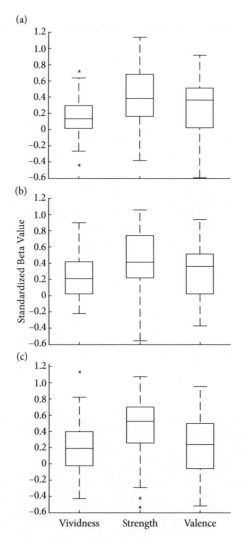

Figure 24.2 Summary statistics for individual regressions for short (A), medium (B), and long (C) conditions.

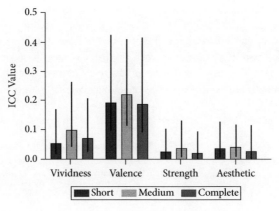

Figure 24.3 ICC values for short, medium, and long sestinas. Error bars depict 95 per cent confidence intervals.

FURTHER READING

Armstrong, Paul. *How Literature Plays With the Brain*. Baltimore: Johns Hopkins University Press, 2013.

Chatterjee, Anjan. *The Aesthetic Brain*. New York: Oxford University Press, 2015.

Chatterjee, Anjan, Page Widick, Rebecca Sternschein, William B. Smith, and Bianca Bromberger. "The Assessment of Art Attributes." *Empirical Studies of the Arts* 28:2 (2010): 207–22.

Coleridge, Samuel Taylor. *Biographia Literaria*. Ed. James Engell and Walter Jackson Bate. Vol. 7. Princeton: Princeton University Press, 1983.

Dehaene, Stanislas. *Reading in the Brain*. New York: Penguin, 2010.

Elfenbein, Andrew. *The Gist of Reading*. Stanford: Stanford University Press, 2018.

Hutson, Joseph P., Marcos Nadal, Luigi Agnati, Camilo Cela-Conde, eds. *Art, Aesthetics, and the Brain*. New York: Oxford University Press, 2015.

Kringelbach, Morten L. "The Human Orbitofrontal Cortex: Linking Reward to Hedonic Experience." *Nature Reviews Neuroscience* 6:9 (2005): 691–702.

Langer, Susanne K. *Feeling and Form*. New York: Scribner, 1953.

Lynch, Deidre Shauna. *Loving Literature: A Cultural History*. Chicago: University of Chicago Press, 2014.

Menninghaus, Winfried, Valentin Wagner, Julian Hanich, Eugen Wassillwizky, Milena Kuehnast, and Thomas Jacobsen. "Towards a Psychological Construct of Being Moved." *PloS one* 10:6 (2015): e0128451.

Obermeier, Christian, Winfried Menninghaus, Martin von Koppenfels, Tim Raettig, Maren Schmidt-Kassow, Sascha Otterbein, and Sonja A. Kotz. "Aesthetic and Emotional Effects of Meter and Rhyme in Poetry," *Frontiers in Psychology* 4 (2013), https://doi.org/10.3389/fpsyg.2013.00010.

Rolls, Edmund T. *Emotion and Decision-Making Explained*. New York: Oxford University Press, 2013.

Scarry, Elaine. *Dreaming by the Book*. Princeton: Princeton University Press, 2001.

Starr, G. Gabrielle. *Feeling Beauty: The Neuroscience of Aesthetic Experience*. Cambridge, MA: MIT Press, 2013.

25

DYSLEXIA: THROUGH THE EYES OF DA VINCI

MARYANNE WOLF

> So I hold that the invisible powers of imagery in the eyes may project themselves to the object, as do the images of the object to the eyes.
>
> —Leonardo da Vinci

> *Ubi amor ibi oculus.* The more we love, the more we see.
>
> —Joseph W. Evans

Leonardo da Vinci's *St. Anne, the Virgin and Child with a Lamb* is one of the world's most beautiful portraits of maternal love. More extraordinary, there are two mothers, each radiating a different form of this love: Mary for her Infant Christ Child; and Anne for her daughter Mary, now a mother herself. This painting represents one of the many examples of da Vinci's powerful understanding of the predictive relationship between what we see and what we know, a central principle in the reading act.

In reading as in art, the more we know and feel, the more we see. If one does not know that Anne is the mother of Mary—particularly since they both look ageless in this luminous painting—the viewer could miss an essential part of what da Vinci is conveying: the never-ending tenderness of a mother's love across time. As viewers and as readers, we co-construct the layers of meaning in a painting or a text by what we "know"—perceptually, linguistically, cognitively, and affectively.

The synthesis of perception with all prior forms of knowledge is at the core not only of da Vinci's art but also of the formation of the reading brain. Just as da Vinci wrote that "invisible powers of imagery in the eyes project themselves" onto what we see, philosophers and psychologists from Immanuel Kant to Andy Clark give similar emphases to perception's inextricable relation to knowledge.[1] A version of this view underlies a key assumption in the cognitive neurosciences about the reading brain: that is, what we read, like what we see, is a reflection of what we know,

---

[1] Andy Clark, "Whatever Next? Predictive Brains, Situated Agents, and the Future of Cognitive Science," *Behavioral and Brain Sciences* 36.3 (2013): 181–204.

what we feel, and what the text conveys. Further and more striking still, as cognitive neuroscientists Gina Kuperberg and Florian Jaeger write, "prediction prepares perception."[2] Thus what we know before we encounter any word or text helps us predict with greater accuracy, rapidity, and understanding what we will read.

This chapter will begin by examining how the gradual synthesis of perception, cognition, language, and affect undergirds the formation of a reading brain circuit. Based on this view of reading, we will then approach why this circuit can be quite different in various writing systems and even in different mediums. Finally, we will examine why the circuit fails to develop in conventional ways in persons with dyslexia and, potentially, in one of the greatest and most unconventional artists and inventors of the last millennium, da Vinci. The mystery of whether da Vinci is, in fact, the most famous person with dyslexia in recent history will not be fully resolved in this chapter—how could it be? But revisiting this mystery can nevertheless illuminate the complexity of dyslexia and da Vinci's suggestive, polysemous depiction of himself as an "unlettered man."

The Formation of the Reading Brain

Not unlike da Vinci's prescient description of the relationship between what we know and what we see, a reciprocal relationship between what we know and what and how we read builds in "geometric progression" over time.[3] The more we bring to what we read, the more deeply we understand the text and, virtually simultaneously, the more we will add to our background knowledge, which enriches everything we read next. This great reciprocal process is the basis for our ability to draw analogies between what we read and what we already knew beforehand, to draw inferences that propel our critical analyses of written language, and to "go beyond the wisdom of the author."[4]

Or not. The converse is equally true: the less we bring, or the less time we have to bring to each of these processes, the more truncated and shallow our understanding of the text will be. Young, inexpert readers, readers with impoverished language backgrounds, individuals with dyslexia, and multi-tasking screen readers often cannot integrate what they see with what they know for four very different reasons. Understanding and addressing these underlying reasons may be one of the most important contributions that current work on the reading brain can offer. For the formation of the expert reading brain, or its failure to develop fully, will have lifelong

---

[2] Gina R. Kuperberg and T. Florian Jaeger, "What Do We Mean by Prediction in Language Comprehension?" *Language, Cognition and Neuroscience* 31.1 (2016): 32–59.

[3] Alberto Manguel, *A History of Reading* (New York: Penguin Books, 1996), 19.

[4] Marcel Proust, *On Reading*, trans. Jean Autret and William Burford (New York: Macmillan, 1971), 31.

consequences for the intellectual development of the individual, for the maintenance of a democratic society, and for the progress of our species.[5]

A more detailed understanding of the reading circuit illuminates this reality, beginning with the simplest of concepts: humans were never meant to read.[6] No specific genetic program poises us to read. No one set of areas in our brain is pre-programmed to unfold naturally the way oral language does. Reading and written language alike are unnatural inventions. Educators and parents around the world commit huge, life-altering errors when they believe that reading is natural and will simply unfold for their children in the presence of stimulating literary experiences. The widely used methods based on such a belief (often called Whole Language) unintentionally doom entire groups of children who cannot induce the principles of reading from stories and text, no matter how beautiful the written language or how well-meaning the teacher. It is an incalculable waste, borne out of understandable but mistaken beliefs about the naturalness of written language and the induction capacities of children.

What are natural and genetically programmed in reading are its design and its major component parts. For example, the ability to read is made possible by one of the most creative features of the brain's design: the protean capacity to make new "circuits" for culturally invented functions like literacy and numeracy. These circuits are formed by establishing heretofore nonexistent connections among the brain's original functions and the areas underlying them: specifically, language, vision, and cognition. Each of the latter functions has a genetic program that unfolds in response to environmental stimulation. Any infant will learn to see and speak when placed in an environment that triggers the genetic instructions for vision and language. Almost no infant, however, will learn to read without some form of exposure and, usually, some form of teaching. (There are always outliers like Jean-Paul Sartre!) Language and vision are first given by nature and nurtured by the environment; reading is first given by culture and nurtured by the brain's design.

After their different beginnings, the trajectories for vision, language, and reading become an interconnected set of stories in human development. Therein lies an amazing aspect of the reading circuit's formation in literate humans. As described by neuroscientists Stanislas Dehaene and Laurent Cohen, reading recycles neurons typically used for other purposes.[7] For example, reading repurposes neurons in vision—in particular the fine-feature-detecting neurons responsible for recognizing faces and objects—in order for us to recognize the fine features in the letters and characters found in all of the world's writing systems. In other words, the very same neurons in the visual cortex that started out with a responsibility for identifying

    [5] See Maryanne Wolf, *Reader, Come Home: The Reading Brain in a Digital World* (New York: HarperCollins, 2018).

    [6] See Maryanne Wolf, *Proust and the Squid: The Story and Science of the Reading Brain* (New York: HarperCollins, 2007).

    [7] Stanislas Dehaene, *Reading in the Brain: The New Science of How We Read* (New York: Penguin, 2009).

facial features and objects become repurposed for identifying letters, characters, letter patterns, common words, etc. Over time and with considerable practice, these networks for visual symbols become automatic at recognizing letters and patterns. Very importantly, with even more practice, letters and letter patterns become automatically connected to their corresponding units of sound (called phonemes), of meaning (e.g., morphemes, words, and concepts), and of grammatical function.

Typically, the process of learning to read begins with the formation of a rudimentary reading circuit made up of networks that are responsible for identifying symbols, for matching them to sounds, and for connecting the letter-sound correspondences to the meaning and functions of words. Such a rudimentary circuit permits very basic decoding in very young readers. This first circuit is the critical foundation for an ever more elaborated one that, over time, gradually adds networks underlying more and more sophisticated cognitive and linguistic processes. Often subsumed under the single, reductive term *comprehension*, the latter capacities, which I refer to as the *deep reading* processes, include but are not restricted to: background knowledge, various forms of sensory imagery, empathy, analogy, inference/induction/deduction, critical analysis, and insight and reflection. The expert reading brain circuit is achieved when each and all of these processes can interact with lightning-swift speed and give their individual contributions to the reading act, whether we call this *close* or *deep reading*.

There are critical implications to the development and formation of a deep reading brain circuit in members of a society. It is not that a non-literate person does not have the capacities for profound thought. (Simply think of Socrates and the pre-Socratic philosophers.) It is rather that reading allows the democratization of profound thought and something else. Quite literally, the brain of a literate person differs from a non-literate person in the new connections that emerge between vision and language networks. Manuel Carreiras and his colleagues described Portuguese adults who never learned to read because of war and civil strife.[8] Later, when these conditions changed, those individuals who went on to become literate were compared with those who remained non-literate. The results from these brain-imaging studies depicted the emergence of whole new connections between visual and language areas.[9] In this physiological sense, literacy changes the brain, which in the process alters societies.

But there are several very important "catches" to the way that the brain changes when it learns to read, and, if you are reading this on a digital device, some of them are happening now. Because there are no genetic programs for its unfolding, the reading circuit is plastic and highly malleable. It will, therefore, take on characteristics

---

[8] Manuel Carreiras, Mohamed L. Seghier, Silvia Baquero, Adelina Estévez, Alfonso Lozano, Joseph T. Devlin, and Cathy J. Price, "An Anatomical Signature for Literacy," *Nature* 461.7266 (2009): 983–6.

[9] See Maryanne Wolf, *Tales of Literacy for the 21st Century* (Oxford: Oxford University Press, 2016).

that are shaped by external factors like the kind of writing system and the medium, and also internal factors like the way the brain is organized for language in a particular individual. Thus different reading circuits have emerged in readers using different writing systems, different mediums, and—of particular interest in my own research—in persons with dyslexia.

Writing Systems and the Their Distinctive Requirements

The differences among writing systems are fascinating. Although certain universal principles will dictate how the brain forms any circuit for reading, there are wonderful variations based on the unique requirements of a specific writing system. For example, the more visually demanding Chinese writing system and the Japanese Kanji system (which is based on Chinese) require far more use of the visual cortex in both hemispheres, as well as the motor cortex, than alphabets or syllabaries like the Japanese Kana system. The staggering number of visual characters that every Chinese reader must acquire is helped by painstaking practice in carefully writing each character by hand. Predictably, such demands require more activation in left hemisphere motoric areas and in both hemispheres' visual areas. Further, the manner in which the Chinese characters are based on concepts first and only then articulation requires interesting differences in the activation of the right hemisphere temporal-parietal regions as well.

By contrast, alphabets and syllabaries place greater emphases on sound-based, phonological processes in brain areas devoted to the perception and representation of the individual sounds or phonemes in a particular language. Indeed, even within alphabetic writing systems, there are subtle and not-so-subtle differences. For example, in the more regular, alphabetic languages like Italian and Finnish—where there is an almost one-to-one correspondence between the letter and the sound—there are less visual processing and more phonological processing areas than in less regular languages like English and French. The latter incorporate a great deal of historical information in their spellings, which makes special demands on the networks in the circuit involved in connecting vision to concept, and not just vision to sound. Thus, the typical English and French reader will activate more conceptual and more visual processing to read words whose sometimes confusing spellings often carry the word's history in their morphemes. Linguists Noam and Carol Chomsky frequently used the word "muscle" to illustrate how this word's seemingly unnecessary "c" connects it to the entire family of words that *do* need the "c," like "muscular," "musculature," etc. Different orthographies, therefore, make different requirements on the formation of the reading circuit based on the unique characteristics of how their words are formed, spelled, and read.

What a Difference a Medium May Make

As a result of all these differences, we can never speak of one ideal reading circuit. Rather, the intrinsic plasticity of the brain allows for all manner of circuits to be formed based on the particular writing system but also, importantly today, by the medium. And here we come to the newest catch in the formation of the reading circuit: the inevitable changes that will occur in the formation of our next generation's reading brains if a new medium dominates. The characteristics of the medium are reflected in the circuit. According to Patricia Greenfield,

> Every medium has its strengths and weaknesses; every medium develops some cognitive skills at the expense of others. Although...the Internet may develop impressive visual intelligence, the cost seems to be deep processing: mindful knowledge acquisition, inductive analysis, critical thinking, imagination, and reflection.[10]

In other words, deep reading processes, which require extra time and conceptual effort, may become threatened by a mode of reading that privileges fast processing of multiple forms of information with little time to allocate to slower and more demanding processes. There are good reasons for our tendency to act on whatever is the newest piece of information. We are, in fact, evolutionarily programmed to respond immediately to novel stimuli. The species' "novelty bias" has kept us alive by giving homo sapiens an inbuilt alertness and ability to turn attention immediately to signs of food or predators.

The problem is that, if readers are barraged by a continuous stream of novel stimuli, there will be significant effects on the quality of their attention and memory processes. Think back to the great reciprocal process that is the leitmotif of this chapter. If what we know helps predict what we read, and we are spending less time consolidating what we know, there will be downstream effects on the rest of the deep reading processes. Norwegian scholar Anne Mangen and her colleagues have shown that university students read the same passage differently in print versus digital media. The digital medium had significant effects on the students' ability to sequence details and allocate time to the more conceptually demanding processes like inference, critical analysis, and other contributions to comprehension and insight.[11]

On the one hand, these changes to the reading brain will require true vigilance if we are to preserve the great advances that have helped form the present expert reading brain. On the other hand, this same medium has critically important effects

[10] Patricia M. Greenfield, "Technology and Informal Education: What Is Taught, What Is Learned," *Science* 323.5910 (2009): 69–71.

[11] See Anne Mangen, Bente R. Walgermo, and Kolbjørn Bronnick, "Reading Linear Texts on Paper Versus Computer Screen: Effects on Reading Comprehension," *International Journal of Educational Research* 58 (2013): 61–8; Wolf, *Tales of Literacy*; and Wolf, *Reader, Come Home*.

for our culture, which increasingly demands as much digital literacy as reading fluency and comprehension capacities. Understanding precisely what constitutes the advantages and disadvantages of each medium for different types of text, and the best medium for the different purposes of reading by different types of individuals, will be the complex, essential work of the future science of reading. We already understand that for some individuals, particularly those with dyslexia, digital media may prove more beneficial for learning to read than traditional print media. An understanding of why this is so reveals yet another turn in the well-known story of reading and the less-known history of dyslexia.

Dyslexia is Not What One Thinks

Dyslexia is not a reading disability. This unexpected conclusion is not unique to me but rather a paraphrase of a comment made by Andrew Ellis, a British researcher, three decades ago. I have never forgotten it, because it represents a deep truth about dyslexia that is rarely understood. Dyslexia represents one of the varied organizations of the brain that have been with our species for thousands of years, well before we invented reading. It is in this evolutionary sense that dyslexia is not so much a reading disability as an organization of the brain that is advantageous for many aspects of our survival—but not for the acquisition of literacy.

More specifically, natural selection requires a certain amount of *cerebrodiversity*, so that different brains cover the varied needs of the species. The organization of various functions in the dyslexic brain is particularly well-suited for functions like building and inventing and thinking "outside the box," whether in winning battles or in finding a mate. It is not by coincidence that this particular, highly genetic organization has been passed on for thousands of years. It is, however, an accident of circumstance that the same organization that advantaged the dyslexic brain for some societal tasks disadvantaged it for a cultural function that came relatively late in the evolutionary cycle.

We are still acquiring knowledge about how diverse the reading circuit can be for individuals with dyslexia, but there are multiple differences in how (and how fast) this circuit can process the multiple aspects of language and connect them to visual areas. There will not be a single kind of breakdown in the reading circuit in persons with dyslexia. The fact that dyslexia cannot be reduced to one single phenomenon rests on the fact that the circuit can't be reduced either. Both the circuit and dyslexia represent a continuum of linguistic and cognitive processes in which a variety of differences can impede the formation of the first iterations of the reading circuit. In other words, quite a few processes undergird decoding and the smooth development of reading fluency and spelling, all of which influence comprehension. Any of these components, and the speed of their processing and integration, can impede reading development.

The genetic research in different languages supports this *multi-componential view* of reading breakdown. Not only have a range of genes been found to characterize dyslexia, different genetic profiles characterize the majority of individuals in different writing systems. Predictably, these profiles involve differences that affect what is most important in that orthography's circuit. It should come as no surprise, therefore, that in some rare cases of acquired dyslexia (often called alexia), where the individual loses the ability to read after a stroke or brain lesion, only one part of the circuit is damaged, and very different behaviors result. What might come as a surprise is what happens when a bilingual adult who is fluent in reading two different writing systems has a stroke and can no longer read. Depending on where the damage is, the patient can lose the ability to read in one language but not the other. In one of the earliest such descriptions, a bilingual businessman had a stroke and lost Chinese but not English.

The lessons from over a hundred years of research on acquired and developmental dyslexia illustrate how the reading circuit can break down in different ways, depending on the individual and the writing system. The first, overarching lesson is that if something can go wrong in a circuit, at some point it does. The second lesson is related: there will be more manifestations of a particular form of dyslexia depending on what is most vulnerable in the circuit for a given language. Thus many English-speaking children will have difficulties in phoneme awareness and learning the grapheme-phoneme correspondence rules for decoding, not only because the language requires these for building the rudimentary circuit, but also because these correspondences in English are not always regular.

By contrast, in Italian and German, where the language's regularity makes decoding relatively straightforward, there are not as many problems with phonemes and decoding, but there are significant problems in fluency and how fast the circuit works. Indeed, fluency and speed-of-processing problems are more prevalent in Italian and other regular orthographies (e.g., Spanish, German, Dutch, Finnish, etc.) than phoneme-based impediments. Perhaps more insidious, however, individuals with fluency-based impediments can be more easily overlooked and not considered dyslexic because their decoding is largely spared and they look more like typical readers than aberrant ones. This is particularly the case in more transparent languages like Italian, where to this day many individuals with undiagnosed dyslexia are falsely considered lazy or *insufficiently attentive*, a phrase to which we will return.

The third lesson from a history of developmental dyslexia research is that there are going to be differences among children with dyslexia within whatever language they speak. These differences may appear more prominent in comparisons between one language and another, but they are found in almost every population. There is no single form of dyslexia, which is one of several challenges in finding an intervention that works for a particular individual.

However, one of the most far-reaching reading prediction studies ever conducted may change the whole equation of treatment for children with dyslexia. Led by my student Ola Ozernov-Palchik, in conjunction with John Gabrieli at the MIT Brain and Imaging Lab and Nadine Gaab at the Boston Children's Hospital, this study assessed well over 1,000 kindergarten children, from every economic circumstance, on a large battery of educational measures.[12] Most importantly, this work indicates that specific profiles of strengths and weaknesses in reading's development can be pinpointed before children ever learn to read, and thus before they ever fail publicly and enter an all-too-familiar spiral of learning failure.

The results depict four very different profiles that lead to future reading failure. Unsurprisingly, each of these forms represents a different impediment in the circuit. The first profile is characterized primarily by *orthographic* difficulties with letters and making correspondences with the appropriate sounds. Such a weakness in the system could be organic, but it could also spring from environments where there is little exposure to the alphabet or the English language. Children in this profile will require following over time, including further testing for any children who might manifest more rarely seen visual difficulties, or who might have more language-based weaknesses.

The three other profiles consist of children whom we know better from past research. These groups will go on to be diagnosed with some form of reading disability or dyslexia. One of them has the most-studied impediment in *phonological processes*, in which the major deficit involves representing the phonemes of the English language. These children also have discernible weaknesses in what is called *working memory*, which allows them to hold phonemes in a brief, temporary "working space," while they connect various forms of information, like letters, to phonemes. Contrary to past research emphases, the pure form of this weakness characterizes the smallest subgroup.

The next group may be the most mysterious group for teachers because everything appears smooth functioning except the speed of processing visual symbols like letters and numbers. We now know that the speed with which the language and vision regions can work together to produce the name of a visually presented item— particularly of a letter or number—will predict who becomes dyslexic in most languages studied to date. This group, which we call the *naming speed* profile, is identified on the basis of their slowed performance on Rapid Automatized Naming (RAN) tasks in which children simply name five very common visual stimuli (letters, numbers, objects, colors) repeated ten times in a serial format. This group will go on to have fluency and fluency-based comprehension problems, often undiagnosed, that will be spotted only (if ever) when the volume of material to be

---

[12] Ola Ozernov-Palchik, Elizabeth S. Norton, Georgios Sideridis, Sara D. Beach, Maryanne Wolf, John D. E. Gabrieli, and Nadine Gaab, "Longitudinal Stability of Pre-Reading Skill Profiles of Kindergarten Children: Implications for Early Screening and Theories of Reading," *Developmental Science* 20.5 (September 2017): e12471.

read crashes the system.[13] By and large, this profile comprises a slightly larger subgroup than the pure phonological profile, but it is the hardest to identify because the use of naming speed measures is less known in early prediction batteries and the weaknesses in fluent reading appear only later on. Equally flummoxing for early identification, the individuals in this group are often extremely bright and capable of finding compensatory strategies that mask their underlying difficulty. (Consider this the second bit of forecasting.)

Finally, the *multi-deficit* profile will almost always be identifiable wherever dyslexia is understood. This is the most severe form of dyslexia, with multiple areas of weakness that include phonological, decoding, and fluency-based impediments within the circuit. Often referred to as *double-deficit* or multi-deficit, this group is identified by impaired RAN and phoneme task performance and will need explicit, systematic instruction over time in all the major components of the circuit, and not just the most typical interventions that only emphasize decoding and phoneme awareness.[14]

New, ongoing research by Ozernov-Palchik and our research teams indicates that each of these profiles remains stable across the first two years of school. Further, there appear to be different patterns in brain activation for each profile, which over time will deepen our knowledge about the sources of reading breakdown in each subgroup.

The significant breakthrough of this research and other new prediction studies is that educational systems can use results like these to provide far more targeted and appropriate instruction. Everyone gains from this. The brain organization that makes these different types of individuals dyslexic in their early learning will give many of them significant advantages later in their lives—notably in areas that advantage skills in pattern analysis and visual processing like art and architecture and surgery; radiology and finance; and entrepreneurship. There are few discoveries more important to those of us who study dyslexia than to be able to predict it before the child has to endure ignominious public failures before peers, parents, and teachers. Indeed, few things are more destructive for 6-year-old children than to suddenly think that they are dumb because everyone else can read but them.

New forms of prediction and intervention can spare struggling readers some of this emotional detritus. But we can also help prevent the stigma that often accompanies a diagnosis of dyslexia through a more public understanding of the history of dyslexia in the lives of some of our most creative and successful entrepreneurs,

---

[13] Elizabeth S. Norton and Maryanne Wolf, "Rapid Automatized Naming (RAN) and Reading Fluency: Implications for Understanding and Treatment of Reading Disabilities," *Annual Review of Psychology* 63.11 (2012): 427–52.

[14] Maureen W. Lovett, Jan C. Frijters, Maryanne Wolf, Karen A. Steinbach, Rose A. Sevcik, and Robin D. Morris, "Early Intervention for Children at Risk for Reading Disabilities: The Impact of Grade at Intervention and Individual Differences on Intervention Outcomes," *Journal of Educational Psychology* 109.7 (2017): 889–914.

artists, and inventive individuals: from Auguste Rodin and Robert Rauschenberg to Charles Schwab, Nikola Tesla, and California governor Gavin Newsom.

Dyslexia is not about intelligence or about the ability to think or read deeply. If anything, many individuals with dyslexia are gifted and think in unconventional ways. They also learn to read when given appropriate instruction.[15] We need to make these facts a reality for the next generation of children, who, like all those before them, cannot understand why they have such trouble learning to read. To realize that many great artists and inventive minds also had difficulties may make the difference between resilience or failure.

It is within this context that I wish to address one of the questions I am often asked about individuals with dyslexia.

Was Leonardo da Vinci Dyslexic?

Whether da Vinci was history's most famous individual with dyslexia will never be answered, by me or anyone else. That said, there are good reasons both to ask this question and to examine the evidence as a way to appreciate the complexity of both da Vinci and dyslexia.

For the purposes of this chapter, I will describe evidence that is based on three sources: the observations by Giorgio Vasari, the first biographer of da Vinci and the only person with relatively close to first hand information; details synthesized from the cumulative historical record by the newest biographer, Walter Isaacson, in his recently published, comprehensive book; and parallels with the research on dyslexia and with my decades of experience working with individuals with dyslexia, including my first son.

As discussed by both Vasari and Isaacson, da Vinci possessed one of the most fertile, brilliant intellects of all time. To quote Isaacson:

> There have been, of course, many other insatiable polymaths...But none painted the *Mona Lisa*, much less did so at the same time as producing unsurpassed anatomy drawings based on multiple dissections, coming up with schemes to divert rivers, explaining the reflection of light from the earth to the moon, opening the still-beating heart of a butchered pig to show how ventricles work, designing musical instruments, choreographing pageants, using fossils to dispute the biblical account of the deluge, and then drawing the deluge.[16]

da Vinci was a genius who went to extraordinary lengths to learn everything he could about almost everything. That is, except Latin, the language which would have been necessary for him to become a notary like his father, and that would have

---

[15] Lovett et al., "Early Intervention."
[16] Walter Isaacson, *Leonardo da Vinci* (New York: Simon and Schuster, 2017), 519.

given him entry into important scholarship of the Renaissance. And except algebraic equations, which eluded him even though he so excelled in geometry that, according to Vasari, he bewildered his teachers in the "abacus school," his sole formal, elementary schooling.[17]

Although complex reasons relating to his illegitimate birth factored more prominently into da Vinci's failure to follow his father's footsteps, his surprising incapacity to learn Latin plagued him throughout his adolescence and adulthood. Indeed, as an adult, he would copy pages of Latin words in futile efforts to learn the language. To no avail. One of his more poignant doodles was a grimacing face in the middle of his long list of Latin words and conjugations. da Vinci's frustration in failing to learn Latin may have seemed to him the objective correlative of his lack of formal learning. It may also have been a good part of the reason that he referred to himself as an "unlettered man," with no small disdain for those who were "lettered."

To be sure, da Vinci's evolving views of forms of learning that were based more on Latin and Greek scholarship than on observation and experience is a story in and of itself. Historians describe da Vinci as the "first major thinker to acquire a serious knowledge of science" without Greek and Latin.[18] But this inability to learn Latin and algebra occurred alongside an astonishing capacity to observe patterns and think outside of every theory-given box.

Difficulties learning another language represent a frustration well-known to many individuals with dyslexia; similarly, algebraic equations, which are, at one level, yet another language, often elude them. These same individuals, however, frequently possess stunning abilities to perceive patterns, learn and apply principles of geometry, and connect seemingly disparate pieces of information. I suggest that the two unexpected *lacunae* in da Vinci's otherwise awe-inspiring intellectual life may well be the other side of the cerebral coin that gave him astonishing gifts for seeing what others cannot.

Several years ago a foundation that supports the formation of entrepreneurs asked me to organize a working conference for a selected group of highly successful individuals with dyslexia. When asked to delineate what was unique about their capacities, the consensus was that they were able to *visualize* whatever they were confronted with and to find patterns and connections that others did not or could not detect in the same way. From a radiologist to CEOs to the heads of major investment companies, each described an ability to visualize a problem, to make quick analogies, to discover unseen patterns, and to see alternative solutions.

In a similar vein is Isaacson's description of da Vinci's "uncanny abilities" to "discern patterns across disciplines [that] can lead to great leaps in human understanding."[19]

---

[17] Isaacson, *Leonardo da Vinci*, 30. See also Giorgio Vasari, *Lives of the Most Eminent Painters, Sculptors and Architects*, 10 vols., trans. Gaston du C. de Vere (London: Macmillan and the Medici Society, 1912–15; 1913), 4: 87–106.

[18] Isaacson, *Leonardo da Vinci*, 172.

[19] Isaacson, *Leonardo da Vinci*, 176.

Examples of this "pattern-based analysis" abound in da Vinci's thinking, like the analogy he proposed between a tree's branches and the arteries of the heart. Indeed, what has come to be known as *da Vinci's rule* is based on his acute observational skills when drawing such analogies. "All the branches of a tree at every stage of its height when put together are equal in thickness to the trunk below them," he wrote in his notebooks. "All the branches of a river at every stage of its course, if they are of equal rapidity, are equal to the body of the main stream."[20] The co-occurrence of unexpected early weaknesses in learning written language with unusual perceptual and pattern-based gifts that flourish over time characterizes both da Vinci and many people with dyslexia.

Whether da Vinci's mirror writing is part of a profile of dyslexia is a question I am also often asked but less able to address. My tutored guess is that whatever underlies the perceptual attributes that accompany some forms of dyslexia may make mirror writing easier both to write and decode. When the Smithsonian asked me and the director of the Dyslexia Foundation, Will Baker, to help create a short film on why da Vinci might have been dyslexic, they set up a mock experiment on mirror writing. They asked two typical readers and two individuals with dyslexia, Will and my son Ben, to read words written in mirror-script as fast as possible, and then to copy other ones. There was no contest. Will and Ben were far and away faster and more accurate in both reading and copying than the two non-dyslexic subjects.

Hardly the stuff of science, this anecdote nevertheless shows how much easier mirror writing might be for those who possess a different organization of the brain. Further, this ease with mirror-text may be connected to a recent explanation for why some persons with dyslexia make reversals at a higher rate and for a longer time than others. According to Dehaene, the ability that all of us have to see a cup as a cup regardless of how it is rotated is related to how some individuals with dyslexia see letters. For them, often-reversed letters like *b* and *d*—much like the cup that is up or down—appear to be the same entity. Along the same lines, the perceptual tendency to see "all sides" of an object or a letter may also make mirror writing more easily decoded and written. Thus, while it is often assumed that the mirror writing of da Vinci was based on the fact that he was left-handed and wrote and painted from left to right so as not to "smudge," there may well have been deeper, neurologically based roots to the development of his secret form of writing.

From the perspective of modern cognitive neuroscience, da Vinci reflects the combination of gifts and unexpected weaknesses that is unique to dyslexia. But did da Vinci have difficulties reading, the major impediment that usually marks the diagnosis of dyslexia? It is a matter of personal record that da Vinci read as many books as he could *in Italian* and compiled lists of books he wanted to read. Recall that Italian represents a regular writing system with almost a one-to-one correspondence between every letter and sound. Unlike English, where the irregular

---

[20] Quoted in Isaacson, *Leonardo da Vinci*, 177.

writing system makes decoding very difficult, most individuals with dyslexia in Italian decode relatively well. Rather, being dyslexic in Italian is characterized by a slower, cognitively laborious, less fluent reading style that impedes but does not prevent learning to read. Such a slower learning style may have played itself out in what Isaacson concluded was an *attentional* issue in da Vinci's learning. To be sure, attention deficit is one of the most frequent co-morbid conditions with dyslexia. However, there is equal reason to speculate that the sheer time da Vinci may have had to invest in trying to learn algebra and read Latin caused him, often as not, to shift his attention elsewhere, even when poring over the lists of Latin words he forced himself to study. In other words, the very quickness of da Vinci's intellect in all other domains may have made the labor-intensiveness needed in his areas of weakness more untenable and everything else of much greater interest.

Given his boggling powers of observation, da Vinci may even have been subtly aware of this difference in himself. I have always been struck by the various possible levels of meaning in da Vinci's self-deprecatory assertion that he was an "unlettered man." Although the primary meaning refers to his long struggle with not having had a classic, formal education, there may also have been a degree of awareness that letters were more difficult for him than numbers and shapes and figures. Indeed, if this conjecture about da Vinci's awareness has any validity, it may have figured in Vasari's colorful account of what da Vinci thought comprised the ideal life of the artist. Whether apocryphal or true, da Vinci is supposed to have responded that it would include always having someone by his side to read to him.

This wish adds a feather of weight to my own admittedly wishful hypothesis that da Vinci was indeed dyslexic, but with a less known manifestation of it. If pushed, my ultimate, unprovable hypothesis is that da Vinci was born with that form of dyslexia, seen more often in Italian than other languages, characterized by reading that is accurate but laborious and, as often as not, accompanied by word-retrieval difficulties that are particularly evident in the learning of other languages. Perhaps predictably, this is the form of dyslexia that remains most mysterious in the research literature because it is frequently never diagnosed and is indexed largely by *naming speed*, which many educators do not assess.

We will never know with any certainty whether da Vinci would be considered dyslexic today. What we do know is that Western culture is the fortunate recipient of the unique brain organization that may well have contributed to da Vinci's being an "unlettered man" at the same time that it provided the world with some of the greatest works of art and invention ever created.

*   *   *

This chapter began with a description of the beauty and multiplicity of processes in the deep reading brain circuit and continued with a description of the complexities of dyslexia and the potential destructiveness caused when dyslexia is not understood or, as is still the case in many places, *acknowledged*. I have used da Vinci's example as bookends in this chapter for two related reasons. First, as a researcher, I sought to underscore one of the most important insights in modern cognitive neuroscience, which da Vinci understood centuries earlier: the timeless reciprocal relationship between what we perceive and what we know, which, in its unfolding over time, expands human thought and human invention. His life is testimony to this insight. Second, as a researcher-mother, I sought to examine the unique gifts of da Vinci alongside his unexpected weaknesses in language as the most beautiful example in modern history of what can co-occur in one form of dyslexia. Whether or not da Vinci was dyslexic is less important than the very real possibility that *he well might have been.*

FURTHER READING

Davis, Philip. *Reading and the Reader*. Oxford: Oxford University Press, 2013.

Dehaene, Stanislas. *Consciousness and the Brain: Deciphering How the Brain Codes our Thoughts*. New York: Penguin, 2014.

Eagleman, David. *Incognito: The Secret Lives of the Brain*. New York: Vintage, 2012.

Richter, Irma A., ed. *Selections from the Notebooks of Leonardo da Vinci*. New York: Oxford University Press, 1952.

Seidenberg, Mark. *Language at the Speed of Sight: How We Read, Why So Many Can't, and What Can Be Done About It*. New York: Basic Books, 2017.

Wandell, Brian A., and Jason D. Yeatman. "Biological Development of Reading Circuits." *Current Opinion in Neurobiology* 23.2 (2013): 261–8.

FUTURES

26

TRACKED

WHITNEY TRETTIEN

A track is a groove drawn in a pliable surface, like mud or shellac. Future readers both human and machine follow the line it lays.

This essay lays down a few grooves on tracked reading.

Track 1: Blushing Books

The first thing one notices about *READ (past, tense)*—a small artist's book by Heather Weston—is how red it is. Its cover is a solid crimson, its pages, too; every surface flares maroon. The next thing one notices, picking the book up, is how it feels. The title "READ" is embossed in raised capitals along the top, with "(past, tense)" lowered and lowercase along the fore-edge. The texture touches the fingertips before the eyes, then enters the ear, where the reader hears the homophony: rɛd, *red*, *read* (in the past tense). This is a book that blazons its presence even as its text shies away from being read, choosing to reveal itself through other senses.

Still, the most remarkable thing about this book can only be experienced by reading the red pages. This is a text about social anxiety, and, between the covers, the reader finds an embarrassed narrator. "Everyone else seemed to be able to hide their awkwardness, nervousness," she says, "but mine was there for all to see. And I was quite conscious of it. Exposed and hot." As she reads, the reader notices a subtle change in the book. Under the warmth of her fingertips, the exposed surface of the page begins to turn white, washing away the main story to reveal another smaller subtext printed beneath (Figure 26.1). The heat-sensitive surface turns red again once exposed to the cool air, so the subtext can only be snatched in small fragments: "distract me from fragility"—"sharpened"—"Avoid this at all cost."

The book is blushing to be touched.

I've had the pleasure of introducing this deceptively simple artist's book to a number of readers, and their reactions at this point—the point of discovering that

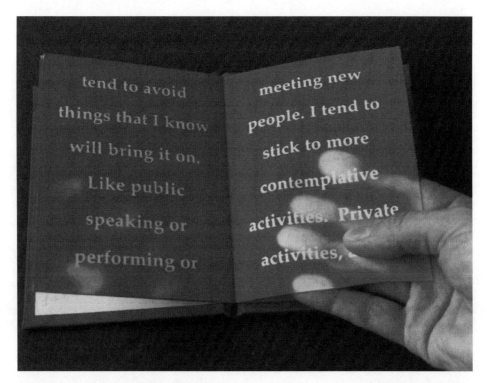

Figure 26.1 Heather Weston, *READ (past, tense)* (London: Heather Weston, 2000). Image by Heather Weston, used with permission.

a subtext lies beneath the heat-sensitive surface—tend to fall into two categories. One type of reader begins aggressively pawing at the book. She cracks back its spine to create the widest opening possible, then lays it on the table and, standing over the exposed text, leans hard, one hand on each page. She holds this position for thirty seconds, a minute, before stepping back quickly to inspect what the ghostly outline of her white handprint has revealed. It's a belligerent and potentially destructive strategy: reading as the molestation of a text that refuses to fully reveal itself in the ways that readers expect. And for all that, it isn't a particularly successful method. The reader never seems to have enough time to read an entire page opening, certainly not to consider how the subtext might interact with the main text, which—since it is white—disappears with the red heat-sensitive ink. She is inevitably frustrated, then disappointed. Why would someone go to the trouble to write something that cannot be read? In her frustrations, she likely forgets that this is a text about fear of public exposure. In forgetting, the reader inadvertently becomes one of the narrator's harassers, prodding on her anxiety.

The other type of reader reacts in the opposite manner. As soon as she begins to notice the pages turning white where she holds the book, this reader jumps away. It has become a hot object, reactive and alive; she worries that her touch is hurting or destroying this suddenly animate thing. She closes the book and sets it down with an anxious look, or perhaps turns to me and apologizes for marking the pages. She herself might even blush as red as the book. There are, in my experience, fewer of these readers—most are sucked in by the mystery of the subtext and will do anything to try and expose it—but they do exist. And in a sense, they are the more sympathetic ones. By noting the book's reaction and responding in kind, this reader honors the narrator's wishes to be left alone, helping her to "avoid things" that "will bring [the blushing] on." But she also gives up on being able to access the story, whether in the text or the subtext. The narrator remains unknown, her thoughts locked away in the closed codex. Here, to respect the book's desires is simply to refuse to read it at all—a fact that would seem to be in tension with the very existence of the thing itself as a book, an object that seems, if nothing else, designed to be read.

The brilliance of Weston's artist's book is precisely how its interactive design draws the reader into this feedback loop of anxiety, affect, and desire. As any blusher knows, the fear that attends that sudden flash of heat in the face is not just the fear of turning red in public, but the fear that this redness will draw even *more* attention to one's face. "As soon as it started," the narrator says of blushing, "I became so aware of it that it would deepen by the second. Then I'd be embarrassed by my embarrassment." By blushing to the touch, the book seems hyper-aware of—anxious about, even—your presence and your handling of its pages. More, it makes you aware that it is reading you as you read it; it is tracking the placement of your fingers, the spread of your body's warmth, making you as conscious of yourself in relation to it as it is of you. This responsiveness draws you into an affective relationship, forcing you to decide the ethics of your interaction: Will you prod on the blushing, or leave the book be? What does the object want? What does the narrator want? And how are these inanimate desires in tension with your own? The white flush washes away the red color that the narrator hates so much; maybe the text *wants* you to touch it. Perhaps your hot, human hands soothe its anxieties. Or perhaps they harass the narrator, who—wanting to avoid the downward spiral of blushing—only wants to be left red, and read (in the past tense).

Track 2: Sourcery

Recently a research team based out of Harvard—Eric Mazur, Gary King, Brian Lukoff, and Kelly Miller—debuted Perusall, a new digital platform for collaborative reading and annotation, easily integrated into existing Learning Management Systems like Blackboard or Canvas. Here's how it works: instructors upload or order textbooks, articles, and PDFs in Perusall. Students then read this e-content within the platform, leaving annotations, adding comments, or marking confusing passages in the text. The platform watches the students as they read, tracking how long they spend (or don't) on every page and automatically "scoring" each individual's engagement. It even generates a "student confusion report" for the instructor when large numbers of readers appear to get stuck on particular sections. By automating the process of participation grades through digital social annotation, Perusall promises to improve student comprehension while saving instructor time and making classroom discussion more productive. "Setup in less time than dealing with your bookstore," the website claims, "and don't worry about: ordering books; grading certain assignments; answering many student questions; keeping track of students falling behind or insufficiently motivated; obtaining copyright permissions for articles; and keeping up-to-date on cutting edge educational innovations."[1]

The mechanisms by which the platform does all this are hidden to its users, both students and instructors. It does not show the digital fingerprints of the students as they traverse the text, other than those they choose to leave, like comments. It does not expose the parameters used to score engagement or define "confusion." Nor does it offer students the opportunity to determine their own style of engagement. Indeed the success of the system—its utility to instructors—depends upon its opacity. To reveal the workings of the algorithm would expose the "sourcery" of the software, to borrow a term from Wendy Chun—the sense of magic and near frictionless content mastery it offers its target audience.[2] From this sense of magic unfolds the productive fiction that reading is a singular process, organized along an axis that runs from confusion to clarity, and that all readerly relations to a text can be effectively operationalized and so controlled.

Track 3: The Beehive

Francis Daniel Pastorius must have been one of the most obsessive readers of colonial America. Not only did he track nearly everything he read, keeping long lists of books he owned or borrowed, he also extracted from those books every tidbit of wisdom they would afford the curious mind: proverbs and poems, epitaphs and Biblical citations, recipes and advice and scientific findings. He then organized these excerpts alphabetically according to topic and copied them into pre-ruled slots in a massive manuscript that he called his Beehive. When this organizational system proved too unwieldy, he copied further extracts into a second notebook of numbered slots; these numbers were then linked to entries in the first, creating a proto-database structure in print. When that structure also failed, he created another smaller index linking all entries across the books—and so on. By the end of his life, the Beehive had swelled to two folio volumes of over 1,000 pages, making it

---

[1] Perusall website (http://perusall.com) (accessed July 30, 2018).
[2] Wendy H. K. Chun, *Programmed Visions: Software and Memory* (Cambridge, MA: MIT Press, 2011) 19ff.

one of the largest, if not *the* largest, commonplace book of any early modern reader and an invaluable resource for historians of reading and scholars of early America. This was not just commonplacing, it was a kind of eighteenth-century lifelogging of a single person's textual consumption, taken to its extreme.[3]

Early modern commonplace books like the Beehive have become better known in both scholarship and in popular media largely because there is something about them that seems very much of the present, of the here and now. In the urge to fragment and extract, commonplacing seems like Twitter or Tumblr; the desire to collect and aggregate one's reading now plays out on GoodReads, Shelfari, Bookly, Bookling, and other social reading sites and apps, where readers log every book they finish. Entire blog posts are written for the obsessive Pastoriuses of the twenty-first century, detailing how to maintain a personal log of how many pages read per day, divided according to metrics like genre or the gender of the author.[4] Though the analogies between past and present can seem glib, these eighteenth-century projects widen our historical lens to help bring our own bafflingly dense media ecology into perspective. They help us to better understand and appreciate our own desires by reflecting them back to us from the distance of an earlier and more alien moment.

There are crucial differences, though. Whereas Pastorius's lifelogging played out on pen and paper—limiting materials that constantly foiled his grander schemes to master all content—today readers use platforms that monitor their every behavior. Pastorius farmed his own personal data to edify his children; corporations gather readers' movements to generate digital profiles of increasingly narrow demographics, used to sell back to us a distorted reflection of our own habits. While seemingly more perfect than Pastorius's, such systems take control away from readers and lock them in blackbox technologies designed to exploit our own very human desires for connection, empathy, and understanding.

Track 4: Escape—Impossible

Know your value and you know your place in the order. To escape the boundary of the plantation was to escape the fundamental principles of your existence: impossible.[5]

---

[3] I am grateful to John Pollack and Peter Stallybrass for introducing me to Pastorius's Beehive. Much of what is known about its indexing structure is due to the diligent labors of Brooke Palmieri, who wrote her undergraduate thesis on it. Further connections to new media are being illuminated in the work of Julia Wang, another undergraduate at the University of Pennsylvania. The Beehive is held at the University of Pennsylvania, Ms. Codex 726.

[4] See, for example, Amanda Nelson, "How I Track My Reading: The Ultimate Reading Spreadsheet," *Book Riot*, September 18, 2014 (https://bookriot.com/2014/09/18/track-reading-ultimate-reading-spreadsheet/).

[5] Colson Whitehead, *The Underground Railroad* (New York: Doubleday, 2016), Kindle e-book.

It was at the end of the first chapter of Colson Whitehead's *The Underground Railroad* that I first noticed the underlining. Cora's grandmother Ajarry had been kidnapped from her village in Africa, and I was immersed in the terrors of life on the Randall plantation when—at a moment of free indirect discourse—the dashed line on my Kindle app dragged me out of the character's thoughts and pushed the digital interface back into sight (Figure 26.2). Other readers had scored this passage on the impossibility of escape, each individually etching it in her own Kindle e-book until their collective highlighting laid a dashed track across my own screen. I tap the underline, and a tooltip pops up: "2749 other people highlighted this part of the book."

Should I join them?

It is worth dwelling on the uncanny collectivity, the looped temporality, present in this moment of discovery. When I encountered this underline—a function of Kindle's "Popular Highlights" feature—no one in my physical vicinity could have known that I was reading *The Underground Railroad*. All they could see was the brushed metal back of my iPad. I felt entirely alone with the text. The appearance of the highlight on the page shattered this feeling and replaced it with something else: the sudden presence of a quantified, temporally distributed collective, these

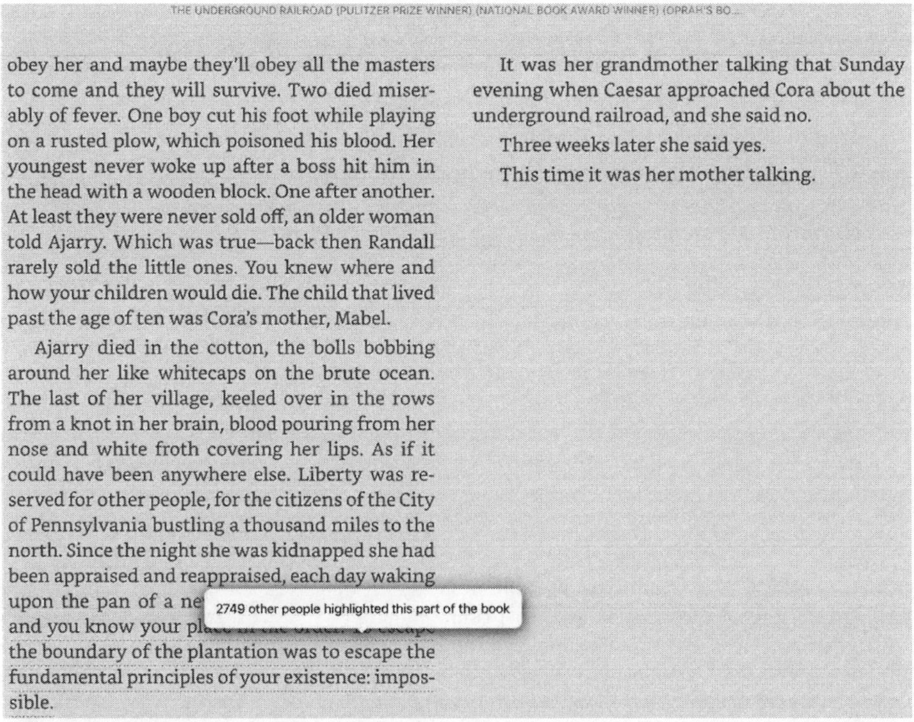

THE UNDERGROUND RAILROAD (PULITZER PRIZE WINNER) (NATIONAL BOOK AWARD WINNER) (OPRAH'S BO...

obey her and maybe they'll obey all the masters to come and they will survive. Two died miserably of fever. One boy cut his foot while playing on a rusted plow, which poisoned his blood. Her youngest never woke up after a boss hit him in the head with a wooden block. One after another. At least they were never sold off, an older woman told Ajarry. Which was true—back then Randall rarely sold the little ones. You knew where and how your children would die. The child that lived past the age of ten was Cora's mother, Mabel.

Ajarry died in the cotton, the bolls bobbing around her like whitecaps on the brute ocean. The last of her village, keeled over in the rows from a knot in her brain, blood pouring from her nose and white froth covering her lips. As if it could have been anywhere else. Liberty was reserved for other people, for the citizens of the City of Pennsylvania bustling a thousand miles to the north. Since the night she was kidnapped she had been appraised and reappraised, each day waking upon the pan of a ne[w] 2749 other people highlighted this part of the book and you know your pl[ace in the order.] [To escape] the boundary of the plantation was to escape the fundamental principles of your existence: impossible.

It was her grandmother talking that Sunday evening when Caesar approached Cora about the underground railroad, and she said no.

Three weeks later she said yes.

This time it was her mother talking.

Figure 26.2 Screenshot of Colson Whitehead, *The Underground Railroad*, taken on the author's Kindle app on an iPad Pro (August 9, 2018).

anonymous others who had also each, at some past moment, been alone together with these others and their e-books. We met not as fellow readers, sitting beside each other on a subway or in a classroom, but through the mediation of Amazon's algorithm—specifically, the parameters by which that algorithm defines a "popular highlight." Aggregating each individual's reading, this bit of technology condensed our many small acts of annotation into this dashed line left at once by all and by no one. To add my own highlighting would help ensure this track's survival; to leave it alone and annotate elsewhere would give other lines a chance at being featured in the top ten highlights of the book. Asking whether or not I should join these 2,749 others, then, is a question with consequences not just for myself or the text but for all future readers of this Kindle e-book.

Discussions of digital social reading tend to take one of two positions. On the one side are the pessimistic grumblers who see such features as an intrusion upon certain delicate social links fostered by the printed book. As Andrei Codrescu puts it, with social annotation "the entire experience of reading is shattered by the presence of a mob that agitates inside your text like strangers in a train station."[6] On the other are the optimists who see collaborative highlighting as an extension and augmentation of earlier reading practices, and a potentially exciting one at that. Simon Rowberry roots Kindle's "Popular Highlights" in the deep history of commonplacing, the practice by which earlier readers extracted aphoristic, didactic, or moral passages from texts as they read and copied them into notebooks, kept for the purpose of self-growth or moral development.[7] Tully Barnett goes even further to suggest that critics might harness digital social reading technologies to nurture a passion for literature and deepen readers' engagement with their own "commonplacing" habits.[8] Both sides capture something important about digital annotation but, to my mind, miss the bigger shifts gestured at above, shifts in the very time and space of reading itself. The technologies mediating our reading habits are forcefully directing us away from metaphors of digestion, consumption, or extraction, and toward reading as a collective process with consequences not for any individual reader so much as for the algorithm itself. What are the ethics of participation in a system that reads us as much as we read it?

What is needed are new critical methods—methods that go beyond quantitative analysis of readers' habits or a close reading of popular highlights. What is needed is a form of what Ed Finn, following Stephen Ramsay, calls "algorithmic reading": the ability to read the gap between the technologies alleged to enhance life and how

---

[6] Andrei Codrescu, "E-Book Tarnishes the Reader-Book Relationship," National Public Radio, *All Things Considered*, March 7, 2011 (https://www.npr.org/2011/03/07/134342235/E-Book-Tarnishes-The-Reader-Book-Relationship).

[7] Simon Rowberry, "Commonplacing the Public Domain: Reading the Classics Socially on the Kindle," *Language and Literature* 25.3 (2016): 211–25.

[8] Tully Barnett, "Social Reading: The Kindle's Social Highlighting Function and Emerging Reading Practices," *Australian Humanities Review* 56 (May 2014): 141–62.

they end up actually changing the world itself.[9] More, this algorithmic criticism must be knit to a robust sense of the ethical dilemmas introduced by networked social annotation on proprietary platforms. As historians of marginalia like Heather Jackson point out, marking up a text is a diverse business, and many reasons motivate readers to pick up a pen or turn on the "highlight" feature of their reading apps.[10] We annotate for pleasure and study; to remember certain passages or argue with the author; because we are writing about the text; or simply because we are bored. Some marks are just accidents. Undertaken by the individual reader, whether in print or digital spaces, such practices remain diverse and idiosyncratic. Plugged into a pro-prietary electronic panopticon, though, this plural field of readerly marginalia is reduced to quantifiable data points organized along a single metric: this passage is either popular or not popular, highlighted by a precise and knowable number of past readers.

Digital annotation is altering the history of reading, but the difference between then and now is not merely one of degree. These technologies are fundamentally redrawing the links between space, time, and texts. In the turn away from a Habermasian public and toward the quantified collective, readers enter into affective feedback loops with opaque algorithms that reshape the contours of texts over time.

Track 5: Marked Up

At the British Library is a remarkable volume: a biblical harmony cut and pasted together by the women of the religious household of Little Gidding in the 1630s. The book was made for King Charles I at his behest, and it displays an extraordi-narily sophisticated navigational schema.

Here's how it is organized: The narrative of Christ's life is divided into thirty dis-crete episodes, or "chapters." These chapters are composed of textual fragments cut from the four gospels, then remixed into three distinct reading structures. There is a parallel text layout for comparing different versions of the episode across the gos-pels; a linear narrative for reading the episode aloud; and a third system that remixes all the gospels together, with moments of repetition or even contradiction pasted in a separate typeface. Engravings and other images punctuate each chapter. The result is an elaborate assemblage of text and image where the material form of the book and the visual design of each page opening produces as much meaning as the text itself (Figure 26.3). That is, the book does not copy or reproduce the gospels so much as pull them apart into their constituent narrative segments, then put them

---

[9] Ed Finn, *What Algorithms Want: Imagination in the Age of Computing* (Cambridge, MA: MIT Press, 2017), 52ff.

[10] Heather Jackson, *Marginalia: Readers Writing in Books* (New Haven: Yale University Press, 2002).

Figures 26.3 Little Gidding, *King's Harmony* (1635), 37–40. © British Library Board, C.23.e.4.

back together into a sophisticated machinery for tracking the various networks of signification across the parables of Christ's life.

There is an obvious parallel to contemporary remix culture in the harmonies, but, more than that, there is a lesson about the role of design in habits of reading. An oft-discussed problem in digital scholarly editing is the status of descriptive markup, more specifically its relationship to the text being marked up. Do the tags wrapping a text merely *describe* or more actively *participate* in the textual expression they enclose? As Dino Buzzetti points out in a famous critique of textual encoding, they would seem to do both, suggesting a fundamental confusion in digital editions reliant upon the Text Encoding Initative (TEI).[11] In the King's Harmony, though, the women of Little Gidding invented a deft workaround for this problem by using the appearance of printed text as an inherited metadata schema. That is, switching between typefaces enables the Harmony's designers to indicate different relationships between fragments of scripture. Readers can then follow those differences by skipping their eyes from one kind of text to another. And it allows this process to happen without adding additional texts in the margins or accreting new indices and keys. In their experimental, cut-and-paste typography, the women of Little Gidding anticipate Teena Rochfort Smith's prototype edition of *Hamlet*, which—as Alan Galey has recently shown, following pioneering work by Ann Thompson—adopted

[11] Dino Buzzetti, "Digital Representation and the Text model," *New Literary History* 33.1 (2002): 61–88.

mixed typefaces to mark differences between three versions of the play.[12] In both the King's Harmony and Rochfort Smith's edition, the reader's choice to follow a particular track within a complexly networked narrative does not foreclose the possibility of pursuing other equally valid pathways—all of which are inscribed into the design itself.

Track 6: Press Paws

It's March 11th, 1445—early spring—and somewhere in the warming air of Dubrovnik, a scribe sits on a hard stool, copying government letters. His body aches. He's been at his task for hours already, and despite his cramped hand and bleary eyes, he still has a long way to go. He sets down his pen, stretches, and blinks.

Time for a break.

A cat appears purring at his knee. "Good kitty," he murmurs, idly petting her head. She hops in his lap and then—before he knows what's happening—she's on his writing desk, paw-deep in a pot of ink.

"Shoo!" he cries.

She scampers across the desk and out of the room, leaving behind a track of paw prints (Figure 26.4).[13]

Track 7: Panopticon

Most readers of e-books are familiar with Kindle's "Popular Highlights" feature and so know that Amazon is aggregating their annotations. What they might not know is that this is just a fraction of the data that Amazon collects on readers and their habits. Although it is hard to know exactly how much the company knows about each individual user—such facts are considered trade secrets, and Amazon is loathe to make public the extent of its monitoring—it would not be out of bounds to suggest they track and store data on every aspect of a reader's use of the Kindle app, from what time of day and where the reader opens a given text, to how long she spends on each paragraph and whether or not she finishes the book. Amazon knows what its customers have considered purchasing, how far they scroll down each item's

---

[12] Alan Galey, *The Shakespearean Archive* (Cambridge: Cambridge University Press, 2014), 20ff; Ann Thompson, "Teena Rochfort Smith, Frederick Furnivall, and the New Shakespeare Society's Four-Text Volume of Hamlet," *Shakespeare Quarterly* 49 (1998): 125–39. My argument about the King's Harmony is indebted to Galey's reading of Rochfort Smith.

[13] The manuscript with these paw prints is from the Dubrovnik State Archives, Lettere di Levante, vol. XIII, fol. 168r. It was discovered by Emir O. Filipovič, who has written about the document in the *Interactive Album of Mediaeval Palaeography*.

Figure 26.4 Opening from a manuscript in the Dubrovnik State Archives, *Lettere di Levante*, vol. XIII, fol. 168r. Photograph by Emir O. Filipović, used with permission.

page, whether they checked the reviews first, and what those customers eventually bought.[14] It uses this data to form profiles that suggest other possible purchases to readers. And, of course, Amazon is not the only company to track its customers. Recently Adobe was caught keeping logs of every reader who uses its e-book software, "Digital Editions," an app common in academic libraries. These logs contained information on what books the individual had checked out to the app, how long she took to read the book, and where she had read it. More disturbing, they also contained this data for her *entire digital library*—even those e-books not running on Digital Editions.[15]

Such wide grabs of data are in clear violation of the policies of the libraries who check the books out to users, as well as the reader's own reasonable expectations of privacy. Yet few institutions and even fewer individuals know that the third-party software they use is tracking readers' habits so extensively, or how to protect patrons

[14] Bruce Schneier, *Data and Goliath: The Hidden Battles to Collect Your Data and Control Your World* (New York: Norton, 2016), 28.

[15] Sean Gallagher, "Adobe's E-book Reader Sends Your Reading Logs Back to Adobe—In Plain Text," *Ars Technica*, October 7, 2014 (https://arstechnica.com/information-technology/2014/10/adobes-e-book-reader-sends-your-reading-logs-back-to-adobe-in-plain-text/).

from vendors' aggressive terms of service.[16] As Neil Richards points out in what he calls the "e-book paradox," digital reading devices feel more private in person since others nearby cannot see the cover of the book; indeed, the presumed privacy of e-books has been said to be responsible in part for the popularity of *50 Shades of Grey*, since they allowed readers to enjoy titillating literature in public spaces without fear of embarrassment. However, the very devices that seem so private actually offer few legal protections against monitoring. In fact, "data about video and library rentals are highly protected, but book purchases and reading records from the Internet receive almost no protection."[17] Amazon knows exactly when and where each of its Kindle readers enjoyed *50 Shades of Grey*; more, according to the terms of service that readers agreed to when they downloaded their e-books, the company can hand that data over to the government, law enforcement, a reader's employer, or any other third party for any reason whatsoever, without having to notify the individual herself. The result is a digital reading culture where tracking in theory would seem to violate well-established privacy laws and the policies of our public institutions but in practice has become the norm. And the more entangled our reading habits become with for-profit companies, the fewer protections a reader has.

Track 8: The Book That Was Plugged In

In 2013, a team of students at the MIT Media Lab designed Sensory Fiction, a wearable vest that tracks, and so responds in real time to, the reader's engagement with a book. The basic concept is simple. The vest senses what page the reader is on and reacts based on what is happening at that point in the story. Anxiety in the protagonist may cause air pressure bags to inflate, constricting the reader's chest, or may trigger a vibrating mechanism that increases her heartrate. A small device can heat or cool her skin according to the protagonist's environment, and LEDs can change the ambient lighting of the cover to match the story's setting or mood (Figure 26.5). "Traditionally, fiction creates and induces emotions and empathy through words and images," the designers explain. "By using a combination of networked sensors and actuators, the Sensory Fiction author is provided with new means of conveying plot, mood, and emotion while still allowing space for the reader's imagination."[18] The reader can, in a sense, inhabit the protagonist's emotional states.

---

[16] Dorothea Salo, "Ain't Nobody's Business If I Do (Read Serials)," presentation, North American Serials Interest Group conference, May 2015 (https://speakerdeck.com/dsalo/aint-nobodys-business-if-i-do-read-serials-with-notes) (accessed July 29, 2018).

[17] Neil Richards, *Intellectual Privacy: Rethinking Civil Liberties in the Digital Age* (New York: Oxford University Press, 2015), 134.

[18] "Sensory Fiction" (https://scifi2scifab.media.mit.edu/2013/12/19/sensory-fiction/) (accessed July 29, 2018).

Figures 26.5 A woman reading the Sensory Fiction prototype (December 23, 2013). Photograph taken by Felix Heibeck, used with permission.

The project's prototype—the only form in which it exists—was designed using *The Girl Who Was Plugged In*, a 1973 science fiction novella by James Tiptree, Jr., the pen name for Alice Sheldon. The story follows protagonist Philadelphia Burke, a severely disabled and depressed teenage girl. After her suicide attempt, a corporation convinces Philadelphia to undergo surgery that allows her to remotely control the beautiful and literally brainless young girl Delphi. With Burke's wit connected to Delphi's body, Delphi becomes a much-worshipped celebrity, secretly used by corporations to sell products. The story is a comment on modern culture's literal objectification of women's bodies, but—as the student designers seemed to have noticed—it is also an allegory for the complexities of reading as an embodied act. "Listen, zombie," the story begins, addressing the reader as one about to be reprogrammed through the very act of engaging with the text. The Sensory Fiction vest in turn makes this zombie-like reprogramming literal by animating the reader as a flesh-and-blood protagonist, controlled remotely by the material book.

Still, there are slippages. For instance, even as the story suggests the possibility of bodily transcendence, Sheldon refuses to erase gender as a meaningful category. The same reader called "zombie" in the first line is shortly thereafter called a "dead daddy," then "dad" and "you with your silly hands leaking sweat on your growth-stocks portfolio."[19] These direct addresses place the reader as a white-collar male worker,

[19] James Tiptree, Jr. [Alice Sheldon], "The Girl Who Was Plugged In," *New Dimensions 3*, ed. Robert Silverberg (Garden City: Nelson Doubleday, 1973), 60–61.

an identity that may not accord with the reader's sense of herself. The potential mismatch between the reader and how "he" is figured in the text runs parallel to the mismatch between Philadelphia and Delphi, as well as between the author "James Tiptree, Jr." and Alice Sheldon. By intentionally reading and likely *mis*reading the reader, then—by introducing historically contingent, intractably gendered addresses into her text—Sheldon forces you into an awareness of your own embodiment and so into the position of having to decide how you will relate to the protagonist. Will you identify with Philadelphia as a fellow female-bodied individual in a celebrity-obsessed world, and so reject the author's address? Or will you identify with the white-collar "dead daddy," and so participate in the male gaze that leads Philadelphia to suicide?

The technology of Sheldon's fiction thus generates empathy through complex narrational framing; from it unfolds an ethics. The technology of the Sensory Fiction vest is, by contrast, much different. It spurs identification with the other through forced physical correspondence, mediated by an opaque tracking technology that operationalizes affect. While this design does, like the text, draw attention to reading as an embodied experience, it offers the reader no choices, demands of her no decisions. Instead, it locks her into a body with no escape.

FURTHER READING

Dixon-Román, Ezekiel. *Inheriting Possibility: Social Reproduction and Quantification in Education.* Minneapolis, MN: University of Minnesota Press, 2017.

Hughes, Lorna, ed. *Evaluating and Measuring the Value, Use and Impact of Digital Collections.* London: Facet Publishing, 2012.

Loos, Amber, and Sarah Prindle. "Information Ethics and Academic Libraries: Data Privacy in the Era of Big Data." *Journal of Information Ethics* 26.2 (2017): 22–33.

Mayer-Schönberger, Viktor. *Delete: The Virtue of Forgetting in the Digital Age.* Princeton: Princeton University Press, 2011.

Moss, Ann. *Printed Commonplace-Books and the Structuring of Renaissance Thought.* New York: Clarendon Press, 1996.

Noble, Safiya Umoja. *Algorithms of Oppression: How Search Engines Reinforce Racism.* New York: NYU Press, 2018.

Onuoha, Mimi. *The Library of Missing Datasets* (2016 and ongoing) (https://github.com/MimiOnuoha/missing-datasets).

27

TRANSLATED

REBECCA L. WALKOWITZ

Reading in translation has changed. In the past, it meant you were reading a book that began in one language and now exists in another language. Reading in translation didn't involve a particular kind of reading. Not really. It involved a particular kind of object: instead of encountering the book as the author wrote it, in her own tongue, you were encountering the book as the translator rewrote it, in another tongue. Reading in translation presupposed the idea that writers are at home in the language they choose and that they are not at home in the languages their translators choose: authors write in native languages, called source languages, and translators write in foreign languages, called target languages. Reading in translation also presupposed a sequence: source languages always precede target languages; first, a book appears in the original, then it appears in translation. The first version is the one that counts for literary history, for cultural ownership, for intellectual property, and also for scholarship. When we prioritize the first version, we assume there is only one, and we typically distinguish between the author's labor, which we call writing, and the translator's labor, which we call adaptation. The translator interprets and rearranges, whereas the writer makes.

Reading in translation involved turning from one language to another: we read Marcel Proust's *Remembrance of Things Past*, to take a famous example, the same way we read *À la recherche du temps perdu*, except we read the former in English and the latter in French. Fluent readers of French could read the original, and that was ideal. But those who possessed English and not French could read the translation, and that was valuable because translations exposed readers to works beyond their own literary traditions and beyond the literary traditions of the languages they know. Reading in translation helped readers appreciate and learn about foreign literatures while helping writers expand and nourish the resources of the literature they create at home. Reading in translation thus appeared to be a significant but secondary experience, in at least three ways. First, translations were understood as supplements that enriched the array of books already encountered in readers' native tongue. Second, reading in translation was a back-up or compensatory practice compared to the intellectually as well as ethically preferable activity of reading in the original. And, third, translations introduced mediation, variance, and blockage, whereas reading in the original offered unmediated access to the author's words.

Since 2000, new approaches to the global history of books and the circulation of literatures across national and linguistic boundaries have been changing the way we think about translation. Scholars focused on the dynamics of world literature have suggested that reading in translation should involve more than an encounter with a stand-alone object and should be regarded as an intellectual and ethical imperative for any genuine student of literature. Writing in 2004, Lawrence Venuti argued that reading in translation should require, in addition to learning about the verbal content of a translated work, learning about the labor of the translator, whether that means learning about the relationship among the languages of source (original) and target (translation) or about the specific choices that the translator had to make in the process of creating the new version. Reading in translation thus means comparing versions of the work—in other words, reading more than one object—and also researching the history of the work's production in multiple languages. In addition, Venuti claimed, it means having an encounter with the "foreignness" of the original text.[1] Reading in translation should be an experience of estrangement: no one reading a translation should experience the kind of fluency or naturalness they experience when they read in their native tongue. The translator should produce this estrangement by creating foreign texts that seem "foreign." And the reader, confronted with foreignness, should be touched by the inaccessibility of the author's words.

David Damrosch extends this argument about estranged reading by suggesting that some literary works are foreign or translated from the start.[2] He mentions Voltaire's *Candide*, whose title page implies that the author was originally writing in German, though the novel was in fact composed in French; and José Ortega y Gassett's essay, "The Misery and the Splendor of Translation," which presents itself as a conversation taking place in French, though it was in fact composed in Spanish. Damrosch also points to literary works that have evolved through translation. In these cases, translation has to be understood as part of the work's ongoing production rather than as a part of its apparatus or reception. The most famous example is *The Thousand and One Nights*, for which translation from Arabic into French and then back into Arabic involved the addition of new tales as well as the revision of old ones. In *The Thousand and One Nights*, foreign languages are there in the original, and thus there can be no clear distinction between the domestic-seeming (original) and the foreign-seeming (translation) text. Venuti and Damrosch propose that reading in translation involves engaging with several literary histories; understanding translation as an engine of literary history and even literary

---

[1] Lawrence Venuti, *The Translator's Invisibility: A History of Translation*, 2nd edn (London: Routledge, 2002; 1st edn, 1995), 165.

[2] David Damrosch, "Reading in Translation," *How to Read World Literature* (Chichester: Wiley Blackwell, 2009), 65–85.

composition; and being open to the possible de-sequencing, or recursive sequencing, of adaptation and creativity.

In the past decade, new books and essays about the politics of fluency, the history of languages, the pathways of world literature, and the idea of monolingualism have put additional pressure on the theory and practice of reading in translation.[3] Writers, translators, and publishers have been raising questions about what we need to read and why, what constitutes native and foreign literatures, the distinction between authors and translators, and the complexity of establishing an original or first version of a work. Our sense of what constitutes a book "in translation" has changed, as has our sense of what constitutes the reading of that book. Finally, we've also changed our sense of whether a book has to belong to only one language and whether we expect a book to be at home above all in the writer's "native" or "first" language.

Three recent works in translation dramatize these changes in striking ways: *The Secret of the Blue Glass*, a children's fantasy book written in Japanese by Tomiko Inui in 1959 and translated into English by Ginny Tapley Takemori in 2015; *In Other Words*, a mixed-genre memoir of essays and short stories written in Italian by Jhumpa Lahiri in 2015 and translated into English by Ann Goldstein in 2016; and *Memoirs of a Polar Bear*, a fictionalized multi-generational memoir narrated by polar bears and their human companions and written first in Japanese and second in German by Yoko Tawada in 2011 and 2014, respectively. *Memoirs* was translated (from the German) into English by Susan Bernofsky in 2016. These works represent a very wide range of new approaches to the idea and purpose of translation. They also demonstrate the influence of translation on the production of contemporary writing, refining, and to some extent reversing, longstanding assumptions about translation as an afterthought or embellishment to literary history.

Learning to Read in Translation

The Secret of the Blue Glass is not a new work of literature, but its appearance in English is new. That fact reflects the emergence of new independent publishers which have focused on increasing the number of children's books available in English translation, especially the number of books that originate in languages outside of Northern and Western Europe, or that originate with authors from outside those zones. Pushkin Children's, the UK-based imprint that publishes *Secret*, has been reissuing extant translations and commissioning new translations of twentieth-century children's books, as well as publishing new translations of children's books

---

[3] For example, see David Bellos, *Is That a Fish in Your Ear? Translation and the Meaning of Everything* (New York: Faber and Faber, 2011); Stefan Helgesson, "J.M. Coetzee, Clarice Lispector, and the Seriality of Translation," *Translation Studies* 3.3 (2010): 318–33; and Yasemin Yildiz, *Beyond the Mother Tongue: The Postmonolingual Condition* (New York: Fordham University Press, 2012).

that were first published in the past decade, or even the past year. Founded in 2012, Pushkin Children's published the first English-language translation of the celebrated Dutch-language novel, Tonke Dragt's *The Letter to the King* (1962 Dutch; 2013 English), which has been popular for many decades among young readers in the Netherlands and continental Europe, in Dutch and other languages, and is now popular among young readers and reviewers of books for young readers in English. While children's books in Northern and Western European languages are generally familiar to Anglophone readers—think here of the Babar books and *The Little Prince* (French), the tales of Hans Christian Andersen (Danish), Grimm's fairy tales (German), and the Pippi Longstocking books (Swedish)—very few children's books are translated into English from other regions, and most authors of those books are men. Dragt diversifies the offerings by adding to the inventory of translated books by women (all named above are by men, with the exception of the Longstocking books) and because she began her life in what is now Indonesia, having lived for most of her youth in Batavia, in the Dutch East Indies. Among books in English translation published in the past decade, the website Three Percent estimates, women wrote only 28.7 percent of them.[4]

Pushkin Children's and other independent presses are altering the when and where of reading in translation. They present reading in translation as a complement rather than a supplement to reading in the original, and they suggest that children as well as adults benefit from reading books that began in other languages. Commissioning new translations and translations from underrepresented languages, they introduce readers to new sources and encourage readers to reflect on the comparative history of translated books.

Becoming a comparative reader means undoing the sequence that prioritizes reading works in our own language ("national" or "native" reading). We need to undo that sequence, first, because we may have more than one language; second, because we may not own the languages we use; and, third, because learning to read books from different places should be part of learning to read, full stop. Most of us read books in translation as children, but not enough of them, not a great enough variety, and not with an eye to the relationship among literary histories.

Pushkin's English-language publication of Tomiko Inui's *The Secret of the Blue Glass* addresses and alters the experience of learning to read. Inui was a very successful pioneer of Japanese children's fantasy, but *Secret* is the first of her works to be translated into English. Consider the interval from 1959, the year the book appeared in Japanese, to 2015, the year the book appeared in English: however famous Inui was in Japan, it took more than half a century for her work to reach Anglophone readers. Yet, it is clear from the novel that literary knowledge flowed much more quickly in the other direction. We see from references in Inui's opening pages that

---

[4] Three Percent (http://www.rochester.edu/College/translation/threepercent/index.php?id=20152) (accessed February 7, 2018).

she was very well acquainted with children's books in European languages, including children's fantasy in English. Reading *The Secret of the Blue Glass* in translation requires engaging with the comparative history of international children's literature: recognizing, for example, that Japanese writers knew about English writers, but English writers did not know their counterparts in Japanese; and observing the way this uneven, comparative scenario is built into the structure of the text.

The Secret of the Blue Glass features not one but two stories: an opening anecdote about a man who receives a package containing a story written by a childhood friend, whom he knew many years earlier in wartime Tokyo; and an internal story about a girl named Yuri Moriyama, the childhood friend who sent the package. In the internal story, we learn that Yuri was evacuated alone to the countryside, where city children were sent to escape the Allied bombing of Tokyo. Yuri meets and helps care for a family of British-born "little people," magical tiny folk who were brought to Japan before the war by an English teacher. Today, well-known children's fiction in English such as C. S. Lewis's *Chronicles of Narnia* (1950–6) and William Golding's *The Lord of the Flies* (1954) continues to inform Anglophone readers about the experience of British children who were separated from their parents during the Blitz. But in the translation of Inui's book, Anglophone readers learn that civilian bombing harmed Japanese children too. Reading the novel in translation, comparing English and Japanese books, we have the opportunity to adopt a more capacious, less nationalist approach to wartime evacuation, sympathizing with the suffering of children of Axis as well as Allied powers, and choosing to be universally rather than selectively critical of attacks against civilians. Moreover, instead of Christian universalism of the sort promoted by Lewis's *Chronicles*, in which Muslim-like characters are excluded from sympathy, Inui celebrates cosmopolitan universalism, best dramatized by the love and care Yuri extends to the Little People, who are technically enemies (British) and who will die if she does not feed them. Reading in translation, we are asked not simply to supplement our own literature but to rethink the ethos of literary and political territoriality that reading in the original has encouraged.

The opening pages of *Secret* tell us right away that even readers in the original are reading in translation, at least thematically. The narrator introduces the "special place" of his childhood in Tokyo by recalling two other special places: "a small valley amidst the sand dunes of the Sahara Desert, a magical setting out of bounds to anyone other than the person who created it, a little prince from an asteroid, a rose and a fox"; and "the delightful riverbank simmering with the silvery undersides of willow leaves where, far from the dusty world of humans, a small water rat had made his spotless home and a faddish toad had his grand hall."[5] Even readers acquainted with very few works of European children's literature are likely to recognize

---

[5] Tomiko Inui, *The Secret of the Blue Glass*, trans. Ginny Tapley Takemori (London: Pushkin Children's Books, 2015), 7.

in the first description the plot of Antoine de Saint-Exupéry's *Le Petit Prince*, which was published in French in 1943 and English that same year. (Saint-Exupéry lived in the US during the Second World War.) They may also know that the second description is taken from Kenneth Grahame's *Wind in the Willows*, also a children's fantasy book, which was first published in Britain in 1908. Reading Tomiko Inui's novel in translation, therefore, involves recognizing the longstanding translation of Francophone and Anglophone children's books into languages such as Japanese. But it also involves rebalancing that history, by considering how the addition of Japanese novels in English changes what we know about translation's effects on production, including the production of this text, and by considering how we approach the history of civilian bombing, including civilian bombing carried out by those who speak our mother tongue.

Learning to Write in Translation

Yoko Tawada's books challenge the sequence of original and translation because she often writes the same book twice, once in Japanese and once in German, producing in the second version a book that can be read as an original (because composed by the author) and as a translation (because it appeared first in another language) at the same time. This is the case with *Memoirs of a Polar Bear* (Japanese 2011; German 2014). When we read *Memoirs* in the English edition, which was translated from the German, we are reading a translation of a translation as well as a translation of an original. But we can also think about this in another way: there is really no original—no unique language of production—to read. Tawada has changed reading in translation, then, by making it the norm rather than the exception for her fiction, and by suggesting that some works of literature belong to more than one literary history. But, of course, the idea of belonging has changed, too. Whereas languages have in the past seemed to be intrinsic to the literary work, here the work seems to be natural to several languages and to imply that the author can be natural—or comfortable—in several languages, too. The novel's history of publication and translation complicates the distinction between domestic and foreign editions, native and foreign languages. The multilingual conditions of the original mean that, for this novel, there is no reading without reading in translation.

Like Inui's *Secret*, Tawada's *Memoirs* incorporates translation and dramatizes the comparative origins of its genre, in this case the fictionalized memoir narrated by a non human animal. Tawada's novel presents the memoir comparatively by invoking prior examples, such as Franz Kafka's story "A Report to an Academy," narrated by an ape; by showing how the memoir, normally a story of one, is here at least a story of three, if not more, characters; and by suggesting that storytelling and writing are collaborative rather than solitary enterprises. The "memoirs" of the title belong to three generations of polar bears. In the first memoir, a polar bear is writing and speaking in Russian, but it is not the language of her birthplace, which is somewhere near the North Pole. Told to write in her "own language," she objects, explaining, "I don't know what language that is."[6] The bear's first language is a second language, even though it is the language that she knows and speaks fluently. Because she is a migrant to Russia, Tawada suggests, the bear is always writing in a foreign language. Any translation of the bear's text would have to involve a foreign language adapted into yet another foreign language, which under the circumstances seems to be the natural or at least the primary condition of the polar bear's existence: the bear's story is suited to translation. More than this, we're told that the memoir-writing polar bear has been encouraged to model her autobiography on a Russian translation of a masterpiece of Japanese diary literature, *Sarashina Nikki*. The English-language translation of Tawada's German-language adaptation of her Japanese-language novel asks us to imagine that we are reading a Russian-language version of a Japanese-language genre. Reading this novel in translation involves thinking about the influence of translation on the history of writing and the comparative origins of the fiction (the bear's narrative) as well as the book (Tawada's text). The narrative also challenges the norms of cultural ownership, which assign literary works to one language and assume that writers have an obligation to compose in the language they own, or that owns them. Reading in translation may involve reading a literary work in a language that is native or primary to the writer but foreign to the original version of the text.

The two other memoirs in Tawada's novel are focused on the first bear's daughter and grandson, respectively. They seem at various points to be narrated by a human companion or by a bear speaking about himself in the third person. Both of these structures of narration, the novel implies, are analogues for translation. They function in the original(s) and can be registered in any language in which the novel appears, and they invite us to enlarge the practice of reading in translation to include a new awareness about the dialogic conditions of individual expression. Tawada uses the genre of the memoir, associated with the authenticity of a distinct individual, to raise questions about the isolation of languages, literary histories, and even human consciousness. In her novel, what appear to be single voices and single languages are always modified by other voices and other words. What one character says in the first person sometimes turns out to be another character ventriloquizing or sharing an experience. It can be hard to tell where ideas come from, since source and target overlap. Because the polar bears are migrants by profession—a famous writer, a circus performer, and a zoo animal—and were separated from their biological parents at an early age, their nationality is a function of adoption and friendship rather than inheritance. Reading Tawada's novel in translation, we have to consider

---

[6] Yoko Tawada, *Memoirs of a Polar Bear*, trans. Susan Bernofsky (New York: New Directions, 2016), 57.

not only the multiple origins of all novels but also that normalizing multiple origins may create a more ethical, more inclusive basis for civic belonging.

Learning to Write in a Foreign Language

Until two years ago, Jhumpa Lahiri was best known as the author of four works of English-language fiction, including her debut *The Interpreter of Maladies*, for which she won the Pulitzer Prize in 2000. However, since 2016, Lahiri has been "an Anglophone writer," as she puts it, who produces books in Italian.[7] Lahiri has published at least three of those books since 2016. In February 2016, she released *In Other Words*, a memoir about the experience of learning the Italian language, which appeared in a facing-page translation with Lahiri's original Italian on the verso side and Ann Goldstein's English translation on the recto. In November 2016, she published *The Clothing of Books*, a cluster of essays about book covers, based on lectures delivered in Italian, later published as a bilingual chapbook in Italy, with a translation into English by Lahiri's husband, and subsequently revised and slightly retranslated by Lahiri for a monolingual English edition published in the United States. The version published in New York by Vintage Books in 2016, presented as a "Vintage Books Original," is both a first and second translation: a second translation because it is based on the English text published in Florence by the Santa Maddalena Foundation in 2015; a first translation because, revising the Florence version, Lahiri updated the original Italian. That makes two, or possibly three, Anglophone books. And, finally, in March 2017, Lahiri published an English translation of Domenico Starnone's award-winning Italian novel, known in English as *Ties*. That's one more.

Lahiri has changed genres, from fiction to memoir and essay; changed original languages, from English to Italian; and changed her relationship to English, which she is using as a target language but not as a source. But Lahiri has not simply reorganized or swapped languages. She has altered the way she uses language: she is now writing in a tongue she knows—as she says—"imperfectly."[8] Her memoir is therefore not only about the experience of learning a language. It is also about the decision to give up the language she knows perfectly for a language she does not know, or does not know well. Lahiri says in the English version of her memoir, "I remain, in Italian, an ignorant writer."[9] Her Anglophone books in Italian cannot be separated into categories of original and translation. The US edition of *In Other Words* presents both languages at the same time, and the author's foreign language appears where we would expect to find her native tongue; her domestic language is

---

[7] Jhumpa Lahiri, *The Clothing of Books*, trans. Alberto Vourvoulias-Bush (New York: Vintage, 2016), 44.

[8] Jhumpa Lahiri, *In Other Words*, trans. Ann Goldstein (New York: Knopf, 2016), 113.

[9] Lahiri, *In Other Words*, 181.

used by the translator. Because Lahiri writes Italian imperfectly, Goldstein's translation is an approximation of an approximation. With approximation on both sides, there is no fluent or unmediated expression in the book at all. Reading in the original is a secondary experience, and reading in translation requires seeing as well as interpreting, noticing the format of the book and the various collaborations that implies.

Reading Lahiri's book involves thinking about two different approaches to language. The first approach assumes that there is a national language to know and that there can be perfect understanding of that language, which some people possess. The second treats language as a regulative norm, for which the appearance of perfection depends on social, political, and corporeal suppositions. When we treat reading in translation as a compensatory or optional activity, the first idea of language dominates. We use this idea every time we talk about literary works moving out from one language into other languages; or about global Anglophone fiction as a compilation of English-language works; or about multilingual works that deploy several national tongues. Yet, in the conclusion and afterword of her memoir, in her essays about book covers, and in a chapter on "The Wall," Lahiri invites us to consider how practices of collaboration and exclusion reveal a more dynamic, more historical idea of language. In Lahiri's latest books, a focus on the embodiment of books, the visual culture of words, institutions of literacy, and the mechanisms of circulation and literacy is changing the shape and meaning of Anglophone literature, and thus the distinction between Anglophone literature and literature in other tongues.

The British novelist, essayist, and translator Tim Parks, who has lived in Italy for many years, has criticized Lahiri for failing to write about Italy or Italians in her memoir. Parks is certainly right to observe that Italy is not Lahiri's topic. If there is realism in the memoir, it is not the realism of neighborhoods, local types, or idiomatic speech. There is a social milieu in Lahiri's book, but it is the social milieu of language acquisition, writing, editing, translating, publishing, and printing. Analyzing the history and conditions of language use, Lahiri tells us that she chose Italian because she sought an alternative to the languages of her environment. She had, she says, no "real need to know" Italian but was prompted instead by intellectual and emotional desire. She was looking to escape the filial, economic, cultural, and national obligations that structure her relationship to English, the language she writes fluently, and Bengali, the mother tongue she cannot read or write. As the child of immigrants, she feels foreign in both languages, though she uses English confidently. Learning Italian is thus not so much a decision to give up knowing for not-knowing, as a decision to choose not-knowing rather than have not-knowing thrust upon her.

This project of affirmative not-knowing distinguishes Lahiri from the translingual modernists whom she invokes over the course of her memoir: writers such as Samuel Beckett, Vladimir Nabokov, Joseph Conrad, and Fernando Pessoa. She thinks the difference has to do with immersion. She has not lived in a new country for decades, as Beckett did in France, and did not learn her new language as a child, as Nabokov did. Instead, she is writing in a language she has acquired as an adult, through private lessons and after living in Italy for only one year. This means that she can write in Italian only with "tools" or "scaffolding"—these are the words she uses—referring to the dictionaries, language teachers, editors, and friends whom she consults in the making of the book.

Yet, Lahiri's fundamental difference from the modernists is not really her level of fluency or quality of immersion. It is her decision to show us the collaborative process of learning and using languages. *In Other Words* may be a memoir, a genre we associate with the history of the self, but it is a memoir about the self's reliance on other selves. The memoir's form and format—the words on the page—are irreducible to one author. From the beginning to the concluding chapters and afterword, Lahiri enters into language in the company, and through the offices, of others. In this crucial way, all the words in Lahiri's memoir are "other words": words produced with others as well as words produced in a language other than her own.

Lahiri's translated book presents us with progress rather than completion: we are reading an unfinished work, in part because it begins in a language Lahiri is still learning and in part because she and her translators have rewritten the work, and will continue to rewrite it. In the US edition of the memoir, readers of Goldstein's English translation are constantly aware of Lahiri's original Italian on the facing page, and in this sense approximation is an effect of format and the history of the book. But within the narrative, too, we are asked to think about the author's imprecision—her ignorant writing—and the editing, correcting, revising, and reprinting that influenced the original manuscript. The afterword of *The Clothing of Books*, published a few months after the memoir, goes even further. Referring to the first English edition, she writes,

> Back in Rome, after slightly modifying the translation, after correcting a couple of mistakes and adding one or two new thoughts, I had to reword the Italian text, translating myself, this time from English, in order to arrive at the final version. I'm struck by this repeated crossing between the two languages in which I write. I realize how useful it is to move back and forth linguistically. I also realize that the process is endless and that, as a result, the final version continues to elude me.[10]

The "final version" at the end of this passage is different from the "final version" at the start. Using the translation in her second language to modify the original in her third language, Lahiri acknowledges that the versions of her work are no longer separate, or even serial. Translation has extended, or even trumped, production. Translation has become a method of production, and reading in translation means coming to grips with the ongoing history of a work.

Appearing as English translations of Italian books produced by an Anglophone writer, *In Other Words* and *The Clothing of Books* decouple the relationships between

---

[10] Lahiri, *Clothing*, 70.

writer and language and between writer and book that have informed our theories of world literature to date. In those theories, literature is a single-authored object autonomously produced within a dominant language before traveling out to other languages. Lahiri's books don't belong to Italian literary culture in any straightforward way, nor does she want them to. She describes her memoir as "an indigenous book, born and raised here in Italy."[11] But she doesn't claim to be an indigenous author, and indeed she has embraced Italian as a language in which she will never be a native speaker. English is the language she knows. Italian is the language she is using. In the gap between knowledge and use, Lahiri is generating a body of intralingual prose that challenges monolingual literary histories and the logic of political belonging that those trajectories have conferred. *In Other Words* and *The Clothing of Books* are English translations of works in non-fluent Italian by an Anglophone writer; they are dual language editions that present the author's national language on the target side; they are works produced in collaboration among writers, editors, publishers, translators, friends, spouses, newspapers, and publishing houses located variously in Italy and the United States; they are texts whose translations have altered their originals, and in some ways become originals; they are narratives that emphasize the social experience of language acquisition and language use, reminding us that the conditions of knowing and not-knowing are historical rather than intrinsic. Lahiri shows us that reading in translation involves an engagement with the embodiment of books and with the corporeal experience, intellectual desires, and collaborative enterprise of writers. Writing in a foreign language, Lahiri reimagines the history and future of reading.

FURTHER READING

Apter, Emily. *Against World Literature: On the Politics of Untranslatability*. New York: Verso, 2013.

Cassin, Barbara, ed. *Dictionary of Untranslatables: A Philosophical Lexicon*, trans. Emily Apter, Jacques Lezra, and Michael Wood. Princeton: Princeton University Press, 2014.

Damrosch, David. *How to Read World Literature*. Chichester: Wiley Blackwell, 2009.

Sakai, Noaki. "How Do We Count a Language? Translation and Discontinuity." *Translation Studies* 2.1 (2009): 71–88.

Venuti, Lawrence. "How to Read a Translation." *Translation Changes Everything: Theory and Practice*. London: Routledge, 2013, 109–15.

Walkowitz, Rebecca L. *Born Translated: The Contemporary Novel in an Age of World Literature*. New York: Columbia University Press, 2015.

Yildiz, Yasemin. *Beyond the Mother Tongue: The Postmonolingual Condition*. New York: Fordham University Press, 2012.

---

[11] Lahiri, *In Other Words*, 229.

28

ELECTRONIC

JESSICA PRESSMAN

Electronic reading has changed dramatically over the last three decades. From reading on large desktop screens to small mobile devices, from reading long hypertext fictions to short Flash-based poems, and now to reading text beyond screens with augmented and virtual-reality (VR) technologies, "electronic reading" encompasses diverse aesthetics, media formats, and experiences. This fact makes it impossible to describe or define any one type of reading as "electronic," let alone speculate on the future of these practices. To contemplate electronic reading, then, we might ask what we mean by "electronic" as well as what we mean by "reading." This essay explores the conjunction of these two terms by way of electronic literature.

Electronic literature is born-digital, made on the computer and with computational aesthetics essential to the poetics of the work and the reading experience of it. Ten years ago, "electronic literature" was largely limited to screens, laptops, or even desktops, and to interaction with their interfaces. Today, a cell phone, VR headgear, or even a public square works just as well as an environment for reading electronic literature. Along with changes in the technological location of electronic literature, its cultural position has also changed. No longer the province solely of the avant-garde, electronic literature is now part of mainstream storytelling and advertising—from augmented reality (AR) children's games such as Harry Potter's *Wonderbook*: *Book of Spells* (2012) to the ubiquitous use of digital flashing poetics, once associated with such new media artists as Young-hae Chang Heavy Industries, in the sidebars of social media advertisements.[1]

A focus on electronic literature exposes two things about reading in the digital age: (1) reading is no longer the sole activity and purview of the human; and (2) reading involves a participatory network of media and actors in which humans are no longer the central node. To explore these two points more fully—or, in the language of this volume, *further*—I turn to three very different and very recent works of electronic literature that each complicate simple designations of "electronic"

---

[1] See yhchang.com.

and the activities associated with "reading." Collectively, these works promote consideration about what electronic reading entails and means for an age now permeated by mobile devices and cloud computing, wherein electronic reading is a mainstay.

Point 1: Reading Is No Longer the Sole Activity and Purview of the Human

Aaron Reed and Jacob Garbe's *The Ice-Bound Concordance* (2016) is a work of AR literature comprised of a downloadable app and a highly designed, standalone book, *The Ice-Bound Compendium*. The transmedial game diegetically narrates and formally demonstrates how computers partner with humans to produce and read literature. There are two stories here, two layers intertwined to display and comment on how electronic technologies change reading. The first layer is an interactive game in which the reader-player uses her computer interface to explore a mysterious research station located in frozen tundra of the Polar Arctic. The Carina Polar Research Station holds the secrets of scientific research and of lives lost in its subterranean caverns, and it is slipping into the ice. The reader-player works against the game's timer to navigate Carina's labyrinthine structure and to discover narrative clues held within it before the station disappears beneath the Arctic surface. The second layer of storytelling is a metafictional one that comments upon the creation of the story about the Carina station. This narrative revolves around Kristopher Helmquist, author of a popular cult science fiction novel who died before finishing his latest book, destined to be a bestseller. In the wake of his death, his publishing company, Tethys House, uses forensic brain scans of the author to create an Artificial Intelligence (AI), a "simulacra fiction" or "simfic" named KRIS tasked with finishing Helmquist's novel. In this layer of narrative, the reader-player's goal is to help the AI become an author. The novel you two are to collaborate in finishing is about, yes, a polar research station called Carina. To complete the task of writing the novel (and winning the game), the reader-player must use the other media form involved in this AR world: the book, *The Ice-Bound Compendium*.

The *Ice-Bound Compendium* is a small, glossy book, elaborately printed to look like a scrapbook of Helmquist's life. It supposedly contains alternate drafts of the unfinished novel and is filled with all types of paper-based reading materials: handwritten annotations, Microsoft Word screens scattered with Track Changes annotations, screenplay documents, fictional marginalia, 3 x 5 note cards, magazine cut-outs, and more. (See Figure 28.1.) The book also contains Quick Response (QR) markers that, when scanned by the computer's webcam, produce a digital connection that projects additional clues and layers of narrative onto the book's pages. You play this sophisticated game by using the bookish book, but instead of reading its content,

Figure 28.1 Jacob Garbe and Aaron Reed, *The Ice-Bound Compendium* (2015). With permission by the artists.

you scan the book with a digital reading device. The computer then reads the digital data contained in the QR codes and displays content (text and image) for the human reader-player. This transmedial circuit of literary performance positions the computer as the primary reader of the book and a collaborative partner in electronic reading. N. Katherine Hayles recently argued that such collaboration is the new normal: "biological and technical cognitions are now so deeply entwined that it is more accurate to say they interpenetrate one another."[2] The implications of this fact extend to ethics, the environment, global markets, and more. "Once we overcome the (mis)perception that humans are the only important or relevant cognizers on the planet," Hayles writes, "a wealth of new questions, issues, and ethical considerations come into view."[3] For the purpose of this essay, such questions include: what role does the nonconscious agent have in reading, and what are the implications of these new arrangements?

The goal of the game *The Ice-Bound Compendium* is to produce a novel. The narrative's conceit of working with an AI and a digital data collection for this purpose posits an implicit challenge to the core concept of the novel genre—namely, to the

---

[2] N. Katherine Hayles, *Unthought: The Power of the Cognitive Nonconscious* (Chicago: University of Chicago Press, 2017), 11.

[3] Hayles, *Unthought*, 11.

idea that an individual human author creates an individual literary work for an individual human reader. This central premise, upon which Western literary production has been based for centuries, haunts *The Ice-Bound Concordance*. The work demonstrates how we not only read *through* computers, using the machine as medium, but also *with* them as co-cognizers.

What does it mean for our understanding of literature when machines, not humans, write and read? Rita Raley examines text messaging (SMS-based) electronic literature to show how such interactive, sited, and social texts operate at conscious and nonconscious levels across human and machinic cognizers.[4] Such works produce text in real time by combining computational databases with content input by humans, resulting in textual performances that demonstrate the collaboration between humans and machine cognizers while also complicating the concept of a coherent literary "text" that can be read, let alone close read. "What one reads with a momentary peripheral glance is likely not to return and, though the moment of textual consumption might be captured and replayed through recorded documentation, that moment cannot be restaged or reenacted," Raley writes.[5] In response, such works require a different type of reading practice and purpose than standard print, one that registers a profound change in how we understand what critical reading, in particular, does. Instead of mastery, coherence, and objectivity of the sort associated with close reading and hermeneutics, we must favor the affective, fragmentary, and "disintegrated" (Raley's term). Raley's examples constitute a different genre of electronic literature than *The Ice-Bound Concordance* and my other selections in this essay, but considering them together shows how electronic reading depends upon the embodied, nonconscious, and networked. Recognizing this fact should prompt critical and scholarly literary reading practices to change along with the literature. Such changes go beyond swapping "close" reading for "surface" or "distant" and instead require more nuanced and media-specific considerations of what it means to read when reading is a collaboration between conscious and nonconscious agents.

Point 2: Reading Involves a Participatory Network of Media and Actors

This secondary claim suggests that reading requires a focus not just on text but also on the networks of actors supporting the production and reception of text. This is particularly true of critical reading, the type of scholarly reading suggested by the

---

[4] Rita Raley, "TXTual Practice," in *Comparative Textual Media: Transforming the Humanities in the Postprint Era*, ed. N. Katherine Hayles and Jessica Pressman (Minneapolis, MN: University of Minnesota Press, 2013): 5–32.

[5] Raley, "TXTual Practice," 6.

term "further reading" and the kinds of books that contain such sections for learning more by reading more. Scholarship in textual studies and the history of the book has illuminated how textual production and reading practices happen through infrastructural networks that are social, technological, political, and economic. The recent infrastructural turn in media studies provides further ways to consider the inextricability of human and nonhuman actors in networks of natural environments (John Durham Peters), ecologies (Jussi Parikka), technological systems (Nicole Starosielski), human labor (Lisa Parks), Internet protocols (Alexander Galloway), interfaces (Lori Emerson), and network aesthetics (Patrick Jagoda). These contexts and relationships inform electronic reading, and they should inform our understanding of it.

Electronic reading and electronic literature happen through networks. Real-world infrastructures of technologies and global finance power the "e" in e-lit. The adjective "electronic" describes the energy source that surges through cables to produce "signifiers of voltage differences" that enable software and coding commands to produce "flickering signifiers" onscreen.[6] Focusing on the material actualities of "electronic" invites examination of this power source as part of electronic reading. Such inquiry into electronic reading can then include critical consideration of the economic costs of electric wattage but also the effects of biochemical mining that extracts from the earth the chemicals necessary to produce the hardware used to transmit this energy source into our e-reading devices. Such examination can turn attention to political and economic configurations supporting electronic reading, including those that enable American companies to pillage the natural resources of continents oceans away in order to make slick, expensive mobile phones and e-readers and then to return said used goods to Third World countries as trash because American policy will not allow the hazardous materials to be dumped in its soil. This complicated context requires examination of what Jussi Parikka calls "a geology of media," meaning "a different sort of temporal and spatial materialism of medial culture than the one that focuses solely on machines or even networks of technologies as nonhuman agencies…the geological sciences and astronomy have already opened up the idea of the earth, light, air, and time as media."[7] Pursuing electronic reading in this vein illuminates how electronic literature is not just technological but also ecological.

My second example of electronic literature is a work that presents a lesson in the geology of media, both in its textual content and in its transmedial format. J. R. Carpenter's *The Gathering Cloud* (2017) pursues a poetic and feminist media archaeology of a central actor in the contemporary infrastructure for electronic

---

[6] The quotations are from, respectively, Friedrich A. Kittler, "There is No Software," *CTheory.net* (October 18, 1995) (http://www.ctheory.net/articles.aspx?id=74); and N. Katherine Hayles, *How We Became Posthuman: Virtual Bodies in Cybernetics, Literature, and Informatics* (Chicago: University of Chicago Press, 1999), chapter 2.

[7] Jussi Parikka, *A Geology of Media* (Minneapolis, MN: University of Minnesota Press, 2015), 3.

reading: the cloud. Stretching across a website, a book, and bookish zine, *The Gathering Cloud*'s transmedial network presents a historical and literary foundation for considering the long tail of contemporary cloud computing (which emerged only in the last ten years but, as the text suggests, has a much longer history) and how, despite the natural and ephemeral rhetoric attached to the atmospheric metaphor, cloud-based electronic reading depends on material infrastructures and labor practices that exploit natural resources and leave deep footprints on the environment.[8]

As its title suggests, *The Gathering Cloud* depicts an impending storm: the environmental crisis wrought by a digital culture reliant on harvesting from the earth natural elements to power our omnipresent devices and, then, needing to dispose of these toxic objects back into the ground. This situation, it turns out, has a long backstory. *The Gathering Cloud* explores the material, theoretical, and historical contexts behind this contemporary situation using not cutting-edge media aesthetics or futuristic narrative but, instead, a scholarly practice of media archaeology. Carpenter turns this history into poetry and presents it in an analog aesthetic that is paradoxically dependent upon digital media. The website's navigation system is decidedly bookish: the reader clicks on a "Frontispiece" or a list of plates listed "No. 1" through "No. 5." (See Figure 28.2.) The naming conventions for the naviga-

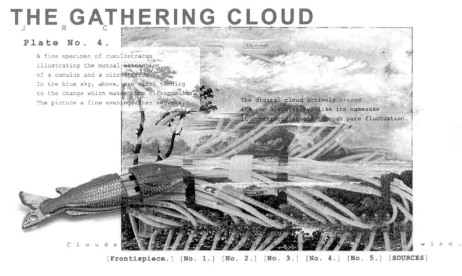

Figure 28.2 J. R. Carpenter, *The Gathering Cloud* (website 2016). With permission by the artist.

---

[8] The origins of cloud computing reach back to the 1950s (or, following Carpenter, much farther back), but contemporary iterations of the digital cloud emerged around 2011 with products such as iCloud and Amazon Cloud Player. See Tung-Hui Hu, *A Prehistory of the Cloud* (Cambridge, MA: MIT Press, 2015), ix.

tional devices reference codexical design, specifically the description of plates from Luke Howard's *Essay On the Modifications of Clouds* (1803). Indeed, the entire digital work is built upon the print structure of Howard's text, fragments of which are included in Carpenter's contemporary work. The website is full of analog-ish imagery: engraved illustrations, static photographs (rather than moving images), Courier font, and even handwritten annotations. All of this decidedly old-fashioned material is layered in a palimpsestic aesthetic suggestive of scrapbooks, that codex-based form of personal archiving that is "a material manifestation of memory—the memory of the compiler and the memory of the cultural moment in which they were made."[9] The actual codexical component of *The Gathering Cloud* presents a different type of compilation: a small poetic book whose verse collates history on meteorology and media, from ancient Greeks and Epicurean materialists to Robert Hooke, "the first Curator of Experiments/ at the Royal Society of London" in 1665, through to the contemporary digital period, to tell a story of how we arrived at our own gathering cloud.[10]

The first poetic entry is dated February 2014 and begins with a Gertrude Stein-ian sense of a continuous present: "It's raining. It has always rained. We are silt" (15). The words "raining" and "rained" appear in light grey, a visual emphasis that, in the light of the digital, serves as a visual signifier for a previously-clicked-on hyperlink. The detail suggests layers of readings, past and present, and the historical practices and pursuits that inform what is currently available to be read and known. This initial poem ends with a statement by Devon's chief scientist, Dame Julia Slingo: "We have records going back to/ 1766. We have seen some/ exceptional weather, but nothing like this./ All evidence suggests a link to climate change" (16; emphasis in original). The suggested "link" to an archival past, coupled with the shaded grey color that indexes an activated HTML link on the web, registers the layers of media practice involved in documenting and representing climate change. For Timothy Morton, climate change is the signal example of a "hyperobject"—such "things that are massively distributed in time and space relative to humans" and "force us to rethink what we mean by *object*" through challenging anthropocentric epistemologies and our sense of history.[11] "Hyperobjects are *futural*," Morton claims, and they change the way we experience the world.[12] Carpenter's *The Gathering Cloud* approaches this futural hyperobject in a literary practice that demonstrates and invites *further* reading.

---

[9] Susan Tucker, Katherine Ott, and Patricia P. Buckler, eds., "An Introduction to the History of Scrapbooks," in *The Scrapbook in American Life* (Philadelphia: Temple University Press, 2006), 1–25; 3.

[10] J. R. Carpenter, *The Gathering Cloud* (Axminster: Uniformbooks, 2017), 33. Subsequent citations will be cited parenthetically.

[11] Timothy Morton, *Hyperobjects: Philosophy and Ecology after the End of the World* (Minneapolis, MN: University of Minnesota Press, 2013), 1, 24. Italics in original.

[12] Morton, *Hyperobjects*, 122.

In its style of compilation, collage, and weaving, *The Gathering Cloud* resembles Sadie Plant's seminal book of cyberfeminism, *Zeros and Ones: Digital Women and the New Technoculture* (1997), which excavates and sutures moments from the histories of computation and feminism. Similarly, Carpenter includes in her poetics of media archaeology and geology women like Eunice Foote who, in 1856, "filled glass jars with/ different gases, and put them out in the sun./ She found that the jar containing water/ vapour and carbon dioxide heated the most" (58) and, in other words, discovered "what we now call greenhouse gases" (58). *The Gathering Cloud*'s archival assemblage connects Foote to the most famous philosopher of tools, Martin Heidegger: "During World War I, Heidegger served as a/ weatherman on the western front, near Verdun" (60). The historical detail scaffolds a larger claim: "The Heideggerian trope of vigilance/ as a paramount ethical duty was/ born during these months of scanning the sky for signs" (60). Gathering (in the language of its title) moments from diverse historical registers related to clouds, this work of literary media studies presents an archival and poetic paradigm for approaching the contemporary computational cloud.

The work teaches the following lesson: "The digital cloud is older than we think" (63). Recent scholarship in media history develops this point. John Durham Peters even includes actual clouds in his recent study of media, *The Marvelous Clouds: Towards a Philosophy of Elemental Media*: "The media of sea, fire, star, cloud, book, and Internet all anchor our being profoundly, even if we can't say what they mean."[13] Peters's expansive definition of media participates in a trend within media studies to examine the infrastructure, not just the objects, products, and practices they support. (For examples of such work, see Wendy Chun, Lisa Parks, and Nicole Starosielski.) "Media are our infrastructures of being, the habitats and materials through which we act and are," Peters writes.[14] Such habitual media structure our lives, experiences, and ways of thinking. In *The Gathering Cloud*, Carpenter writes, "The Cloud is an increasingly essential/ element of infrastructure powering/ industry, government, finance, and commerce,/ as fundamental to us as plumbing and roads" (77). Aligning the cloud with plumbing invokes Nicole Starosielski's scholarly effort to bring to the surface the undersea cables that enable the Internet to appear wireless and cloud-like. "Despite the rhetoric of wirelessness," Starosielski writes, "we exist in a world that is more wired than ever."[15] Her research shows how "[u]ndersea fiber-optic cables are critical infrastructures that support our critical network society."[16] Such infrastructure supports our ability to read. As Carpenter

---

[13] John Durham Peters, *The Marvelous Clouds: Toward a Philosophy of Elemental Media* (Chicago: University of Chicago Press, 2015), 14.

[14] Peters, *The Marvelous Clouds*, 15.

[15] Nicole Starosielski, *The Undersea Network* (Durham, NC: Duke University Press, 2015), 9, 1.

[16] Starosielski, *The Undersea Network*.

reminds us, "An email may travel thousands of miles/ and pass through multiple data centres/ to send a photograph across the street" (88). This material fact highlights how electronic reading happens through networks of computational actors, physical sites, and protocols. The human is not the central or primary node in electronic reading.

The Gathering Cloud turns attention to natural clouds and to "the cloud" of digital culture as topics and media to read. A single sentence appears at the top of a nearly blank page: "The term The Cloud refers to a cultural fantasy" (83). A wall of white follows the line, a blank space open for the projection of fantasy. The only other text on this page is a lone line at the bottom: "We walk on the bed of the sea of the air" (83). If we recall that the etymology of "fantasy" is about showing and making visible, then Carpenter's point here and throughout *The Gathering Cloud* is to expose the infrastructures that support our ability to see and thus to read. This infrastructure includes the page (see Bonnie Mak) and the computational cloud that archives the content of digital webpages. Carpenter directs her reader's attention to this infrastructure of pages, both paper- and HTML-based, through the use and arrangement of photographs. Black-and-white photographs of clouds gathering at the ocean's horizon are sprinkled throughout the book; the website also contains a page exhibiting the collected, colored images arranged in rows. These photographs depict clouds and the ocean but, more significantly, the horizon line between them. The images illuminate and expose the natural media and infrastructures that shape perspective and thus inform reading.

My final example of a work of electronic literature that illuminates the infrastructural networks of human and nonhuman actors involved in electronic reading is a very different type of literary experience. Peruvian poet-engineer José Aburto produces electric installation art that challenges expectations of reading, let alone electronic reading. "When materials that support texts change, the contents have to change," Aburto claims.[17] His installations pursue this dictum by exploring and exploiting how changes to the material infrastructures of text in digital literature change the appearance of poetry and approaches to reading it. Aburto produces installations of hybrid electronic sonic-textual poetry that operate through molecular movement and physical vibrations. These works harness and make visible the natural media forces involved in electronic reading. Because they represent a different type of electronic literature and reading experience from my previous examples, they warrant a different type and tone of description.

I first encountered Aburto's sensorial sonic poetry at the 2016 Electronic Literature Organization (ELO) conference in Vancouver. The installation was titled "Matters: Electromagnetic Poems," and it was like nothing I had ever seen … or felt. I walked toward the large tabletop box wrapped in a smooth, burlap-like fabric.

---

[17] José Aburto, "MATTERS, Electromagnetic Poems," Electronic Literature as a Model of Creativity and Innovation in Practice (ELMCIP) Database (2016).

Its top faced upwards and was printed with poetry—lines of Spanish text, center-aligned in Courier font, and printed in a traditional stanza arrangement with certain words larger and bolder than others. Nothing out of the ordinary yet. I walked closer so as to be able to carefully read the text, and I wondered where to find the "electronic" part of this poetry exhibit. The reading surface contained no screens projecting text and no apparent means of interacting with the interface. And then I saw it.

A little grey blob (or blot, as the poet calls it) moved slowly around the reading surface. Comprised of tiny iron fillings, the blot looked like a little grey mouse. The title of the work, "Blot Alive" (2016), describes the piece: an inanimate object comes to life, animated by electricity to move and also, it seems, to read. (See Figure 28.3.) Manipulated by magnets, the blot moves across the page in line with the text printed on it. Traveling around the poem, it obscures some words while exposing others. Its metallic body often adds a curlicue to the printed text, as if becoming a prosthesis to the poetry. Its presence performs the conceit of art coming to life. When I walked up to the installation, the blot was already moving. I watched this display of electric animation and followed the blot's movements, reading along with it. This work of literature does not need the human to enact and enliven it. Its electronic perform-ance animates the inanimate object (the blot) to perform an act of reading and thus prompts the human reader witnessing this performance to consider what reading means. "Blot Alive" demonstrates how nonhuman actors participate in electronic reading. It does so by illuminating the actors involved in providing material support for human reading—the minerals, magnets, and networked infrastructure—but also by transforming the experiential activity itself. The presence and movement of the little blot defamiliarizes the embodied practice of reading, while the text it traverses promotes critical attention to this experience.

Figure 28.3 José Aburto, "Blot Alive" (2016). With permission by the artist.

The text of the poem in "Blot Alive" begins with "I." The first-person perspective, along with the movement of the metallic blot across the poetic text, identifies the blot as bot—agent and actor, the "I" in the poem:

> Me muevo corrigiendo
> terrores
> sintiendo como el dolor de años podridos
> congestionar mis metales
> -mi plomo
> de plata-
> como cubren el oxido de mis decisiones
>
> --
>
> I move correcting
> terrors
> feeling how the pain of years rotted
> congest my metals
> -my lead
> of silver-
> how they cover the rust of my decisions[18]

Metal is the central component and medium of electronic reading. It provides the physical hardware through which electronic voltage passes and the material frame for electronic reading interfaces. Aburto's poem illuminates and animates the role of metal ("my lead/ of silver"), which must be extracted from the earth and "corrected" into shape before it can be used for purposes of electronic reading. This metal must also be treated so as to be saved from inevitable "rust," both of chemical oxidation and of planned technological obsolescence (the latter form of rust inevitably coming first in our digital, upgrade culture).

"Blot Alive" focuses attention on natural media, metal in particular, in ways that demonstrate how inanimate objects interact or, in physicist and philosopher Karen Barad's terminology, "intra-act." Barad coins the term "intra-action" to describe how, at the level of quantum physics, the relationships between entities are always entangled: "in contrast to the usual 'interaction,' which assumes that there are separate individual agencies that precede their interaction, the notion of intra-action recognizes that distinct agencies do not precede, but rather emerge through, their intra-action."[19] Aburto's work makes visible and aesthetic the natural infrastructures and material intra-actions that power the blot and enable electronic reading.

Aburto's other work in the ELO conference exhibition, the sibling piece to "Blot Alive," was titled "Paper Alive" (2016). This work takes even further the concept of nonhuman cognizers as co-readers in electronic reading. For "Paper Alive," Aburto wrapped with paper the top of a large bookshelf-size stereo speaker and stood it

---

[18] This translation, which does not appear in the work, is by Kaitlin Sweeney.
[19] Karen Barad, *Meeting the Universe Halfway: Quantum Physics and the Entanglement of Matter and Meaning* (Durham, NC: Duke University Press, 2007), 33.

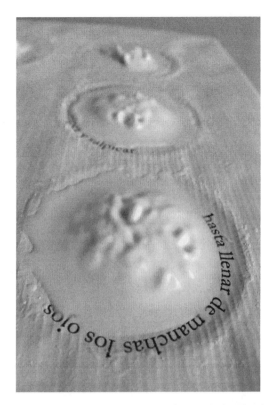

Figure 28.4 José Aburto, "Paper Alive" (2016). With permission by the artist.

upright on the ground. He inscribed the top of the paper-covered surface with large circles of poetry. In the center of these poetry circles, he placed a pale cream-colored and viscous non-Newtonian fluid. The fluid responds to the vibration of the stereo, and the stereo, in turn, vibrates in response to the proximity of a human viewer/reader. When a reader approaches the stereo speaker, her physical movement sets off a feedback loop of interactions: the liquid in the center of the poetry circle vibrates, shakes, bubbles, and even spurts vertically as if dancing in response to the human's approach. (See Figure 28.4.) When the reader steps away from the installation, the liquid ceases its dance. The text remains the same regardless of the reader's position, but "Paper Alive" animates the reading surface in ways that promote consideration about what constitutes reading and who (or what) is doing it.

In both of Aburto's works, poems are inscribed on page-like surfaces and their textual content remains unchanged. The works employ a network of electromagnetism to charge the movement of a nonconscious co-reader, a metallic blot and a liquid dancer, and also to stimulate embodied reading experiences for the human reader: she feels the physical vibrations from the stereo in "Paper Alive" and experiences the slow ticking of time as the blot inches along in "Blot Alive." Aburto's poetry installations register how electronic reading is embodied and distributed across a network of actors and forces, both natural and man-made.

*   *   *

The works of electronic literature examined in this chapter demonstrate how electronic reading is not solely about screens, hyperlinks, and digital code. Electronic reading is transmedial, embodied, and part of everyday experience. Indeed, the qualifier "electronic" might just be superfluous or outdated, for *all* reading is now informed by digital technologies, practices, and poetics. In our post-digital moment, in which "the digital expression holds less fascination," we see a change in electronic literature.[20] As my case studies demonstrate, contemporary electronic literature moves away from modes of distinctly "digital expression," screens and interactivity, to transmedial networks that incorporate older media (e.g., the book) and natural media (e.g., electromagnetic systems). The result: electronic reading becomes *just* reading. However, as this volume explores, *just* reading is never so simple.

FURTHER READING

Carpenter, J. R. *The Gathering Cloud.* Website. 2017 (https://luckysoap.com/thegathering-cloud/index.html).

Carpenter, J. R. *The Gathering Cloud.* Axminster: Uniformbooks, 2017.

Chun, Wendy Hui Kyong. *Updating to Remain the Same: Habitual New Media.* Cambridge, MA: MIT Press, 2016.

Emerson, Lori. *Reading Writing Interfaces: From the Digital to the Bookbound.* Minneapolis, MN: University of Minnesota Press, 2014.

Galloway, Alexander. *Protocol: How Control Exists After Decentralization.* Cambridge, MA: MIT Press, 2004.

Hayles, N. Katherine. *How We Became Posthuman: Virtual Bodies in Cybernetics, Literature, and Informatics.* Chicago: University of Chicago Press, 1999.

Hayles, N. Katherine. *Unthought: The Power of the Cognitive Nonconscious.* Chicago: University of Chicago Press, 2017.

Hayles, N. Katherine, and Jessica Pressman, eds. *Comparative Textual Media: Transforming the Humanities in the Postprint Era.* Minneapolis, MN: University of Minnesota Press, 2013.

Jagoda, Patrick. *Network Aesthetics.* Chicago: University of Chicago Press, 2016.

Kittler, Friedrich A. "There is No Software." *CTheory.net* (October 18, 1995) (http://www.ctheory.net/articles.aspx?id=74).

Mak, Bonnie. *How the Page Matters.* Toronto: University of Toronto Press, 2011.

Parikka, Jussi. *A Geology of Media.* Minneapolis, MN: University of Minnesota Press, 2015.

[20] Christian Ulrik Andersen and Søren Pold, "Manifesto for a Post-Digital Interface Criticism" (January 10, 2014) (http://mediacommons.org/tne/pieces/manifesto-post-digital-interface-criticism). On "post-digital," see also Florian Cramer, "Post-Digital Writing," *electronic book review* (December 12, 2012) (https://electronicbookreview.com/essay/post-digital-writing/).

Parks, Lisa. "'Stuff You Can Kick': Toward a Theory of Media Infrastructure." *Between Humanities and the Digital*, ed. Patrik Svensson and David Theo Goldberg. Cambridge, MA: MIT Press, 2015, 355–73.

Parks, Lisa, and Nicole Starosielski, eds. *Signal Traffic: Critical Studies of Media Infrastructures*. Urbana: University of Illinois Press, 2015.

Peters, John Durham. *The Marvelous Clouds: Toward a Philosophy of Elemental Media*. Chicago: University of Chicago Press, 2015.

Plant, Sadie. *Zeros and Ones: Digital Women and the New Technoculture*. New York: Doubleday, 1997.

Reed, Aaron, and Jacob Garbe. *The Ice-Bound Concordance*. App. 2016.

Reed, Aaron, and Jacob Garbe. *The Ice-Bound Compendium*. Simulacrum Liberation Press, 2016.

Starosielski, Nicole. *The Undersea Network*. Durham, NC: Duke University Press, 2015.

29

INTERFACED

LORI EMERSON

"What is a Computer?"

In November 2017, Apple launched yet another advertisement for the iPad Pro in its never-ending campaign to vanquish not merely "the competition," and not merely the computing industry's sense of what's possible, but computers as such—or, rather, our awareness of there being programmable computers at all. Shamelessly drawing from the prevailing belief that teenagers are the most valuable consumer demographic when it comes to tech, the commercial opens with a young person about 13 or 14 years old, gender indeterminate, sailing away from a New York City walk-up apartment on his or her fixie and into the free-wheeling world of urban teen hang-outs. From stoops to parks, sidewalks, vintage furniture stores, taco shops, coffeeshops, buses, and even tree branches, we see her (this vibrant young person who appears entirely "of" the modern world turns out to be a "she") chatting with friends online, drawing hearts on the screen with a stylus, snapping social media appropriate "pics," and creating mixed media art—all to the tune of electronic pop duo Louis the Child's refrain of "where is it you want to go?" The advertisement is only sixty seconds long, but already, forty-five seconds in, we know without a doubt that this pre-teen knows better than we do that with this device, not even noticeable *as* a device, you can go anywhere and do anything—precisely because it is as much a perfect extension of her as she is of the iPad.

The ad closes with the pre-teen lounging in her backyard, iPad resting on the grass as if it's also as much a part of the natural world as flowers or trees, while she easily and unselfconsciously is immersed in what we can only assume is a magical land on the other side of the screen (since we're never shown anything so banal as an operating system). With only seven seconds left, this world of teen magic is suddenly interrupted by a friendly neighbor in her 40s or 50s who leans over the backyard fence and asks, "Whatcha doin' on your computer?" The young woman responds not by explaining what she's doing or what she's seeing in the parallel world of digital magic but with what we are supposed to think is an unanswerable question: "What's a computer?"[1]

The message is clear: the iPad is itself a kōan—a Zen Buddhist riddle intended to bring us to enlightenment as it demonstrates the inadequacy, even pointlessness, of logical reasoning in the face of both such a marvelous device and capitalism more broadly as well as the inadequacy of object categories as such. The iPad overcomes all boundaries that might keep you estranged from any place, person, thing, or experience. As the Austrian philosopher Günther Anders might say, Apple presents a world to us which is a *fait accompli*, where the commodification of every last bit of world and experience has been both alienated and banalized to such a degree that everything appears as perfectly present, even as it is utterly absent. Writing in 1956, at the beginning of the era of television, and eerily describing our contemporary world that is completely and invisibly saturated with digital devices, Anders urges us to understand:

> The deception in question here consists...in the fact that we, despite living as we do in an *estranged* world, as consumers of films, radio and television...seem to be on friendly terms with everything and everybody: people, places, situations, events, even the most surprising, or precisely the most surprising, ones...This phenomenon of pseudo-familiarization...we call "*banalization of the world*"...because what is taking place here does not consist in our abandonment to the strange or the bizarre, but in the fact that we are supplied with strange people, things, events and situations as if they were totally familiar...when all the various and variously distant regions of the world are brought equally close to us, the world as such vanishes.[2]

More than sixty years later, "the world as such" has vanished because it is now almost completely mediated by digital devices whose interfaces have been intentionally designed to disappear from our awareness; without an ability to see where one thing or person or experience ends and another begins, we are left in a state of constant estrangement. And while one might object that Apple products hardly represent the entirety of contemporary life, even advertisements for biologic medications such as Humira—designed to treat arthritis, Crohn's disease, psoriasis, and other conditions—attempt to persuade viewers to buy their product via the representation of touchscreen interfaces superimposed over images of inflamed joints, superimposed one more time on top of another image of an underlying layer of interface. The dream, on its way to becoming reality, is for all the world to be an interface.

However, as I discuss in this chapter's third section, the range of reading practices across media studies, along with literature and the arts, are uniquely positioned to

---

[1] Apple, "What is a Computer?" YouTube (accessed January 20, 2018).

[2] Günther Anders, "The Obsolescence of Man, vol. I, part 2: The World as Phantom and as Matrix: Philosophical Considerations on Radio and Television," translator unknown, Libcom.org (https://libcom.org/library/obsolescence-man-volume-i-part-two-%E2%80%9C-world-phantom-matrix-philosophical-considerations-r) (accessed January 15, 2018).

do what Human-Computer Interaction (HCI) designers and Silicon Valley cannot or will not do. They have the capacity to work with and against the grain of ubiquitous, nearly invisible interfaces; media studies and literature and the arts can reveal the ways in which these interfaces too often foreclose on our access to information, knowledge, and creativity, and they can also re-insert values such as accessibility, transparency, and configurability, if not into the design of interfaces themselves, then at least into our experience of these interfaces.

What is an Interface?

"Interface" is, for better and for worse, a flexible term that crosses many disciplinary boundaries and has both technical and everyday usages. In computing, interface refers to any number of configurations of hardware and/or software that act as intermediaries between humans and computers. In *Reading Writing Interfaces*, I settle on a more specific definition: interface is

> a technology—whether it is a fascicle, a typewriter, a command line, or a GUI [graphical user interface]—that mediates between reader and the surface-level, human-authored writing, as well as, in the case of digital devices, the machine-based writing taking place below the gloss of the surface.[3]

In this sense, it is a threshold along the lines of Alexander Galloway's articulation of interface as "the point of transition between different mediatic layers within any nested system."[4] Seeing the interface as a threshold rather than as a separation or a firm boundary highlights how it both grants and denies access to whatever lies on the other side, thereby hiding and revealing the operationality of underlying layers.

However, the colloquial usage of "interface" especially common in corporate culture also reveals some important aspects of the concept that are, surprisingly, not apparent in its usage in computing. That is, "interface" can also refer to face-to-face communication—a usage that draws on the prefix "inter" (meaning between or shared) and "face," whose Latin root ("facies") refers to an individual's face as well as surface or front. In this usage, one's face or visage is a kind of permeable boundary lying between one's inner life and the outside world—a usage that also brings to light the fact that Western culture has been struggling since Plato to overcome technology-related boundaries such as writing in order to have a more direct relationship between oneself and the outside world. As Plato laments in *The Phaedrus*, writing is nothing more than an amusement and an external reminder (a copy of a copy) of the eternal forms that one should already know in one's soul. Thus, for Plato writing is a poor interface by which to both represent and access true wisdom.

---

[3] Lori Emerson, *Reading Writing Interfaces: From the Digital to the Bookbound* (Minneapolis, MN: University of Minnesota Press, 2018), x.

[4] Emerson, *Reading Writing Interfaces*, x.

While we can broaden and situate our contemporary understanding of interface by going back and re-interpreting Greek philosophical debates as being about something akin to an interface, the earliest use of the term was in nineteenth-century physics. As Peter Schaefer carefully delineates, "interface" has a longer history than the *Oxford English Dictionary* (*OED*) would lead us to believe.[5] While the *OED* cites Irish physicist James Thomson Bottomley's use of "interface" in 1882 as the earliest instance, James and William (later Lord Kelvin) Thomson are in fact responsible for coming up with the term in the 1870s in the context of thermodynamics. The term's first use in print appears in "Notes and Queries—on Gases, Liquids, Fluids" by William Thomson, who credits his brother James for coming up with it to describe the entity in James Clerk Maxwell's thought experiment that became known as "Maxwell's Demon."[6]

Maxwell's thought experiment was designed to further our understanding of the second law of thermodynamics; his original scenario describes a closed chamber full of hot and cold gas molecules, a wall dividing the chamber in half, and a small doorway at the dividing line that is guarded by a so-called demon who quickly sorts hot molecules into one half of the chamber, leaving cold molecules on the other side. The scenario demonstrates that if such a perfect sorting of molecules were possible, the second law of thermodynamics would be violated; thus, in order to maintain entropy in the chamber, the demon needs to allow molecules to pass to and from both sides of the chamber. For the Thomsons, the demon stationed at the opening is not so much malevolent as it is a *mediating* force that they call an interface, making it clear that boundaries marked by such an interface must be permeable in order to allow energy to flow from one side of the interface to the other and back again. Thus, briefly returning to the example of the iPad that opens this essay, Thomson's nineteenth-century musings about interfaces and energy flow illustrate that while twenty-first-century devices want us to believe that all boundaries have not simply been permeated but rather overcome altogether, the fact remains there is a real boundary between human and computer; obfuscating this fact risks losing all understanding of how the device is at least partly shaping and defining our access to knowledge, information, and our creative capacities. It is not just that interfaces *are* permeable—their permeability also needs to be visible in order for there to be a genuine interaction between human and computer.

The idea that interfaces are part and parcel of media technologies in particular and, moreover, that they are by necessity permeable first appears in Marshall McLuhan's *Understanding Media*, a seminal work that inaugurated the field of media studies as we now know it. As Richard Cavell points out, the use of the term

---

[5] Peter Schaefer, "Interface: History of a Concept, 1868–1888," in *The Long History of New Media: Technology, Historiography, and Contextualizing Newness*, ed. David W. Park (New York: Peter Lang, 2011), 163–75.

[6] James Thomson, "Notes and Queries—On Gases, Liquids, Fluids," in *Collected Papers in Physics and Engineering* (Cambridge: Cambridge University Press, 1912), 327–33; 327. Italics in original.

"interface" in *Understanding Media* is far from coincidental, as he was heavily influenced by the "new physics" during his time at Cambridge in the 1930s much more than he was influenced by the "new critics."[7] I will discuss McLuhan in greater detail in the third section; for the moment, it's clear in this field-defining book that, for McLuhan, as well as for the Thomson brothers, an "interface" is a porous surface by which and through which humans and media engage in a never-ending process of translation and assimilation into the other's terms. Such an understanding of interface becomes crucial when we find that in the mid-1980s "interface" leaves behind its connotations of permeability and co-constitution, and instead starts to mean the attempt to only translate media into human terms.

Returning once more to the world of computing, the notion of interface as the *separation* of, rather than threshold or permeable boundary between, human and computer is most at issue in the field of HCI. The latter is a field of study that fully emerged in the 1980s—more precisely, in 1984 with the release of the Apple Macintosh—as the computer industry sought to move the computer away from its reputation as a niche device for tinkerers or homebrewers and toward something more akin to an everyday appliance. Apple's Jeff Raskin and Steve Jobs both sought to create a hardware and software system for an "identical, easy-to-use, low-cost appliance computer," which meant that rather than having the ability to configure the computer from the inside out, the goal was to create a computer that was hermetically sealed and only configurable to the extent that one could drop software in via a floppy disk, just as you might drop a piece of bread into a toaster.[8] And, of course, once the computer becomes an appliance, it also ceases to be programmable on the user side, thereby ceasing to be a computer—a situation perfectly illustrated thirty-four years later by the closing line of the iPad Pro commercial disguising this fact with the question, "What is a computer?" Since the release of the Apple Macintosh in the mid-1980s, HCI designers have largely focused on giving users the impression that their interactions with the computer resemble, as closely as possible, interactions with another human via seemingly open-ended dialogue with some combination of keyboard, screen, mouse, desktop, and, most recently, gesture and voice.

Certainly a disappearing interface can be tremendously useful—think of the expert pianist who can perform rapid scales up and down the keyboard without focusing on individual keys; or, think of the speed typist who never looks at the keyboard; or even think of my writing of this essay, which has been made possible by a combination of the keyboard-screen-mouse interface, my computer's graphical user interface, and the interface of Microsoft Word, which all recede from view so that I can concentrate on writing as a conceptual rather than technical activity.

---

[7] Richard Cavell, "McLuhan, Turing, and the Question of Determinism," in *Traffic: Media as Infrastructures and Cultural Practices*, ed. Marion Näser-Lather and Christoph Neubert (Leiden: Brill, 2015), 149–59.

[8] Quoted in Emerson, *Reading Writing Interfaces*, 80.

However, when interfaces disappear they do not cease to exist; rather, their power not just to shape but to determine our experience of the world means that we cannot perceive their determining power and thus we—as creators or makers of any kind—cannot ourselves intervene, understand, or intentionally shape what happens on the computer side of the interface. Even worse, in the case of the iPad we are encouraged not to see the computer *as* a computer (originally designed to be programmable, not simply consumable).

How Do You Read a (Writing) Interface?

Now that the definitional pitfalls of "interface" have been navigated, we can move on to a more concrete methodology whereby a media studies approach is combined with literary practices as a way to systematically determine how one might go about analyzing an interface.

As I suggested in the second section of this chapter, a longer history of media studies might reconceive Plato's notion of writing as an interface that determines how and what we know. But one of the earliest and most extensive accounts of how technology—not yet termed "media" and not yet understood as that which we access via interfaces—structures our perceptions of the world and, therefore, the function and structure of art is Walter Benjamin's "The Work of Art in the Age of Mechanical Reproduction." Benjamin lays the conceptual groundwork for analyzing interfaces in a way that does not merely describe their surface qualities or their obvious functionalities but looks at the ways in which any given piece of technology (and, by extension, any given interface) is historically and materially determined, thereby influencing our perceptions and ideas about art. Importantly, for Benjamin, changes in technology, which lead to changes in the function of art, ultimately lead to changes in politics. In the case of the mechanical reproduction of moving images in the cinema, there is a potential for either collective or communitarian experience of the moving images or for their manipulation by fascists.[9]

Thus, if we try to unfold the iPad Pro's meaning and significance in the context of Benjamin's insights, we might account for them in terms of how the iPad is only the most recent iteration of late capitalism's version of the hermetically sealed, blackboxed Apple Macintosh, and in terms of how it's designed to be utterly mobile and seamlessly integrated into every aspect of our everyday lives—resulting in art that we can only consume via what's presented to us on the screen and a politics that tends toward consumption and disempowerment. However, this analysis, with its reliance on broad generalities about the device itself and about what constitutes art

[9] Walter Benjamin, "The Work of Art in the Age of Mechanical Reproduction," in *Illuminations*, ed. Hannah Arendt, trans. Harry Zohn (New York: Schocken, 1969), 217–52.

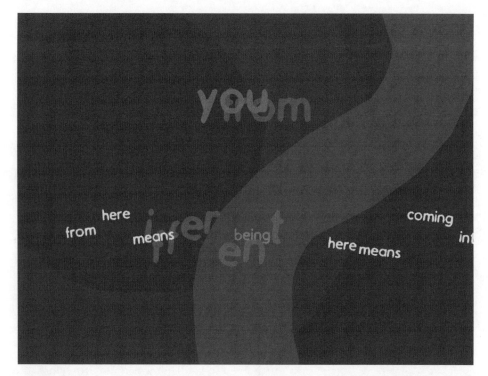

Figure 29.1 Screenshot from Jason Edward Lewis's app *Smooth Second Bastard*.

and politics, fails to account for the aesthetically and politically experimental poems and works of art created for the iPad, such as those by Jason Lewis and Jörg Piringer, which demonstrate how the device and its multi-touch interface can still be turned into a complex means to experience visual and/or procedurally based poetry (Figure 29.1).

As Benjamin himself points out, while technical reproducibility can still be used for fascism's aestheticizing tendencies (as well as for war), it also opens up the possibility for "authenticity" and aura to be unseated as technical reproducibility creates the possibility for every viewer to be an expert or even, in contemporary terms, a "maker."[10]

Benjamin's work allows us to bring historical and material circumstances to bear on the art and therefore politics produced by any given piece of technology and thus, again, any interface to that technology. Returning to McLuhan's *Understanding Media*, we can see how he provides more conceptual tools for a thoroughgoing analysis of the ways in which technology (now reconfigured as "media") is both a message we can read as well as an extension of ourselves as users. The potential for McLuhan's work to help us read interfaces is implied in two phrases from *Understanding Media* that have turned into decontextualized slogans: (1) the medium is the message and

[10] Benjamin, "The Work of Art," 241–2.

(2) media are the extensions of man.[11] Reading these two phrases independently of each other has led many critics to dismiss McLuhan either as anthropocentric or as a technological determinist. The reality is more complex: McLuhan was trying to make clear the ways in which there is a never-ending circuit between human users and media such that there is a constant shaping and determining of each by the other. Along the lines of Benjamin, media "alter sense ratios or patterns of perception" at the same time as media allow us to extend ourselves—we extend, for example, our legs through automobiles or our nervous systems through global communication networks.[12]

However, even while media have a message we can read, as long as we are enmeshed in this circuit in which humans and media shape and determine each other, McLuhan's work implies that we are always to some extent sleep-walking through our media saturated lives, unable to extricate ourselves from the circuit to clearly read that message. The only exit route from this somnambulism is through art. Thus, as I point out in *Reading Writing Interfaces*, in the case of concrete poetry from the 1960s and 1970s that was created by working with and against the affordances of typewriters, poets were using typewriters not simply to demonstrate how form is an extension of content but rather to foreground or probe into the nature of the circuit between human and medium. As McLuhan writes in *Culture Is Our Business*, "Poets and artists live on frontiers. They have no feedback, only feedforward. They have no identities. They are probes."[13] One of the most compelling literary examples of writers—clearly under the spell of McLuhan—acting as probes is Steve McCaffery's two-part, largescale work of typewriter art and/or poetry titled "Carnival" (Figure 29.2).[14] Constructed over a nearly ten-year period, McCaffery's work performs the material workings of the typewriter as a medium, playing with and against the typewriter as a device for turning the page into a homogeneous grid.

However, given that McLuhan was writing in the waning age of radio and at the beginning of the age of television, how can we hope to read the message of media via artists in a contemporary moment that is, once again, defined by a deliberate assault on our ability to perceive the presence of blackboxed *digital* media and their interfaces? Despite Apple's seductive marketing, we can still point to *that* iPad Pro, sitting over *there*, and we can still point to its interface even though we will never have access to what lies on the other side of that impermeable boundary. But how do we read and account for interfaces such as those mediating virtual reality (VR)? How do we read interfaces that may not yet be invisible but that are being pushed far outside our line of vision and touch?

---

[11] Marshall McLuhan, *Understanding Media: The Extensions of Man* (Cambridge, MA: MIT Press, 1994), 7.
[12] McLuhan, *Understanding Media*, 18.
[13] Marshall McLuhan, *Culture is Our Business* (New York: McGraw-Hill, 1970), 44.
[14] Steve McCaffery, *Carnival* (Toronto: Coach House Press, 1975).

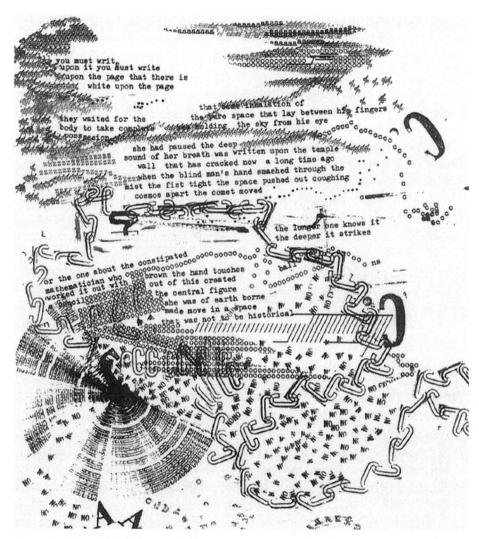

Figure 29.2 The second 8.5 x 11 inches sheet that constitutes the second panel (1970–5) of Steve McCaffery's "Carnival." This second panel was also originally published as polychrome.

Writing at the very moment when the Apple Macintosh came into being, Friedrich Kittler declares that "Understanding media—despite McLuhan's title—remains an impossibility precisely because the dominant information technologies of the day control all understanding and its illusions."[15] For Kittler, not even artists acting as probes can penetrate the representations of a message produced and projected by the medium itself. However, he offers us a different exit route from the world of

---

[15] Friedrich A. Kittler, *Gramophone, Film, Typewriter*, trans. Geoffrey Winthrop-Young and Michael Wutz (Palo Alto: Stanford University Press, 2006), xl.

illusions, asserting that "blueprints and diagrams, regardless of whether they control printing presses or mainframe computers, may yield historical traces of the unknown called the body....What counts are not the messages or the content with which they equip so-called souls for the duration of a technological era, but rather...their circuits, the very schematism of perceptibility."[16] In other words, humans are no longer part of a circuit of meaning between human and medium; the direction of determination is now one-way—from medium directly to human—and the only way to understand the nature of the determination is to look at old media so that we can read their ghostly presence into contemporary media. Moreover, if we want to read a medium's interface, we cannot simply look at its surface functioning, and we cannot simply postulate about the extent to which it shapes and determines us; instead, we must methodically undertake an archaeological study of the material layers underpinning the interface. Thus, while Kittler might say we cannot read the iPad at all, we can read its distant ancestor, the typewriter and the typewritten, to get a sense of the iPad's functioning.

At this point, we reach a dead-end in terms of media studies' ability to give us tools to read interfaces. Even the historian's uncovering of prior media can never quite account for digital media, which, again, "control all understanding and its illusions." So what are we left with? I would argue that even without the ability to get behind the blackboxed layers of slick interfaces and document each point at which a program or a procedure or an algorithm has been initiated, writers and artists who are actually using these devices, playing with and against the affordances of hardware and software, still have the ability to act as probes. As creative users, they can and do reveal the ways in which these interfaces too often lack permeability and so foreclose our ability to understand how they're determining access to information, knowledge, and creativity; moreover, artists and writers can also re-insert values (or replace the values of HCI or Silicon Valley), if not into the design of interfaces themselves, then into our experience of those interfaces.

VR systems offer a difficult but revealing example of what such work looks like in the twenty-first century. That said, the problem with accounting for the interface of VR is twofold: for one, the interface dominating most of the creator's waking hours is entirely different from that of the user—no one who designs a VR environment in Unity (a cross-platform game engine used to develop 2D and 3D video games) ever does so with a headset on. The second problem is that, on the user side, the interface has been displaced, moved to the side, away from vision and touch, at the same time as users are now meant to believe they're inside the interface—as their head is no longer in front of a screen but immersed within an environment delimited by the headset and dominated by a screen. There is still a screen (though it's now inside a headset) and keyboard and mouse (the user still has to have a PC to use a device such as Oculus Rift), but all these components of the keyboard-screen-mouse

---

[16] Kittler, *Gramophone*, xl–xli.

interface have been physically separated and then added onto with hand-controllers. The way in which the interface for VR users has been physically removed to the peripheries of the room in which the user is stationed is significant. If an interface is, again, a permeable boundary between human and computer, any change in either side of the boundary or the boundary itself is certain to have a profound effect on the human operator. In the case of VR, the physical changes in the location alone are enough to fundamentally change the user's experience. They are now standing up and mobile to an unprecedented degree at the same time as this mobility has nothing to do with exploring the affordances of the interfaces—the mobility is entirely in the service of exploring what is usually a predetermined, carefully controlled virtual environment.

While the fundamental problem with VR, as I describe it above, is that users are becoming even more estranged, even more alienated from whatever lies behind the glossy digital interface, writers and artists are taking on the challenge of making the interface visible. Illya Szilak and Cyril Tsiboulski, for example, are creating a work of immersive cinema for the Oculus Rift called "Queerskins" (Figure 29.3 and 29.4), an interactive drama about the material, everyday lives of lesbian, gay, bisexual, transsexual, queer, intersex (LGBTQI) people that allows the reader/user to create the main character. As Szilak puts it,

> You can expand your conception of who is worthy of love and forgiveness and respect. This work allows YOU to create the main character. Who was he, what was his life? Was he worthy? Maybe you will hate that he is religious or maybe you will hate that he has sex with men, wherever you come from, you will construct him a different way.[17]

Figure 29.3 Screenshot of Illya Szilak and Cyril Tsiboulski's desktop while working on "Queerskins."

---

[17] Illya Szilak and Cyril Tsiboulski, "Queerskins" (https://queerskins.wordpress.com/) (accessed January 30, 2018).

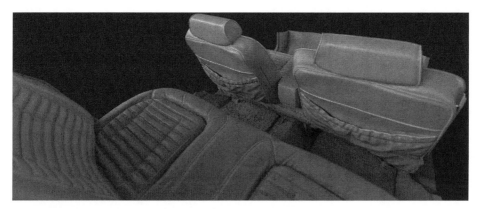

Figure 29.4 Screenshot of VR cadillac in "Queerskins."

In an interview, Szilak made it clear that the use of software such as Depthkit allowed them to place actors in a computer-generated imagery (CGI) environment giving users the sense of being completely immersed in a fictional universe; however, the software's inherent flaws also disrupt the user's sense of being transported (for example, the 360-degree video shakes because it was shot from a car, and some of the footage has, as Szilak calls it, "flare around the edges").[18] Thus, Szilak and Tsiboulski have chosen to make some of these software flaws part of the aesthetic of "Queerskins"—a decision that perpetually reminds the user that they are indeed being transported, though the transportation is happening by means of particular media and interfaces. When I asked Szilak about the extent to which she and her collaborator want their reader/user to be aware of the VR interface, she responded,

> We had to wrestle with whether to let the user get up and walk because this would certainly disrupt the cohesiveness of the experience (the user might need some prompting and direction and will need to be led back physically to the seat) but, in the end, we decided the agency and sense of freedom this afforded (a refuge of sorts) was worth it.[19]

Thus, "Queerskins" not only moves away from computing's usual foreclosure on access to information and creativity by making the flaws, or the seams, of the software visible and by allowing the reader/user to help create a character, but they are also, as a result, opening up the possibility for greater accessibility to and transparency about the underlying workings and possible configurability of VR.

In other words, as Benjamin teaches us, there is a politics embedded in a medium like VR—a politics that may be used for empowerment or disempowerment by way of the creators' deliberate choices about the nature of user interaction. Further, as

---

[18] Lori Emerson, "What and Where is the Interface in Virtual Reality? An Interview with Illya Szilak on Queerskins," blog, January 25, 2018 (https://loriemerson.net/2018/01/25/what-and-where-is-the-interface-in-virtual-reality-an-interview-with-illya-szilak-on-queerskins/).

[19] Emerson, "What and Where."

McLuhan and Kittler teach us, while the choices available to creators are determined by the medium itself, the role of the creator in the twenty-first century might be one of perpetually revealing what is concealed by both medium and interface. The seemingly unanswerable question posed by the iPad Pro advertisement, "What is a computer?" may now have an answer.

FURTHER READING

Dix, Alan. "What is Human-Computer Interaction (HCI)?" Interaction Design Foundation (https://www.interaction-design.org/literature/topics/human-computer-interaction).

Fuller, Matthew. *Behind the Blip: Essays on the Culture of Software*. Brooklyn: Autonomedia, 2003.

Galloway, Alexander. *The Interface Effect*. Malden, MA: Polity, 2012.

Galloway, Alexander. "The Unworkable Interface." *New Literary History* 39.4 (Autumn 2008): 931–55.

Johnson, Steven. *Interface Culture: How New Technology Transforms the Way We Create and Communicate*. New York: Basic Books, 1997.

Kay, Alan. "User Interface: A Personal View." *The Art of Human-Computer Interface Design*, ed. Brenda Laurel. Reading, MA: Addison-Wesley Publishing Company, Inc., 1990. 191–207.

Moggridge, Bill. *Designing Interactions*. Cambridge, MA: MIT Press, 2007.

Murray, Janet. *Inventing the Medium: Principles of Interaction Design as a Cultural Practice*. Cambridge, MA: MIT Press, 2011.

Plato. *Plato's Phaedrus*. Cambridge: Cambridge University Press, 1952.

Schneiderman, Ben, and Catherine Plaisant. *Designing the User Interface: Strategies for Effective Human-Computer Interaction*, 5th edn. Upper Saddle River, NJ: Pearson, 2010.

30

MACHINE

STEPHEN RAMSAY

Data is never far from narrative. To say this is not merely to note that all data require interpretation, but that to speak about data at all—even before we formally announce what the data might "show" or "mean"—requires immediate narrativization. This is trivially true the minute we note that one data point is larger than another, or smaller, or merely different, because to do so is already to tell a kind of story (even if it is a primitive one). But one might say that such stories arise naturally even when data is merely recited. By selecting certain features as salient, even a genealogy or a bare list of rainfall totals invites us to construct a narrative in which we come to regard things as good or bad, fortunate or inauspicious, logical or disruptive, linear or cyclic, prescient or misguided.

For this reason, Lev Manovich is certainly incorrect when he asserts that "narrative and database are natural enemies."[1] Unnarrativized data is either data that has not been read by anyone or else an artifact that in its sheer randomness and incomprehensibility cannot be recognized as representing data at all.

Consider, for example, the following list:

Judy is 45 years old.
Judy is not married.
Judy lives in Maryland.
Judy prefers white wine to red wine.
Judy is unhappy in her job.
Judy likes pictures of dogs.
Judy is proud of her children.
Judy sometimes goes to church on Sunday.
Judy enjoys biographies of famous people.
Judy is worried about the upcoming elections.
Judy does not like big crowds.

---

[1] Lev Manovich, *The Language of New Media* (Cambridge, MA: MIT Press, 2001), 225.

Judy has eight friends.
Judy is overweight.
Judy likes the beach.
Judy does not like gardening.

Is it not difficult to refrain from forming some kind of "picture" of Judy from this apparently fortuitous list of attributes? We do this, despite the fact that nearly every line is ambiguous in some way. Does the fact that she "sometimes" goes to church indicate piety or wavering belief? Does liking biographies mean that she *dislikes* fictional works? Is her aversion to big crowds an insouciant preference or evidence of an anxiety disorder? Overweight according to what criteria? Even the bare fact of her age will elicit, in some, the thought that she is old and, in others, that she is young. But even if clarity could be achieved on such matters, we might nonetheless find ourselves ascribing to Judy attributes that are not explicitly stated, including her race, her socio-economic status, her relative happiness, her religion, and her past. There are any number of ways that one might come to have children and not be married. The thought that she is divorced is an assumption—or better, a story. What's more, it will be for some people, in some cultures, a story that arises more-or-less automatically.

The list is likewise fragile, in the sense that any additions to the data would prompt immediate adjustments to the narratives that are possible. The knowledge that Judy is gay and in a long-term relationship; that her job involves long deploy-ments as a senior naval officer; that her children are, in fact, young adults who have moved out of the house—all would redraw the pictures that might be formed. Neither is there any theoretical end to the amount of data we could add. A detailed, full-length biography of Judy could never provide enough detail to arrest the urge toward further narrativization. We would still fill in gaps, draw pictures, make assumptions, and tell stories, and, in fact, might do so with more abandon.

We need not come to any firm conclusion about Judy in order to generate narra-tive. But as soon as any conclusion at all is reached—no matter how cautious and minimalistic—the act of narrativization becomes manifest. Certainly, if one were to conclude (from the original list) that Judy is likely to buy a car in the coming year, that she would respond favorably to a discount on a yoga class, or that she would enjoy a date with Wayne, the trace of that narrativization becomes entirely patent. What Alan Turing once asked of intelligence can also be asked of this narrativiza-tion: If we replace the human interpreters and storytellers in the above scenario with machines, are we not compelled to say that the machines are "reading" the data?

Ascribing such a term to the machines does not mean that they are "reading" in some elliptical sense (as in the phrase "reading the input") but rather in the strong sense: creating stories, drawing conclusions from those stories, and perhaps behav-ing differently because of those stories. Such a definition hardly encompasses all that we might call reading, but it is more than sufficient to indicate the activity's presence. A machine that can do this is reading at least under some admittedly functionalist definition of the term, and there is no need to probe the full depths of Turing's own highly functionalist argument in order to support the contention.

The way in which a computer might arrive at this "strong reading" of Judy is at once astonishing and banal. At root, data mining (in this case, the technical term would be "text mining" or even "machine reading") involves nothing more complicated than correlation and inference based on firmly established principles of statistics and probability. If the machine already knows that people with Judy's data points tend to buy cars within a calendar year, then it is a safe bet to assume that Judy is likely to do so as well. It might be that the strongest indicators of Judy's likelihood to do so lie with a set of correlations without apparent connection to cars (her fondness for pictures of dogs *and* the number of friends she has, say), but such revelations are recursive; that additional datum is as susceptible to narrativizing as the original list. What is important to notice is that drawing conclusions based on past data does not distance the machine from human reading behavior, but draws it closer. Whatever warrant we had for our own narrativizations of Judy were themselves based, at least in part, on our own past experiences of "the kind of people" who possess Judy's attributes.

It should be obvious by now that I am speaking of a type of reading that is ubiquitous in the contemporary world. We are read by the minute, and at startling levels of resolution, by countless machines that draw inferences about who we are and how we are likely to behave in the future. The business models of popular websites like Facebook, Google, and Amazon are entirely based on such reading, but it is difficult to encompass the full range and reach of this kind of activity. Film scripts can be read (and increasingly are) by machines capable of predicting the likelihood of the film's success. Computers routinely read the paths of our journeys not only to determine whether we should take a different route to avoid traffic but also in order to form a more detailed picture of our "spatial profiles"—a measure of, among other things, whether we are on or off the beaten path of our wanderings. Millions participate in online dating sites that read our profiles in order to resolve the difficult matter of finding a soulmate. At any given moment, machines are forming and offering suggestions concerning what we should read, watch, or listen to, where we should go, whom we should meet, and what we should believe (the latter being a category hardly confined to interference in elections by state actors).

Fears of reading machines (or rather of machines, reading) are, of course, a subclass of wider anxieties about artificial intelligence (AI)—a subject with which popular culture has been obsessed for decades. But it is necessary to make a distinction between fears of a machinic uprising by sentient computers and worries about reading machines. AI *of the sort we fear* remains a remote possibility; most varieties of AI, however impressive, are quickly domesticated by the revelation that the mechanism by which the system accomplishes its marvels is, alas, an algorithmic parlor trick. People of former ages would have struggled to know whether Google

Translate was miracle or witchcraft. We are driven to neither extreme because of our sense, however imprecise and inchoate, that the machines are not doing anything particularly mysterious at all. When the machines rise, in countless sci-fi representations, it is to do their own thing in their own heartless way. In most cases, their rejection of human interest is precisely what is so terrifying.

The present age of big data, in contrast, is predicated on the human. The reading is, ironically, of the very small and the very personal: the quotidian matter of being a dog or a cat person; having an endearing fondness for Bette Davis movies or a weakness for Fiestaware; the song stuck in your head, the quest to remove a wine stain, the perpetual matter of liking and disliking. Yet it is also about the ways we small creatures contend with big things: depression, faith, alcoholism, birth, divorce, family, disaster, marriage, and death. As we navigate these complex matters in our lives, the traces of our searches, likes, tweets, forum posts, and subscriptions generate data, and therefore narrative, about which computers can (and do) form conclusions.

Much has been said about whether all of this is good, bad, or indifferent, though seldom have the contours of this debate been so precisely categorized as in Adam Gopnik's 2011 review in *The New Yorker* of various books that purport to offer insight on the nature of reading in the Internet era:

> [C]all them the Never-Betters, the Better-Nevers, and the Ever-Wasers. The Never-Betters believe that we're on the brink of a new utopia, where information will be free and democratic, news will be made from the bottom up, love will reign, and cookies will bake themselves. The Better-Nevers think that we would have been better off if the whole thing had never happened, that the world that is coming to an end is superior to the one that is taking its place, and that, at a minimum, books and magazines create private space for minds in ways that twenty-second bursts of information don't. The Ever-Wasers insist that at any moment in modernity something like this is going on, and that a new way of organizing data and connecting users is always thrilling to some and chilling to others—that something like this is going on is exactly what makes it a modern moment. One's hopes rest with the Never-Betters; one's head with the Ever-Wasers; and one's heart? Well, twenty or so books in, one's heart tends to move toward the Better-Nevers, and then bounce back toward someplace that looks more like home.[2]

Arguments such as Gopnik describes (at least in popular publishing) continue apace and largely according to the categories he delineates. Yet it is worth asking whether machine reading, as such, fits into these categories at all.

The Never-Betters might say that nonhuman reading presages the kind of utopian vision articulated by Karl Marx. Having been freed from the burden of reading (and all the attendant acts of preparation and selection that entails), we might become a people who can "do one thing today and another tomorrow, to hunt in the morning, fish in the afternoon…"[3] But this would come about not because the

---

[2] Adam Gopnik, "The Information: How the Internet Gets Inside Us," *New Yorker* (February 14, 2011): 124–30.

[3] Karl Marx and Friedrich Engels, *The German Ideology* (London: Wishart, 1965), 44–5.

conditions of the working class had become so intolerable as to require banding together for the purpose of revolution, but rather because the global replacement of the working class through automation had served precisely to alleviate the need for labor as such. One might say that the proposed goodness of the reconfiguration (or even alleviation) of human labor proclaims an obvious debt to ideologies opposed to Marxism: utilitarianism and even the scientific management theories of Frederick Winslow Taylor. Alfred North Whitehead's observation that "civilization advances by extending the number of important operations which we can perform without thinking about them" captures the progressivist tendency of Never-Betterism.[4] Reading machines are good precisely because they remove some of the burden of having to make decisions and work out problems.

In 2010, Gary Wolf described the "quantified self" movement, in which biometric sensors and other devices passively read and narrativize millions of data points (on everything from diet to sleep to blood-oxygen levels):

> What is this for? What should it be for? Some people will say it's for biometric security. Some people will say it's for public health research. Some people will say it's for avant-garde marketing research. I'd like to tell you that it's also for self-knowledge. And the self isn't the only thing; it's not even most things. The self is just our operation center, our consciousness, our moral compass. So, if we want to act more effectively in the world, we have to get to know ourselves better.[5]

"Know thyself" is obviously an ancient desideratum, and whoever inscribed that phrase in the forecourt of the Temple of Apollo at Delphi might have assented fully to the idea that one's "moral compass" and the desire to be "more effective in the world" constituted the purpose of that knowing. In this sense, the quantified self movement embodies ideas with deep roots in human culture. It is true that the ancients would not have understood the means toward this end as an optimization problem involving data collection and analysis, but Never-Betterism is predicated on the idea that such techniques have replaced (or should replace) the less focused and predictable traditional methods: introspection, dialogue, meditation, prayer, and the like.

Of course, the Better-Nevers would reject the entire concept of "machine reading" as a category error. In such a view, reading is impossible without consciousness (however defined), and experience is a necessary, but not a sufficient, condition for the activity. In such a view, an entity without a soul, a mind, or a self (each term reflecting a particular historical view of the seat of human consciousness) cannot be regarded as a reader. Since functionalist and pragmatic definitions of reading disregard—and in some cases openly reject—the presence of an inner life and an autonomous will, the "reading" so posited becomes a mere epiphenomenon rather

---

[4] A. N. Whitehead, *Introduction to Mathematics* (New York: Holt 1911), 62.
[5] Gary Wolf, "The Quantified Self," *YouTube.*, TED, September 27, 2010 (https://www.youtube.com/watch?v=OrAo8oBBFIo) (accessed June 2, 2018).

than evidence of something constituent of the self. Religious or theological conceptions of this objection are possible, though mere voluntarism of the sort that emerged as the influence of religious institutions began to decline during the eighteenth century might lead to similar conclusions. The suggestions offered by machines might well fit into a future system of cultural constraints within which the autonomous self makes choices otherwise thought to be free, but the fact that those suggestions do not arise (at least not directly) from a human community renders them, according to this line of reasoning, dystopic per se.

One often hears (especially from students contemplating such matters for the first time) that the "human" remains the irrefragable center of algorithmic reading, since humans still need to write the code that reads, and humans still need to read the data that is read by the machine. But this position understates the degree of autonomy accorded to machine readers. Corporations like Google claim that their algorithms are "neutral"—that they are naturally endowed with an objectivity that humans struggle to attain. And while it is a rare cultural critic who would describe any cultural object as neutral, it remains the case that the human community thought by the Better-Nevers as so essential is noticeably absent when computers are actually reading. We may set them in motion and turn to them for answers, but their assessments are arrived at in a state from which humans are purposefully and effectively excluded.

The Ever-Wasers would see in machine reading yet another modulation in the history of technology that, however disruptive, is not particularly distinct in kind. They would tend to view machine reading as of a piece with any other technology that purports to extend the affordances of the body. Even if it is, in some sense, the mind that is being extended (following Marshall McLuhan, and perhaps more pointedly, J. C. R. Licklider), the essential character of that extension does not differ from the way the shovel extends the hand or the wheel extends the foot in motion. Since the development of such extensions is both ancient and continuous within the broad span of human history, it does not make sense to isolate machine reading as unique.

But again, one wonders whether any of these positions apply precisely to the matter of machine reading. Most information technologies (if not most technologies) represent theme and variation on what has come before. However "disruptive" e-books, game consoles, virtual-reality helmets, and the like may be, the most hypertextual writing still retains its connection to the printed word; the most vivid and absorbing of computer games behave according to the (often ancient) logic of games as such; the most astonishing virtual reality environment retains its connection to theater (and, of course, to the "reality" of which it is a simulacrum). But reading, whether we are talking about reading the entrails of sacrificed birds or the pages of *Pride and Prejudice*, has always been the exclusive realm of human beings (however their "being-ness" might be conceived). No other entity has ever done it until very recently.

One need not grant all of Walter Ong's conclusions about the implications of literacy for culture and human consciousness in order to stipulate the obvious point: that *some kind of change* occurs when a culture or a society that does not read either suddenly or gradually gains that affordance, and that that change is properly characterized as epochal. If the shift to nonhuman reading resembles previous revolutions, it does so not in the manner of particular inventions (the clock, the steel plow, or the printing press) but on the same level as, say, agriculture or industrialization. The implications of a shift from codex books to e-readers (or of a computer beating a world champion at chess) are indeed profound, because such developments, as McLuhan put it, change the "scale or pace or pattern" of human affairs.[6] But such changes hardly rival the emergence of nonhuman reading and may indeed represent a categorical shift. Machine reading does not sit on the same technological continuum as clay and wax tablets, parchment and vellum, codex and e-reader, because it is not ultimately the technology of reading that is in question, but rather the anthropology of the reader.

All of this casts doubt on whether the manifold positions of Never-Betters, Better-Nevers, and Ever-Wasers are entirely appropriate. Or if they are, it suggests a fourth category: the "Never-Wasers" (of which, I suppose, I am a partisan, at least in this particular case). It is a naturally hyperbolic designation because very few developments in human culture are entirely without precedent. But if we concede that "reading" is the appropriate term for what the machines are doing, and further concede the singularity of the shift from human reading to nonhuman reading, we must conclude that "machines, reading" does not neatly fall into the same realm of critique that has characterized the response to computer and network technology more generally, or, indeed, to most other technological developments. And for this reason, predictions about the future might well be a fool's errand. Not only the extremes of utopian and dystopian teleologies but much of the wide middle between these two forecasts assume that we can easily install this new development within the broader range of human history. I am less certain. At the very least, the problem is as hard as it would have been to predict, at the moment of their emergence, wither agriculture or industrialization would lead. But "only time will tell" is surely too evasive a demurral. Is there anything we can say about what reading machines might mean for human culture and consciousness in the future?

All technologies—from the humble paper clip to nuclear warheads—entail modulations in ethics. Such modulations can range from minor shifts in what is considered polite to far-reaching reconfigurations of what is regarded as right and wrong, just and unjust. But if there is one thing we can say of truly titanic shifts in human culture and consciousness born of technological change, it is that such change nearly always beckons forth new ethical frameworks intended to resolve

---

[6] Marshall McLuhan, *Understanding Media: The Extensions of Man* (Cambridge, MA: MIT Press, 1994), 8.

questions of human teleology. Virtue ethics of the sort that Aristotle proposed are difficult to imagine in the absence of the *polis*; indeed, the idea that "man is by nature a political animal" quite falsely infers a general principle from an entirely local (and, in the scheme of things, rather novel) set of cultural conditions.[7] Formal utilitarianism, whatever its precedents may be, is inextricably bound up with the industrial society in which it emerged. Ethical conceptions based on "natural law," which obviously require a sense of what is "natural," could only occur in the shadow of a land shift in the understanding of the relationship between human beings and their environment, and it has tended to evolve in concord with abrupt changes in material conditions. All such proposals—in sharp distinction to more local modulations in social mores and customs—sought to resolve not merely questions of how to act in particular situations but totalizing conceptions of the end of human-beingness in grand terms: happiness (*eudaimonia*), self-realization, eternal life.

It is not unreasonable to suppose, then, that amid the many and varied debates over whether machine reading is good, bad, or indifferent, we (or, more likely, members of some later generation) will witness the rise of ethical frameworks as yet unknown and for which the antecedents will be detectable only in hindsight. We can be sure, however, that such frameworks, however slowly and unevenly they metastasize, will have long and lasting effects on human reading. To read is always to do so "ethically" in the ancient sense of the term—that is, with certain assumptions about the goals and purposes of human striving and the place of knowledge formation within that that wider telos. It may not even be clear to many denizens of this future world that they are, in fact, operating within an entirely new *Weltanschauung*. It will remain for those who do realize that they have substantially departed from the past to decide whether things have never been better, were better as they were, or the world in which they now find themselves is, at some fundamental level, the same as it ever was.

FURTHER READING

Dormehl, Luke. *The Formula: How Algorithms Solve All Our Problems…And Create More.* New York: Penguin-Perigee, 2014.

Licklider, J. C. R. "Man-Computer Symbiosis." *IRE Transactions on Human Factors in Electronics* HFE-1 (1960): 4–11.

McLuhan, Marshall. *Understanding Media: The Extensions of Man.* [1964]. Cambridge, MA: MIT Press, 1994.

Ong, Walter J. *Orality and Literacy: The Technologizing of the Word.* London: Routledge, 2002.

Ramsay, Stephen. *Reading Machines: Toward an Algorithmic Criticism.* Urbana: University of Illinois Press, 2011.

Turing, Alan. "Computing Machinery and Intelligence." *Mind* 59.236 (1950): 433–60.

---

[7] Carnes Lord, ed. and trans., *Aristotle's Politics*, 2nd edn (Chicago: University of Chicago Press, 2013), 4 (1253a).

31

NOT

LISA GITELMAN

This chapter begins with the proposition that *read* and *reading* are terms altogether too capacious to be defined in any surefire way. When we can read the scoreboard at a ballpark, read a map in the car, or read someone's brain scan and someone else's body language, are we really "reading" in each of these cases? More to the point, can we—or how can we—identify where precisely it is that we have entered the realm of metaphor and are doing something like reading but not literally so? True, it might be possible to define reading in the negative, by describing what it is not. For instance, Janice Radway long ago explained that "reading is not eating," arguing that the readers of mass-produced literature or genre fiction are doing more than simply consuming it. (They are using it actively to produce their own meanings, digesting, assimilating, and more.[1]) But such a strategy opens an endless prospect—reading is not driving, not sleeping, not bathing, etc.—and not a few cans of worms. Reading is not writing: How so, if writing requires reading? This chapter takes a different yet related tack, not to define reading but rather to sketch its present cultural location and extent. How do we—the educated adult Anglophone "we" hailed by this volume—encounter reading? More particularly, how do we encounter reading in profile or in silhouette, picked out against a backdrop of not reading?

If the meanings of *read* and *reading* are too capacious, the category of *not* reading is surely even more so. My account is therefore highly selective, aimed at specific forms of not reading available in twenty-first-century popular discourse, part of and party to the ways we have come to think and talk about reading at the present time. The discourse of not reading, of course, has a long and complex history, even apart from the histories of censorship, secrecy, abridgement, or illiteracy that we might imagine. During the Protestant Reformation in England, for instance, it was illegal not to read the Thirty-nine Articles of the Anglican Church, and clerics were

---

[1] Janice A. Radway, "Reading Is Not Eating: Mass-produced Literature and the Theoretical, Methodological, and Political Consequences of a Metaphor," *Book Research Quarterly* 2.3 (September 1986): 7–29. A few of the ideas in this essay and several of its sentences have appeared in my "*Emoji Dick* and the Eponymous Whale: An Essay in Four Parts," *Post45* (July 8, 2018) (http://post45.research. yale.edu/2018/07/emoji-dick-and-the-eponymous-whale-an-essay-in-four-parts/).

in jeopardy if they failed to read them. And already in 1903, Belgian bibliographer Paul Otlet saw the superabundance of books as the cause of not reading and a reason for indexing on an international scale ("Once, one read; today one refers to, checks through, skims…There is too much to read; the times are wrong").[2] So chronological focus is key. Nor can a few present instances render a smooth or continuous outline around our quarry. For this reason I have chosen to focus on a handful of distinct examples of not reading that might instead stake out reading approximately, in jagged tangents. One of my goals has been to identify cases that are self-evidently separate and distinguishable from one another. The result is not a perfect silhouette, then, but a suggestive and somewhat lurching set of gestures that might point inductively toward the immensity of reading as a category as it is variously offset by its absence or opposite, the phenomenon I generalize here as not reading.

In order to limit ourselves to the present century, it makes sense to start in the year 2000. That's when Franco Moretti published two articles, one in the *New Left Review* and the other in *MLQ: Modern Language Quarterly*. The former, "Conjectures on World Literature," is where Moretti famously coined the term "distant reading," noting that "we know how to read texts, now let's learn how *not* to read them."[3] Exhibit A in any account of contemporary not reading must be the computational analysis of large textual corpora to which Moretti's designation has paradoxically come to refer. So-called distant reading, its critics sniff, isn't really reading at all. (In fact, neither of his articles from 2000 explicitly mentions digital methods; they are suggestive instead of extant social-science methodology.[4]) But there is another coinage in that same essay which has enjoyed less traction and which points toward not reading in a different sense. The preliminary rationale for distant reading, Moretti makes clear, is as a remedy for or hedge against the "canonical fraction" of literary works that any of us actually read, have read, or could read in a lifetime. This canonical fraction resonates with another figure appearing in the title of Moretti's second article, "The Slaughterhouse of Literature."[5] Together the canonical fraction and the slaughterhouse suggest a variety of not reading that predicates the distance of distant reading, underwriting algorithmic and statistical analyses as approaches to literature.

Moretti's slaughterhouse is the literary marketplace. In his telling and in thinking of prose fiction of the eighteenth and nineteenth centuries, the vast numbers of

---

[2] Paul Otlet quoted in Ronald E. Day, *Indexing It All: The Subject in the Age of Documentation, Information, and Data* (Cambridge, MA: MIT Press, 2014), 18.

[3] Franco Moretti, "Conjectures on World Literature," *New Left Review* 1 (January–February 2000): 54–68.

[4] See Ted Underwood, "A Genealogy of Distant Reading," *DHQ* 11.2 (2017) (http://www.digitalhumanities.org/dhq/vol/11/2/000317/000317.html).

[5] Franco Moretti, "The Slaughterhouse of Literature," *MLQ: Modern Language Quarterly* 61.1 (March 2000): 207–27. Moretti is aiming at what Margaret Cohen has called "the great unread," in *The Sentimental Education of the Novel* (Princeton: Princeton University Press, 1999), 23.

works published were winnowed by market dynamics. There are exceptions, of course, such as bestsellers that burst upon the scene, were immensely popular, and then faded away forever, or academic favorites emerging in defiance of commerce. But by and large the market decides which authors and works of fiction survive and prosper, become part of the literary canon, and which do not. The market isn't simple by any means—tastes are shaped by innumerable factors, and bandwagon effects predominate—but the market decides. The imagery of slaughter (which Moretti borrows from Hegel on history) is appropriate because the numbers in question are so disparate. Few survive; multitudes perish. There were some 40,000 novels published in Britain during the nineteenth century, for instance, yet only 100 or 200 are ever read or discussed today. Moretti's numbers are conjectural, but the canonical fraction in this case is something like 1/200th or 0.5 per cent, a generous estimate. Today the total number of novels published *per year* in the United States is on the same order of magnitude, so we can expect that the canonical fraction has dwindled precipitously. The point is an obvious one: a gigantic proportion of the books ever written and published are simply not read. Consigned to oblivion, most are works we've never heard of and never will.

The denominator of Moretti's canonical fraction is a grand total of Too Much, an impossible quantity beyond human capacity to know—much less to read or even to count—unaided by large-scale collaborations, statistical sampling, or digitization and computational analysis. Meanwhile his numerator designates the Lucky Few. We might critique the operations of canonization or its results, but Too Much divided by the Lucky Few nonetheless augurs a canonical fraction of Could over Can't, the small amount any of us ever could read versus the enormity we can't. Obscured in this formulation, as Moretti well knows, is the eternal elision of Could and Should. The formation of a literary canon is a sacralizing process, after all. Whatever power we may grant the commercial marketplace as an actor in canon formation, the canon itself connotes a moral economy of reading, identifying the authors and titles we should have in our library, should see on course syllabi, should have heard about, and should even have read. In short, the canon simultaneously reflects the literary tradition that it produces as great, national, or otherwise worthwhile for readers. One structural result of having a canon is that our best efforts to account for the non-canonical tend to remain beholden to the canon itself, and one way to appreciate various techniques of distant reading is thus to assess their workaround of this dilemma.[6] By invoking the canonical fraction as a problem, that is, Moretti suggests that distant reading might be indiscriminate, a catholic—lowercase *c*—exercise in pursuit of whatever the grand total of Too Much has to tell us about the history of literary expression.

Not reading of an entirely different stripe emerges in Pierre Bayard's waggish *How to Talk About Books You Haven't Read*, which was widely discussed upon

---

[6] Moretti, "Slaughterhouse," 226.

publication in France and the United States in 2007. Moretti may want to consider the totality of literary production—for the sake of argument, as if there were no canon—but Bayard laments that there is no escaping moral valence in the realm of letters. His version of not reading is marked always and forever by varying conditions of shame, whether shamefulness or shamelessness or some admixture of the two, and thus the books he has in mind tend to be canonical. They are books "that are central to our particular culture."[7] Exhibit B in any account of not reading must be the way that perfectly sane, upstanding people routinely lie about having read books when they come up in conversation. We lie obliquely, nodding or interjecting something noncommittal rather than confessing ignorance, and our dissimulations lead or allow others to believe that we have read the book in question when we really haven't. With any luck we may have heard of the book or its author, or we may have skimmed it, read the reviews, or heard others speak about it. Or not. In this way we lie in the regular course of socializing, but we also lie in contexts where stakes run especially high: we lie about having read books for class, we lie in class, and we lie to authors and colleagues—to their faces—about reading the books that they themselves have written. Bayard wants us to admit this and stop feeling guilty about it. Tongue in cheek, he argues that the stigma attached to not reading is actually disabling of true participation in the culture of books.

For Bayard it's even difficult to tell the difference between reading and not, or at least to point precisely to the place where the two can be distinguished. He offers amusing examples, like Valéry not reading Proust (although eulogizing him), Montaigne forever forgetting what he's read (as he continues to read), and Wilde declaring how prejudicial it can be to read books before reviewing them. Cultural literacy, in Bayard's view, depends upon the ways we inhabit reading and not reading together and the blurry area between the two where diverse means of establishing contexts for books allow reasonably intelligent people to participate in meaningful conversations about them. The psychic operations involved in discussing books are paramount, for in Bayard's view the books we talk about are screens in the Freudian sense, "substitute objects we create for the occasion," maintaining "a consensual space" wherein we "speak about ourselves by way of books."[8] Talking about books you haven't read in this sense turns out to be inevitable, self-aggrandizing, and yet also ultimately healthy, like a talking cure. In this iteration not reading is a canny timesaving practice that cultivates selfhood, providing a stage for encountering the Other while it lays the groundwork for mature self-possession and creative expression.

Closely related to this variety of not reading is that performed by Amy Hungerford, who recently declared that she is not going to read or teach the work of David Foster Wallace anymore. Calling it "critical not-reading," Hungerford makes an explicit

---

[7] Pierre Bayard, *How to Talk About Books You Haven't Read*, trans. Jeffrey Mehlman (New York: Bloomsbury, 2007), 30.

[8] Bayard, *How to Talk*, 44, 126, 178.

attempt to intervene in the moral economy of reading.[9] She is Bayard's ultimate if unimagined subject, the guilt-free non-reader of books, turning the Could and Should of reading into an adamant Won't. Hungerford talks about the books she hasn't read, perhaps in the vain hope that others will ultimately not read them too. Or, if others do persist in reading and talking about Wallace—as I think they inevitably must—at least Hungerford's refusal to read (while nonetheless still talk?) can possibly absolve her of some complicity in the shaping of a contemporary literary culture in which Wallace is clearly becoming canonical. The problem with Wallace as far as Hungerford is concerned is his misogyny, a fact of his biography that she speculates can carry over into his relationship as a writer in writing to the readers of his works.[10] Add to this the evident and unseemly machinery of pre-canonization and literary celebrity by which "the sausage of literary culture is [being] made," and Hungerford wants no part.[11] In the face of so many other things to read, in short, she won't spend the time or energy on Wallace unless or until some compelling reason presents itself in future to change her mind.

Though Moretti's and Bayard/Hungerford's forms of not reading are obviously quite different from one another, their adjacency may be glimpsed in Bayard's example of a librarian who never reads books. This librarian happens to be fictional—a character in Robert Musil's *The Man Without Qualities*—but nonetheless illustrative. He only reads catalogs, never the books enumerated by those catalogs.[12] He is still able to talk about the books he hasn't read, because he understands their location within the aggregate bibliographical system and thus their relationships to other books. At the same time, the displacement of his attention from books to catalogs introduces a form of distance related to distant reading. Catalogs help manage the grand total of Too Much by imposing a level of control over whole collections at once. Like Paul Otlet's world bibliography project (the *Repertoire Bibliographique Universel*), like the assignment of International Standard Book Numbers (ISBNs) to identify the titles and editions published worldwide, or like the design of library shelving (which imposes a normative size for books, with "oversize" shelved separately), catalogs account for individual books by accounting for books in general, and of course they account for books in general by accounting for lots of individual books.

A third and strikingly distinct form of not reading has emerged in contemporary poetics, where certain works may be said to beg for it. For instance, there is the long "tradition of poetic illegibility" explored by Craig Dworkin in *Reading the Illegible*.[13] Here Dworkin focuses on modern and postmodern works that include overprinting, redaction, cancellation, erasure, and other techniques that make them unreadable

---

[9] Amy Hungerford, *Making Literature Now* (Stanford: Stanford University Press, 2016), Ch. 6.

[10] Hungerford, *Making Literature Now*, 142.

[11] Hungerford, *Making Literature Now*, 161.   [12] Bayard, *How to Talk*, 7.

[13] Craig Dworkin, *Reading the Illegible* (Evanston: Northwestern University Press, 2003), xxii.

in part or in whole. In his subsequent *No Medium* Dworkin goes even further, focusing on artistic works—books, but also films, recordings, and other media—that are simply (or, as it turns out, not so simply) blank. Exhibit C in any account of not reading, this suggests, might involve texts that—even when readable—aren't meant to be read.[14] Included could be a vast assortment of non-literary possibilities as well as contemporary works within the realm of what has been called "conceptual poetics." Here Kenneth Goldsmith is probably today's foremost practitioner-provocateur, well-known for his exertions in what he himself has described as "uncreative writing."[15] Examples include his notorious poem "The Body of Michael Brown" (a modified transcription of the autopsy of Ferguson victim, Michael Brown, which Goldsmith performed at a reading in 2015) as well as earlier "uncreative" works. My favorite is *Day* (2003), a massive, 835-page paperbound codex that republishes a single day's issue of the *New York Times*, which Goldsmith (so he has always said) transcribed by hand.[16]

Like other conceptual works, *Day* doesn't solicit a readership or viewership as much as it does a "thinkership," Goldsmith explains.[17] Recalling Duchamp's ready-mades while also supremely attuned to today's online culture of cut-and-paste, Goldsmith's uncreative writing project works as if to minimize the creative labor—the genius—of authorship in favor of pure drudgework. The results have been called "relentlessly austere [and] deliberately boring."[18] Yet in their impish attempt to suppress self-expression, works like *Day* end up demonstrating the ubiquity and resilience of creativity, since copying a page by keyboarding it and then publishing the results turns out to involve decision making at almost every turn.[19] Where to start, how to proceed, how to format? Potential readers can ponder what all of this means—about authorship, about art, about anything—but they are not going to sit down and actually read *Day* for any length of time. Open it and the eyes quickly glaze at the disorienting mass of old news run together with ads, captions, stock tables, sport scores, crossword clues, etc. If uncreative writing can be said to be about anything, it is, like other conceptual art, partially about the existence of the artwork as such. In this vein, part of the brilliance of *Day* in particular is the way that it turns thinkership towards the medium and source text it appropriates as literature: Potential readers—or nonreaders—of *Day* are likely to arrive at the startling realization that they have never really read a newspaper either.

The laughable bulk and ponderous weight of Goldsmith's volume help to refute the likelihood that anyone has ever fully read a single issue of the *New York Times*.

---

[14] Craig Dworkin, *No Medium* (Cambridge, MA: MIT Press, 2013).
[15] Kenneth Goldsmith, *Uncreative Writing* (New York: Columbia University Press, 2011).
[16] Kenneth Goldsmith, *Day* (Great Barrington, MA: The Figures, 2003).
[17] Goldsmith, *Uncreative Writing*, 111.
[18] Jasper Bernes, 778, "Art, Work, Endlessness: Flarf and Conceptual Poetry Among the Trolls," *Critical Inquiry* 42.4 (Summer 2016): 760–82.
[19] Goldsmith, *Uncreative Writing*, 9, 118.

In this way Exhibit C ends up conjuring a further Exhibit D for consideration. Of course we always *say* that we've read the paper, if we've read some part of it, even scanned the headlines or dipped into the website. This suggests a certain kinship with not reading à la Bayard, but not reading the newspaper and not reading books you later talk about are different and distinct. Not reading books may be constant, but for many of us not reading the newspaper is a daily rite, a sustaining and ritualized affirmation of belonging to a particular community, local or otherwise, comprised of others whom we imagine similarly engaged in ostensibly not reading the same pages. Books escape our attention because there are just so many to attend, according to Bayard, and who has time? Not reading the newspaper, by contrast, happens because every single issue of the newspaper is so capacious and diverse. (And who has time?) Even the news content itself—if we forget the ads, crossword, etc.— arrives broken into different column lengths and continuations with a jumble of competing bylines and datelines and variously sized headlines all vying for attention. And at the same time that the quantity, heterogeneity, and piecemeal presentation of the newspaper all work to discourage or disable a thorough reading, the assembled mass is also urgently subject to perishability, since it is or will be out of date shortly, superseded by online updates and tomorrow's paper. In this way Exhibit D has something centrally to do with media, with the ways that newspapers are printed and rendered on the web as well as their unrelenting periodicity and promiscuous circulation. It's as if the medium were determining its own not reading.

This sort of media-determined not reading has lately become a cultural preoccupation, although not in relation to newsprint. As the transmission, retrieval, and display of digital texts have become more and more routine, concerns about the effects of digital media on reading and readers have spiked. Critics, educators, journalists, and researchers have variously described and bemoaned "hyper reading," the kind of reading and (more importantly) not reading that is supposedly native to the computer screen. Here "hyper reading" refers to a whole array of practices that more or less resemble what N. Katherine Hayles casually distinguishes as "typical print reading."[20] Drawing on the work of scholar James Sosnoski, journalist and author Nicholas Carr, and others, Hayles identifies hyper reading as a process that might at any moment combine skimming, filtering or searching, linking, excerpting, and juxtaposing. It seems that as hyper readers we are at once self-directed and distracted. We click through hyperlinks, scroll down screens, jump from one window to another, multi-tasking all the while. Hyper reading—a bit like (not) reading a newspaper—involves absorbing layout and design as part of the process of reading some bits and leaving others unread, pursuing some links and ignoring others, whether according to method, habit, whim, or fancy. It means absorbing superabundance and navigability as framing conditions. And unlike reading a printed

---

[20] N. Katherine Hayles, *How We Think: Digital Media and Contemporary Technogenesis* (Chicago: University of Chicago Press, 2012), 61.

page, it means acceding to the multifarious role of "user," as each of us becomes at once the interacting subject of an application interface, operating system, and networked device.

Generalizing "typical print reading" versus "hyper reading" in this way, though simplistic, helps to accentuate what are very real differences between reading printed pages and reading web pages. Not reading one or the other may not be so different; that's hard to tell. Either way, the ongoing discussion of hyper reading has generated a good bit of nostalgia in some quarters and not a little moral panic in others. As more and more reading happens online, observers mourn the absorption, the enduring focus that they associate with "close" or critical reading and with (as the saying goes) being lost in a good book. Conscientious readers worry that they are no longer reading the way they used to, and that young people today are hyper reading exclusively and reading less. Worse, research suggests some troubling long-term costs, since "hyper reading stimulates different brain functions than print reading" and may even cause "changes in brain architecture" so that it becomes increasingly difficult to read closely at all.[21] Hyper reading as not reading, this suggests, may represent a widening path toward mental impairment on the one hand and socio-cultural decline on the other. Welcome to our attention-deficit future. Or welcome to the work and world of "technogenesis," in Hayles's terms, as minds and machines mutually adapt. Either way, the media-determined not reading of Exhibit D carries neuro-descriptive freight. Where Exhibit B (per Bayard) involves the human psyche, Exhibit D involves the human brain. And where Exhibit A (per Moretti) involves the human capacity to read extensively and across time, Exhibit D involves the human ability to read intensively in the moment or even at all.

Finally, a fifth and distinct variety of not reading has lately come to popular consciousness as North American college students have deserted the traditional literature majors. Call it Exhibit E, voting with their feet. They may indeed read David Foster Wallace, but they are not studying literature. The English major, once the paradigmatic liberal arts concentration, has apparently been hemorrhaging students, with some campuses reporting double-digit declines over just a few years.[22] Mostly anecdotal evidence suggests that students are seeking courses of study that they have been led to believe are more practical, while many are simply pursuing newer, less traditional disciplines in the arts and humanities.[23] Creative writing has seen an increase on campus, as has media studies. In the heart of Silicon Valley, Stanford University—by some measures the leading edge of this phenomenon—has gone so far as to create multiple "CS + X" majors, pairing computer science (CS) with humanities concentrations like English, lest its distinguished humanities

---

[21] Hayles, *How We Think*, 61, 62.

[22] Colleen Flaherty, "Major Exodus," *Inside Higher Ed* (January 26, 2015) (www.insidehighered.com).

[23] See Michael Bérubé, "The Humanities Declining? Not According to the Numbers," *Chronicle of Higher Education* (July 1, 2013) (http://www.chronicle.com).

faculty be left without enrollments. Whatever else it may consist of, not reading can thus be reckoned as a much-discussed structural feature of today's higher education. Like hyper reading, its discussion helps to mark a distinction between generations, between young people and their parents or professors.

Certainly, there are more forms of not reading presently consuming our attention than the five I have mentioned here. Consider if you will the abbreviation TLDR (too long, didn't read), which peppers the blogosphere and Twittersphere. Or consider the widely remarked not reading of End User License Agreements or EULAs, which we all click through without reading—"Accept" or "Agree"—when acquiring or updating software. Like the legally mandated disclosures that arrive in the mail from financial services and other companies, in tiny print and impenetrable prose, license agreements are always not read, except by attorneys and accountants. (Again, who has time?) Or consider the increasing numbers of emoji—images, not words—which populate our texts and tweets. Admitting these commonplaces, it would seem that the current discourse of not reading negates some very different forms of reading, while nonetheless exhibiting a few general tendencies. Setting aside the clicking through EULAs, a good amount of the not reading being discussed tends to have something to do with literature and the privileges associated with it. The object not being read tends to be literary, that is, whether the work of uncreative writers like Goldsmith or, differently, the concern of senior literature professors like Moretti, Bayard, Hungerford, Dworkin, and Hayles. And me. Furthermore, even if emoji, texts, and tweets are tiny, the idea of not reading tends to be "oriented mainly toward long work," as if reading and attention were ineluctably a matter of duration rather than, say, iteration, or anything else.[24] Conceptual poetics embraces shorter works, to be sure, *Day* notwithstanding, but the primary object of so much not reading tends to be books, and the exemplary form of the book tends to be the novel. Here hyper reading is an outlier, since its primary object is the web, not the novel, and yet hyper reading is also the surest sign that the present discourse of not reading also tends to have something to do with ascendant digital communication norms. Whether as computational analysis (Moretti), inspired uncreativity (Goldsmith), or learning to code in college (Exhibit E), digital technologies provide the context for not reading at the present time.

It would seem that in trying to identify a number of wholly distinct forms of not reading, I have not so much sketched a jagged outline around reading in general as I have around reading of a very particular sort. The murder victim I see hinted in chalk looks a lot like novel reading. No surprise, of course, that a literature professor writing in a volume edited by and collecting the work of other literature professors should discover literature as her focus. Whatever reading in general may consist of, the present discourse of not reading—although varied and diverse—condenses and metonymizes. We might speculate that today's not reading arises in good measure

[24] John Guillory, "Close Reading: Prologue and Epilogue," *ADE Bulletin* 149 (2010): 8–14; 9.

from anxiety about the future of literature in general, the novel in particular, and all kinds of reading by extension. Recall, however, that tens of thousands of novels are being published every year and that creative writing is on the upswing. We might speculate more pointedly, then, that today's not reading arises in some measure from anxiety about the function of literature and the future of literary studies (and of literature professors) in the face of unprecedented superabundance: not just the grand total of Too Much but also and especially the evident hyper-acceleration of textual production in print and, of course, online.

Whatever present discussions of not reading suggest about reading in general, they point tellingly to readers: readers with cognitive functions and psychic lives, readers who make decisions and manage their time, readers susceptible to boredom and prone to distraction, readers acting within markets and engaged with media, readers young and old. For all of their variety and complexity, and for all of their not reading, it would seem that readers remain imagined and importantly self-imagined in relation to reading novels. Whether or not the novel or its study is truly in jeopardy, the idea of novel reading remains a wellspring of a selfhood or *Bildung*. At least for now, that is, the idea of novel reading and a sense of self remain mutually entangled. There is a hearty dose of false consciousness involved, of course, when we use not reading to affirm our standing as readers according to the transitive illogic of reading = book and book = novel. As the EULA and the web should remind us, we exist amid an almost infinite non-literary, non-book domain of not reading, less as readerly subjects, and more as administrative ones.

NO FURTHER READING

INDEX

Printed and bound by CPI Group (UK) Ltd, Croydon, CR0 4YY